# UNIX
## Step-by-Step

Ben Smith

Consulting Editors: Stephen G. Kochan and Patrick H. Wood

*Howard W. Sams & Company*

*A Division of Macmillan, Inc.*
*11711 North College, Suite 141, Carmel, IN 46032 USA*

*I dedicate this book to Rich Grehan,*
*who taught me that technical writing can be fun and creative.*

International Standard Book Number: 0-672-48469-2
Library of Congress Catalog Card Number: 90-662866

Acquisitions Editor: *Scott Arant*
Development Editor: *Linda Sanning*
Manuscript Editor: *Sam Karnick*
Copy Editor: *Susan Christopherson*
Production Coordinator: *Steve Noe*
Illustrator: *Don Clemons*
Production Assistance: *Claudia Bell, Brad Chinn, Sally Copenhaver, T.R. Emrick, Denny Hager, Tami Hughes, Bill Hurley, Chuck Hutchinson, Cindy Phipps, Joe Ramon, Dennis Sheehan, Louise Shinault, Bruce Steed, Mary Beth Wakefield, Sarah Leatherman*
Indexer: *Sherry Massey*
Technical Reviewer: *Peter J. Holsberg*

*Printed in the United States of America*

## About the Author

Ben Smith is an author and technical editor for *BYTE* magazine, where he formed the BYTE UNIX Lab and UNIX Benchmarks. (*BYTE* is read by 500,000 experienced computer users around the world.) By nature of his position in the UNIX industry, he is constantly in touch with UNIX developments and familiar with all the popular UNIX workstations. Mr. Smith has many years of experience developing commercial programs for UNIX systems and helping UNIX users. He has also taught computer applications to the business and industrial community. Ben Smith was an architect and civil engineer before his full-time involvement in computing.

## Acknowledgments

I want to thank Sam Karnick for making a polished work out of my rough writing. I also want to thank the following for their help and encouragement: Pat Wood, Stephen Kochan, David Fiedler, Bruce Hunter, Rebecca Thomas, and Tom Yager. Linda Sanning made dealing with a publisher much easier and more enjoyable than I ever thought possible. Thank you all.

Hayden Books
UNIX
Library

The UNIX System Library is an integrated series of books covering basic to advanced topics related to the UNIX system. The books are written under the direction of Stephen G. Kochan and Patrick H. Wood, who have worked for several years teaching introductory and advanced UNIX courses and have written many books on the C programming language and the UNIX system.

The first title in the UNIX series is *Exploring the UNIX System*. The text introduces the new user to the UNIX system, covering things such as logging on, working with the file system, editing files with the vi editor, writing simple shell programs, formatting documents, using networks and electronic mail, and system administration.

Another introductory title in the series is *UNIX Step-by-Step*, which uses material from *Exploring the UNIX System*, presented in step-by-step tutorial fashion with exercises and review questions.

*UNIX Shell Programming* uses a clear, step-by-step approach to teach all the features of the standard and Korn shells. Also covered are tools used by many shell programmers, such as grep, sed, tr, cut, and sort, and a detailed discussion on how to write regular expressions.

*UNIX Text Processing* gives a comprehensive treatment of the many tools available for formatting documents under UNIX. The book shows how troff can be used to format simple documents like letters and how to format larger documents like manuals and books. The text shows how to use the popular mm and ms macro packages and how to write custom macro packages.

*UNIX System Administration* is an essential guide to administration for anyone who owns or operates a UNIX system. The text describes how to set up file systems, make backups, configure a system, connect peripheral devices, install and administer UUCP, work with the line printer spooler, and write shell programs to help streamline the administration process.

*UNIX System Security* is the only text devoted specifically to this important topic. Security for users, programmers, and administrators is covered in detail, as is network security. Source code listings for many useful security-related programs are given at the end of the book.

*UNIX Networking* contains practical discussions of several important UNIX networking systems including UUCP, TCP/IP, NFS, RFS, Streams, and LAN Manager/X. Each chapter is written by a noted expert in the field of UNIX networking.

## Trademarks

All terms mentioned in this book that are known to be trademarks or service marks are listed below. In addition, terms suspected of being trademarks or service marks have been appropriately capitalized. Howard W. Sams & Company cannot attest to the accuracy of this information. Use of a term in this book should not be regarded as affecting the validity of any trademark or service mark.

CP/M is a registered trademark of Digital Research Inc.

DEC, DECWindows, ULTRIX, VAX, DEC PDP-7, and DEC PDP-11 are trademarks of Digital Equipment Corporation.

Frame is a trademark of Frame Technology Corp.

HPUX is a trademark of Hewlett-Packard Corporation.

IBM is a registered trademark of International Business Machines.

Interleaf is a trademark of Interleaf, Inc.

MOTIF is a trademark of the Open Software Foundation.

MS-DOS is a registered trademark and XENIX is a trademark of Microsoft Corporation.

NCR Tower is a registered trademark of NCR Corporation.

NFS is a trademark of Sun Microsystems, Inc.

Open Look is a trademark and UNIX is a registered trademark of AT&T.

PICK is a registered trademark of Pick Systems.

PostScript is a registered trademark of Adobe Systems, Inc.

X Window System is a trademark of the Massachusetts Institute of Technology.


The `man` example in Chapter 2 of the present work contains copyrighted material from AT&T's Unix System Laboratories, Inc., © 1988 AT&T. The `help` example in Chapter 2 of the present work contains copyrighted material from the Santa Cruz Operation, © 1988 SCO. These two excerpts are reproduced with permission from AT&T and SCO.

# Contents

# 1

# Introduction to UNIX

## Contents

## Objectives

In this chapter you will learn

1. What an operating system does
2. The differences between multiuser and single-user operating systems

3. The differences between multitasking and single-tasking operating systems

4. The relationship between the kernel, the shells, and application programs

5. The advantages and responsibilities of working in a multiuser operating system

UNIX is an *operating system*. UNIX is also a *computing environment*. These two concepts and a colorful history are what make UNIX the rich and exciting subject it is.

# 1.1   Who Needs an Operating System?

The first and fundamental job of an operating system is to provide an interface between *applications* and computer hardware. Applications are programs written to apply computers in solving problems or facilitating work; for example, accounting programs, computer aided design (CAD) software, word processing programs, database software, and information management systems.

The hardware? Well, it used to be easy to identify the hardware, but now, with operating systems distributed over networks, we can't just point a finger at a box and say, "That's the hardware." But whether the hardware is a personal computer or a network of workstations or supercomputers, the operating system has the responsibility for managing hardware resources, preventing conflicts between different application programs, and, in the case of a multiuser system, preventing conflicts among users' computing needs. Disk drives, input/output communication ports, memory, central processor control — all these resources require management. Application programs do not have to be written to the specifications of each style and model of hardware if they can request services (such as disk file operations and communications) from the operating system.

At the risk of being simplistic, we can say that having an operating system is like using a grocery store. You don't have to know how to grow and ship vegetables, how to raise and milk cows, or how to forest timber and use the wood for manufacturing paper towels. You just need to know how to find the grocery store, put what you need in a shopping basket, and pay for it at the cashier. The grocer knows how to order from each of the producers or processors, who in turn know how to harvest and package the products.

Programs running on top of an operating system that does not give them efficient or conveniently managed resources might have to access the hardware directly, reaching around the operating system. Early PC operating systems were notoriously slow in writing information to the screen. If an application required very fast screen operations but requested these through the operating system, the result was unsatisfactory. Programmers had to directly control the memory and hardware devices that controlled the image on the screen. But there were several different kinds of devices for the PC, each having to be handled differently. A program written for a Color Graphics Adapter (CGA) display would not work on a monochrome display, or on an Enhanced Graphics Adapter (EGA). The application program (rather than the operating system) became responsible for detecting what kind of display was attached to the computer. But then, when new kinds of displays were introduced, the software wouldn't run on them.

A properly working operating system is the only part of the system that has to be modified or enhanced when a new display is introduced. UNIX handles different kinds of displays (or terminals) by using special tables or data files that describe the attributes of the device. Most UNIX systems come with a hundred or more display descriptions. The application program doesn't need to know the specifics of the terminal. It just has to know how to ask the operating system for the desired operation, whether clearing the screen, putting a character on the screen, or whatever.

Some operating systems are designed for a specific kind of data processing. For example, the PICK operating system is designed for database operations. The database "engine" is embedded in the operating system. Manufacturing-control computers usually have special operating systems that give the peripheral devices a far higher priority in their use of the central processor than the reporting aspects and user interface. These are called *real-time* systems.

Embedded systems such as the computer control for a microwave oven do not have operating systems. They are computers that have only one function, and the program that provides the computer with that function directly controls all the resources. As a result, they are usually very efficient at a limited set of tasks.

# 1.2   What Is UNIX?

UNIX is a general-purpose operating system. This fact is its greatest strength. Although there are "real-time" versions of UNIX, the standard version is better suited to general tasks such as document preparation; accounting; information management; typesetting; software development; and mathematical, scientific, and engineering computing.

UNIX is a *multitasking, multiuser* operating system. To qualify as multitasking, an operating system must be able to manage the sharing of the central processor (CPU) among concurrently executing tasks. Concurrency is really a figure of speech, because most processors can only perform one operation at a time.

Therefore, for every task to get a fair share of the processing resources, UNIX must be able to process each task a little bit at a time. Some tasks have high priority, and therefore should be able to grab the CPU when they need to.

UNIX provides ways for tasks to communicate with one another. One of the advantages of a multitasking operating system is the ability to have different tasks work together simultaneously. We will see that tasks work together in different relationships — some are peers and others work as master and slave, or client and server (a much more tender relationship). Some tasks are even called "parent" and "child" (not always the most tender task relationship).

How can a computer be multiuser? A simple example: different users can sit down at the same computer at different times and still keep their information separated. Multiuser also generally means that people can use the same computer *at the same time*, thus requiring that the computer be capable of accommodating more than one simultaneous connection. Traditionally, multiple connections have been made by having several terminals connected to the computer by separate cables. Terminals have little or no processing power of their own. They know only how to capture keystrokes, send them to the computer, and display what the computer sends back.

Now, however, the layout can be far more complex. Instead of terminals, there can be workstations with separate computing resources. At times the workstations might be doing all their own processing. At other times they might ask for computing resources from a *server*, a remote processor that is accessed by a network. On the other hand, the UNIX computer can be a high-performance personal computer (386 AT class), and its single keyboard and screen might appear as several terminals to the operating system. (These are called virtual terminals.) As we will see in Chapter 3, "User Interfaces: Shells and GUIs," a workstation might do something similar by creating virtual terminals in graphical windows, all on the same high-resolution screen.

As a multiuser operating system, UNIX must keep track of the terminal, virtual terminal, or workstation associated with each task. It must also be capable of keeping track of different users and which resources they can access. The operating system must have enough robustness and security to protect against foolish or mischievous user activity. UNIX's multiuser facilities protect files from intrusion by other users while allowing the sharing of files and information by those authorized to access it.

## Kernels and Shells

The basic operations of UNIX are switching tasks in and out of the CPU, checking input/output ports for activity, managing memory and disk drives, and providing the facility for application programs to use the resources. The basic operations are handled by the kernel, a special program that runs continuously. All other programs access their resources through the kernel. (See fig. 1-1.) According to the definition of an operating system at the beginning of this chapter, the UNIX kernel is the operating system. But the kernel does not provide a way for users to tell it what do. The interface is provided by a program external to the kernel: the *shell*.

**Fig. 1-1:**
The UNIX kernel provides a common interface between the hardware and the tasks.

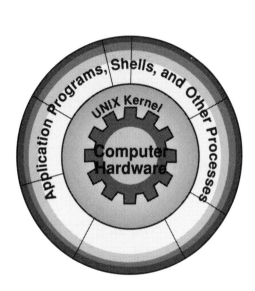

As we will see in Chapter 3, "User Interfaces," there are several different shells. Shells are command interpreters; they accept requests from the user (or command files — known as "shell programs" or "shell scripts"), and translate these commands into requests to the kernel for its facilities. Shells allow users to control the portion of the system to which they are allowed access.

There are several graphical user interfaces (GUIs) that perform many of the same functions as shells. These generally involve a pointing device, such as a mouse or trackball, and windowed areas of the screen and menus from which to select operations.

## Beyond the Basics

UNIX is known for its rich selection of commands. A few commands are internal (and specific) to the shell you are running. Most commands are programs separate from either the kernel or the shell. UNIX systems have several hundred commands (we can call them "tools") for accomplishing everything from reading and sending mail, editing text files, and typesetting, to locating files on remote computers. The majority of the tools are small, single-purpose programs. Most of them can send and receive information from other programs; therefore, simple UNIX tools can be tied together to perform complex tasks.

It is not uncommon to have a UNIX system without any commercial applications programs! (The author's UNIX machine is one. This is becoming less common, however, as more and more commercial UNIX applications emerge.) A complete UNIX system includes all the programs necessary for general computing. Of course, what is included in your UNIX system depends on which machine you are using and what utilities were included by the manufacturer/vendor. Some manufacturers even bundle commercial packages along with their version of UNIX.

Most of this book is devoted to increasing your understanding of UNIX utilities and shells. Appendix B summarizes the utilities discussed in this book. Appendix C lists more than 200 utilities and standard programs you might find on a UNIX system.

# 1.3  Sharing Resources

Unlike operating systems specifically designed for use on a stand-alone personal computer, UNIX is structured around the concept of sharing both hardware and processing time. You share the central processor (CPU), computer memory, space on the disk drive, printers, and other resources with other users. UNIX helps to ensure that there are no conflicts, but you must do your part. Often this requires no more than being patient with less-experienced users.

More important than just sharing hardware, you can also share information. As you will see from the history of UNIX, sharing information is the basic concept around which UNIX was designed. You can link files in your "personal file area" to other users' file areas. A link is not a copy; it makes a single file appear in many different places on the system without using up space with multiple copies. Any additions or changes appear at all links. (See Chapter 4, "Files," for more about links.) On the other hand, each user can control access to files and to what extent they can be accessed to read, write, or execute.

Sharing implies communications. UNIX utilities include electronic mail, electronic bulletin-board communications (UNIX news system), remote program execution, and automatic file transfers with remote machines. Some systems even include phone-message services and FAX generation and reception.

# 1.4   Users

Most UNIX users are not dragons, wizards, or gurus. They are just regular people doing regular sorts of things with their UNIX computers: lawyers and judges tracking cases; statisticians gathering and analyzing data; investment managers keeping track of funds; warehousers tracking shipments and inventories; publishers editing and typesetting periodicals and books. Many users are government workers and military personnel. Retail clerks might be running UNIX if their cash register is a terminal to the storewide inventory and accounting system. Fast-food restaurants use UNIX at the specialized order and cash stations. Many electronic conferencing systems, such as BIX (BYTE Information eXchange), run on UNIX computers. Many of these UNIX users are not even aware that their computer is running the UNIX operating system.

This operating system can be made to appear as simple as you want, by limiting the user activities to those in simple menus. Each user can have a personalized view and set of operations. There is nothing esoteric about this process. UNIX was designed to be customized.

An office or department that has purchased a UNIX computer for some specific application will often, after the users have learned the basics of the application, begin to use the standard UNIX utilities as a reminder service, as a message system, as a communications network for hardware and software support personnel, or even for a little recreational computing. Though many UNIX users are engineers and research people who use the utilities as part of their office operations, authors and business people can easily learn to use them as well. (That is the purpose of this book.) It is unfortunate for any user of a UNIX system to be unaware of its functionality or hesitant to use it to its fullest.

## UNIX Programmers

Many computer programmers enjoy the rich set of software development tools that are traditionally part of UNIX. In fact, many of the traditional UNIX tools are now found on other operating systems, including VMS and MS-DOS. Having programmers on the same system as non-programmers is a mixed blessing. Many programmers, by their very nature, like to experiment with the system they use.

If the programmers also happen to be the system administrators (see below), users might be in for some surprises. (The author knows this only too well.)

You will find that some UNIX programming utilities— for example, the `make` utility described in Chapter 11, "Advanced Utilities"—can be used for other tasks. Many of the complex system operations (such as the mail system, the news system, and the UUCP file transfer system) were developed using the standard utilities and shell scripts.

### System Administrators

The basics of UNIX system administration are no more complex than managing a PC with a hard disk drive. An administrator has to ensure that the machine boots (starts up) properly, that user(s) can access the application programs, that the application programs know where to find their files, and that the disk is backed up regularly. If you are the only user on your system, you will probably be the system administrator for it. No big deal.

On the other hand, UNIX is not as simple to manage as a single-architecture, single-user, single-task operating system such as MS-DOS. Administrators of systems with only a few users have some serious responsibilities. They must be able to install all new software, limiting access to the proper users. They have to delete unnecessary files and programs. In other words, they have to deal with possible conflicts between users and what each might feel is important and fair. Administrators are required to get strange disk drives, tape drives, terminals, and printers to work. They set up new user accounts and delete them when they are no longer needed. If the system is networked with other computers, administrators are responsible for getting along with administrators of other systems, maintaining communications between the machines, and managing efficient use of the network. In short, administrators of large systems can be very busy people; respect their time by not bothering them with trivial questions.

# 1.5   A Little History

UNIX is one of the better things that grew out of the '60s. It has maintained much of the philosophy of "sharing" from that period into the subsequent years. Other operating systems have come and gone as hardware design has evolved, but UNIX has survived, and is getting stronger each year, although security is now more important than sharing.

Most operating systems are designed specifically for marketing, to provide functionality to otherwise worthless computer hardware (CP/M and UCSD-p are exceptions). I don't mean to say that an operating system is usually an after-thought. In fact, typically the operating system and the hardware grow up together, so closely that the operating system can only run on the specific design of hardware, and the hardware can run only that operating system. The two are designed to enhance the features of each other; a sort of mutual enhancement club. If the package sells well, scaled-down and scaled-up versions might appear in a year. UNIX, in contrast, is *hardware independent.*

The majority of computers in the '60s were "batch-oriented" systems, with computer users submitting their programs and data to the system in a queue. When it was that "job's" turn to run, all of the resources were dedicated to the task until it was finished. The system was not interactive. (I use the past tense even though there are still batch-oriented systems all around.) In 1968, Digital Equipment Corporation (DEC) introduced the DEC-10, a pleasant but very expensive mini-computer that ran an interactive time-sharing system. Inspired in part by the DEC operating system, a team of researchers at AT&T, M.I.T, and G.E. worked on developing their own time-sharing system, MULTICS, a user-oriented, rather than machine-oriented, operating system. MULTICS is the acronym for **MULT**iplexed **I**nformation and **C**omputing **S**ystem. But, like its full name, MULTICS was too big and too slow on the General Electric computer it was originally designed for.

Team member Ken Thompson was also working on a space-travel simulation program. The other team members complained that his program took up too many computing resources on the GE, so he was allowed to run it only when nothing else was happening on the system. He decided to move it to its own machine, a little-used DEC PDP-7. While moving this program over to the DEC, he and some friends began the basics of what was to become the UNIX operating system: a file system, a command interpreter (shell), and some basic elements of a multitasking operating system.

As work continued on the PDP-7, the underlying system took on many of the attractive concepts of MULTICS, so much so that Brian Kernighan (one of the originators of the C programming language) referred to this fledgling operating system as the emasculated version of MULTICS. The idea of "eunuchs" led to "UNICS," which led to "UNIX."

In 1970, UNIX was implemented on the DEC PDP-11/20 along with an editing program and a text-formatting program. In 1971, the Bell Labs patent office selected it for their new text-processing system. UNIX — First Edition became official in November of 1971. By June 1972 there were 10 UNIX machines. Dennis Ritchie (the other originator of the C programming language) had also worked on the MULTICS project. In 1973, he and Ken Thompson rewrote the UNIX kernel in C. AT&T released tapes of the source code (free of charge) to Columbia University and several other colleges and universities, and UNIX was out in the world.

By 1975, AT&T had released the Sixth Edition. By this time it was necessary for a site to have a license for UNIX. It had become a commercial product, not just in requiring a license, but also in content. Most of the kernel was now in the C programming language. UNIX included a Portable C Library. The operating-system source code and the libraries were not specific to the underlying hardware. It was feasible to port UNIX to any machine that provided enough resources for a multitasking, multiuser system.

Even then, it had been the licensees' responsibility to implement and maintain the UNIX kernel on the hardware of their choice. In 1977, Interactive Systems Corporation started reselling UNIX as a supported product on DEC computers. Also in 1977, the University of California at Berkeley began distributing some of their work on UNIX: 1BSD—1st Berkeley Software Distribution.

AT&T released the Seventh Edition of UNIX in 1979. The seventh edition proved to be a fountainhead for UNIX development everywhere. It included the complete Kernighan and Ritchie C compiler, the Bourne shell (a major subject of this book), and much more complete documentation, including many technical tutorials and articles about the UNIX utilities. Also in 1979, Version 7 (not to be confused with the Seventh Edition) was ported to the DEC VAX line of computers. Ken Thompson went on sabbatical from AT&T to teach a course on operating systems at the University of California, Berkeley; his students in this course have influenced UNIX ever since. The Department of Defense Advance Research Projects Agency (DARPA) decided to fund more research and development on UNIX for use with their projects in artificial intelligence, very large scale integrated circuit design, and vision research. UNIX came into wide use; its potential was becoming apparent.

## 1.6  Explosion

Since 1979, distribution of UNIX has increased dramatically. Students at Berkeley, Columbia, MIT, the University of Illinois, Carnegie-Mellon, Purdue, and other trend-setting institutions used UNIX. When they went on to work in industry, they wanted to take their UNIX environment with them. DARPA's adoption of UNIX encouraged the organization's contacts and support industry to use UNIX. In the 1980s, Motorola and Intel (integrated circuit manufacturers) developed microprocessors capable of running UNIX. Computer manufacturers such as Sun and Altos began producing machines designed to run *only* UNIX.

By the end of the 1980s, most major computer manufacturers had ported UNIX to some of their computers. Hewlett-Packard adopted UNIX (HPUX) as the preferred operating system for their engineering workstations. NCR's "Tower" line of super micros was very successful. Cray Research, Motorola, Sony, HP/

Apollo, Tandy, Everex, and many others had joined the movement to UNIX. Even DEC and IBM made major commitments to UNIX.

The development of microcomputer-based UNIX by Microsoft, Interactive Systems, and Santa Cruz Operations (among others) has increased the number of applications and their demand. The introduction of relatively low-priced engineering workstations with extremely high computing performance has helped make feasible undreamed-of applications. These workstations all run UNIX. UNIX is now affordable and even more desirable.

In 1989, there were an estimated 100,000 UNIX systems available to 11,000,000 users.

# 1.7 Tradition

Although there are plenty of specifications for standards in UNIX today, this was not always so. Many of today's UNIX standards spring from its history, or in other words, tradition. For example, the awk utility (named for its inventors: Aho, Weinberger, and Kernighan) is used for formatting data and text into reports.

The tradition is that command names are terse, even if obscure, stemming from the difficulty of typing at a Teletype. (The first UNIX machines used Teletype-writers and modified electric typewriters as terminals.)

Another tradition is the use of the dash character in command-line options. For example, the command for listing the files in the current work area (subdirectory) is *ls*. The default is an alphabetic list. To change the sort order to the time that files were last modified, the command would be *ls -t*.

# 1.8 A Personalized World

Another tradition is user configurability; in other words, the UNIX user should always be able to choose personal defaults for the way a program will appear and work. These personal settings never affect the appearance or operation of the program for anyone else.

The ability to create an autonomous personalized computing world while using the same machine and programs is one of the major differences between the UNIX environment and networked personal computers. Each PC must have a separate copy of each personalized program. On a PC network, if a single copy of a program exists that everyone uses, the personality of that program is the same for everyone. No one can change the personality without affecting everyone else. Only if the program has copies on each machine can each user change it with personal modifications. PC applications were not designed for sharing. The only real advantage of a PC network over stand-alone PCs is the ability to move data from machine to machine without making diskettes. (Some electronic mail services almost justify a PC network.)

On a UNIX system, there is one copy of each program. Several people can run the same program at the same time, and each user can give it an entirely different personality. UNIX programs were developed on UNIX machines with multiuser design in mind. As a result, the programs take full advantage of the fact that UNIX is a multitasking/multiuser operating system.

UNIX gives users an efficient way to use their resources, a rich and consistent environment in which to work, and utilities to facilitate sharing.

## 1.9   Summary

Almost all computers that run user-interactive programs have operating systems. Some operating systems allow only one user or one program to run at any time. These are single-user, single-tasking operating systems.

UNIX is a multiuser, multitasking operating system. It allows more than one user to use the computer at one time, and more than one program can be running simultaneously.

UNIX runs on many different kinds of computers; it is a portable operating system. UNIX also includes many utility programs which make for a rich working environment. Many UNIX users do not need anything more than the operating system and its optional packages to do all their computing.

Because UNIX is a multi-user operating system designed for sharing resources, users must be considerate of each others' needs. There are many kinds of users on UNIX systems, including the novice, the programmer, and the system administrator.

UNIX's rich history has led to many traditions that are still part of modern UNIX. One of these is the expectation that any UNIX program is configurable by each user without affecting the configuration of any other user.

# Review Questions

1. What is the fundamental purpose of an operating system?

2. What does UNIX provide beyond the fundamentals of an operating system?

3. What are UNIX shells?

4. What are the responsibilities of each user to other users on a multiuser system?

5. Who developed UNIX?

6. Has UNIX always been a commercial operating system?

7. Name two reasons for the spread of UNIX throughout the computing world.

8. Why is tradition important to UNIX?

# Exercises

There are no exercises for Chapter One. If you want some exercises, read Chapter Two.

# Further Reading

*Life With UNIX*, Don Libes and Sandy Ressler, Prentice Hall, Englewood Cliffs, NJ, 1989. An enjoyable compilation of UNIX history, culture, and esoteric information.

*The Design of the UNIX Operating System*, Maurice J. Bach, Prentice Hall, Englewood Cliffs, NJ, 1986. A technical textbook on the internal design and system services of both System V and BSD UNIX.

*Understanding UNIX: A Conceptual Guide*, 2nd Edition, James R. Groff and Paul N. Weinberg, Que Corporation, Carmel, IN, 1988. An excellent book for beginners.

# 2

# Getting Started

## Contents

## Objectives

In this chapter you will learn

1. How to begin and end a session
2. The value of individual accounts and security
3. Which control keys are used to edit command lines
4. How and where to get help on UNIX

UNIX is a multiuser operating system. To provide you with the correct environment, it must know who you are. To identify yourself to the system, you *log in* by giving the system your account ID and a password. You must also tell the system when you have finished working with it, by *logging out*.

## 2.1   User Accounts and Passwords

Some systems have only one user, in which case the login process can be disabled. Most UNIX systems, however, have at least several users; some systems have hundreds. Each authorized user has an *account* on the system. The system keeps track of the resources used by each user. This process is called *system accounting*. Each user is given a private area in the storage space of the computer—the file system. When you log in, the file system appears to contain only your files. Do not be concerned about the thousands of other files on the system; they are not in your normal view, although you can see the whole system if you want.

The operating system associates a *password* (user ID) with each account. The password is like a key to your files and, to some extent, the entire system. A unique password provides some privacy for your files, but there are other reasons to use one. See Chapter 4, "Files," for a discussion of system security and the concepts of *file ownership*, *groups*, and *permissions*.

### Identifying Yourself

Let's make no assumptions here: Do you know who you are? Joking aside, be sure that you know the name of your UNIX account before you try logging in. You have to know your password as well.

Let's assume that your login (account name) is *felix* and that you were given *thecat* as your password. (When you first receive your account, it might not have a password. In either case, choose a new one. See the next section.) The login process is simple:

```
login: felix              — your account name
Password: thecat          — your password is not displayed
$                         — response is shell prompt
```

Press Enter or Return after you enter the account name and after you enter your password. The exact format of the login prompt varies from machine to machine. Usually the word "login" is on the screen. After you enter your account name, the prompt for the password might appear below the "login" or in a new window. (If there is minimal security, the prompt might not appear at all.) When you enter your password, the characters do not appear on the screen. This prevents other users' seeing your password. Some systems echo dashes or stars; others echo nothing. On large or very busy systems, the system might take a few seconds to start a session for you. User interfaces using windows are notoriously slow to start.

Once you have gained access, there will be a shell prompt, usually indicated by a $ or %. Windowed system interfaces open with some graphic indication of what to do next, showing either a menu or an array of icons.

A sample session with a text-based UNIX system follows.

```
login: felix
Password                    — the password is not displayed

*** System shutdown at 19:00 for preventative maint. ***

$ who
felix   tty22 Oct 29 16:33
pat     tty29 Oct 29 16:20
ben      console Oct 29 9:30
ruth    tty37 Oct 29 10:54
steve   tty25 Oct 29 15:52
$ mail
No messages.
$ date
Sat Oct 29 16:34:47 EDT 1989
$ exit
login:
```

Felix logged in and received a message about the status of the system. He looked for other users on the system with the who command, checked for mail with the mail command, checked the system date and time with the date command, and logged out with the exit command. (The dollar sign is the prompt the shell issues when it is ready for a command.)

## Ending a Session

Never walk away from your terminal or console without logging out (ending your UNIX session). A stray cat could walk across your keyboard and mess up your work. Logging out in UNIX is equivalent to saving your files and turning the computer off on a personal computer. When you log out, you free the computing resources (processing time and memory) allocated for you when you logged in. Logging out protects your files from accidental modification or removal.

The logout procedure varies from system to system. Try the following commands in response to a prompt that is either a $ or a %:

```
exit
```

or

```
logout
```

or

```
^D
```

(That last one, "^D," is the common way of indicating that you should hold down the Ctrl key and press the D key. Read "^D" as "control D.")

If you are in a graphics window environment, look for a menu with the words logout or End Session or exit. Using the mouse, move the pointer to the menu item and click (press and release the left mouse button).

No menu? Try moving the pointer to the background of the screen (outside any active windows) and hold down the left mouse button. If there is no session-manager menu there, look for an icon (graphic symbol) with sm or session manager and click the left mouse button on that. Or try Ctrl-D or the exit command on a command line.

Whereas logging in is fairly consistent across a variety of UNIX systems, logging out varies considerably. Hopefully you can also see the need for Chapter 3, "User Interfaces," and for some standards, particularly with graphic user interfaces, window managers, and session managers. Don't worry. UNIX isn't generally this inconsistent. You just need to learn the basic rules of your system's user interface.

## 2.2 At Least a Little Security

In recent years, computer data and time have become valuable resources that require protection. As a result, security is now a very important part of multiuser systems. One reason for security is to keep unauthorized people from gaining access to a computer system; another is to keep authorized users from tampering with each other's (or the system's) files; still another is to allow some users exclusive privileges to which commands they can use and files they can access. Ideally, all these goals are met with as little bother to users as possible. Security should be available but unobtrusive.

Security on UNIX systems is available through a few simple commands and features that form the basis for a complete, but secure, system. It can be as lax or as tight as desired.

## Changing Passwords

When you log in, the password you enter at the terminal is encrypted (so that no one will know what it is) and checked against the encrypted password for your account ID. If they match, you are allowed on the system; if they don't, you are given the message `Login incorrect`, and you must try again.

When you first log in to a new system, you might be requested to change your password. Even if you don't receive such a request, changing your password the first time, and periodically thereafter, is a good idea. (Some systems inform you when you haven't changed your password for a long time.)

You can always change your password from a shell prompt by using the command `passwd`. Enter `passwd`, and you will receive prompts for the rest:

```
$ passwd
Changing old password for felix
Old password: -----          — your response is not displayed
New password: -----          — your response is not displayed
Re-enter new password: -----  — your response is not displayed
$
```

Asking for the old password ensures that the person using your terminal is really you. If you make a mistake entering the old password, the utility responds with `sorry`, meaning that no change was made and that you should try again. If the old password is correct, `passwd` asks you to enter the new password. Because the passwords are not displayed, the utility asks you to enter your new password a second time, to make sure that you did not make a mistake. If the two entries do not match, the `passwd` utility will ask you to enter the *new* password twice more:

```
$ passwd
Changing old password for felix
Old password: -----          — your response is not displayed
New password: -----          — your response is not displayed
Re-enter new password: -----  — your response is not displayed
They don't match; try again.
Old password: -----          — your response is not displayed
New password: -----          — your response is not displayed
$
```

The `passwd` command is like most other UNIX commands in that nothing is printed when your password has been successfully altered. UNIX simply returns you to the shell prompt.

### Choosing Good Passwords

Although many UNIX systems don't put restrictions on passwords (some don't require them at all), using obscure passwords keeps your user ID secure. First and last names, initials, birth-dates, and the like are poor passwords. Even passwords from ordinary English words can be cracked, given a weekend or two of computer time and an on-line dictionary. Good passwords are at least six characters long, are not based on personal information, and include nonalphabetic characters. `4score`, `adv8ance`, `my name`, `bon1jour`, and `a1b2c3` are unusual enough to make discovery difficult (but not impossible). Misspelled words and two-word combinations make good passwords.

Even better passwords are `dg71m33ex` and `z_1_y_2_x`. These are almost impossible to crack. Unfortunately, they are also almost impossible to remember. If a password is so weird that you have to write it down, it's not a good password—writing down passwords is a bad security practice. Many computer systems require passwords such as `dg71m33ex`, which causes users to write down their passwords and tape them to their terminals!

The only times you need to enter your password are when you log in and when you change it. To keep prying eyes from seeing your password, the screen does not show it at these times. However, someone with sharp eyes and a good memory can find out your password by watching your fingers at the keyboard. When you enter your password, make sure that no one is nearby. If you are standing by someone about to enter his or her password, it is polite to turn your head away (another tradition).

## 2.3 Command Line Controls

If you have already worked with UNIX, you might have had to delete mistakes on the command line. Most terminals have a backspace key, and most systems are set up so that the backspace key does the job. Digital Equipment (DEC) and Sun Microsystems machines traditionally use the Delete key for the same function. To find out how your computer connection is set up, issue the `stty` command:

```
$ stty -a
speed 9600 baud; line = 0; intr = DEL; quit = ^; erase = ^H;
```

```
kill = ^U; eof = ^D; eol = ^@; swtch = ^@ -parenb -parodd cs8
-cstopb hupcl cread -clocal -loblk -ctsflow -rtsflow  -ignbrk
brkint ignpar -parmrk -inpck -istrip -inlcr -igncr icrnl -iuclc
ixon -ixany -ixoff  isig icanon -xcase echo -echoe echok -echonl
-noflsh  opost -olcuc onlcr -ocrnl -onocr -onlret -ofill -ofdel
cr0 nl0 tab0 bs0 vt0 ff0
$
```

There is a little more here than what you're looking for. Note the expressions that include an equal sign; these are the *assignments* (the keypresses assigned to command line operations). All the other information is about communications, protocols, and other things of little interest unless you are trying to make a terminal work with a computer.

The operations assigned to keys are shown in Table 2-1.

**Table 2-1: Command-line keys with special powers**

| Abbreviation | Meaning | Sample assignment |
| --- | --- | --- |
| intr | abort operation | Del (Delete key) |
| quit | abort with core dump | ^\ (Ctrl-\) |
| erase | backspace with delete | ^H (Backspace key) |
| kill | delete entire line | ^U (Ctrl-U) |
| eof | generate end-of-file | ^D (Ctrl-D) |
| eol | optional end-of-line | ^@ (NULL, not assigned) |
| swtch | job-control switch | ^@ (NULL, not assigned) |

You might find that your ^C (Ctrl-C) key has been assigned one of these functions, perhaps intr. If you have a Delete key on your keyboard and want to assign intr to it, the stty command can be used to change the assignment (and any other of its many settings). In the following example, assume that your connection to the computer has erase assigned to the Delete key and intr (interrupt) assigned to Ctrl-C; you want them to be the same, as in the preceding table.

```
$ stty intr "^?" erase "^H"
$
```

A little explanation is required. In the `stty` command, the carat (^) is entered as a literal character. The carat-question mark (^?) expression is the abbreviation for the Delete key. As you will find out later, the hook (nickname for the question mark) is a wildcard character on the command line, and therefore must be enclosed in quotation marks. The quotation marks around the second assignment are there for historical reasons.

## 2.4 Getting Help

The most reliable resource for information on the UNIX operating system is the *UNIX User's Reference Manual*. The printed version of this tome is about as exciting as a dictionary; it's good for resolving arguments in *Trivial Pursuit* but not for light reading at the beach. The real value of the manual is that it is "on line"; that is to say, you can look up commands using the UNIX system. (Some small UNIX systems do not have an "on-line" manual.) To read an entry in the manual, enter `man` followed by the command you want to know about:

man *command*

If `man` is so easy, why are there so many books about using UNIX? Two problems occur with `man`. First, you have to know *what* to look up before you can find it. Second, the "man pages" (entries in the manual) are highly technical; they are not easy for the new UNIX user to read. For example, the `man` entry on using the manual is

```
$ man man
     MAN(CT)                    UNIX 3.0                    MAN(CT)


     Name
          man - Print entries in this manual.
     Syntax
          man [ options ] [ section ] titles
     Description
          Man locates and prints the entry named title in the section
          named section from the UNIX Reference Manual. (For
          historical reasons, the word "page" is often used as a
          synonym for "entry" in this context.) The title is
          entered in lower case. The section number may not have a
          letter suffix. If no section is specified, the whole manual
          is searched for title and all occurrences of it are printed.
          Options and their meanings are:
```

| -t | Typeset the entry in the default format (8.5"x11"). |
| -s | Typeset the entry in the small format (6"x9"). |
| -Tterm | Format the entry using nroff and print it on the standard output (usually, the terminal); term is the terminal type (see term(M) and the explanation below); for a list of recognized values of term, type help term2. The default value of term is 450. |
| -w | Print on the standard output only the path names of the entries, relative to /usr/man, or to the current directory for -d option. |
| -d | Search the current directory rather than /usr/man; requires the full file name (e.g., cu.C, rather than just cu). |
| -12 | Indicates that the manual entry is to be produced in 12-pitch. May be used when $TERM (see below) is set to one of 300, 300s, 450, and 1620. (The pitch switch on the DASI 300 and 300s terminals must be manually set to 12 if this option is used.) |
| -c | Causes man to invoke col(CT); note that col(CT) is invoked automatically by man unless term is one of 300, 300s, 450, 37, 4000a, 382, 4014, tek, 1620, and X. |
| -y | Causes man to use the non-compacted version of the macros. |

The above options other than -d, -c, and -y are mutually exclusive, except that the -s option may be used in conjunction with the first four -T options above. Any other options are passed to troff, nroff, or the man(CT) macro package.

When using nroff, man examines the environment variable $TERM (see environ(M)) and attempts to select options to nroff, as well as filters, that adapt the output to the terminal being used. The -Tterm option overrides the value of $TERM; in particular, one should use -Tlp when sending the output of man to a line printer.

Section may be changed before each title.

As an example:

    man man

would reproduce on the terminal this entry, as well as any
other entries named man that may exist in other sections of
the manual.

If the first line of the input for an entry consists solely
of the string:

'\" x

where x is any combination of the three characters c, e, and
t, and where there is exactly one blank between the double
quote (") and x, then man will preprocess its input through
the appropriate combination of cw(CT), eqn(CT) (neqn for
nroff) and tbl(CT), respectively. If eqn or neqn are
invoked, they will automatically read the file
/usr/pub/eqnchar (see eqnchar(CT )).

See Also
checkcw(CT), checkeqn(CT), eqnchar(CT), nroff(CT), tbl(CT),
troff(CT), environ(M), term(CT).

Notes
All entries are supposed to be reproducible either on a
typesetter or on a terminal. However, on a terminal some
information is necessarily lost.

$

At this point, you might find this kind of help a little disconcerting. (You can see
why there are so many books about how to use UNIX.) But man can be a quick way
to refresh your memory or see the details about a command.

Entries in man have these sections:

- *Name*
- *Syntax* describes how to enter the command to the shell. Information
  enclosed in square brackets ([]) is optional. Usually, options are preceded by
  a dash (−). Any words following the utility/command name are substituted
  with values (parameters). For example, a syntax description of:

```
translate [-f rules] [-d] file [output-file]
```

might be entered in any of the following ways:

```
translate source
translate -f myrules source
translate -d source
```

```
translate source destination
translate -f myrules -d source destination
```

(and others) with different results. The program name, translate, and the name of the source file are always required.

- *Description* describes the action of the utility or command, including the meaning and significance of any parameters and options.

- *See Also* refers to other commands. Following the string of "See Also" can provide insight into the organization of UNIX utilities. Note that cross-references can be difficult to keep track of. The "See Also" section is not always 100% accurate.

- *Files* lists the system files that run the program. These files might provide defaults or be the subject of the program. Some programs require temporary files.

- *Notes* comments on the limitations or dangers of using the program.

- *Bugs* lists known bugs in programs and utilities. Some of these are mentioned in the *Notes* or in another section.

## Fast Help

Some UNIX systems have replaced their man utility by (or supplemented it with) a help utility. The help program is much faster than man (it doesn't require a text formatter). The output usually consists of the program's syntax and a one-line explanation of each option. For example:

```
help more

more:

MORE - View File by Screenful or by Line

$ more [options] [files]
Options:
  + /pat      start two lines before line containing pat
  -c          redraw page one line at a time
  -d          prompt after each Screenfull
  -f          count by newlines instead of screen lines
  -l          treat formfeed (^L) as ordinary character
  -n          window size (default set with stty)
  +n          start viewing file at line n
  -r          display control characters as ^C
  -s          reduce multiple blank lines to one
```

```
    -u          suppress terminal underlining or enhancing
    -w          prompt before exiting (any key terminates)
    ? or h      shows summary of more commands
```

The `help` text often contains abbreviations; however, it is usually easier to read than a full `man` entry.

## People Who Can Help

Large UNIX sites, such as universities and research organizations, often have a staff of *site advisors*. It is the responsibility of these individuals to help you resolve any difficulties you have with the system. Advisors are also responsible for setting up new accounts and maintaining cooperation among disparate users. Their offices usually adjoin public terminal rooms (although, with the proliferation of networked UNIX systems, the site might not have a public terminal room). To get help from the local expert you have to learn the UNIX mail system.

The UNIX electronic mail system is the utility for getting human-generated help. (You won't suffer a penalty if you skip to the section on `mail` in Chapter 11, "Advanced Utilities.") If you don't know whom to ask for help on your system, direct a polite request to "postmaster." If there is no postmaster, ask for the name of an advisor from *root*, the account name for the *system administrator*. (System administrators are typically very busy people; respect their time and avoid making demands on them.)

Once you have acquired some facility with UNIX and `mail`, you can extend your queries outside your system. The worldwide network of UNIX machines has millions of users. If your machine or network connects to this worldwide network, you can get help from just about anyone. Help is also available on other systems such as the McGraw-Hill/BIX (BYTE Information eXchange), BITstream, USENET, CompuServe, and other electronic information services.

## Printed Matter

The printed manuals and documentation delivered with your UNIX system often include far more sections than those available on-line, including:

- User's Guide
- User's Reference Manual
- UNIX System Readings and Applications, Volumes I and II
- UNIX System Software Readings

- The UNIX Systems User's Handbook
- The Vi User's Handbook
- Utilities Release Notes
- The C Programmer's Handbook
- Programmer's Reference Manual
- Programmer's Guide
- Documenter's Workbench User's Guide
- Documenter's Workbench Reference Manual

UNIX and its utilities are well-documented by AT&T, by publishers, and by many of the companies that have implemented it. Most chapters in *UNIX Step-by-Step* end with a brief bibliography of further reading on that chapter's topics. You might discover that the problem isn't finding information about UNIX, but rather selecting the information you need. To that end, you will find the descriptions in Appendix A useful.

## 2.5   Summary

To use a UNIX computer, you have to "log in." When you finish working on the computer, log out.

Each UNIX user has an individual account. The use of individual accounts helps protect the system and the data of each user from being corrupted accidentally or intentionally.

Because UNIX does not assume that only one type of communications link exists between users and the computer, you sometimes have to configure the special meanings of some control keys. The stty command is used to see and set the communications and controls of your connection to the UNIX system.

Most UNIX machines are self-documenting. The man and help commands enable you to read the on-line documentation.

## Review Questions

1. Why do you have to log in to a UNIX system?

2. Why do you log out at the end of your session on a UNIX system?

3. Why are accounts password-protected?

4. How do you end a session on a terminal or console?

5. How do you change your password?

6. What is man?

7. What is the difference between a *site advisor* and a *system administrator*?

# Exercises

*Note:* All exercises require you to have access to a UNIX computer.

Log in to your account and change your password using the passwd command. Then log out. Now log in again with your new password. When you changed your password, did the system put some constraints on the passwords that you wanted to use?

While you are logged in to your account, try the following commands:

```
man man
man help
man passwd
man exit
man who
man date
```

If you have time, follow some of the threads through the manual indicated by the "See Also" paragraphs at the end of the manual entries.

# Further Reading

*UNIX System Security*, P.H. Wood and S.G. Kochan, Howard W. Sams & Company, Indianapolis, IN, 1988. A practical guide to system security, with methods for making sure that your UNIX system is as secure as you want it to be.

*The UNIX System*, S.R. Bourne (Bell Laboratories), Addison-Wesley Publishing, Reading, MA, 1983. Although this book was written when there were but 3000 UNIX systems in the world, and the current version from AT&T was not nearly as robust as it is now, this text remains a valuable resource, if for no other reason than that it was written by the developer of the Bourne shell (see Chapter 3, "User Interfaces"). It was written for a technical audience.

# 3

# User Interfaces:
# Shells and GUIs

## Contents

## Objectives

In this chapter you will learn

1. The role of the UNIX shell
2. How to distinguish between the Bourne, Korn, and C shells
3. The strengths and weaknesses of each UNIX shell

4. The concepts and operations of graphical user interfaces

5. The organization and utilities of the Open Look user interface

6. How to use the OSF Motif window

Although UNIX can batch, it is not a batch-mode operating system. It is a multi*user* system and therefore requires a user interface, a way for each user to communicate with the system. Most modern operating systems have user interfaces. Even in the MS-DOS microcomputer world, PCs have the MS-DOS COMMAND.COM, the program that gives the user the `A>` prompt, `DIR`, and `COPY`. The Apple Macintosh has the folder windows, the file icons, and the arrow pointer that moves with the mouse. UNIX has all these features and more.

This chapter explores some UNIX concepts as they are actually implemented. The examples use commands discussed in depth in later chapters. Don't worry if you don't understand the details of the commands at this early stage.

## 3.1  Shells

A shell is a command interpreter. It is a program that accepts input from a user and interprets it into actions that the operating system kernel understands. Some user instructions require action by the shell only, others involve the kernel as well, and others access other programs. The shell program determines what to do with the user input. As you will read in Chapter 12, "Basic Shell Scripts and the Shell Environment," the UNIX shell programs have variables that you can change. You can create new variables and programs with the shells, just as with any other procedural programming language. The shells vary mainly in the facilities they offer the user, and, to some extent, in the specifics of their syntax.

The shells are line-oriented; they prompt you to enter a command. The Bourne shell prompt defaults to the dollar sign ($); the C shell (Berkeley shell) defaults to the percent sign (%); and the Korn shell, because of other similarities with the Bourne shell, defaults to $. Some commands require more than one line. To indicate that more is expected on the next line, the shells use a secondary prompt, usually the greater-than character (>).

Many UNIX programs have no user interface and rely on the shell program to provide control over the input, output, and options of program operations. Other programs have their own user interfaces, but rely on the shell program to start them up.

The shells are programs. You can start any shell from any of the other shells. The Bourne shell is the sh program; the C shell is csh; and the Korn shell is ksh. You can run more than one shell at a time; for more information on this feature see Chapter 8, "Processes."

## The Bourne Shell

All UNIX systems provide you with the Bourne shell. It is the oldest, most common interface to a UNIX system. It is the least common denominator of all UNIX shells. The facilities of the Bourne shell are available in all the common shells, although the syntax might differ.

There is a version of the Bourne shell, the restricted shell (rsh), that limits some capabilities. This shell was developed to help new UNIX users and to prevent "guests" from doing things that might be inconsiderate to other users.

Using the Bourne shell is like carrying on a conversation with the computer. With the $, the shell prompts you for instructions, and you respond by telling it what you want it to do. When the shell is ready for another command (that is, when it or some other program has completed the task), it reissues the prompt. For example,

```
$ echo "testing"
testing
$
```

The dollar sign prompts the user to enter something; the user responds with: echo "testing". Once the echo has done its work, the shell responds with another prompt.

The echo command is internal to current versions of the shell. This means that the shell does not invoke another program. By contrast, the following is an interaction with a program external to the shell:

```
$ cal
Thu Nov 16 22:42:22 1989
         Oct                    Nov                    Dec
 S  M Tu  W Th  F  S     S  M Tu  W Th  F  S     S  M Tu  W Th  F  S
 1  2  3  4  5  6  7              1  2  3  4                    1  2
 8  9 10 11 12 13 14     5  6  7  8  9 10 11     3  4  5  6  7  8  9
15 16 17 18 19 20 21    12 13 14 15 16 17 18    10 11 12 13 14 15 16
22 23 24 25 26 27 28    19 20 21 22 23 24 25    17 18 19 20 21 22 23
29 30 31               26 27 28 29 30           24 25 26 27 28 29 30
                                                31

    $
```

The command `cal` is the utility program for calculating a calendar. (See Chapter 9, "A Collection of Utilities," for more about `cal`.) Note that you don't have to know whether the command is internal to the shell or is a separate program. The shell takes care of that detail.

To find out which shell you are running (and what other programs you might be running at the same time) use the `ps` (*process status*) command. The dialog with the shell looks like the following:

```
$ ps
   PID TTY   TIME COMMAND
   180  2a   0:00 sh
   182  2a   0:00 ps
$
```

Chapter 8, "Processes," presents more on the significance of `ps`. For now, just note what is in the `COMMAND` column. There are two processes, *sh* and *ps*, the command executed in the preceding example. The point is, when you invoke programs from the shell, the shell continues to run. The following dialog makes this point clear:

```
$ sh                        — Start a new shell from the shell
$ ps                        — See the result
   PID TTY   TIME COMMAND
   184  2a   0:00 sh
   186  2a   0:00 sh
   189  2a   0:00 ps
$
```

(After trying the preceding example, return to having only one shell process by terminating the second shell with `exit` or Ctrl-D.)

Some commands (and programs) take arguments and options. An argument is a word (or value) that follows the command on the line. For example, the `cal` command used earlier can take two arguments, the month and year:

```
$ cal 7 1995
   July 1995
 S  M Tu  W Th  F  S
                    1
 2  3  4  5  6  7  8
 9 10 11 12 13 14 15
16 17 18 19 20 21 22
23 24 25 26 27 28 29
30 31
$
```

An option is an argument that works like a switch, traditionally preceded by a hyphen (-). For example, the a option to the ls command tells it to show all the files in the directory:

```
$ ls -a
$
```

If you make a mistake while entering on the command line, you can backspace, deleting characters as you go. If you really botch up the command, you can interrupt it and get a fresh prompt by pressing the interrupt key. Usually the interrupt is the Del key, but on some systems you might have to use Ctrl-C.

Most utility programs don't require user interaction once they are started. All the shells can invoke programs as "background" processes. Keeping the shell as your foreground process and sending the utility programs to the background allows you to continue to work on other things while the noninteractive programs crank away. To invoke a program as a background process, end the command with the ampersand (&) character as follows:

```
$ cal 1989 > 1989.cal &
```

This command generates a calendar of all of the months in 1989 and puts the output in the file, 1989.cal. This process is called *output redirection* and is explained in Chapter 8, "Processes."

With the Bourne shell, you can terminate a process before its normal completion, but you cannot bring a background process (a process that you have instructed to run noninteractively, in the background) back into the foreground.

Another limitation of the Bourne shell is the lack of a facility to reissue a command used earlier without reentering the entire command line. To circumvent this limitation, programmers at the University of California, Berkeley, created a shell that added a command recorder, command *history*, and other features.

### The Berkeley C Shell

The Berkeley shell is the program csh. Its name derives from the fact that its syntax is similar to that of the C programming language. UNIX system administrators, software developers, and others spend much of their time working at the level of the shell, rather than within an applications program. They wanted a UNIX interface that made reissuing complex commands easier. For example, a software developer might repeatedly edit a program using the vi editor, invoke the compiler (cc) with some options, and then execute the resulting program. With the Bourne shell, the sequence of commands might look like the following:

```
$ vi myprogram.c
$ cc -o myprogram myprogram.c
$ myprogram
$ vi myprogram.c
$ cc -o myprogram myprogram.c
$ myprogram
$ vi myprogram.c
$ cc -o myprogram myprogram.c
$ myprogram
$
```

Wouldn't it be nice not to have to reenter those commands each time? With the Berkeley C shell, you don't have to. Your command list looks something like this:

```
% vi myprogram.c
% cc -o myprogram myprogram.c
% myprogram
% !v              — The user enters only this
vi myprogram.c    — The C shell prints what it has interpreted
% !c
cc -o myprogram myprogram.c
% !m
myprogram
% !v
vi myprogram.c
% !c
cc -o myprogram myprogram.c
% !m
myprogram
%
```

What is going on here? The C shell maintains a list of the commands executed. (The length of the list is determined by a shell variable, history. The usual value is history=20.) The ! character in the command instructs the C shell to look back through the command history for the first command that starts with the characters that follow the !. The shell prints what it has found, and reexecutes that command.

You can reissue any command in the history list (usually the last 20 commands). To pick a command from the history without doing a backward search, prefix the command number with the exclamation point (!). If you don't know the command numbers, use the history command:

```
% history
    1  cal 6 1990
    2  vi myprogram.c
    3  cc -o myprogram myprogram.c
```

```
    4  myprogram
    5  history
% !1
cal 6 1990
    June 1990
 S  M Tu  W Th  F  S
                1  2
 3  4  5  6  7  8  9
10 11 12 13 14 15 16
17 18 19 20 21 22 23
24 25 26 27 28 29 30
%
```

The C shell offers some command-line (and historical-line) editing. For example, to reissue the previous command with substitution, enter a carat (^), the text to be replaced, another carat, and the substitution text:

```
% echo monkey see
monkey see
% ^see^do
echo monkey do          — The shell's interpretation
monkey do
%
```

But the results are not always so obvious. The substitution can be done on only one command-line argument at a time:

```
% echo monkey see
monkey see
% ^monkey see^turkey do
Modifier failed         — An error message from the shell
%
```

You can, however, use quotation marks to combine the arguments of echo into one:

```
% echo "monkey see"
monkey see
% ^monkey see^turkey do
echo "turkey do"
turkey do
%
```

Another feature of the C shell is *aliasing*, or giving an alternate name to a command expression. Enter the alias, and the shell substitutes your expression for the alias before attempting to execute it. As you will learn later, some commands have long argument and option lists. If you use these commands often, you might want to alias the most common invocations to a single word.

If you are accustomed to MS-DOS commands, you might want to alias the UNIX equivalents to the names with which you are familiar:

```
% alias dir ls
% alias del rm
% alias type cat
%
```

The C shell has job-control capabilities beyond those of the Bourne shell. You can send jobs to the background, and you can bring background jobs to the foreground (if your underlying kernel supports these job-control capabilities).

The C shell and Bourne shell can be found on most modern UNIX systems. The C shell has some shortcomings, however. It is not always the most efficient shell, and its programming syntax and key words are significantly different from the Bourne shell. It is common for a UNIX user to use the C shell as the standard interface with the system and use the Bourne shell for complex tasks. Today there is a shell with the features of the C shell and the language and efficiency of the Bourne shell: the *Korn* shell.

## The Korn Shell

The Korn shell, like the C shell, is enhanced with aliasing, history, and command-line editing. The Korn shell, however, has many more options that allow you to customize the shell to your specific tastes. It also has a much simpler syntax than the C shell. This shell was developed by David Korn while he was at AT&T; it is standard issue with UNIX System V.4, and is the preferred shell in many commercial licenses. Rather than diverging entirely from the Bourne shell syntax, the Korn shell retains most of the original syntax.

The Korn shell prompt is the same as the Bourne shell prompt, but it is typically preceded by the current command number in the history list (as a reminder). Unlike the C shell, the historical commands are reissued using the special shell commands r and fc. (Think of *replay* and *fix command*. Also note that r is actually a preset alias to a special case of the fc command.) The single command r is separated from its optional arguments by a space or tab, unlike the C shell's !. A dialog using the command history might look like the following:

```
5$ history
1          cal
2          mail
```

```
3          cp phonelist phonelist.bak
4          vi phonelist
5          history
6$ r v
vi phonelist
```

In addition, you can edit the command line or any available historical command
with either a vi or emacs style of editing syntax. With the editor you can move
your cursor back and forth on the line, one character or one word at a time. You
can also substitute words, expand aliases, and perform many other editing
operations.

The Korn shell has job-control capabilities similar to those of the C shell. You can
send jobs to the background, monitor the status of background jobs, and bring
background jobs to the foreground (if your underlying operating system kernel
supports these job-control capabilities).

Although the Korn shell is relatively new, it is well-designed and well-documented.
You'll find it on many new UNIX systems. However, many new UNIX systems
are graphic workstations or window-display stations. On these you will find an
even newer way of communicating with the operating system: *graphic user interfaces* (GUIs).

## 3.2  Graphic User Interfaces

If your UNIX work involves a graphics workstation, you will encounter some
form of windowed user interface. You can still get at the good ol' UNIX prompt,
but you will probably interact with your system primarily through a window/
session manager. The process of logging on to the workstation is much the same
as described in Chapter 2, but from there on the world is very different.

Each of the graphic user interfaces that we discuss in this book has a significantly
different way of presenting the world to the user. The more sophisticated (read
*mature*) interfaces were created along with a set of "developer guidelines" so that
applications running under the interface would have a consistent way of presenting controls to the user. In this vein, the Apple Macintosh computer has been a
great inspiration to interface designers. Apple provided no alternative for developers other than the visual tools of their operating system. Also, they did not
approve any software that went outside their guidelines. The learning curve for
most Macintosh applications is short because so much is similar from application
to application.

An important property of UNIX GUIs is that they are based on an underlying window system designed to work on networks. When a UNIX window application is running on a workstation, two programs are actually running simultaneously. One program is the main processing element of the application. The second program handles the input and output for the application; it controls the screen operations and accepts the keyboard and mouse entries. The two programs converse continuously. In the language of the X Window System (from MIT), the input/output program is the "server" and the application is the "client."

The server (input/output program) sends messages about the keyboard and mouse activity to the client (application) program. The client does its processing and passes requests for screen operations back to the server. Because one process can be running on one computer in the network and the other process on another computer, the client/server model is ideal. The server process is usually running on a workstation designed specifically for displaying graphics. The client can be on any computer well-suited to the internal operations of the application, such as a computer used as a database engine. The requests and information are passed back and forth between the two processes over the network.

If you are evaluating a graphic user interface for UNIX, take note of whether it has a good set of guidelines (style guide) for developers. Tight guidelines result in applications that display and act similarly. Also pay attention to how well it works in networks, and which aspects of the window operations are expected to be performed on the client and which on the server. A poor division of responsibility results in excessive interprocess communication across the network, resulting in sluggish response.

With a GUI, the interface to the operating system is menu-oriented rather than command-oriented; in other words, you control the UNIX session by making selections from lists displayed on-screen. This method is radically different from the shells discussed earlier in this chapter. The shells require you to remember commands and their syntax, and then enter them with the keyboard. GUIs require only that you select options.

Graphic user interfaces use a pointing device (usually a *mouse*) as well as a keyboard. Moving the device causes a corresponding motion of a pointer symbol on the workstation screen. The position of the pointer in relation to graphic objects on the screen determines the kind of action that results from pressing the buttons on the mouse. Actually, you can do more with the mouse than just point and click. Common mouse operations are as follows:

- *Press*. Press and continue to hold down a mouse button.
- *Release*. Release a mouse button that you are pressing.
- *Click*. Quickly press and release a mouse button.

- *Double-Click*. Quickly click a mouse button twice without moving the mouse.

- *Move*. Move the mouse without clicking or pressing any buttons.

- *Drag*. Press a mouse button and move the mouse without releasing the button.

GUIs use many different visual elements, including windows, borders, buttons, menus, scroll bars, and file and action icons. Most of these elements are more than decorative; they actually effect window operations. For example, dragging the corner of some window borders resizes and reshapes the windows. Dragging the title bar moves the entire window across the screen.

An *icon* is a small graphic representation of some element of the system. For example, a picture of a file cabinet might represent a program for manipulating files. A picture of a file folder probably represents a collection of files (a *directory* in the old language). A sheet of paper might represent a text file. Graphic user interfaces associate operations with the icons. Clicking on an icon launches the application program associated with the icon. Dragging a file icon to a folder icon and then releasing it moves the file to the folder (subdirectory).

If there is more information than can be displayed within the frame of a window or windowpane, there might be a scrollbar. To move the window around in the information area, you slide a knob (drag it with the pointer) or click on an arrow on the scrollbar.

You might use the GUIs discussed later in this chapter just to manage more than one operation at a time, or you might use them as an underlying structure for an application. Generally speaking, any UNIX application that can run on a standard terminal can run within a terminal window. But the best benefit of the GUI comes from applications that are built on top of it, applications that use the GUI's structures and user-interface tools so that the screen and keyboard or mouse resources are consistent with other applications. Some GUIs offer file managers, whereas others require that the file manager be built on top of them like any other application using that GUI. AT&T/Sun's Open Look includes both a user interface to the operating system and graphic file and process management utilities.

## 3.3  Open Look

The *Open Look* graphic user interface resulted from the combined efforts of AT&T and Sun Microsystems. It is a trademark of AT&T (as is UNIX). Only applications that conform entirely to the specifications for "Look and Feel" of the

Open Look interfaces are certified as Open Look applications. The specifications include which fonts and screen devices are to be used, and where, when, and how they are used. Though these conventions cannot be enforced as strongly as the Apple Macintosh guidelines for applications, rules like these are necessary to bring the usability of the Macintosh to UNIX.

The mouse for Open Look applications has three buttons (see fig. 3-1): from left to right, the *Select* button, the *Adjust* button, and the *Menu* button. The Select button (on the left) is the most commonly used. You use it to manipulate controls and make selections from screen representations of buttons and menus. The Adjust button (in the middle) adjusts the size, shape, and position of windows, text, and groups of objects. The Menu button (on the right) is for bringing up *hidden menus*.

**Fig. 3-1:**
*The mouse for Open Look.*

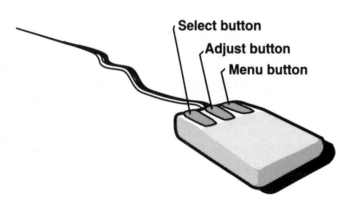

Open Look applications bear a *window mark* on the left side of the window header (see fig. 3-2). The window mark is actually a window-control button; clicking the mouse's Select button while the pointer is on the window mark closes the window, reducing the window to an icon. The window header also contains a window title, usually the name of the application that created the window. Immediately below the window header is the *control area*, with its screen representation of buttons. Many windows have at least a *File* button, a *View* button, and an *Edit* button. Many applications add their own special-purpose buttons to the control area. If no control is appropriate for the application (as with the clock display), there might not be any control buttons.

*Fig. 3-2:*
*An Open Look*
*window.*

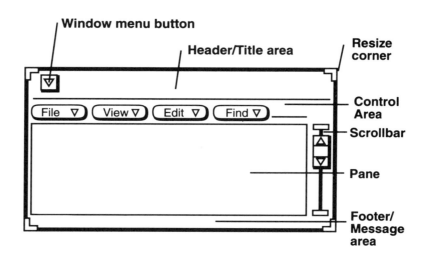

*Fig. 3-2:*
*An Open Look window.*

The display of a button indicates whether it is a simple control button, a *button stack* (which has a line representing additional buttons behind the displayed button), or a *window button*, which has either the window mark slashes or an ellipsis (...) after the title to indicate that there is an associated pop-up window. A double-outlined button represents the default action that is carried out if you press the Enter key on your keyboard (see fig. 3-3). A faded, or ghost, button implies that the button activity is not available at the current level in your activities. A shaded button indicates that the activity associated with the button is currently running.

*Fig. 3-3:*
*Open Look*
*buttons and*
*pins.*

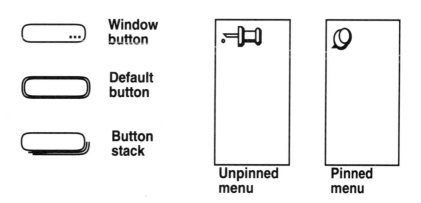

The large open areas below the control area are called *windowpanes*. Application programs use these areas to carry on their activities. In some cases, you converse or enter text or commands in this area. The terminal emulation program, for example, uses a pane as the synthetic screen (a window that looks and acts like a separate terminal). Panes can contain text, graphics, or both.

## Manipulating Open Look Windows

Note that the corners of many windows have what look like pieces of reinforcing tape. If you grab one of these *resize corners* by pressing the Select button and dragging it in any direction, you resize the window. If you grab any other part of a window's border or header and drag it, the entire window moves to the new location.

When you have several windows open simultaneously, it is difficult to avoid having some windows partially obscure others. To bring any background window to the foreground, click Select on any exposed part of the obscured window.

Some windows pop up with information or requests for you to enter data. Pop-up windows usually disappear when their function is complete. If you want to keep a pop-up window alive, click Select on the pushpin icon in the title area of the window (see fig. 3-3). The window becomes "pinned" to the screen. To release the window, click again on the pushpin icon.

## Open Look Menus

Menus appear as a stack of buttons inside a titled box. Each button has a menu item associated with it. The default selection has a double outline. Some selections might represent button stacks, implying that there is a submenu.

No matter what application program you might be running or what its special menus might be, Open Look always provides you with a menu for managing your entire workspace. If you move the pointer outside the applications window to the background area of the screen (the *root*, or workspace area), and press the Menu (right) button on the mouse, the Workspace Menu displays four selections: Programs (the default), Utilities, Properties, and Exit. The first three selections are button stacks, indicating that this simple menu is the base of a tree in your system resource operations. Use the last selection, Exit, to terminate your session in an orderly way, stopping all your applications and closing and saving your files.

The tree in figure 3-4 shows the organization of the operations available from the Workspace Menu. It is generally the entry point to new operations because you launch application programs and manage your files through it. The Programs button provides a menu of the applications installed on your system. The `Properties` menu provides the tools for customizing your personal session workspace. You will find the *File Manager* under `Utilities`.

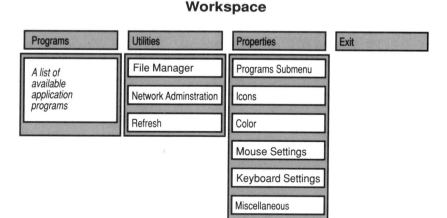

## Open Look File Manager

The Open Look File Manager handles many of the file-management operations discussed in Chapter 4, "Files." The File Manager is a typical Open Look application program; its visual and operational elements are common to many applications. Figure 3-5 shows the File Manager window layout.

The control area contains a `File` button stack, a `View` button stack, an `Edit` button stack, and a `Match` button, plus two input fields: `Directory` and `Pattern`. There are two panes below the control area. The first of these, the *path pane*, describes the path through the directory tree of the file system to the current subdirectory. The lower pane, the *directory pane*, displays the files and directories held by the current directory. The directory pane contains icons for each element found in the directory; there are different icons for different kinds of files. Many directories contain more files than can be displayed in the directory pane. To see the other files, use the scrollbar at the right of the pane.

You can perform some file operations by manipulating the file's icon. You can open a file, for example, by first selecting a file (clicking on its icon) and then "pressing" the Open button in the `File` button stack; or by simply dragging the file icon into the workspace background field, where it opens automatically.

**Fig. 3-5:**
*Open Look file-manager menus.*

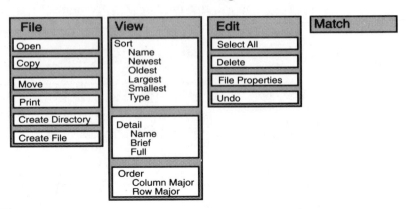

**File Manager**

| File | View | Edit | Match |
|------|------|------|-------|

File:
- Open
- Copy
- Move
- Print
- Create Directory
- Create File

View:
- Sort
  - Name
  - Newest
  - Oldest
  - Largest
  - Smallest
  - Type
- Detail
  - Name
  - Brief
  - Full
- Order
  - Column Major
  - Row Major

Edit:
- Select All
- Delete
- File Properties
- Undo

Use the view stack to configure the directory pane. The edit stack provides miscellaneous functions such as file deletion and operations on all the files in the subdirectory. Using the Match button in conjunction with the `Pattern` input field allows you to select groups of files using *regular expressions*. (See Chapter 5 for an explanation of regular expressions.)

## Open Look Terminal Emulator

Use the Terminal Emulator to use Open Look and a shell (as if you were at a terminal). It is the X Window System's `xterm` program and it's simple: there is no control area and only one pane, with a scrollbar to the right. Any standard terminal-oriented application program will run in the `xterm` window.

If you place the pointer anywhere in the pane and press the Menu button (the right mouse button), you can configure and control `xterm` from the menu: `Redraw`, `Soft Reset`, `Full Reset`, `Properties` (the configuration window), `Interrupt`, `Hangup`, `Terminate`, and `Kill`. The last four buttons send different signals to whatever process you might be running in the `xterm` window. If your interface to UNIX is Open Look, use the Terminal Emulator to experiment with most of the material in this book.

# 3.4  OSF Motif

Without going into the politics of the creation of the Open Software Foundation (OSF), we can just say that Motif was designed to compete with Open Look. Its design has been accepted by many major UNIX vendors, even some who would otherwise be in competition with the Open Software Foundation, a consortium of major computer manufacturers. Motif is not limited to any hardware or operating system. Its only requirement is the presence of MIT's X Window System on the target machine. The X Window System has been implemented on everything from Apple Macintosh, PC computers, and Commodore Amigas to IBM, DEC, and Cray mainframe computers.

The design concept was to produce an attractive, easy-to-use graphic user interface familiar to the PC user. Therefore it has the look of Microsoft Windows and Presentation Manager (IBM), with the elegance of the Hewlett-Packard New Wave screens and the functionality of DECwindows for Ultrix (DEC's UNIX) and VMS operating systems.

Motif is largely a definition of the look and action for application programs. The Motif window manager (mwm) is roughly equivalent to Open Look, but does not include many of the desktop utilities of the AT&T/Sun product. Both Open Look and Motif have strengths and weaknesses.

## Gadgets and Widgets

All Motif application programs share the same set of widgets and gadgets: the graphic screen elements that give you control over your view of the UNIX system. OSF Motif popularized the three-dimensional look of these elements. When you click on a button, it looks as if you actually *pressed* the button. Although there are three-dimensional versions of Open Look, the shaded three-dimensional appearance is most often associated with Motif.

Motif windows have the same actions and icons as Microsoft's Presentation Manager for the OS/2 operating system (see fig. 3-6).

To resize both horizontally and vertically, you press and drag a corner of the frame. To resize in only one direction, press and drag one edge of the frame. Pressing on the title bar of the window allows you to move the window. The smaller of the two buttons in the upper-right corner of the window frame reduces the window to an icon. The larger of the two buttons expands the window to the full screen.

**Fig. 3-6:**
*OSF Motif
window.*

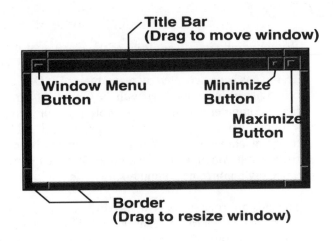

There is always a menu associated with the Window Menu icon button (a dash) in the upper-left corner. This is the system menu. With it, you accomplish the same functions the frame provides. You can also use the system menu to lower the associated window in a stack of windows and to quit the process and destroy the window.

The window that is in *focus* is the one with which any keyboard or mouse button action is associated. Usually some graphic element in the window's frame or title bar signals that it is in focus. (Only one window is in focus at a time.) By default on most systems, Motif automatically changes the focus to whichever window contains the pointer. Changing the focus does not mean that it automatically raises that window to the top of the stack. You must click on the frame to do that. (Almost all these features can be configured to behave however you want.)

As you work with different Motif programs, you will find that there is a multitude of widgets and gadgets, for example:

- The *menu bar* is a horizontal list of submenus. It appears just below the title bar. If you press on any of the items or enter the underlined *key* letter, you get the attached menu.

- *Windowpanes* are dual windows whose shared boundary can be repositioned, changing the size ratio of the two but maintaining the overall size of the combined windows. You can reposition the boundary by dragging it where you want.

- A *slider* is a button that moves along an axis (either vertical or horizontal). Drag it to select a value from a range.

- A *scroll bar* is a gadget that repositions your view in a window. You can either move a slider or press on the appropriate arrow button.

- A *menu* is a list of alternatives. There are many different kinds of menus. (See the next section of this chapter, "Motif Menus.")

- A *push button* is a button used for selection. It appears to have a spring that releases it after it is pressed. Default buttons in a menu are emphasized by having an additional frame.

- *Radio buttons* are sets of buttons in which only one button in the set can be selected at a time. The selected button remains depressed until you press another button.

- *Check buttons* are sets of buttons in which more than one button can be depressed at a time. You toggle the status of a button by clicking on it.

- The *Message area* is the window in which textual information is displayed. Look to the message area for status and error information or for prompts and help.

- A *Dialog box* is an area for keying in information. You are expected to enter data by typing and pressing the Return or Enter key.

Although this list seems long, the intent of the designers was to provide a sufficient variety of gadgets to fill the requirements of any application program. Application programs using Motif thereby display consistent behavior.

### Motif Menus

The Background (root) of the window manager usually has menus associated with it. To see the menus, move the pointer outside all the application windows (and off any icons) and press a button on the mouse. Start with the left button. You can have your own menus associated with the root, but you must develop them by editing the `.mwmrc` file in your home directory.

# 3.5 Summary

The user instructs the operating system through a shell or a graphical user interface (GUI). The most common shells are the Bourne shell, the C shell, and the Korn shell. The most common GUIs are Open Look (from Sun and AT&T) and Motif (from OSF) running with the X Window System (from MIT).

The traditional interface, the Bourne shell, does not make interactive computing easy. The C shell (from Berkeley) is on many UNIX systems, but is hampered by incompatibility with the Bourne shell. The Korn shell (now standard with UNIX System V Release 4) has the features of the C shell and is compatible with the Bourne shell.

The Open Look and Motif GUIs use icons and window elements to provide user control of the operating system. Though the two systems look somewhat different, the basic user actions are quite similar. The greatest difference lies below the look and feel of the GUI, at the programmer's level. Both GUIs use a mouse.

## Review Questions

1. What is a shell's relationship with the user and the UNIX kernel?

2. Which shell has the default prompt of the percent sign (%)?

3. Many UNIX programs have options that can be set from the command line. What is the usual character that denotes a command-line option?

4. What does it mean for a shell to have *command history*?

5. What does it mean for a shell to have *command aliasing*?

6. What are the two most notable differences between the Bourne shell and the Korn shell?

7. What term is applied to operating-system interfaces that use windows, menus, and icons rather than just a command line?

8. When you use a pointing device, what is meant by *clicking on*?

9. When you use a pointing device, what is meant by *dragging*?

## Exercises

Determine what kind of shell or user interface is your default. If you are using a shell within a GUI, determine which shell it is. (*Hint:* use ps.) Also look at what is assigned to Shell in your environment by issuing the env or set command.

Create a C shell by issuing the command csh. Investigate the alias and history properties of your C shell. (You might have to set the length of the history with the command: set history=20.) When you have finished investigating, exit (with exit or Ctrl-D) back to your previous shell.

Create a Bourne shell by issuing the command `sh`. Explore this interface and return to your previous shell in the same way you did in the previous exercise.

Try starting a Korn shell with the command `ksh`. If you don't get an error message, explore this interface and return to your previous shell.

If you have a GUI, investigate all the buttons and icons on your screen. Try clicking each of the mouse buttons on the background (root) of your screen. Note which GUI you are running.

# Further Reading

*AT&T Open Look – Graphical User Interface, User's Guide*, AT&T/Prentice Hall, Murray Hill, NJ, 1989.

*The Kornshell – Command and Programming Language*, Morris I. Bolsky and David G. Korn, AT&T/Prentice Hall, Murray Hill, NJ, 1989 (Chapter 1).

*The UNIX System*, S.R. Bourne, Addison-Wesley, Reading, MA, 1983 (Section 2.6).

*User Interfaces: Shells and GUIs*

# 4

# Files

## Contents

## Objectives

In this chapter you will learn

1. About the UNIX file tree
2. The UNIX commands for copying, moving, renaming, and deleting files
3. How to create and move among directories
4. About the different UNIX file types
5. About file permissions, their meaning, and how to change them

Files in UNIX are organized like an upside-down tree with the root at the top. In fact, the point from which the entire file structure branches out is called the *root*. A branching node is a *directory*. The leaves are *files*. (See fig. 4-1.) A directory can contain other directories, regular files, and special files. The list of directories from the top of the tree (the root) to any file on the branches is the *path*. For example, the path to the file plan in figure 4-2 is /usr/felix/documents/memos/plan. (MS-DOS users should note that the directory names are delimited by a forward slash rather than a backslash.) Everything in UNIX appears as a file in this file structure. This chapter looks at the organization and properties of files, and operations for managing them.

**Fig. 4-1:**
*A partial directory tree, with the root at the top.*

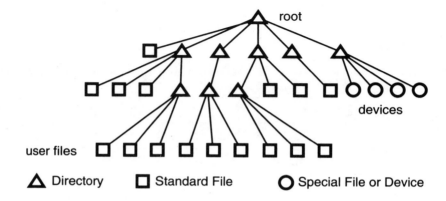

**Fig. 4-2:**
*The directory tree for the* felix *account.*

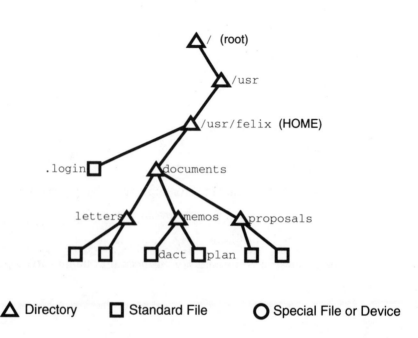

# 4.1   What's In a Directory

When you first log into a UNIX system, you are located in your home directory. The relative location of your home directory varies from system to system, but this variation need not concern you. You are generally interested only in your home directory and the directories below it. This directory is created for you when you are given an account on the system.

You can see what is in any directory by using the ls command. The UNIX system typically provides very terse responses to commands. But when there are no current files stored in your directory, the system displays no message at all. If your account is new, there might not be any files in your home directory:

```
$ ls
$
```

If you give ls an argument that is a directory path, it gives you a list of the files in that directory. Use the -C option to make it format in multiple columns. (On Berkeley-derived systems, ls defaults to multiple columns. On some other systems, the lc command is a shortcut for multiple-column format.)

For example, the root directory might appear as follows:

```
$ ls -C /
Mail            dev             lost+found      tmp
bin             etc             mbox            usr
boot            lib             mnt             unix
$
```

Some of the items correspond to directory names, others to file names. Directories are listed just as if they were files.

If you are not sure which entries are files and which are subdirectories, use the -F option on the ls command:

```
$ ls -CF /
Mail/           dev/            lost+found/     tmp/
bin/            etc/            mbox            usr/
boot            lib/            mnt/            unix
$
```

The subdirectories are listed with the slash character (/) appended. Any files that you can use as programs are listed with an asterisk (*) appended.

The most common directories for executable files are /bin and /usr/bin!EM. Note that due to the number of executable files on most UNIX systems, this command produces more output than can fit on the screen at one time. As the output scrolls, you can make it pause, by pressing Ctrl-S. There are also ways of paging the output of a program (breaking the output into separate screens of information).

Use the ls command to find out what programs and utilities you can use on your system:

```
ls -CF /bin /usr/bin
```

The -l option produces a list with the *long* format:

```
$ ls -l /
total 3166
drwx——      2 root      root          64 Jul 16 08:36 Mail
drwxr-xr-x   2 bin       bin         2496 Sep 23 22:33 bin
-r——         1 bin       bin        24524 Jun 21  1988 boot
drwxr-xr-x   6 bin       bin         2624 Sep 24 23:00 dev
-r——         1 bin       bin          577 Nov  3  1987 dos
drwxr-xr-x   5 bin       bin         1520 Nov 23 20:26 etc
drwxr-xr-x   4 bin       bin         1104 Mar 17  1989 lib
drwx——       2 bin       bin         1024 Aug 30  1988 lost+found
-rw——        1 root      roo         3242 Apr 11  1989 mbox
drwxr-xr-x   2 bin       bin           32 Aug 30  1988 mnt
drwxrwxrwx   2 bin       bin         1248 Nov 23 21:10 tmp
drwxr-xr-x  29 bin       bin          480 Nov  7 21:50 usr
-rw-r—r—     1 bin       bin       341942 Aug  3 21:56 unix
$
```

Later we will explore the significance of much of the information displayed in the long format. Briefly for now, the first column of data shows the file type and the permission flags. The second field is the number of links (entries in the file system for the same file); the third is the name of the owner of the file; the fourth is the group owner. The large number in the next field is the file size in bytes. Then comes the date on which the file was last modified (if it occurred during the current year, the time replaces the year), and finally, the name of the file.

To find information about a specific file (or list of files), include the file name or names on the command line as an argument to the ls command:

```
$ ls -l /unix
-rw-r—r—   1 bin        bin    341942    Aug  3 21:56 unix
$
```

The ls command doesn't usually show *hidden* files unless told to. Hidden files have names beginning with a dot. You can see the hidden files by using the -a option to ls:

```
$ ls -FCa /usr/ben
./              .mgrc           .sbs/           epsilon.stu     poems/
../             .newsrc         .signature      explore/        qs/
.cshrc          .oldnewsrc      Mail/           finance/        resume/
.desk_p         .organization   articles/       linda/          sbs/
.elm/           .phonelist      ayurveda/       list/           scrlib/
.emacsrc        .profile        bin/            ltrs/           tests/
.emacsrc.bak    .pwd            bix/            macros/         text/
.exrc           .rninit         byte/           miscl/          tmp/
.history        .rnlast         calendar        music/          uunet/
.joverc         .rnsoft         coyote/         pasquaney/
.login          .rog_defs       e.src/          pgms/
$
```

Note that there are two hidden directories with unusual names, signified by a dot (.) and two dots (..). These two directories are links to the entries in the file structure for the current directory (.) and the one just above it in the directory tree (..), its parent directory. These names facilitate moving about in the directory and describing paths relative to your current directory.

# 4.2 Files

Directories, memory, input/output ports, disk drives, and other devices appear as files in subdirectories. In UNIX System V.4, even processes appear as files. Under UNIX there are four different types of files:

- *directory* files
- *ordinary* files
- *block special* files
- *character special* files

You have already seen the *directory* file. An *ordinary* file is just that: any file on the system that contains data, text, program instructions, or just about anything else. As its name implies, a *special* file has a special meaning to the UNIX system, and is typically associated with some form of *I/O* or *device*. For the most part, you need not be concerned with these special files—at least not until you become a system administrator.

If you try to display a file that isn't text, you might be in for a surprise. There is no .COM or .EXE suffix to tell you that a file is actually a program. It is best to be sure about the kind of file you are dealing with before you try to treat it like text. To find out, use the `file` command:

```
$ file /unix
/unix:  80386 separate standalone executable not stripped
$ file /etc
/etc:   directory
$ file /etc/passwd
/etc/passwd:    ascii text
$
```

The `file` command looks at the structure of the beginning bytes or lines of a file to determine what kind of file it is. It can usually discriminate between English text, C source code, and shell scripts.

### Making a Copy of a File: The `cp` Command

After you have worked with files for a short time, you will want to be able to make a copy of a file. Once you have made a copy of a file, you can modify the original file without fear of losing it. If you ever need the original information, you can simply *restore* the file from the backup copy.

In order to make a copy of a file, use the `cp` command:

`cp` *source-file destination-file*

The first argument to the command is the name of the file to be copied (the *source file*), and the second argument is the name of the file to place the copy in (the *destination file*). For example, the following entry will make a copy of the file `names` and call the copy `saved_names`:

```
$ cp names saved_names
$
```

Executing this command causes the file called `names` to be copied to a new file called `saved_names`. As with many UNIX commands, after you enter the `cp` command a command prompt appears, indicating successful execution of the command. Of course, you can use the `ls` command to verify that the new file was created:

```
$ ls
names
saved_names
$
```

## Not Quite a Copy: The Link

A *link* is an additional entry in the file structure for the same file. The link is not a copy of the file, but is just another path to the same file. You'll find that links are very convenient when you have a file that you use from several different subdirectories. The most common use of links is between users; if several users want to share a file, there can be a link to each user's file area. Not only is the link a convenience, but it also preserves security that a user might have implemented on his or her file area while still allowing access to individual files. The permissions (control of who can do what with a file) of one link are common to all links.

However, having several points of entry into the same file emphasizes one of the dangers of sharing files (even with one location); that is, more than one person can edit the file simultaneously! (This is true for *any* file, not just for links.) It is not recommended to have more than one person editing a file at one time, because only the last-saved version of the file is retained. The versions from the users who finish editing earlier are overwritten. There are revision-control systems (such as SCCS) that restrict editing to only one user at a time; other users can only read the file.

When you delete a file with multiple links, the actual file remains; only the specified link is removed. There is no hierarchy to links; all are created as peers.

## Renaming a File: The mv Command

Sometimes you need to change the name of a file. You can easily change a name with the mv command, as follows:

mv *source-file destination*

The arguments to the mv command follow the same format as the cp command. The first argument is the name of the file to be renamed, and the second argument is the new name. Therefore, to change the name of the file saved_names to hold_it, for example, the following command would do the trick:

```
$ mv saved_names hold_it
$
```

The mv command actually moves the file. Moving it to another name in the same directory is equivalent to renaming it. You can also use mv to move files to another location in the directory structure. If you want to retain the same name but move a file to another preexisting directory, you need only give the destination directory name. The file is moved to that directory:

```
$ mv dead.letter /usr/tmp
$
```

The same abbreviation can be used for copying (cp) and making links (ln); the destination might be just a directory name. This, then, is one of the applications of the dot notation for the current directory. For example, if you want to copy dead.letter back into the current directory, enter the following command:

```
$ mv /usr/tmp/dead.letter.
$
```

All three of these commands (mv, cp, and ln) can also be used for operating on more than one file at a time, but only if the destination directory already exists. UNIX assumes that the destination is the last argument used with the command. In the following example, we move dp.txt, log, and maps.shar to the subdirectory /usr/tmp:

```
$ ls -C
dp.txt              log           maps.shar       shar.shar
$ mv dp.txt log maps.shar /usr/tmp
$ ls -CF
shar.shar
$ ls -CF /usr/tmp
dead.letter         dp.txt              log             maps.shar
$    .
```

A word of caution when using the cp, ln, and mv commands: the UNIX system does not care whether the file specified in the second argument already exists.

If the file specified in the second argument already exists, then the contents of the original file are lost. So, for example, if a file called old_names exists, then executing the command cp names old_names would copy the file names to old_names, destroying the contents of the previous old_names file in the process. Similarly, the commands mv names old_names and ln names old_names would overwrite the previous old_name.

If you don't have write permissions to the existing file, you cannot overwrite it. (See the section on "Permissions and Protections" later in this chapter.) There is also an environment variable, noclobber, that helps protect existing files. BSD systems protect you from linking over existing files even when noclobber is not set. Environment variables are discussed in Chapter 12, "Basic Shell Scripts and the Shell Environment."

## Removing a File: The rm Command

No system that enables you to create files would be complete without a command that also allows you to remove them. Under the UNIX system, the command to remove a file is rm.

rm *file-list*

The arguments to the rm command are the names of the files to be removed:

```
$ rm hold_it hold_it.bak
$
```

This command removes the files hold_it and hold_it.bak from the current directory.

Although the rm command is conceptually one of the simplest UNIX commands, it is also potentially one of the most dangerous. Because it is easy to accidentally remove *all* your files with this command, be careful when you use it.

## Displaying and Printing Files

The simplest way to dump the contents of a file to your screen is to cat the file. The text pours right out with no paging, filtering, or control other than what you can provide at your terminal.

```
$ cat /etc/motd
Welcome to ronin.
The system is scheduled to be down every Sunday from 8AM to 10AM for
system maintenance.
$
```

You can also use the cat command to create files. If no file name is given to the cat command, it assumes that your keyboard is the source. To terminate the cat command, you must give it the end-of-file character, Ctrl-D (automatically part of any real file, but must be explicitly entered if you are using the keyboard as a file). We will discuss input and output *redirection* more in Chapter 8, "Processes," but you can start using it here by entering the following:

```
$ cat
This is being entered at the keyboard rather than from a
file.
This is being entered at the keyboard rather than from a
file.
To end, I need to type a CTRL-D.
^D
To end, I need to type a CTRL-D.
$ cat > names
Susan
Jeff
Henry
Allan
Ken
^D
$ cat names
Susan
Jeff
Henry
Allan
Ken
$
```

You have seen how the cat command is used to display a file at the terminal. This approach works fine for relatively small files. Most video terminals can display 24 lines of information; therefore, if your file is larger than that and you try to cat it, all but the last 24 lines will "fly" right off the screen.

The UNIX system provides a program called pg that allows you to view your file one screenful at a time. The format of this command is simple enough:

pg *file-list*

in which *file-list* is the name of the file or files you want to look at. The program automatically displays enough lines from the file to fill up your entire screen, and then waits for you to type a key before continuing. This feature gives you as much time as you need to read the information on the screen. When you are ready to view the next screenful, press Enter. After displaying the next screenful of data, the program once again waits for you to press Enter. If you decide that you've seen enough, enter q to stop the display; otherwise, press Enter again to cause the next screenful to be displayed.

If you're not running UNIX System V, you won't have the pg program. However, chances are that you have a program called more that performs the same function. In contrast to pg, more displays the next screenful from the file when you press the space bar, rather than Enter. It also accepts a q as an indication that you've seen enough of the file.

To get a hard-copy printout of your file, use the lp command. (See Chapter 9 for more information about lp.)

# 4.3 More About Directories

To work with directories, it is necessary that you learn about the pwd command. This command helps you get your bearings, by telling you the name of your *present working directory* (pwd). Although you start at the same place in the UNIX directory tree every time you log in, you can move around the tree. Think of yourself as a squirrel (sorry if this isn't very flattering) whose home is a knothole in a big maple tree. You don't have to spend your life on that one branch. You can scramble back to the trunk and explore other branches to gather the treasures that might be growing out there. Your present working directory is the description of the path from the root to wherever you might currently be working.

The special directory you are placed in upon logging into the system is called your home directory. If your account is "felix," your home directory is /usr/felix. Therefore, whenever you log in as felix, you are automatically placed inside this directory. To verify that you are in the right directory, issue the pwd command:

```
$ pwd
/usr/felix
$
```

The output verifies that felix's present working directory is /usr/felix. Now that you know how to find out where you are with the pwd command, you can go "exploring."

## Changing Directories

A very common UNIX command changes your present working directory. The command is cd (change directory):

cd *directory-path*

Its argument is the name of the directory you wish to change to.

Let's assume that you are felix and have just logged into the system. You have been placed inside felix's home directory, /usr/felix. You can see from figure 4-2 that there is one directory directly *below* felix's home directory: the documents directory.

To make documents your current working directory, issue the cd command, followed by the name of the directory to change to:

```
$ cd documents
$
```

If the directory doesn't exist, cd gives you an error message. For example:

```
$ cd mungbean
mungbean: No such file or directory
```

After executing the correct command, you are placed inside the documents directory. You can verify at the terminal that the working directory has been changed by again issuing the pwd command:

```
$ pwd
/usr/felix/documents
$
```

and you can list the files contained in the current directory with the ls command:

```
$ ls
letters
memos
proposals
$
```

Now we'll change to the memos directory:

```
$ cd memos
$ pwd
/usr/felix/documents/memos
$ ls
dact
plan
$
```

The path between the home directory and the memos directory is highlighted in figure 4-3.

**Fig. 4-3:**
*Getting to the*
memos
*directory from*
HOME.

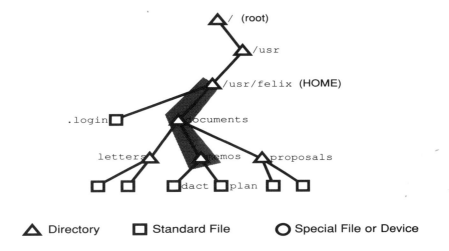

△ Directory    □ Standard File    ○ Special File or Device

The easiest way to get back up one level in the directory path is to issue the following command:

```
cd ..
```

because, by convention, the double dot (..) always refers to the directory one level up, the parent directory. Issuing the cd .. command once more brings you up one more level to the home directory:

```
$ pwd
/usr/felix/documents/memos
$ cd ..
$ pwd
/usr/felix/documents
$ cd ..
$ pwd
/usr/felix
$
```

Now suppose that you wanted to go to the letters directory. You know that you can get there by issuing cd twice:

```
$ cd documents
$ cd letters
$ pwd
/usr/felix/documents/letters
$
```

Alternatively, you can get to the `letters` directory with a single `cd` command by specifying the relative path, `documents/letters`, or the full path, `/usr/felix/documents/letters`:

```
$ cd documents/letters
$ pwd
/usr/felix/documents/letters
$ cd ../..
$ pwd
/usr/felix
$ cd /usr/felix/documents/letters
$ pwd
/usr/felix/documents/letters
$
```

You can always return to your `home` directory by issuing a single `cd` command (without any parameters):

```
$ cd
$ pwd
/usr/felix
$
```

Remember that you always have a choice between a full and a relative path name. For now, choose the one that is easiest for you to understand; later—after you become more experienced using UNIX—you will naturally choose the one that is easiest to enter.

### Creating and Destroying Directories

A directory provides the structure for a collection of files and perhaps other directories below it, *subdirectories*. You should organize your files in a manner similar to that used for the rest of UNIX: a directory tree. You will find it useful to have your own `tmp` directory. Use this directory for files that you know you will use for only a brief time. Periodically, go in and clean out your personal `tmp` directory. (No need to burden your account and the system with unnecessary files.) The system's `/tmp` and `/usr/tmp` directories are automatically swept clean every time the system does its maintenance.

Build a directory tree that reflects the way you organize your information. If you want to change the organization later, there are plenty of UNIX utilities to help you do that.

To create a directory, use the `mkdir` (make directory) command:

`mkdir` *directory-name*

The argument to this command is simply the name of the directory you want to make. For example, assume that you are still working with the directory structure shown in figure 4-2. Suppose further that you wish to create a new directory called `misc` *on the same level* as the directories `documents` and `programs`. If you were currently in your `home` directory, entering the command `mkdir misc` would achieve the desired effect:

```
$ mkdir misc
$ ls -F
documents
misc
programs
$
```

This is the equivalent of the command `mkdir /usr/felix/misc`. The directory structure now appears as shown in figure 4-4.

**Fig. 4-4:**
*Felix's directory
tree after
adding the
`misc` directory.*

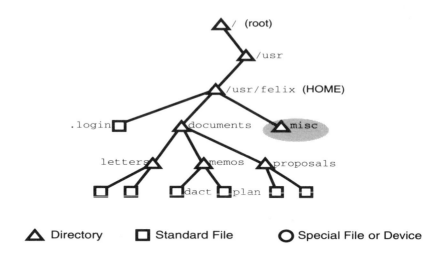

△ Directory          □ Standard File          ○ Special File or Device

Just as you can easily create a directory with the `mkdir` command, so can you easily remove one with the `rmdir` command. The only stipulation involved in removing a directory is that no files be contained in the directory. If there *are* files in the directory when `rmdir` is executed, you will not be allowed to remove the directory. To remove the `misc` directory you created earlier, you could enter the following:

```
$ rmdir misc
$
```

Entering rmdir /usr/felix/misc does the same thing. Although more typing
is necessary, the full path name gives you a little extra insurance against
accidentally deleting the wrong misc directory when you are removing files and
directories.

If you want to remove the misc directory when there are files in it, you must
remove all the files contained in that directory before issuing the rmdir command.

An alternate method of removing a directory and the files contained in it is to use
the rm command but with the -r (recursive) option. The format is DANGER-
OUSLY simple, as follows:

rm -r *dir*

in which *dir* is the name of the directory that you want to remove. rm removes the
indicated directory and *all* files in it. CAUTION! You can easily remove all your
files with rm -r if you're not careful.

# 4.4   *Permissions and Protections*

Look again at the ls command with the long format:

```
$ ls -l
total 8
drwxr-xr-x   5 felix      group1       96 Dec 25 11:54 documents
drwxrwxrwx   2 felix      group1       80 Dec 25 12:11 misc
-rw-r-r—     1 felix      group1       69 Dec 25 12:06 names
drwxr-xr-x   2 felix      group1       32 Dec 25 11:50 programs
-rwxr-r—     1 felix      group1     1234 Dec 25 12:04 zombie
$
```

Note the permissions field: it uses the characters -, *r*, *w*, and *x*. Each position in
this field represents a "permission flag." As shown in figure 4-5, the permission
field allows you to specify a single file-type character and one of three character
positions (*read*, *write*, and *execute*) for each type of user: the file owner, the group,
and all other users.

Look again at the `ls` command with the long format, and note the file-list entry for `misc`; it has a full line of permissions: `drwxrwxrwx`. This means that it is a directory, and the owner, the group, and all others have permission to do anything they want with that directory. (More on directory permissions later in this chapter.)

For the file `names`, the owner is `felix`, the third field. The file group is `group1`, the fourth field. This entry in the file list is *not* a directory; no one has execute permissions (it is not a program and therefore not executable); the group and the world (everyone else) have only read permission; the owner, `felix`, can both read and write to this file.

If one of the permissions is denied, a minus sign (`-`) shows up in place of the appropriate letter. For example, `rw-` means you can read and write, but not execute (good for plain text files that you have no need to execute as programs); `r-x` means you can read and execute, but not write (good for a program you don't want someone to overwrite).

## Changing File Permissions

It should be obvious that there is a way to control the accessibility of your files for each of the three types of users: owner, group, and all others. The command is `chmod`. Let's say, for example, that you are `felix`, the owner of the file `zombie`, and you don't want any user other than yourself to be able to write into (and thereby alter or destroy) `zombie`. On the other hand, because you feel `zombie` is a useful program, you want it to be available to all users to examine and execute. Therefore, you want the new mode of `zombie` to be `rwxr-xr-x`, thus allowing users in your group and others to read (or copy) and execute the file, but not to tamper with it.

**Fig. 4-5:**
*The permission field from ls -l.*

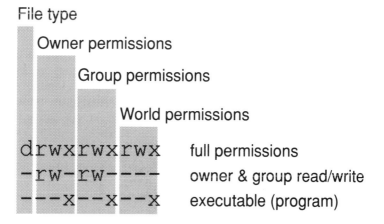

File type

Owner permissions

Group permissions

World permissions

```
drwxrwxrwx    full permissions
-rw-rw----    owner & group read/write
---x--x--x    executable (program)
```

There are two ways to use the chmod command, *symbolically* and with *absolute* (numeric) permissions. The symbolic argument format is this:

chmod *[who] op permission*

in which *who* is an optional combination of the letters u, g, and o. u is for the owner's permissions (think of this as the *user*), g is for the group's permissions, and o is for others' permissions. *a* can be used to specify all of these (ugo) and is the default used when no *who* is specified. The *op* can be a plus sign (+) to add *permission* to the mode, a minus sign (-) to remove *permission* from the mode, or an equal sign (=) to assign *permission* to the mode. The *permission* is a combination of the letters r, w, and x, meaning read, write, and execute, respectively.

Therefore, to change the mode of zombie to -rw-rw-rw-, you would enter:

```
$ chmod a=rw zombie
$ ls -l zombie
-rw-rw-rw-  1 felix   group1   70 Jul 28 21:12 zombie
$
```

Note that the a can be omitted. To add execute permission you can enter:

```
$ chmod +x zombie
$ ls -l zombie
-rwxrwxrwx  1 felix   group1   70 Jul 28 21:12 zombie
$
```

Finally, to remove write permission from others, you would use o-w:

```
$ chmod o-w zombie
$ ls -l zombie
-rwxrwxr-x  1 felix   group1   70 Jul 28 21:12 zombie
$
```

One of the main advantages of the symbolic mode is that you can add or remove permissions without knowing what the old ones are. For example, when you first create a shell program, the permissions don't include execute. This can be added with a quick chmod +x command without knowing what the original read/write permissions are. The absolute (numeric) mode can be much faster when you have a specific permission in mind, but you need to understand octal (base 8) counting.

To alter the mode of zombie with absolute (numeric) mode, you must use the chmod command with the new mode and the file name as arguments. The new mode is not specified to chmod as rwxr-xr-x, but as a *three-digit octal number* that is computed by adding together the numeric equivalents of the desired permissions (see fig. 4-6). In this case, the new mode is 755, where the 7 is rwx for the owner, the first 5 is r-x for the group, and the second 5 is r-x for others.

**Fig. 4-6:**
*Numeric
equivalents of
permissions.*

$$x=1$$
$$w=2$$
$$wx=2+1=3$$
$$r=4$$
$$rx=4+1=5$$
$$rw=4+2=6$$
$$rwx=4+2+1=7$$

To change the mode of zombie to rwxr-xr-x, use the chmod command with the three-digit number:

```
$ chmod 755 zombie
$
```

Looking at the mode of zombie now, you can see that it has indeed changed.

```
$ ls -l zombie
-rwxr-xr-x  1 felix  group1  70 Jul 28 21:12 zombie
$
```

Some other examples of chmod are shown here with the resultant modes. Note that only the owner or the system administrator can change the mode of a particular file; thus, if other users can't access the file, they cannot use chmod to gain access.

```
$ chmod 700 zombie
$ ls -l zombie
-rwx─────  1 felix  group1  70 Jul 28 21:12 zombie
$
```

Now only felix is allowed any kind of access to zombie.

```
$ chmod 711 zombie
$ ls -l zombie
-rwx─x─x  1 felix  group1  70 Jul 28 21:12 zombie
$
```

Now group members and others are allowed to execute zombie, but not to copy or examine it.

```
$ chmod 771 zombie
$ ls -l zombie
-rwxrwx-x  1 felix  group1  70 Jul 28 21:12 zombie
$
```

Now users in group1 are allowed the same privileges as felix, but others can still only execute zombie.

The permissions can prevent accidental overwriting or removal of an important file. All you have to do is change the mode to -r-xr-xr-x and you can't change the file even though you are the owner. You have to change the mode to give yourself write permission before you can alter the file:

```
$ chmod 555 zombie
$ ls -l zombie
-r-xr-xr-x  1 felix  group1  70 Mar 18 16:57 zombie
$ echo hi there > zombie
zombie: cannot create
$
```

Here the shell cannot redirect the output of the echo command into the file zombie because the write permission isn't set.

Even rm does not immediately remove the file; it asks for confirmation first:

```
$ ls -l zombie
-r-xr-xr-x  1 felix  group1  70 Mar 18 16:57 zombie
$ rm zombie
zombie: 555 mode?                     — Do you really want to remove it?
```

If you type a y when rm asks for confirmation, the file is removed *regardless of the mode*; any other input causes rm to quit without removing the file:

```
$ rm zombie
zombie: 555 mode ? n                  — I don't want to remove it
$
```

## Changing Group and Owner

As the owner of zombie, you can change the group associated with it by using the chgrp command:

```
$ chgrp group2 zombie
$ ls -l zombie
-rwxrwxr-x  1 felix  group2  70 Jul 28 21:12 zombie
$
```

Now group2 has full read, write, and execute permission, and group1 no longer does. (Members of group1 now fall into the "others" category.)

You can even change the owner, although that is a little risky, because after you change the owner, you cannot change it back—the new owner would have to do that. (Berkeley UNIX systems allow only the administrator to use chown.) To change ownership of zombie, use the chown command:

```
$ chown lizard zombie
$ ls -l zombie
-rwxrwxr-x  1 lizard group2  70 Jul 28 21:12 zombie
$
```

As you can see, lizard is now the owner of zombie. To change the group, owner, or permissions, you would have to log in as lizard.

For the commands chmod, chgrp, and chown, you can specify more than one file name to change the appropriate file attributes of all the files specified, provided you own the files to begin with:

```
$ chmod 666 *.c
$
```

This entry makes all C programs in this directory readable and writeable by all users. The following denies access to files x, y, and zzz to all users but the owner, who can read, write, and execute the file:

```
$ chmod 700 x y zzz
$
```

The following makes lizard the owner of all files in this directory:

```
$ chown lizard *
$
```

## Directory Permissions

Directories also have modes that work in ways similar to ordinary files. You need read permission (r) to use ls on a directory; you need write permission (w) to add

```
```

or remove files from a directory; and you need execute permission (x) to change to a directory (cd) or use it as part of a path. Note that to use any file, you must have the proper access permissions for the file *and all the directories* in the path of that file.

If you do not have execute permission in all directories along the path to a file, you cannot use the file, regardless of what the file's permissions are. If you do not have read permission to a directory, an echo * will not work. You can still access a file in such a directory if the execute permission of the directory is set, but you must use its full name; file-name expansion does not work. If you don't have write permission in a directory, you can't create files in that directory, nor can you move or remove them. The opposite is also true: if you do have write permission in a directory, you can remove a file, no matter what the file's permissions are or who the owner is. (As of System V, Release 3.2, a directory can be set up so that only the owner of a file can remove or rename it, even if everyone can write to the directory.)

Let's look at some possible directory modes:

```
$ ls -l
total 5
drwxrwxrwx   2 felix   group1   32 Aug 4 18:03 anyone
drwxrwxr-x   2 felix   group1   32 Aug 4 18:03 group
drwxr-xr-x   2 felix   group1   32 Aug 4 18:03 me
drwx------   2 felix   group1   32 Aug 4 18:03 just_me
d--x--x--x   2 felix   group1   32 Aug 4 18:03 nobody
$
```

The directory anyone is available to all users—anyone can create and remove files from this directory. The directory group is open to the owner and members of group1 for creating and removing; other users can list its contents and read from or write to *existing* files (if the permissions on those files allow access), but they cannot create new files. In the directory me, only the owner can create or remove files. The directory just_me is accessible only to the owner. No other user can access any files in it. The last directory, nobody, is only searchable; nobody can create or remove files, nor can anyone use ls on it; however, if you know the name of a file in nobody, you can access that file because you can search (execute) the directory.

The process for changing the access modes of a directory is the same as for a file. If you want to change the mode of nobody to rwx for all classes of users, enter the following:

```
$ chmod 777                                    nobody
$ ls -ld                                       nobody
drwxrwxrwx   2 pat   group1   32 Aug  4 18:03 nobody
$
```

As you can see, it is now open to all users. The -d option to ls tells ls that information about the *directory*, rather than information about its *contents*, should be listed.

## 4.5 Summary

UNIX organizes files in a tree structure in which directories can contain subdirectories and files. Use the ls command to get information about the files in a directory. To specify a path to a directory or file, separate the directory names and file name with a slash (/).

UNIX manages everything as a file. A directory is a special kind of file; so are devices (memory) and even processes (as of UNIX V Release 4).

The UNIX file system allows a single file to appear in several places in the file tree. The ability to be in several places at the same time is called a link.

Files have three levels of permission: owner, group, and all. Each level has three kinds of permission: read, write, and execute.

The most common file and directory commands are mkdir, rmdir, cp, ln, rm, ls, and chmod.

## Review Questions

1. What pattern represents the structure of UNIX directories and files?
2. What is the name of the file-system structure that holds a collection of files?
3. What is the command used for listing basic information about files within a directory?
4. Which commands are used for copying, creating links, moving, and deleting files?
5. What are the shortcut names for the current directory and its parent (used for describing paths relative to the current directory)?
6. What is the simplest way to display a small text file?
7. What are the commands for paging and printing files?

8. What is the significance of the *present working directory*, and how do you find out which directory that is?

9. How do you move about in the directory tree? (Describe both absolute and relative motion.)

10. How do you create a directory?

11. How do you destroy a directory, and what is required before you can destroy it? What is the quick (and dangerous) way of destroying a directory and all the files and directories contained in it?

12. What are the three kinds of file permissions?

13. What command is used to change file permissions, ownership, and group?

14. What is the significance of the three kinds of permissions for directories?

# Exercises

Use the command `ls -CF /etc` to list the files in that directory. (The `/etc` directory is used for system information and programs. It isn't of much interest to you, but it is easy to find on most UNIX systems.)

Use the `file /etc/*` to see what kind of file each of the system information files is.

Using circles to denote directories and vertical lines to denote the connections between directories, draw a picture of the path from the `root` directory to your `home` directory. (Draw the `root` at the top.) You need to use the `pwd` command to get the information for this drawing.

Using `cd ..` and `ls -CF`, move up one directory at a time and note on the previous drawing the number of files and directories off each of the directories in the path to your `home` directory. If there are more than a dozen from any point, just estimate the numbers.

Make sure that you are in your `home` directory: `cd` with no arguments. Now make a directory called *learn* by issuing the command `mkdir learn`. Move to the directory with `cd`. In the `learn` directory, create the subdirectories *one*, *two*, *three*, and *four*. Now make a copy of the file `/etc/motd` and `/etc/passwd` by using the `cp` command. Use `ls -l` and `file *` to see the permissions and file type of everything in your *learn* directory. (You can use the subdirectories for your exercises in each of the chapters. Add subdirectories as you need them.)

# 5

# Regular Expressions, Special Characters, and Wildcards

## Contents

## Objectives

In this chapter you will learn

1. About characters that give special meaning to file names and commands

2. About variables used by the shell

3. A shorthand for describing `groups` of text, called *regular expressions*

4. How to send text

Historically, UNIX users communicated with their computers using standard character-based terminals. It was customary to use the standard printable characters to perform basic editing and control functions. Today, your connection might still include some of these controls; therefore, you should be aware of them and know how to override their special meanings with other special characters. Other special characters, quotations, and accents used as quotations have their own meaning. All these special characters lead to the most sophisticated group of special characters, those that define regular expressions. Regular expressions are used for describing groups of ordinary textual characters. With this set of tools you will be well equipped to do some serious searching with the `grep` family. (If `grep` seems weird, wait until Chapter 11, in which you start writing scripts for `awk`.)

# 5.1  Special Shell Characters

As we mentioned earlier, many punctuation characters are inappropriate in file names, because these characters have special meaning. UNIX has been accused of being an "alphabet soup" of commands; actually, it is more an alphabet soup of special characters, only a few of which we discuss in this chapter. Table 5-1 shows what each of these special characters is used for.

**Table 5-1.  Special Shell Characters.**

| Character | Use | Shell |
|---|---|---|
| ! | Reference commands in the history list | C |
| # | Begin a comment (in a script) | C, Bourne, Korn |
| $ | Prefix to a shell variable name | C, Bourne, Korn |
| % | Pattern substitution<br>Job control | C<br>C, Korn |

**Table 5-1. Special shell characters.** *(continued)*

| | | |
|---|---|---|
| ^ | Pattern substitution | C |
| & | Put command in background | C, Bourne, Korn |
| ( ) | Command or expression grouping | C, Bourne, Korn |
| ~ | Abbreviation for a user's home directory<br>Alias expansion | C, Korn<br>Korn |
| \| | Pipe between commands | C, Bourne, Korn |
| { } | Execute in current shell<br>Shell variable substitution | Bourne<br>C, Bourne, Korn |
| [ ] | Synonym for `test` | C, Bourne, Korn |
| : | History modifier prefix<br>Null command (no action) | C<br>Bourne, Korn |
| ; | Separate sequential commands | C, Bourne, Korn |
| \ | Defeat special meaning of next character<br>(Escape to literal) | C, Bourne, Korn |
| ? | Single character wild character | C, Bourne, Korn |
| * | Multiple character wild character | C, Bourne, Korn |
| " " | Combine to a single argument with shell<br>variable substitution | C, Bourne, Korn |
| ' ' | Combine to a single argument and take<br>all characters as literal | C, Bourne, Korn |
| ` ` | Use output of enclosed command as<br>argument to another command | C, Bourne, Korn |
| < | Redirect standard input to come from<br>a file | C, Bourne, Korn |
| << | Redirect standard input to come from the<br>following lines (up to a key word) | C, Bourne, Korn |
| > | Redirect standard output to a file<br>(Will replace any existing file) | C, Bourne, Korn |
| >> | Redirect standard output to a file,<br>appending to existing file | C, Bourne, Korn |
| . | Read file and execute as a shell script | Bourne, Korn |

In Chapter 8 we discuss the significance of the special characters used for redirecting the input and output of programs. These characters are >, <, and |. We also discuss the characters used for process control, in particular the &. In this chapter we introduce the use of shell variables and then go into them more thoroughly in later chapters on shell programming and customizing your environment. The C shell has different syntax for many of the same special characters as the Bourne and Korn shell, but it adds a few of its own.

## 5.2  Shell Variables

Although this chapter is primarily about the magical properties of special characters, you should understand some basic concepts of shell variables first. A *variable* is temporary storage for data or information. Variables are referenced by *variable names*. A variable name does not necessarily reflect the data stored in the variable; it is just a handle for the storage.

Shell variables have no "type," meaning that the shell does not discriminate between numbers and strings of characters. Nor do you have to "declare" shell variables before you store data in them. (Most programming languages require you to specify what you are going to use as variables, and what types they are.) The only requirement of the shells is that you reference shell variables by prefixing the variable name with the dollar sign. However inconsistent it might seem, when you assign (store) data to a variable, you do not prefix the variable name with the dollar sign. The following are examples of assignments to variables:

Bourne and Korn Shell

```
$ myname=felix
$ mygoal=learn
$ echo myname
myname
$ echo $myname
felix
$ echo $mygoal
learn
$
```

C Shell

```
1% set myname=felix
2% set mygoal=learn
3% echo myname
```

```
myname
4% echo $myname
felix
5% echo $mygoal
learn
6%
```

The obvious question is, "What do you need variables for?" Shell variables are useful in shell scripts. But you can use variables even before you learn about shell scripts. If you anticipate using a string many times with commands, you can easily put the string into a variable (with a shorter name) and use it in each of the command lines.

In the following example, the paths of a source directory and destination directory were assigned to two shell variables, src and dest. These two variables were then used in the remaining commands, as follows:

```
$ src=/usr/lib/X11/examples
$ dest=/usr/felix/learnX
$ ls $src
Xdefaults    maze.c         octa.c     plaid.c
$ cp $src/octa.c $dest
$ cp $src/Xdefaults $dest
$
```

## 5.3   Wildcards

Many of the commands we have seen so far allow the argument *<file-list>*. The implication is that you can apply the command to more than one file at a time. For example:

```
$ cat file1 file2 file3 file4
```

There are, however, *wildcard* characters you can use as shortcuts to entering all those file names. The concept of wildcards comes under the more technical title of *regular expressions*.

UNIX uses two different syntaxes for regular expressions. The first is restricted to *file name expansion* (also referred to as *globbing*), the expansion of abbreviated file names to a list of files. The second regular-expression style is used for searching in text. You use this second style with the editors and text-search commands such as grep (*g*lobal *r*egular *e*xpression and *p*rint) described later in this chapter.

File names can be globbed together by using the single-character wildcard ?, the multiple-character wildcard *, the range-of-characters enclosed in square brackets ([ ]), and explicit characters. Unlike MS-DOS and other similar operating systems, UNIX treats the dot character as a standard character in file names. It is commonly used in file names, and wildcards include it in their range of valid characters. The dot gives a special power to file names when it occurs as the first character in the file name. File names that start with the dot as the first character are invisible to the asterisk wild character. In the following examples, the ls command is applied to a directory with some hidden files (some file names start with dot):

```
$ ls -C  pgms/a*
pgms/a.out          pgms/amort.c        pgms/ascii2.c
pgms/alpha          pgms/ascii          pgms/ascii2fl
pgms/alpha.c        pgms/ascii.c        pgms/ascii2fl.c
pgms/alpha.o        pgms/ascii.tab      pgms/auto
pgms/alpha.out      pgms/ascii2         pgms/auto.c
$ ls -C  pgms/*.c
pgms/alpha.c        pgms/chop.c         pgms/intr.c
pgms/amort.c        pgms/clean.c        pgms/keylog.c
pgms/ascii.c        pgms/col_fltr.c     pgms/label.c
pgms/ascii2.c       pgms/cscript.c      pgms/laser.c
pgms/ascii2fl.c     pgms/dospaint.c     pgms/laze.c
pgms/auto.c         pgms/envelope.c     pgms/lex.yy.c
pgms/b2h.c          pgms/fl2ascii.c     pgms/loadfont.c
pgms/bchop.c        pgms/fromwp2.c      pgms/main.c
pgms/branch.c       pgms/fuel.c         pgms/maketab.c
pgms/calc.c         pgms/getopt.c

$ ls  *
Mail
News
bin
docs
letters
pgms
tmp
$ ls -d .*
.
..
.cshrc
.emacsrc
.exrc
.login
.logout
.newsrc
```

```
.oldnewsrc
.organization
.profile
.rninit
.rnlast
.rnsoft
.signature
$
```

The hook (?) is a wild character that means "any *one* character." In contrast to the asterisk (*), the hook *requires* a character in whichever position it is used, as in the following examples:

```
$ ls -Cd *
a           b           report1
aa          bb          report2
aax         c           report3
alice       cc
$ ls -Cd ?
a           b           c
$ ls -Cd report?
report1     report2     report3
$ ls -cd *[!0-9]
```

Another limited sort of wild-character notation comes from enclosing desired characters within square brackets ([ ]). For example, [abc] matches the *single* letter a, b, or c. It is similar to the ?, but it allows you to choose the characters to be matched, as in the following examples:

```
-Cd   $ ls -Cd [abcd]
a b c
$ ls -Cd report[13]
report1 report3
$ ls -Cd [ab]*
a           aax         b
aa          alice       bb
$ ls -Cd *[0-9]
report1     report2     report3
$
```

The second ls matches any file whose name is a, b, c or d. In the next case, files whose names begin with report and end with either 1 or 3 are matched. The fourth case matches any file whose name begins with an a or b. The last case introduces a new twist. The specification [0-9] matches the characters 0 *through* 9. The only restriction in specifying a *range* of characters is that the first character must be alphabetically (using the order of the ASCII character table) less than the last character. (A character is alphabetically less when it occurs earlier in the ASCII character set.) In other words, [z-f] is not a valid specification for the letters *f* through *z*, but [f-z] is.

By mixing and matching ranges and characters in the list, you can perform some very complicated expansions. For example, [a-np-z]* will match all files that start with the letters a through n or p through z (simply stated, any lowercase letter but o).

If you put an exclamation point (!) immediately after the left bracket, the sense of the match is *inverted*. For example, [!a-z]* will match all files that start with any character *except* a lowercase letter (a through z). The pattern *[!0-9] matches all files that end in any character other than a digit.

# 5.4 All about Quotations

The shell is a unique programming language with respect to the way quotation signs work. The shell interprets four different characters on your keyboard as *quotation characters*:

- the double quotation mark (")
- the ending single quotation mark, hereafter referred to as the apostrophe when used singly (')
- the backslash mark (\)
- the beginning single quotation mark, hereafter referred to as the grave accent when used singly (`)

Each of these marks has a special and *different* meaning to the shell. Understanding the distinctions between them is important. To introduce them, we use the echo command. (This command writes its arguments to the standard output—your terminal in this case. It is usually used in shell scripts to generate literal output.) Recall that the asterisk (*) by itself as a file name matches all the file names in the directory.

## The Apostrophe

Assume that your current directory contains the following files:

```
$ ls
boring_stuff
junk
```

```
treasures
$
```

Now consider the output from the following two echo commands:

```
$ echo *
boring_stuff junk treasures
$ echo '*'
*
$
```

In the first case, the shell substituted * with the names of all the files in the directory. In the second case, no substitution occurred. Obviously, the apostrophe had something to do with this. The fact is, if the shell sees a pair of single quotation marks (apostrophes), *no file-name substitution will occur between the pair of quotation marks*.

The following example implies that an even greater generalization can be made:

```
$ echo >
syntax error: 'newline or ;' unexpected
$ echo '>'
>
$
```

In the first echo, the shell thought you were redirecting the output from the echo and looked for a file name to follow. Because none was specified, the (rather cryptic) error message was generated. In the second case, the apostrophes surrounding the > had the effect of *removing the special meaning* the character had to the shell.

This is the key behind quotation characters (in this case, the apostrophe): any character that is otherwise special to the shell (such as *, ?, >, <, >>, and |) loses its special meaning when it appears between quotation marks. Quotation marks also preserve *white-space* characters by removing their special meaning to the shell. White-space characters are blank spaces, tab characters, and newline characters. You will see quotation marks used for this when we discuss grep at the end of this chapter. Because white space is the shell's way of delimiting arguments, quotations pass all the enclosed text as a single argument. The following example shows how the use of an apostrophe ties together several words into one argument:

```
$ echo a     b c
a b c
$ echo 'a     b c'
a       b c
$
```

You can also use the `banner` command to illustrate how the apostrophe changes arguments. `banner` places each of its arguments on a new line:

```
$ banner one two
```

```
  ####     #     #  #######
 #     #   ##    #  #
 #     #   # #   #  ######
 #     #   #  #  #  #
 #     #   #   ##   #
  ####     #     #  #######


 #######   #     #  #####
    #      #     #  #     #
    #      #     #  #     #
    #      # ### #  #     #
    #      ###  ##  #     #
    #      #     #   #####
```

```
$ banner 'one two'
```

```
  ####     #     #  ########      ######   #     #  #####
 #     #   ##    #  #             #     #  #     #  #     #
 #     #   # #   #  ######        #     #  #     #  #     #
 #     #   #  #  #  #             #     #  # ### #  #     #
 #     #   #   ##   #             #     #  ###  ##  #     #
  ####     #     #  ########      #     #  #     #   #####
```

```
$
```

The shell processes no characters enclosed within apostrophes; that is, the characters are guaranteed to remain unchanged.


## The Double Quotation Mark

The following example uses shell variables discussed in more detail in Chapter 8:

```
$ message='hello there'        —Assign to shell variable
$ echo $message                —Use shell variable
```

```
hello there
$ echo '$message'                   — Use single quote marks
                                       (apostrophes)
$message                            — Literal interpretation
$ echo "$message"                   — Now try the double quotes
hello there                         — The shell variable expands
$ echo "SAY ** $message **"
SAY ** hello there **
```

In both cases, with the double quotes the value of the shell variable message
— hello there — was echoed at the terminal, because the shell substitutes the
value of shell variables *inside* double quotes. $ is still special, even inside the
*double quotes*. Also note that the file name wildcard * was not expanded. Now
look at the following:

```
$ echo '$message'
$message
$
```

As you can see, when a shell variable is enclosed within *single* quotation marks,
its value is not substituted by the shell. Furthermore, special shell characters
enclosed within apostrophes are also ignored, as in the following example:

```
$ echo '< > * ? >> |'
< > * ? >> |
$
```

The *exceptions* to this rule are as follows:

- The dollar sign $

- The grave accent ` (discussed later in this chapter)

- The backslash \ (if it precedes a $, ", `, newline, or another \; otherwise it
  *does* lose its special meaning to the shell)

Study the following output carefully to see the subtle differences among the
effects of using no quotation marks, double quotes, and single quotes.

```
$ echo *
boring_stuff junk treasures
$ echo * "*" '*'
boring_stuff junk treasures * *
$ var=hello
$ echo $var "$var" '$var'
hello hello $var
$
```

In the first case, the asterisk was expanded to include all the file names in the current directory. But when the asterisk was enclosed in either single or double quotes, it had no special meaning. In the example using `hello`, the dollar sign (shell variable name) was expanded to reveal its contents when it was used either bare or enclosed in double quotes. When enclosed in single quotes, it loses its special meaning.

## The Backslash Character

Preceding any character by a backslash removes the special meaning of that character only. In other words, \ followed by any character *x* is similar to writing `'x'`. Here are some examples:

```
$ echo \$foo
$foo
$ echo \< \> \" \' \` \$ \| \* \?
< > " ' ` $ | * ?
$ echo \\
\
$
```

The last example shows that even a backslash can be preceded by a backslash to remove its special meaning.

Do not be misled, however, to believe that the backslash neutralizes any special properties of characters. It can make an *ordinary* character take on special properties (depending on the command it is passed to). The `echo` command in the Bourne shell has the special interpretations shown in table 5-2.

In Chapter 12 you will use these special characters in your shell scripts. The most common is the `\c`, which suppresses the newline at the end of the echo, as in the following examples:

```
$ echo "Act on which file?"            — Without the \c
$                          <           — The cursor goes to the next line
$ echo "Act on which file? \c"         — With the \c
Act on which file? $  <                — The cursor stays right here
```

**Table 5-2.   The special backslash meanings for the Bourne shell** echo **command.**

| Character | Meaning |
|---|---|
| \b | Backspace |
| \c | Print arguments without trailing newline |
| \f | Form feed |
| \n | Explicit newline |
| \r | Carriage return |
| \t | Tab |
| \v | Vertical tab |
| \\ | Explicit backslash |
| \nnn | The 8-bit character with the octal ASCII number of *nnn*. The number can be one, two, or three digits, but the first digit must be zero. |

## The Grave Accent

One of the most unusual features of the shell is the way it handles grave accents
(`). Enclosing a command inside a pair of grave accents causes the command to
be executed and its output to be inserted at that precise point on the command line.
For example, consider the following:

```
$ echo The date is `date`
The date is Tue Jan 30 07:38:29 EST 1990
$
```

When the shell processes the command line, it notices the grave accents. The shell
then proceeds to execute whatever is enclosed between these grave accents; in this
case, the date command. The shell substitutes the output from date, Tue Jan 30
07:38:29 EST 1990, at that point on the command line, and executes the echo
command. echo is not even aware that any of this is happening. In fact, echo sees
as its arguments The date is Tue Jan 30 07:38:29 EST 1990 because the
shell does its work with grave accents *before* it calls on the echo command. It is
a good idea to enclose the entire series of arguments to echo in apostrophes to
prevent any characters with special powers from being expanded:

```
$ echo 'The date is <`date`>'
The date is <Tue Jan 30 07:38:29 EST 1990>
$
```

Take a look at another example:

```
$ echo 'Your current working directory is `pwd`'
Your current working directory is /usr/felix/programs
$
```

In this case, the pwd command was executed and its output inserted in the command line. To be more precise, the standard output of pwd was inserted by the shell. Once you are writing shell scripts, you will find countless applications for the facilities of the grave accent.

Do not worry if this discussion of quotation marks seems a bit complicated, because it is! Even experienced UNIX users still have difficulty getting their quotation marks straight at times. You can expect to experience the same difficulties.

## 5.5 Regular Expressions

Understanding regular expressions is the most important key to gaining the full power of many UNIX utilities. Regular expressions are used wherever searching is required: in editors, in report formatters; and in the text-search utilities. Regular expressions are an expansion on the idea of wildcards. Remember the use of the asterisk (*) and hook (?) wildcards when describing file lists? Regular expressions perform similar functions, but with greater detail, describing collections of words and conditions. They are composed of combinations of special characters and literal characters.

Regular expressions use the dot (.) for any character in a single character position, which constitutes an important difference between fully implemented regular expressions and the wildcard expressions used on the command line. The dot in regular expressions takes the place of the hook in file-name globbing. For example, the regular expression any .og describes the following (among other, more ridiculous) possibilities:

```
any cog
any dog
any fog
any hog
```

```
any jog
any log
any nog
```

As in file expansion, ranges of characters are enclosed in square brackets. All lowercase letters are represented by [a-z], all uppercase letters by [A-Z], and all digits by [0-9]. Negation of a set is described with a carat (^) rather than the bang (the exclamation point, !). Therefore, to describe any character that is *not* a digit, the regular expression is [^0- 9].

## Number of Occurrences

The asterisk (*) is not a wildcard for a regular expression, but rather a modifier, or a kind of multiplier. The asterisk means any number, *zero* or more, of the previous character or subexpression. The cross (+, also called the plus sign) means any number, *one* or more, of the previous character or subexpression. Therefore, the regular expression a*b is valid for the following:

```
b
ab
aab
aaab
aaaab
aaaaab
```

The regular expression a+b represents one or more of the a character. In the previous example, it is valid for all those except the last, the b without any leading a.

The ultimate regular expression wildcard is the combination of the dot and asterisk, .*. It means *any* number of *any* characters. In other words, any string of zero or more of any set of characters. For example, if we searched the first two lines of this paragraph with A.*, we would match the entire first line. The notation .*B is equivalent to just the * in filename expansion.

An exact number or range of occurrences is specified by enclosing the value in curly braces. For example, the regular expression ab{1,3}c is valid for only the following:

```
abc
abbc
abbbc
```

An exact number of occurrences is entered without the comma and second digit; for example, {5}.

### The Beginning and End of a Line

The beginning of a line and end of a line are represented by the carat (^) and the dollar sign ($), respectively. If you do not use either of these symbols, your regular expressions have no restrictions on where in the line they will find their match. The simplest use of these special characters is in searching for patterns at the beginning and end of the line. You can, however, combine the curly braces with either the carat or the dollar sign for some very useful searches. ^Fro matches Fro at the beginning of the line, but does not match the same characters when they occur later in the line: many Fro. The following expression specifies exactly where the string is to occur: ^.{20}Fro, beginning at the twenty-first character. The dot and curly brace indicate that the first twenty characters can be any character.

The best way to learn about regular expressions is to experiment with the UNIX search utilities, grep and egrep.

## 5.6  Searching Text With grep

The grep utility searches files for patterns described as regular expressions. There are three forms of the grep command:

- grep. General purpose search utility, limited regular expressions
- egrep. Extended search with full regular expression
- fgrep. Fast search for literal strings, no regular expressions

Oddly enough, egrep is faster than either grep or fgrep on some systems. The fgrep command is smaller, but by only 10 to 20 Kbytes, which is not much these days.

The general format of the command is the following:

grep *pattern files*

Every line of each file that contains *pattern* is displayed at the terminal. If more than one file is specified to grep, each line is also immediately preceded by the name of the file, thus enabling you to identify the particular file in which the pattern was found.

We will start with an example of searching a single file for a particular pattern. Assume that you have a directory filled with text files that make up a chapter of a book (this book, perhaps), and you want to find every occurrence of the word shell in the file ed.cmd. The resulting output is as follows:

```
$ grep shell ed.cmd
files, and is independent of the shell.
to the shell, just enter a q.
$
```

This output indicates that two lines in the file ed.cmd contain the word shell.

If the pattern does not exist in the specified file (or files), the grep command displays nothing, and the shell displays the following prompt:

```
$ grep cracker chapter1
$
```

Assume that you have a file called phone_book in which you keep the phone numbers of people you call frequently, as follows:

```
$ cat phone_book
Farber, Ethan          445-4343
Iansito, Toby          937-1232
Levy, Steven           (907) 843-4432
Mead, John             864-5378
Sander, Rick           343-2109
Smith, Ben             723-2205
Snellen, Bart          331-9974
Weather info           976-1212
Wood, Pat              421-3193
Wood, Sam              778-3321
$
```

When you want to look up a particular phone number, the grep command comes in handy:

```
phone_book$ grep Sander phone_book
Sander, Rick           343-2109
$
```

Look what happens when we look up Wood:

```
$ grep Wood phone_book
Wood, Pat              421-3193
Wood, Sam              778-3321
$
```

Two lines are printed because there are two lines containing Wood. To obtain a single match from the directory, you can be more specific:

```
phone_book$ grep 'Wood, Pat' phone_book
Wood, Pat          421-3193
$
```

In this case, single or double quotes are *required* around the name because of the space that separates the two patterns, Wood, and Pat. The quotations serve to join the two words together so that the grep command sees them as a *single* pattern. See what happens if you omit the quotations:

```
$ grep Wood, Pat phone_book
grep can't open Pat
phone_book:Wood, Pat          385-3193
phone_book:Wood, Tom          778-3321
$
```

The grep command sees Wood, (and *only* Wood,) as the pattern, and Pat and phone_book as the files to be searched. Because there is no file called Pat, grep displays the message grep can't open Pat. grep then searches the file phone_book for the pattern Wood,. Because this pattern is in the file, the matching lines are displayed at the terminal.

The grep command is useful when you have a lot of files and you want to find out which ones contain certain words or phrases. The following example shows how the grep command can be used to search for the word shell in all the files in the current directory:

```
$ grep shell *
cmdfiles:shell that enables sophisticated
ed.cmd:files, and is independent of the shell.
ed.cmd:to the shell, just enter a q.
grep.cmd:occurrence of the word shell:
grep.cmd:$ grep shell *
grep.cmd:every use of the word shell.
$
```

As mentioned previously, when more than one file is specified to grep, each output line is preceded by the name of the file containing that line.

It is generally a good idea to enclose your grep pattern inside a pair of *single quotes* to "protect" it from the UNIX system. For instance, to find all the lines containing asterisks inside the file stars, enter the following:

```
grep * stars
```

will not work as expected because the UNIX system sees the asterisk and automatically substitutes the names of all the files in your current directory!

Enclosing the asterisk in apostrophes, however, removes its special meaning from the system. Double quotes do not prevent it from being expanded by the shell *before* being passed to grep:

```
grep '*' stars
```

## Options to the grep Utility

Sifting through the output of grep can be tedious sometimes, particularly when there are many occurrences of the pattern and you are interested in the names of the files only. Fortunately, grep has the -l option to make it print just the names of the files containing the pattern, as in the following example:

```
$ grep -l '[Ss]hell' chapter3/*
3-1
3-2
3-4
3-title
contents
temp
$
```

The name of a file is printed only once if the pattern is found in it, no matter how many times the pattern occurs. In this example, the [Ss] is the regular-expression syntax for the single character of upper- and lowercase *s*. In this expression, we have specified that we want to match occurrences of *Shell* and *shell*.

A similar option, -c, instructs grep to output only the file name and the count of matched lines, as follows:

```
$ grep -c '[sS]hell' *
3-1:83
3-2:4
3-3:0
3-4:3
3-all:0
3-title:5
contents:4
firstpage:0
nextpage:0
notes:0
temp:1
$
```

The use of a third option, -n, tells on which line number the expression is found.

```
$ grep -n '[sS]hell' contents
1:Shells
2:The Bourne Shell
3:The Berkeley Shell
4:The Korn Shell
$
```

You can even reverse the "hits" by using the -v option. The lines that do *not* match are used in the output. You can combine the options to get the effect you want. The following example shows how to find out how many lines DO NOT have *shell* in them:

```
grep -vc '[sS]hell' *
3-1:300
3-2:275
3-3:125
3-4:36
3-all:7
3-title:18
contents:4
firstpage:1
nextpage:1
notes:2
temp:397
$
```

A simple way to find both upper- and lowercase versions of the search pattern is to use grep with -i, the *ignore case* option. As with all UNIX commands, your manual tells you about all the options and syntax.


## Regular Expressions: *grep* **and** *egrep*

As we have seen, you can search for every occurrence of shell and Shell with grep using the square brackets: grep '[Ss]hell' *. The standard grep command implements only some (but not all) of the regular expression abbreviations.

The egrep version allows you to use succinct expressions such as [0-9]+. The plus character specifies *one or more* occurrences of the previous character:

```
$ cat testlist
I have 9 cats in my yard
There are 144 different ways of saying the same thing
Ben Smith loves cold snowy mornings.
Brad Smith photographs dried flowers.
Johannes Smith collects herbs.
Kevin Jones understands 15 languages but speaks only 3.
Ben Jones understands only 3 languages but speaks all 3.
$ egrep '[0-9]+' testlist
I have 9 cats in my yard
There are 144 different ways of saying the same thing
Kevin Jones understands 15 languages but speaks only 3.
Ben Jones understands only 3 languages but speaks all 3.
$
```

Note that the exact-count syntax using curly braces ({  }) is not implemented in egrep.

Other features of egrep include using the logical OR operator (|), and using parentheses to make regular subexpressions. The OR operator allows you to specify more than one possible match in your expression. For example, to find all Smiths and Jones in a list of names, use the expression Smith|Jones with the vertical bar (|) indicating a logical OR. You can string together any number of alternatives using OR, as follows:

```
$ egrep 'Smith|Jones' testlist
Ben Smith loves cold snowy mornings.
Brad Smith photographs dried flowers.
Johannes Smith collects herbs.
Kevin Jones understands 15 languages but speaks only 3.
Ben Jones understands only 3 languages but speaks all 3.
$
```

You can designate subexpressions, bracketed by parentheses, to use with the other regular-expression characters. For example, to use either *Brad* or *Johannes* with *Smith*, make a subexpression out of the OR expression and add the *Smith*:

```
$ egrep '(Brad|Johannes) Smith' testlist
Brad Smith photographs dried flowers.
Johannes Smith collects herbs.
```

With any flexible system, there is more than one way to specify the same thing. Choosing a style is up to you; do what you find easiest. Consider the following examples of how to locate words with the combination of f and t in the fourth and fifth position:

```
egrep '^...(tf|ft)' /usr/games/lib/words
draftee
postfix
rooftop
snifter
```

The carat (^) ties the search to the beginning of the line. The three dots indicate that the first three characters can be anything. The parentheses enclose the subexpression of tf OR ft. Unfortunately, even egrep does not recognize the curly braces (specific number of occurrences) specification. You will have an opportunity to use curly braces with awk, sed, and ex.

## Fast Searches for Lists of Targets: fgrep

What if you wish to search for a list of key words? You could put them all together in an OR expression and send for egrep. Or you could put the list in a file and use the fgrep command.

The egrep command can also use lists in files, but it is very memory-hungry (requires more memory) because it uses full regular expressions. The fgrep command is optimized for this kind of search.

The syntax of the fgrep command is as follows:

fgrep -f *key-list search-subject*

Regular expressions are not implemented in the fgrep utility, which handles only literal strings. To search for a list, you must spell out each possibility in the key list; there are no abbreviations. See, for example, the following searches:

```
$ cat keylist
cat
dog
frog
bird
worm
germ
$ fgrep -f keylist /usr/games/lib/words
bulldog
catalpa
catbird
catcall
catchup
catfish
cathode
```

```
catlike
cattail
cowbird
cutworm
dogbane
dogfish
dogging
doggone
dogtrot
dogwood
educate                  —Note the imbedded cat here and below
germane
placate
polecat
redbird
toccata
wildcat
$
```

For any of the grep family, never assume that you are going to find only individual, stand-alone words unless you specify them with leading and trailing spaces. This method is not ideal, however, because it does not catch the target word if it occurs at the beginning (there is no leading space at the beginning of the line.) Nor does this method catch the word if it occurs at the end of a line or with any adjacent punctuation.

Each grep utility has its strengths and weaknesses, but all are very fast. You pay a price for the flexibility of the egrep utility in that it uses a great deal of memory. Therefore, be careful not to make your regular expressions too complex. Only experience will tell you what is "too complex."

## 5.7 Summary

The shell uses variables (names that point to information) to store temporary information to use in your UNIX session, telling where to search for files, or any other use you or a program want to put them to.

The shell and UNIX utilities interpret some characters with a special meaning; for example, the asterix may be a wildcard character.

Apostrophes, quotation marks, grave accents, and backslashes have different meanings to UNIX shells. Apostrophes group words on the command line into a single argument and prevent the shell from expanding any wildcards. Quotation marks group words like the apostrophe but still allow the shell wildcards to expand.

Regular expressions are a shorthand way of describing groups of non-determinate character strings. Regular expressions give special meanings to some characters and are used by UNIX shells and many UNIX utilities.

The `grep` family of commands is used to search for strings in UNIX text files. Some versions of `grep` use regular expressions.

## Review Questions

1. What is the significance of the asterisk (*) character in a file name when applied to the command line?

2. What general class of characters has special meaning to the shell?

3. What is a shell variable?

4. What are three mechanisms that can be used to escape the special meaning of the characters used by the shell for special purposes?

5. What is the difference between how the shell treats several command-line words within quotations and without quotations?

6. What meaning does the shell give to expressions enclosed in grave accents?

7. What is a regular expression?

8. What does the asterisk (*) mean in a regular expression? What does the dot (.) mean in a regular expression?

9. What regular-expression characters are used to represent the beginning and end of a string or a line?

10. What characters are used to enclose a set of characters to be specified for a single character position?

11. What family of utilities is used for searching files using global regular expressions?

## Exercises

Try each of these `echo` commands in your home directory:

```
echo *
echo \*
echo "*"
echo '*'
```

Change directories to /usr/lib, then use the shell's echo command with *, .*, [a-m]*, and other wildcard combinations of your choice. Examine the output of each to understand what you are seeing.

Use the grep command on the /etc/motd file to find all lines with words that start with the letter a (upper- or lowercase).

Use the grep command on the /etc/passwd file to find all lines with words (alphabetic characters only) that have exactly five characters.

# 6

# The Standard Editor

## Contents

## Objectives

In this chapter you will learn

1. The differences between editors, word processors, and desktop publishing systems

2. About the operations and organization of the `vi` editor

3. The major vi editing commands

4. About the relationship between the vi and ex editors

5. How to customize and extend the capabilities of vi

It is easy to think that computers are used to do little more than compute and calculate. This might be true for supercomputers running batches of computations, resolving the motion of distant star systems, analyzing the optimum production of entire oil fields, and balancing the checking accounts of hundreds of thousands of bank customers. But most UNIX systems are used for more personal work: preparing reports, searching databases, refining budgets, mathematical modeling, simulations, and software development. Users spend most of their time editing text. This has been true since the first UNIX system left the development lab. UNIX was used for writing patent documents as its first application outside the laboratory. Even programming, however, requires that you edit the source code. Much of the information of this age is in the form of text. An editing program is usually used to generate the informal messages of electronic mail.

# 6.1   About Editors and Word Processors

Although there is no fine line that distinguishes editing programs from word processing programs, they have different approaches to manipulating text. People who work with text in the personal-computer world use word processing programs; WordStar, Microsoft Word, and WordPerfect are well-known examples. These programs display text basically in the format in which it will eventually be printed. If you insert a word in the middle of a line with a word processor, it might affect all the following lines as well. A word processor reformats as you write. Some word processing programs display different fonts and point sizes so that you preview the printed output while you enter the text.

At one end of the word processing spectrum are desktop publishing systems. Desktop publishing systems can show graphics as well as text. They can wrap text around graphics, alter the spacing between characters (kerning), and drive typesetting machines with their output.

At the other end of the spectrum are line-editing programs such as UNIX ex and ed. Closer to center are the screen-oriented editors such as vi and emacs.

One of the major differences between word processing programs and editing programs is how each program stores the text. The text of a word processing program seems perfectly simple when you look at it through the screen of the word processor. However, the program is actually coding the information you type. It has a special way of keeping track of breaks between words, sentences, and paragraphs. It has hidden codes to indicate which words you want italicized, boldfaced, indented, and so on. If you were to dump a word processor's file to a terminal screen or a printer (without using the word processor) you would see some very strange characters. You might even send the terminal or printer into confusion.

Editing programs are not as devious with their text as word processors are. The files they generate are easily dumped to the screen or printer. There are no hidden control codes in files created with editors. They are just plain ASCII text. This means that the files can be easily moved from one application to another.

A curious point: the vi editor uses temporary files that you do not see unless you look for them. These are not quite as straightforward as what you normally see.

There are many popular word processors for UNIX, but the traditional way to generate text is with an editor. The text you enter on the UNIX command line is plain ASCII. Similarly, the shell scripts that you write in Chapter 10 will be plain ASCII. You can actually do all your text work without using any word processing program; just an editor and text formatter. In UNIX, text formatting and typesetting are traditionally done with programs that process the plain text files (nroff and troff).

The TEX typesetter is also popular. Some people even write in the printer/ typesetter control language PostScript.

It is important to know at least one UNIX editor. You need it to use the mail system, edit your personal configuration files, and get the maximum use of the Korn shell, which has a command editor embedded in it. The two most common editing programs in UNIX are emacs and vi.

The emacs editor is found on many university systems and wherever there are emacs enthusiasts. Even though it is not a standard part of UNIX, it is very popular. The emacs editor is extensible; it includes a programming language for creating extensions for special tasks. There is a story about an MIT student who wrote an emacs extension that called the elevator to his floor when he was ready to go home. Extensible editors can be difficult to learn, because of their flexibility. The environment you build for them totally affects how they look and how they act.

# 6.2  The *vi* Family

Every UNIX system has vi, the visual editor and its relatives: ex, the line-oriented version (vi is just a screen shell to ex); ed, an early version of ex; and sed, the stream editor.

A line editor is appropriate for use on printer terminals rather than display terminals, although nothing prevents you from using a line editor on a screen. A line editor doesn't use up-and-down cursor motion. It always prints on the next line. When you use a line editor, you specify what line you want to edit, and then you insert, append or replace on that line. For editing tasks involving repetition or few corrections, line editors are faster than screen editors.

A stream editor gives you no interactive control of the editing. It applies a *script* of editing commands on a file. Each command is applied to the entire source file. A stream editor is more of a filter than an editor. As with the line editor, some editing tasks are far easier with a stream editor than with a visual editor. That is why UNIX has all three. You always have the right tool for the job.

A visual editor such as vi or emacs is the most common tool for working on text. With it, you have an entire screen of text in view at all times. You can move up and down through the lines and the screens. With vi, the process of editing is much more visual than cerebral. There is no guesswork involved as you edit. You see your additions and changes where and when you make them.

In this chapter, we start with vi and then show how you can access the special powers of ex and sed from within vi. If you find that vi doesn't work for you on a terminal because the terminal controls are unknown to your UNIX system, you can always use ex or ed.

The vi editor has many commands. It is a sophisticated editor. It is a good editor for both writers and programmers. Most of this book was written using vi. (The rest was written using emacs.) Do not think, however, that you can learn vi just by memorizing the commands. That is a waste of time; many of the commands are rarely used. It is far easier to learn a few basic commands and concepts at first, work with those, and then build on that understanding. As you learn more about vi, you will find faster and easier ways of doing editing tasks. But don't be concerned with efficiency until you have become familiar with the basics.

# 6.3   Basic Concepts of the vi Editor

The vi editor has two modes: *command mode* and *text-entry mode*. Keystrokes in command mode do not enter text into a file; rather, they specify commands. The commands do such things as move the cursor (the current point in the file), delete text, copy text, save the file, exit the program, etc. Keystrokes in text-entry mode, however, enter text into the file.

To get to the text-entry mode from the command mode, press an appropriate command key such as i for inserting text at the cursor, a for appending text after the cursor, or R for replacing text from the cursor on. You leave the text-entry mode and return to the command mode by pressing Esc (the Escape key).

A major advantage of having two modes, command and text entry, is that the commands are unembellished key strokes using the standard touch-typing keys. Because your fingers never have to leave their normal positions, editing with vi can be very fast. The impediment to this is the Escape key. And to make matters worse, terminal manufacturers have no standard place for this key.

Many vi commands are mnemonic, however. There is a general organization and sense to all of them. For example, cw is for *change word*, dw is for *delete word*, and yw is for *yank word*. Similarly, 10cw means *change ten words*. Most of the vi commands can be prefixed with a numeric value, as in the previous example. The 10 in the 10cw command acts like a multiplier. It instructs vi to execute the attached command *ten* times.

As you learn new vi commands, keep an eye out for similarities. If some attribute of one command combination appeals to you, try the same combination on a similar command; it will probably work even if it isn't documented. The parallel organization of vi commands helps you learn to construct new combinations of complex commands.

## Editing a File

The command-line syntax to invoke vi is

    vi *file-list*

As implied, you can edit many files at a time. The limitation is that only one file is visible at a time; the current cursor or editing position is maintained for only two files at a time.

From the command line:

```
$ vi myfile
```

produces a screen like that in figure 6-1.

**Fig. 6-1:**
The vi
screen with
no text in the
file.

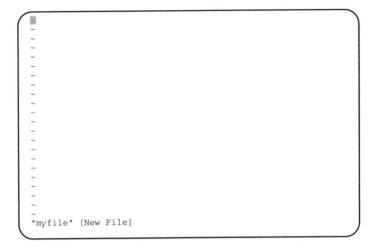

```
▓

~
~
~
~
~
~
~
~
~
~
~
~
~
~
~
~
~
"myfile" [New File]
```

The column of tildes will fill the entire screen except the last line, the status/ex line. The tildes indicate that there is nothing in the file at that point.

The initial (default) mode of vi is command mode. If you start typing before entering a command, you receive error beeps until by chance you press a key representing a valid command.

Before entering text, set up vi to have automatic word wrap. In command mode, press the colon (:) key. Notice that a colon appears at the bottom of the screen in the status/ex line. Enter set wrapmargin=10<CR>. (This can be abbreviated to set wm=10<CR>.) Now when you enter text, new lines will be started any time there is a word break between column 70 and column 80 (the default vi screen width). Later in this chapter you'll see how to set up vi so that it defaults to your preferences.

To begin entering text, use the i (insert) command. There is no indicator that you are in text-entry mode; such terseness is typical of UNIX. (If you want to tell vi to display the mode it is in, issue the command :set showmode<CR>.)

If you are uncertain as to whether you are in command mode or in text-entry mode, press the Escape key. Pressing Esc ensures that you are in command mode. Your terminal beeps if you are already in command mode. No harm done.

There are many different cursor-motion commands, but the basic four are h, j, k, and l (see fig. 6-2).

*Fig. 6-2:*
*The basic*
*cursor-motion*
*keys for* vi.

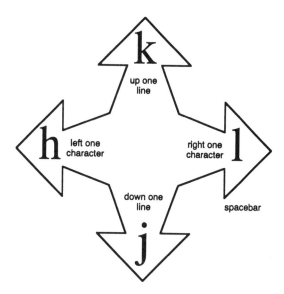

There are no mnemonics for these operations. You have to teach your fingers that h is left one character, j is down one line, k is up one line and l is right one character. Note that all these keys are on the same line. (The arrow keys might work on some terminals, but you should learn the alphabetic keys to facilitate moving from terminal to terminal. Besides, you can work faster if you keep your hands in touch-typing position.) Cursor movement commands work only in command mode. If you press these keys when you are in text entry, those characters are entered as text.

You use the cursor-motion keys to move around the text you have created. You can use the spacebar or the l key to move to the right. The a (append) command lets you append text after the cursor position. The i (insert) command lets you insert text at the cursor position, a subtle but useful difference (see fig. 6-3).

**Fig. 6-3:**
*Before and after insert* ( i ).

```
┌─────────────────────────┐   ┌─────────────────────────┐
│ I want to insert        │   │ I want to insert        │
│ an extra word           │   │ an extra word           │
│ ▓ight here.             │   │ PRECISELY ▓ight here.   │
│ ~                       │   │ ~                       │
│ ~                       │   │ ~                       │
│ ~                       │   │ ~                       │
│ ~                       │   │ ~                       │
│ ~                       │   │ ~                       │
│ ~                       │   │ ~                       │
│ ~                       │   │ ~                       │
│ ~                       │   │ ~                       │
│ ~                       │   │ ~                       │
│ ~                       │   │ ~                       │
│ "myfile" [New File]     │   │ "myfile" [New File]     │
└─────────────────────────┘   └─────────────────────────┘
```

In text mode, the backspace key destructively backspaces as expected, but only back to where you first started during this text command or the beginning of the current line, whichever is nearest. On some terminals, the characters are actually erased from the screen as you backspace. On many terminals, the characters don't disappear until you either type over them or exit the text mode with an Escape.

## Replacing and Deleting Text

Editing implies some replacements and deletions. If you move your cursor to the beginning of a word you wish to replace, you can use the command cw (change word). You will notice that a dollar sign $ appears at the end of the word (see fig. 6-4).

You can enter as much as you want for the change. You are in a text mode similar to insert, except that everything after the dollar sign is pushed out in front of you.

The command to change the text from the cursor position to the end of the line is C (note use of uppercase). You may replace a single character with the r command without leaving command mode. Just press r followed by the new character. (See, for example, fig. 6-5, in which you place the cursor on the *a* of *affect* and enter re to change *affect* to *effect*.)

Uppercase R is used for editing in replace (overwrite) mode. But because vi is really a line editor, you can only replace to the end of the line.

**Fig. 6-4:**
*Change
word (cw).*

```
The computer is the mirro$
of the mind.  It can reflect
your thoughts, and it
can poison.  The affect
results from your attitude
when you use it. If you use
the computer to explore and
facilitate, you will become
an explorer and a facili-
tator.  But if you fear the
computer, it will always be
your master.
~
~
~
~
~
```

```
The computer is the mercury
of the mind.  It can reflect
your thoughts, and it
can poison.  The affect
results from your attitude
when you use it. If you use
the computer to explore and
facilitate, you will become
an explorer and a facili-
tator.  But if you fear the
computer, it will always be
your master.
~
~
~
~
~
```

**Fig. 6-5:**
*Replacing a
character (r).*

```
The computer is the mercury
of the mind.  It can reflect
your thoughts, and it
can poison.  The affect
results from your attitude
when you use it. If you use
the computer to explore and
facilitate, you will become
an explorer and a facili-
tator.  But if you fear the
computer, it will always be
your master.
~
~
~
~
~
```

```
The computer is the mercury
of the mind.  It can reflect
your thoughts, and it
can poison.  The effect
results from your attitude
when you use it. If you use
the computer to explore and
facilitate, you will become
an explorer and a facili-
tator.  But if you fear the
computer, it will always be
your master.
~
~
~
~
~
```

To delete a word, move the cursor to the beginning of the word and enter dw (delete word). To delete to the end of the line, use the uppercase D. To delete an entire line, enter lowercase dd (two ds). To remove a single character to the right, the command is merely x. An uppercase X deletes a single character to the left of the character.

Figure 6-6 shows what happens if you place the cursor at the beginning of the word *thick* and press dw. The word disappears and the line closes up.

**Fig. 6-6:**
*Deleting a*
*word (dw).*

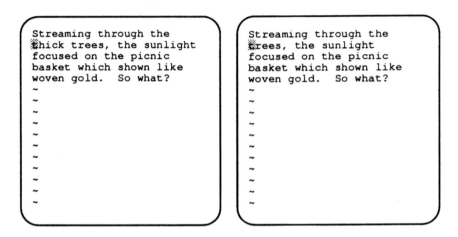

Figure 6-7 shows how to delete to the end of a line. Place the cursor on the first character you want to delete, and press uppercase D. All the characters up to the end of the line are deleted.

Figure 6-8 shows how to remove a character: place the cursor on the character that you want to remove, and press x.

**Fig. 6-7:**
*Deleting to the end of a line (*D*).*

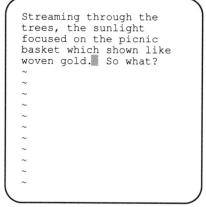

**Fig. 6-8:**
*Removing a character (*X*).*

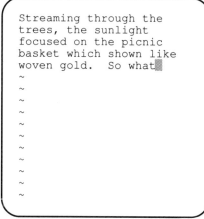

As mentioned before, many vi commands can be prefixed by a number multiplier. For example, to change 5 words, the command is 5cw. To delete 6 characters, the command is 6x. (See fig. 6-9, in which you change through the next two words by pressing 2cw and entering the text.)

**Fig. 6-9:**
*Prefixing a command with a multiplier.*

```
Contains: Carbonated Water,        Contains: Carbonated Water,
High Fructose Corn Syrup           High Fructose Corn Syrup
and/or Sugar,                      and/or Sugar,
Natural Flavor$,                   Nasty Taste,
Potassium Citrate, Gum             Potassium Citrate, Gum
Arabic, Malic Acid, Potas-         Arabic, Malic Acid, Potas-
sium Sorbate,                      sium Sorbate,
Ascorbic Acid, Salt,               Ascorbic Acid, Salt,
Artificial Color, Glycerol,        Artificial Color, Glycerol,
Ester of Wood                      Ester of Wood
Rosin, EDTA, and BHA.              Rosin, EDTA, and BHA.
~                                  ~
~                                  ~
~                                  ~
~                                  ~
~                                  ~
```

### Saving and Exiting

You can write your file to disk at any time. The command is :w<CR>. (That is actually three key strokes: the colon and lowercase w followed by the carriage return.) The command to quit is simply :q<CR>. There is a shortcut to save and exit: ZZ. Note that the command is two uppercase Zs. (This must be the mnemonic for some private joke of Bill Joy's, the author of vi; something like, "Now it's time to catch some Zs.")

The commands so far explained are more than sufficient for you to do basic editing. They do not, however, demonstrate any of the power or shortcuts of vi.

## 6.4 Quick Moves, Searches, and Shortcuts

Let's look at some different ways of moving around in a file. The w (word) command moves you forward one word a time (see fig. 6-10). Each time you press w, the cursor moves to the *beginning* of the next word. To move to the *end* of a word, use the e (end) command (see fig. 6-11). The cursor moves forward, but each time you press e, it moves to the end of the next word. Moving backwards is accomplished with the b (see fig. 6-12). The cursor moves to the beginning of the previous word. (There is no command for moving to the end of the previous word.)

*Fig. 6-10:*
Moving
forward one
word at a
time with w.

```
The vi editor has many
commands for moving the
cursor. The reason for
this is that the older
computer terminals had
very slow incremental
cursor motion. Vi speeds
up the cursor positioning
by allowing you to do natural
jumps based on the text. It
then gives the terminal the
code for moving the cursor
to a specific location.  The
cursor jumps to the new posi-
tion.
~
~
```

```
The vi editor has many
commands for moving the
cursor. The reason for
this is that the older
computer terminals had
very slow incremental
cursor motion. Vi speeds
up the cursor positioning
by allowing you to do natural
jumps based on the text. It
then gives the terminal the
code for moving the cursor
to a specific location.  The
cursor jumps to the new posi-
tion.
~
~
```

*Fig. 6-11:*
Moving
forward one
word at a time
with e.

```
The vi editor has many
commands for moving the
cursor. The reason for
this is that the older
computer terminals had
very slow incremental
cursor motion. Vi speeds
up the cursor positioning
by allowing you to do natural
jumps based on the text. It
then gives the terminal the
code for moving the cursor
to a specific location.  The
cursor jumps to the new posi-
tion.
~
~
```

```
The vi editor has many
commands for moving the
cursor. The reason for
this is that the older
computer terminals had
very slow incremental
cursor motion. Vi speeds
up the cursor positioning
by allowing you to do natural
jumps based on the text. It
then gives the terminal the
code for moving the cursor
to a specific location.  The
cursor jumps to the new posi-
tion.
~
~
```

**Fig. 6-12:**
*Moving backward one word at a time with* b.

```
The vi editor has many
commands for moving the
cursor. The reason for
this is that the older
computer terminals had
very slow incremental
cursor motion. Vi speeds
up the cursor positioning
by allowing you to do natural
jumps based on the text. It
then gives the terminal the
code for moving the cursor
to a specific location.  The
cursor jumps to the new posi-
tion.
~
~
```

```
The vi editor has many
commands for moving the
cursor. The reason for
this is that the older
computer terminals had
very slow incremental
cursor motion. Vi speeds
up the cursor positioning
by allowing you to do natural
jumps based on the text. It
then gives the terminal the
code for moving the cursor
to a specific location.  The
cursor jumps to the new posi-
tion.
~
~
```

Zero (0) takes you to the beginning of the current line. The dollar sign ($) takes you to the end. Neither will take you to the next or previous line. You can use your familiar j and k keys to do that. The j and k keys attempt to move to the same column in the next or previous line. If you want to move to the beginning of the next line, the Enter key (<CR>) does that.

To move forward to the next occurrence of a specified character within the current line, use the f command followed by the target letter. For example, to move to the next occurrence of Q, the command is fQ. (See fig. 6-13, in which we enter fd to move to the letter "d".) Uppercase F takes you to the previous occurrence of the target character. (There are t and T commands that operate similarly to the f and F commands. They take you only as far as the character adjacent to the target.)

You can jump to any specific line number by using the uppercase G (goto). Without a numeric prefix, the G command takes you to the end of the file. The beginning of the file is line one, so the command to go to the beginning is 1G.

If you are scanning text, you'll probably want to move in fairly large increments, a half or full page at a time. The usual way of doing this is with one of the few Control-key combinations in vi: Ctrl-F (screen forward). The reverse is Ctrl-B (screen back). Think of *F* for forward and *B* for back. These two commands actually move two lines less than a full screen. This way you can read continuously in either direction, having two lines of reference for the previous or next page. You can actually scroll up and down with Ctrl-U and Ctrl-D. (Guess which is *up* and which is *down*.) The amount of scroll defaults to half a screen, but you can set the value you want by using the normal numeric prefix. For example, if

**Fig. 6-13:**
Moving ·
forward to
the first
occurrence
of a charac-
ter.

```
The vi editor has many
commands for moving the
cursor. The reason for
this is that the older
computer terminals had
very slow incremental
cursor motion. Vi speeds
up the cursor positioning
by allowing you to do natural
jumps based on the text. It
then gives the terminal the
code for moving the cursor
to a specific location.  The
cursor jumps to the new posi-
tion.
~
~
```

```
The vi editor has many
commands for moving the
cursor. The reason for
this is that the older
computer terminals had
very slow incremental
cursor motion. Vi speeds
up the cursor positioning
by allowing you to do natural
jumps based on the text. It
then gives the terminal the
code for moving the cursor
to a specific location.  The
cursor jumps to the new posi-
tion.
~
~
```

you want to scroll only 5 lines at a time, enter the command 5Ctrl-D. From then on (until you reset it) the scroll commands move only 5 lines.

There are so many cursor-motion commands because it has been so common to use vi with display terminals connected to a central UNIX computer using relatively slow (1200 baud) communication lines. Moving the cursor line by line and character by character was tedious at best. Now, with faster communications (9600 baud and up) and workstations, many of these commands seem superflu-ous.

## Searches

One of the most common ways to jump through text is to search for a word or regular expression. When vi searches your file, it searches the entire file as if it were a loop of text. Therefore, if you ask it to search for an expression, it finds the *next* occurrence of the expression. If there are no more occurrences of the expression from your current cursor location to the end of the file, *next* means that it continues to search back at the beginning of the file and on around till it has either completed a loop of the entire file or found a match for the search.

To enter a search, enter the regular expression after the slash (/) command. For example, to search for the next occurrence of "mugwart," you enter:

```
/mugwart<CR>
```

When you enter the slash command, the slash character (and cursor) appear on the status/ex line. You must terminate your search string with the Enter (<CR>) key.

To search for the previous occurrence of an expression, use the question-mark (?) in place of the slash. The search moves backward through the file, using the same rules as the forward search. Whichever way you search, forward or backward, the search expression is retained in memory. To continue the search with the same search string, press n. To reverse the direction but use the same string, press uppercase N. You can do any sort of editing between instances of the search, and the string remains the same until you enter a new search string.

The search strings are actually regular expressions. (See Chapter 5 for an introduction to regular expressions.) Therefore, to search for *mugwart*, *mudwart*, or *muzwart*, you could use the search expression mu.wart or even mu[gdz]wart. Remember that most punctuation characters have magical properties. To ensure that you use any of the characters such as the dollar sign, the carat, parentheses, and brackets as literals in a search, preface the character with the magical antidote, the backslash.

## Some Good Stuff

Later in this chapter we will discuss the *power user* way of doing search-and-replace; for now, you can do an item-by-item version of search-and-replace by combining the slash command with the handy repeat-last-text-operation command, better known as the dot ( . ) command. To facilitate an explanation, let's take this scenario: You are editing some text that uses the expression *magnificent* far too often. (Obviously you didn't write this piece; you're just trying to make it readable.) These are the steps to improve the writing:

1. Search for *magnificent* (you don't have to spell it all the way out): /magnif<CR> is probably good enough. The cursor moves to the beginning of the next occurrence of *magnificent*.

2. If this looks like a good candidate for change, change word as follows: cw followed by the new word, *fine*. (Remember the cw command?)

3. Search forward to the next occurrence that is a candidate for change: n.

4. Execute the dot command; just press the dot ( . ). *Voila*, the same change-word command is performed again.

With this newfound power, you need some insurance to protect yourself from your own enthusiasm for the dot command. This insurance is found in the u (undo) command. Even though vi keeps track of only one command at a time, that is usually enough to prevent most major catastrophes. Any time you change your mind or a command takes an unexpected turn, just press u to get things back to the way they were. With this protection you might even be ready for some really serious commands.

You can always reverse your long-range mistakes. The dd command deletes an entire line. Prefix it by a number, and you have just deleted that many lines! A less extreme form of delete is the uppercase D command for deleting to the end of the current line.

The change (c) command is parallel to delete in many respects. For example, uppercase C changes to the end of the line. Both *delete* and *change* can also take the t search as a range. For example, to change to the next occurrence (in the current line) of uppercase *J*, you can issue the command ctJ, change-to-J.

Surely you now realize that vi has more than a few good points.

## 6.5  Text-moving Equipment

No word processing program or editor is complete without tools for cutting and pasting blocks of text. The vi tools for moving text are far more flexible than those found on many popular word processors. As with many of the vi commands, there are several ways to accomplish block operations. Some require you to drop into the ex editor (we discuss how to do that later in this chapter), but the simplest are like any other vi command. In fact, you will be able to use one command you already know: delete.

Whenever you use the d command (dd, dw, etc.), the text that you deleted is placed in a *delete buffer*. You put what is in the delete buffer wherever you want by moving the cursor to the new position and pressing p. The deleted text is put after the cursor position. (The uppercase P puts the text before the cursor.) Be sure to *put* as soon as possible, because other commands besides d also use the delete buffer.

Two command pairs perform swapping. To transpose two letters, the commands are x and then p. You can think of it as one compound command: xp. Transposing lines is done with ddp.

The action of copying text into the delete buffer without deleting it from the original position is called *yanking*. The command character for yanking is y (surprised?); it follows the same range rules as change (c) and delete (d). To yank five lines, the command is 5Y; to yank five words, y5w. After you have yanked text, you can put it where you want in the same way as with deleted text. (See figs. 6-14 and 6-15.)

Figure 6-14 shows what happens when you delete text and put it somewhere else. With the cursor on the first of the two lines you are going to move, you press d2d to delete two lines. You move the cursor to the line you want below the pasted text and press uppercase P to paste.

**Fig. 6-14:**
*Deleting text and putting it where you want.*

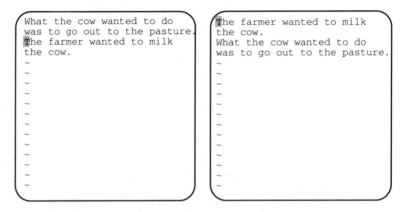

Figure 6-15 shows that yanking is similar to deleting and pasting, in that it leaves the original text where it is. With the cursor on the first of the two lines that you are going to move, press 2Y to yank two lines. Move to the line you want below the pasted text and press uppercase P to paste.

**Fig. 6-15:**
*Yanking text and putting it where you want.*

## Marks

Unlike many wimpy editors that allow you to mark only one point in the text at a time, vi allows twenty-six placemarks. You can use *marks* as reference points for jumping around in the file or as reference points for cut or copy operations. A mark points not only to a line, but to a position within a line. To create a mark, enter m (mark) followed by any lowercase letter. (Some implementations of vi also allow you to use uppercase letters.)

You can jump to a mark by pressing the single quote (') or grave accent (`) followed by the letter of the mark. The grave accent is usually found on the same keycap as the tilde ~. The grave accent takes you to the character position at which you made the mark. The apostrophe takes you to the beginning of that line. (See fig. 6-16.)

**Fig. 6-16:**
*Jumping to marks.*

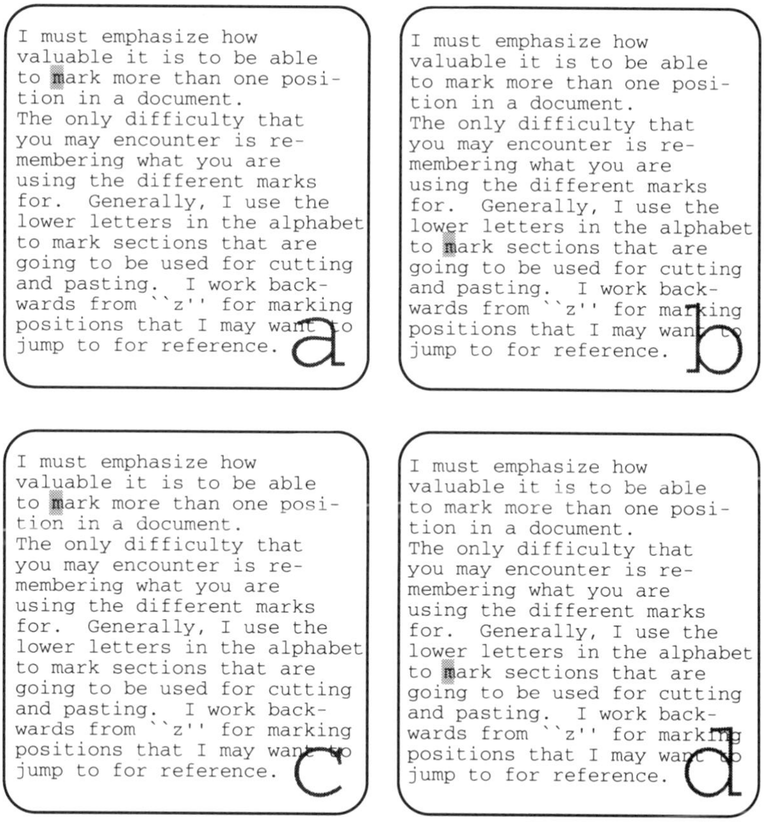

Figure 6-16 shows the following steps for jumping to a mark:

1. Mark the current position (panel a) as "x" by pressing mx.

2. Move the cursor to another position (panel b).

3. Return to your "x" position by pressing 'x. The cursor jumps back to the original spot (panel c).

4. To jump back and forth between the two positions, press the apostrophe twice (''). (See panels c and d.)

*Note:* There is always an unnamed mark at the previous editing position. You can jump to that point by issuing two apostrophes or grave accents.

You can also use marks for changes, deletions, and yanks. For example, if you want to delete a block of text, you can mark the beginning or end of the block, move the cursor, and then delete to the mark. Assuming that you marked with an x (mx), you would delete with the following expression: d'x. (Pay attention to whether you use the grave accent or the single quote; as with jumping to a mark, they behave differently when you delete or yank to a mark.)

**Fig. 6-17:**
*Yanking and pasting with named buffers.*

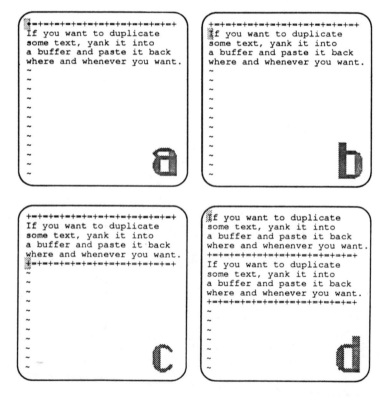

## Named Buffers

Edit buffers are scratchpads for storing pieces of text. Like marks, buffers also have labels a through z. You can yank, delete, or change text into a buffer, and *put* (p or P) it from a buffer. Whichever operation you are doing, prefix it with the double quote (") and the buffer letter. For example, the command for yanking 5 words to the named buffer a is "ay5w. If you have a mark x and want to yank to that mark (you can be above or below the mark), the command is "ay'x.

Let's look at "ay'x piece by piece. The double quote followed by the lowercase a is the buffer you are going to yank into. The lowercase y is the yank-to-a-position command. (The uppercase Y is limited to numbers of lines.) The single quote followed by the lowercase x is the mark to which you want to yank. Now you can put the text in the x buffer wherever you want with "xp or "xP. (See fig. 6-17.)

Figure 6-17 shows the following steps for yanking into a named buffer:

1. To yank into the named buffer "x", preface your yank command with "x. For panel a, this is "xY. For (b), yank four lines into "z" with "z4Y.

2. Move the cursor to a new location (see panel c).

3. Paste with "xp and "zP (see panel d).

You don't have to be as careful with named buffers as you do with the unnamed delete buffer. The text in named buffers remains there until it is overwritten by another command pointing to that specifically named buffer. When you edit more than one file (see the following discussion), you *must* use named buffers to move text from file to file.

# 6.6   Dropping into Ex

Whenever you issue a command that starts with the colon (:), you are actually dropping into the ex editor around which vi is built. For example, the :w command, which writes your file without exiting, is the same as ex w. All ex commands must be terminated by <CR>, the Enter key.

## Search and Replace

The most common reason for dropping into ex is to issue *global commands*, commands that affect the entire file or a range of lines all at once. For example, if you want to change all occurrences of the name "Smith" to "Jones", you issue the command `:g/Smith/s/Smith/Jones/g`, and all occurrences of Smith are changed to Jones.

Before you can use global commands, you need to understand the UNIX construct of *regular expressions*. You might want to review that section in Chapter 5.

Most `ex` commands have the following format:

> [optional *range of lines*] <*command* >[optional *range within line*]

The *range of lines* specifies on which lines the command is to be applied. If it is omitted, the command applies only to the current line. When specified, it can take three forms: a single line number; a pair of line numbers separated by a comma (this is a range); or global indicator—g followed by a regular expression limiting the global action to those lines that contain strings matching the regular expression.

A note on the use of the global g range: it too can be prefixed with a range. In this way you can combine the concept of operating on a range of lines, and specifically on lines matching a regular expression specified with g. There is real power here. It might take a minute to think up a command like `:'a,'bg/^X/s///`, but it might save you several minutes of editing each line in that range to remove the uppercase "X" if there is one.

When specifying line numbers, you can use absolute line numbers such as 1 (the first line) and 5. The dollar sign ($) is the symbol for the last line in the file. The dot (.) is the symbol for the current line number. You can also specify relative line numbers by adding and subtracting from any of the above. For example, the expression `.+4` specifies the fourth from the current line; the expression `$-10` specifies the tenth from the last line.

The ranges can be specified with search strings. This method requires taking care to use search strings that are unique, and therefore is best suited to working with lists or with text that includes comment lines, such as programs or formatting commands.

Sometimes you might want to include a nonprinting note in your text. The UNIX formatter and typesetting programs, `nroff` and `troff`, do not produce output from lines that begin with dot-backslash-quote ( . \ ' ). You can put unique section marks in the text as comments and they will not be output.

As an example of using search strings, suppose that you want to delete all the lines from one that includes the key words "Section V" through a line that has the key words "Section VII." The command is

> `:/Section V/,/Section VII/d`

You can also use any marks you have placed in your file. Assuming that you have placed marks "a" and "b" (having used the vi commands ma and mb), you can specify these points as lines in ranges by prefixing the mark name with a single quote (the apostrophe, '). The range from mark "a" to mark "b" would be specified by 'a,'b.

The ex command to delete a line is d. The ex version of delete is equivalent to the vi dd delete-line command. Several examples of the possibilities of ranges follow:

- :d deletes the current line because no range is specified.
- :3,5d deletes lines 3 through 5.
- :.,.+5d deletes the current line plus the next 5.
- :1,$d deletes the first line through the last; in other words, ALL the lines.
- :g/nasty/d deletes all lines with the word *nasty*.
- :'a,'bd deletes all the lines from mark a through mark b.

The ex substitute command has the following format:

s/*target-string*/*replacement*/[*optional-range — g*]

Therefore, if you want to substitute *cat* for *dog*, the command is

```
s/dog/cat/          — Just the first occurrence
s/dog/cat/g         — All occurrences on the line
```

The regular expressions used with ex substitution have some special abilities that were only touched on in Chapter 5. You can specify sub-expressions within the regular expression and then use the sub-expression matches in the following substitution. For example, you might want to capitalize all occurrences of *star* if and only if it is followed immediately by a number, as in Star-14 and Star-132. Specify the subexpressions in the target regular expression by enclosing them in parentheses, but you must prefix the parentheses with the backslash (\) to give the parentheses that special meaning. The subexpression is referenced by its position number, also prefixed with the backslash. The star substitution is done as follows:

```
s/star-\([0-9]+\)/Star-\1/
```

This subexpression describes any string of digits. The process of using this substitution in a global substitution is shown in figure 6-18. The first subexpression is the [0-9]+ and is referenced later in the substitution command with \1.

To help you visualize this substitution, let's take it in steps.

- The global search finds a line with `star-221`.
- The string `22` is saved as subexpression number 1.
- The literal string `Star-` is substituted for `star-`.
- Subexpression number 1 is substituted at the `\1`.

**Fig. 6-18:**
*A replacement using a subexpression.*

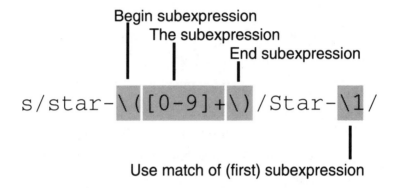

As you can visualize, subexpressions make search and replace very flexible. You can reverse the order of words using subexpressions. As shown in figure 6-19, you reverse the first and second words of all lines with the following:

```
g/\([^ ]*\) \([^ ]*\)/s//\2 \1/
```

**Fig: 6-19:**
*Global replacement for swapping the first and second words in each line.*

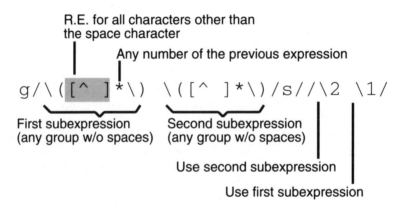

The first subexpression covers everything from the beginning of the line up to, but not including, the first space. The second subexpression starts after the space and continues to the end of the line. When `ex` makes the substitution, whatever is matched by the first subexpression is placed after a space following whatever is matched by the second subexpression.

## Limiting Globals to Ranges

You can probably see how to combine the range command with the substitute command, `:g/Smith/s/Smith/Jones/g`. This command can be shortened to `:g/Smith/s//Jones/g` because a null target for substitution implies that the target should be the same as the previous regular expression in the command; in this case, the global search string. Still another way to do the same thing is `:1,$s/Smith/Jones/g`; in fact, this syntax is a little more obvious than the other two.

## Block Operations

Using the same range-definition methods we discussed in the "Search and Replace" section of this chapter, you can move and copy blocks of text. Use any of the range-definition methods to define the block and any way of describing a single line position to define the destination. (*Note:* The grave accent is not recognized by the `ex` editor for *mark* operations.)

The command is `mo` and the syntax is as follows:

> *range-of-block* `mo` *destination*

As an example, if you want to move the block of lines bound by the marks "a" and "b" to be after mark "c", the command is

> `:'a,'b mo 'c`

The syntax of the copy command, `co`, is exactly the same as that of the move command, `mo`:

> *range-of-block* `co` *destination*

As an example of this command, to copy the block of lines 5 through 15 to the position after the current line, the command is

> `:5,15 co .`

The advantage of using the `ex` commands over the `vi` equivalents is that you don't have to use buffers to do these operations.

One command that doesn't have a `vi` equivalent is write, specified with `w`. The `w` command without any parameters merely writes the current file to its file name, essentially *saving* the file without exiting the editor. (You should do this any time you are about to take a break from editing or if you have been working for a half-hour or so, just for safety's sake.)

You can use the w command to create a new file or append to an existing one. You can prefix the command with a range so that only the lines in that block are written. (Without a range, the entire file is written.) The syntax is

*optional-range* w *optional-file-name*

To append to an existing file, the syntax is

*optional-range* w >>*file-name*

You might find it necessary to cut pieces out to another file. To do this, mark with your favorite letters of the alphabet the beginning and end of the section to be cut. Then, write the block and delete it. Figure 6-20 shows the steps to do this.

**Fig. 6-20:**
*Cutting text out to a file.*

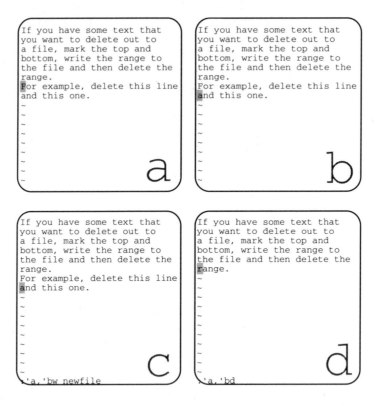

Let's look at the procedure step by step.

1. You mark the top of the text with `ma` (full lines only) (See panel a.)

2. Mark the bottom of the text with `mb`. (See panel b.)

3. Write the text with `'a, 'bw newfile`. (See panel c.)

4. Delete the region using `'a, 'bd`. (See panel d.)

You might want to do just the opposite: patch another file into the file that you are editing. The command is r (read), and the syntax is

*optional-position* r *file-name*

If you do not indicate where you want to patch the file (optional-position), the patch starts immediately after your current line.

*Note:* when using ex commands from vi, if you have several ex commands to issue, it might be more efficient to move from vi to ex. You can accomplish this with uppercase Q. The ex command to return to vi is simply vi.

## Editing More Than One File

As noted at the beginning of this chapter, you can use vi to edit more than one file at a time. If you invoke vi with more than one file name, it generates a list of the files that you want to edit. When you finish editing the current file and are ready to move on to the next, save the current file with :w and bring up the next file in the list with :n (next). Your most recent search string and action (the one that was redone with the dot command) will still be available as you work in the next file. Your delete buffer is cleared, however. If you want to move a buffer from file to file, you must store it in a named buffer (a through z). Either delete or yank the text into the named buffer, then put it in the new file with the put command, P or p.

If at any time you want to start back at the beginning of the list, enter :rewind. You don't have to do :w (write) before going to the next file or rewinding if you have not made any changes to the file — in other words, if you have been using vi only to look at the files.

To switch to editing any other file (not necessarily in the list, just any file) use :e *filename*. You can do this even if you specified only one file when you started your vi session. Although you can view and manipulate only one file on your screen, vi can keep track of your position in two files at a time: the current file and the previous file. You can switch between these two by using the hash mark (#) in place of the file name with the command :e#. The current position and several other parameters are maintained for these two files (but not the delete buffer). Switching between two files makes it convenient to borrow pieces of one file while editing another.

If you discover that you have made unwanted changes to a file and want to exit the vi editor without saving, issue :q!. If you prefer to stay in vi and read in a fresh copy of the original, issue :e!. Don't confuse this use of the exclamation point (!) with the vi shell escapes described in the next section.

## Working with the Shell

The vi editor, like most other programs that are part of the standard UNIX programs, is designed to work with the shell and other programs. But vi is unlike the other utilities in that it is an interactive program rather than one that uses its standard input and output to connect to other programs.

The simplest interface with other programs is the ability of vi to escape to a command. To run another program from vi, use the exclamation point (!) with this syntax:

> :! *program-name*

For example, if you want to look at the calendar while you are running vi, enter :! cal. When cal is finished generating its output, vi gives you the message:

```
[Press return to continue].
```

If you want to escape to the shell without losing your vi session, you can get a whole new shell with :sh. You get a regular shell prompt, just as if you had just logged in. But your vi session is still there (you can check by using the UNIX ps command). To return to your vi session, respond to the shell prompt with exit or Ctrl-D. You end up in the editor, right where you left off. (It is a good idea to save your file with :w before you escape to a shell.)

Another thing you can do with the UNIX shell is insert the output of a UNIX command into your file. You already know the commands to do this, but how to put them together might not be obvious. The commands are the :r command and the !. The syntax is

> : *optional-line-position* r! *command*

As with any other use of the r (read) command, the line-position is optional; if omitted, the current line is assumed. As an example of an escape-and-read command, suppose that you want to insert the current date and time after the current line in the file you are editing. The command is :r!date.

The most interesting interaction between vi and the shell is the ability to ship a range of lines out to a UNIX command and replace the current block with the output from that command. The syntax is simply

> : *range* ! *command*

This trick can be used for sorting a range of lines within a file. Using our now-familiar marks a and b, the command is :'a,'b!sort. Don't forget that if you don't like the results, you can always use the u (undo) command.

This little combination of ranges and external programs allows you to enable vi to do just about anything you want. You can write shell scripts (see Chapters 12-14) that use any of the UNIX utilities, or use nroff (see Chapter 11) to format a paragraph or two. These become your extensions to vi. For example, a technical author or editor might often have to modify texts with the double-quote character (") to use the double apostrophe (' ') and double grave accent (` `) where appropriate. This whole editing process can be automated by using a simple sed script. The author or editor can then invoke sed with this script from within vi. (The stream editor, sed, is described later in this chapter.)

## Creating Your Own Commands

There are two other ways to extend and modify vi: maps and abbreviations. The first of these is similar to what many other editing programs call *macros*. You can map a series of keystrokes to a command letter.

The syntax for creating a key map is as follows:

:map *key string-of-characters*

A simple example uses the uppercase G (go to line number) command: "go to line number one." You enter the following:

:map g 1G

After defining this map, whenever you press the lowercase g you move to the beginning of the file. The uppercase G still takes you to the end. (The next section of this chapter shows how to put maps and other personal embellishments in your default vi environment so that you won't have to re-enter them every time you start an editing session.)

A map can include a sequence of key strokes. If you are entering text along with the commands, you will probably want the map to include the Escape key at the end of the text, to return to command mode. To enter Esc into the sequence, precede it with Ctrl-V. Actually, you can use Ctrl-V to enter any literal control character. An example of text included in a map is

:map M I!SUBHED^[A!ENDSUBHED^[

(The ^[ is the way vi displays the escape character.) The example is a map for the uppercase M key. It inserts "!SUBHED" at the beginning of the line and appends "!ENDSUBHED" at the end.

When you map a key to a new command, be careful not to overwrite a standard vi command that you might need. If by chance you do make this mistake, you can always *unmap* the key. The syntax is simply

    :unmap *key*

Unfortunately, some complex key maps do not work as expected or at all. This weakness seems to be dependent on the version of vi you are running.

You can use the mapped key only while you are in command mode. But there is a text-entry equivalent: *abbreviations*. The syntax for creating an abbreviation is similar to that for maps:

    :abbr *abbreviation expansion*

Suppose, for example, that you use the expression "in the first part" frequently. Who wants to type that over and over? Instead, you can do as follows:

    :abbr p1 in the first part

Now, whenever you enter text and type "p1" as a word, it expands out to "in the first part".

## Setting Your Environment

Besides the buffers, marks, abbreviations, and keymaps, vi maintains more than 40 flags and variables that define the editing environment. You can set these from within vi with :set followed by the setting. For example, earlier in this chapter in the section "Editing a File," near the beginning of the discussion about vi, I pointed out that :set wrapmargin=10, makes lines automatically wrap to the next line when a word ends in the last 10 character places on the screen (after character position 70 for a screen 80 characters wide). If you set the wrapmargin to zero (the default), the lines no longer wrap.

The wrapmargin is far from being the only setting. If you want to see all of the settings, issue the command :set all to get the following display:

```
:set a
noautoindent        nonumber                noshowmode
autoprint           open                    noslowopen
noautowrite         nooptimize              tabstop=8
nobeautify          paragraphs=IPLPPPQPP     taglength=0
directory=/tmp      prompt                  tags=tags/usr/lib/tags
noedcompatible      noreadonly              term=tvi965
noerrorbells        redraw                  noterse
```

```
hardtabs=8          remap                           timeout
noignorecase        report=5                        ttytype=tvi965
nolisp              scroll=4                        warn
nolist              sections=NHSHH HUnhsh   window=8
magic               shell=/bin/csh                  wrapscan
mesg                shiftwidth=8                    wrapmargin=15
nonovice            noshowmatch                     nowriteany
[Press return to continue]
```

Without going into all of these, let's explore a few.

Many of the settings are toggles; for example, number/nonumber, which displays line numbers at the left of the text. This is useful when you are editing from someone else's directions. The process usually includes printing the text with pr -n, a page-formatting program (see Chapter 11 for details). The person specifying the corrections uses a copy of the file with the line numbers to mark up, and then gives directions using these numbers. The person entering the corrections can then find the point at which to make the corrections without having to make repeated use of the vi command *linenumber*G or Ctrl-G, which displays the current position in the file. Although the line numbers are visible, they are not in the text of the file.

As with most of the settings, number can be abbreviated. In this case, the abbreviation is nu, therefore the commands

```
:set nu
:set nonu
```

set the number to either state, on or off.

When learning vi, you might find it helpful to have a clue as to whether you are in text-entry mode. The command :set showmode enables a message at the bottom right of the screen whenever you are able to enter text. The reverse command is :set noshowmode.

Another useful setting is ignorecase (abbreviation ic). The default setting of the slash and hook (/ and ?) searches is to be case sensitive; in other words, you must specify whether you want to look for uppercase or lowercase characters by describing the search string with regular expressions. Turn this sensitivity off by using the following:

```
:set ignorecase
```

The section in this chapter on searching indicated that searches wrap around through the beginning of the file, all the way back to the current position. This can be turned off. The command is :set nowrapscan. (The abbreviated form is :set nows.)

Check your UNIX manual or just experiment to learn about all the possible settings. Many have special uses for programming; for instance, lisp, showmatch, and autoindent.

## Personalizing the Defaults

When the vi editor starts up, it looks for a file named .exrc in your home directory. If it finds that file, it runs the commands in that file as a script of ex commands before you begin editing. You can personalize your vi by putting settings, abbreviations, and key maps in your .exrc file. (Because the file name begins with a dot, you will not see it in your directory unless you use the ls -a command.)

An example of this file follows:

```
set showmode
set wm=15
map ] /^ /
map [ ?^ ?
map g 1G
map = :w^V^M:e#^V^M
abbr !i !ITAL
abbr !m !MONO
abbr !s !SUBHED
abbr !b !BOLD
abbr !e !END
abbr U UNIX
```

Note that, even though these are ex commands, none of the lines begins with the colon ( : ). The commands in the .exrc file don't require a colon because they are executed in ex mode, not visual mode.

The first line in the example sets the editor so that it shows what mode it is in: insert or append. No message means that you are in command mode.

The second line, set wm=15, means that the editor automatically wraps to the next line after the 65th character (80 minus 15 is 65).

Now we come to some key maps. The first key map is for moving to new paragraphs that begin with a space. Press the right bracket (]) and you move to the next line beginning with a space. The next entry searches backward— in other words, to the previous line beginning with a space. The map for lowercase g takes you to the beginning of the file.

The map for the equal sign looks complex, but all it does is switch you back and forth between two files if you are editing more than one file. Before you can edit another file, you must write the one you are currently editing (assuming that you have made some changes). The :w accomplishes this task. When you issue an ex command from vi, you must terminate it with the Enter key. The ^V (Ctrl-V) tells the editor to take the following character literally. The following character is the ^M (Enter). The colon begins another ex command, e#, which means to edit the alternate/previous file.

The list of abbreviations that include a bang (exclamation point: !) in the example are quick ways of entering instructions to a typesetter to change fonts.

The abbreviation signified by a single uppercase U means that the word "UNIX" never has to be entered in full. Not all uppercase U characters are expanded, only those that stand alone as a word.

You can see why these macros and abbreviations are in the editor initialization script, .exrc.

# 6.7  The Stream Editor: sed

A stream editor is more like a text filter than what you might ordinarily consider an editing program to be. The key word here is *stream*. The concept is one of text flowing in one end of the editor and out the other, somewhat changed. The control comes from either shell command line parameters or a file of editing directives. The two most common syntaxes for invoking sed are:

    sed -e *directive text-file*

and

    sed -f *directive-file text-file*

The version using the -e option can have more than one editing directive, but each must be preceded by -e. If you have only one sed editing directive on the command line, you may omit the -e. For example, sed.

Unless specifically instructed to operate on only a range of files, sed applies its editing to *all* lines in the text. You will recognize the syntax for most sed commands from the description of editing with ex. The basic sed commands are as follows:

| | |
|---|---|
| s/*pattern*/*replacement*/ | substitution |
| d | delete line |
| a*text* | append after line |
| i *text* | insert before line |

There are nearly two dozen sed commands, but most of the time you will use only these four.

Obviously you don't want to apply the d, a, and i commands to every line. Therefore, sed allows you to restrict commands to specific lines or ranges, much like the global commands in ex. Therefore if you want, for example, to delete all lines with the word *funky*, give sed the following directive:

```
sed '/funky/d'
```

Typically, you use sed to make substitutions. For example, a writers' style guide might specify that certain acronyms and abbreviations are not to be used. The sed script might look like the following:

```
s/DEC/Digital Equipment Corporation/g
s/IBM/International Business Machines/g
s/GE/General Electric Corporation/g
s/OSF/Open Software Foundation/g
s/Inc./Incorporated/g
```

A more complex example substitutes typesetter quotes for the quote character. The problem here is to determine which pair of typesetting quotes is appropriate, opening quotes or closing quotes. Regular expressions allow us to deal with the problem in a sensible way:

```
s/" /" /g
s/;"/;"/g
s/:"/:"/g
s/,"/,"/g
s/\."/."/g
s/\?"/?"/g
s/!"/!"/g
s/"$/"/
s/ "/ "/g
s/^"/"/
```

The ex substitution for most closing quotes might be much simpler:

```
:1,$s/\([ ;:.!?]\)"/\1"/g
```

Chapter 10, "Networks," provides more information on how to create your own UNIX commands. Some of these commands actually use sed and scripts. For example, you might create a command requote that uses the previous example. Then, from within vi, you invoke requote over a range of lines, say from mark a through mark b, as follows:

```
:'a,'b!requote
```

In this way you have just extended vi with your own commands that far exceed the potential of a key-mapped macro. When you study the emacs editor, keep in mind that you can extend vi with regular UNIX utilities; you don't have to resort to using a special macro language.

## 6.8  Summary

All modern UNIX installations include a set of standard text editors: the ed, ex, vi, sed family. The first two of these are line editors; vi is a screen editor. The last of these editors, sed, is a non-interactive stream editor.

The vi editor is a dual-state editor; there is a command mode and a text-entry mode. You generally go into text entry mode with the a (append) or i (insert) command. You return to command mode with the Escape key.

Most of the commands of vi are character, word, or line oriented. There are also many commands for blocks of text.

You can search forward with the slash (/) and backwards with the hook (?). Searches use regular expressions. You can use named buffers (and single unnamed buffers) for moving and copying text.

To use the ex commands from vi, preface the command with a colon. You can customize vi with a wide selection of settings, your own command key maps, and automatically expanding abbreviations. You can also extend vi with external commands. These commands can be standard UNIX utilities or your own creations.

The non-interactive stream editor is used to edit files that must be altered in a predictable way. It is often used with other UNIX utilities in shell scripts (programs).

# Review Questions

1. What kind of application program is used more than any other?

2. Which kind of text-entry program reformats text as you write?

3. Which kind of text-entry program does not embed any special characters in the text? (In other words, which kind produces the simplest text files?)

4. What are the differences between line editors, visual (screen-oriented) editors, and stream editors?

5. What are the two basic states of the vi editor?

6. How do you get in and out of *insert* and *append* modes?

7. What are the four commands for moving the cursor to the previous and next character and line?

8. What are three forms of the command for changing text?

9. What are four delete commands?

10. How do you specify the number of times a command is to be applied (the command multiplier)?

11. What are two ways to save and exit vi?

12. How do you search forward and backward? How do you find successive occurrences of the search target?

13. How do you jump to the next and previous screen?

14. How do you jump to the beginning, end, and specific line of a file?

15. How do you move forward or backward one word at a time?

16. How do you undo the previous command?

17. How do you copy or move lines of text (without using ex)?

18. How do you mark a position in the text?

19. What are two ways to use marks?

20. What are *named buffers* and how do you reference them?

21. What is the relationship between the ex editor and vi?

22. How do you drop down to ex for a single command and for a series of commands?

23. What are three ways to define ranges in ex?

24. What are the ex commands for reading in and writing out a file?

25. What kind of editor is sed? What is it used for?

# Exercises

Use the `vi` editor to enter the following text:

```
It was night in the city. Broken bottles caught the
colors of street lights and flashing signs. The con-
gested streets had drained to the suburbs. Soon, the
real urban people would come out on the streets.

Our friend, Borgonne, listened to what he thought was
the murmur of a family at dinner. But the sound grew
full and heavy. Maybe it was a crowd gathering. But now
the pitch rose. Hollow, like tubular bells. The sky
changed from blackness to strobes of rose and lime-green
light. Light and sound surrounded Borgonne as the alien
spaceship lifted him into its jaws.
```

Change the sentence, *Light and sound surrounded Borgonne as the alien spaceship lifted him into its jaws*, to read *Light and sound lifted Borgonne into the jaws of the alien spaceship*.

Move the first paragraph to a new file named *pieces*.

Without exiting `vi`, change to the new file. (Shortcut hint: the file you just wrote to is now the *alternate file*.)

With an `ex` global command, change all the spaces to new lines. (Hint: the newline is entered as Ctrl-V Ctrl-M and appears as ^M on your screen.)

Sort all the lines in the file without leaving `vi`.

# Further Reading

*UNIX Text Processing*, D. Dougherty and T. O'Reilly, Howard W. Sams & Company, Indianapolis, IN, 1987. An in-depth reference covering all aspects of text processing in the UNIX environment.

*Vi — The UNIX Screen Editor*, August Hansen, Brady, Prentice Hall, New York, 1986. A thorough and easy-to-read reference text on `vi`, exclusively.

*Guide to Vi Visual Editing on the UNIX System*, D. Sonnenschein, Prentice Hall, Englewood Cliffs, NJ, 1987.

*Learning the Vi Editor*, Lamb, O'Reilly & Associates, Inc., Cambridge, MA, 1987. One of the Nutshell series of handbooks.

"An Introduction to Display Editing with VI," W. Joy. An introductory guide to `vi`.

"Ex Reference Manual," W. Joy. A complete description of the `ex` text editor, which underlies `vi`.

# 7

# Editing with emacs

## Contents

# Objectives

In this chapter you will learn

1. The differences between a single-state editor like emacs and a dual-state editor like vi

2. The basic operations for starting and entering an edit session with emacs

3. About the block/buffer operatives of emacs

4. About emacs keystroke macros and the emacs macro language

The debate over which is the better editor, vi or emacs, reaches the intensity of a religious war. Ultimately, which one you should use comes down to your personal preference and needs. The vi editor, found on all UNIX systems, is relatively easy to learn and use, but it cannot be customized and extended nearly as much as emacs can be. In fact, the full name for this editor is "Emacs, the advanced, self-documenting, customizable, extensible real-time display editor." In short, if your UNIX system has emacs and you like it, use it.

Touch typists probably find vi easier than emacs because vi requires minimal use of the key combinations outside the typist's keyboard. Hunt-and-peck style typists, on the other hand, adapt easily to the emacs style of commands. Microcomputer users familiar with the many Alt and Ctrl function key operations of PC word processing programs have no problem adapting to emacs commands.

The emacs editor is self-documented; you can get help on the editor from within the editor. But this is a Catch-22 situation. If you don't know how to get started, there is little likelihood you will learn much about emacs. Making your way through the first part of this chapter will help you use emacs effectively. But don't stop reading, because the rest of the chapter shows you things that you never thought an editor could do for you!

# 7.1 Variations

You probably found both strengths and weaknesses in the vi editor; if so, you'll find that the same is true with emacs. There is no perfect editor. But emacs can be made into your perfect editor. That is its greatest strength. It is so flexible that it can even emulate vi. If you think you know what the perfect editor would be like, start with emacs and build from there. But it is going to take some work. Also, it will probably hog system resources; a full implementation of emacs can require a great deal of memory and disk space.

An attractive feature of emacs is that you can edit many files (not just two) simultaneously. In fact, you can divide the screen into multiple windows. Each window can have a different file in it. While learning emacs, you might keep one window open with a "cheat sheet" of emacs commands while you edit in another window.

There are many implementations of emacs. Two popular commercial ones are *Epsilon* from Lugaru Software, Ltd. and UniPress *Emacs*. We will describe a standard implementation, GNU emacs from the Free Software Foundation, Richard Stallman's organization. He is the author of the original emacs editor, so it is fitting that we use his implementation for the model. Incidentally, the manual he wrote (see *Further Reading* for details) is complete and clear once you gain familiarity with emacs. Stallman recommends that you run the emacs tutorial as an introduction to the editor. You can do this with the following command:

```
$ emacs -t
```

## 7.2  Basics

The emacs editor is not a dual-state editor like vi. With emacs, you are always in text-entry mode. You can issue commands from this state because they all start with either a Control-key combination or a meta-key combination. Generate Control-key combinations by holding down the Ctrl key while pressing another key. You are probably already familiar with Ctrl-D from other UNIX programs. Meta-key combinations depend on your system and the implementation of your terminal in emacs. On some systems, the meta key is the Alt key, in which case you hold down the Alt key while pressing the appropriate combination key. More often, however, the meta-key combination is implemented with the Esc key. In this case, release the Esc key before pressing the combination key. In the emacs nomenclature, the Control-key combinations are written as C-*key*. The meta-key combinations are written as M-*key*. We follow this style in this chapter.

All these key combinations bind to underlying commands, all of which have names. For example, the key combination C-o is used for opening a new line (or breaking a line at the cursor). It is actually bound to the command *open-line*. There is an organization to the default-key bindings: C- operations act on the screen and cursor position independent of the text, whereas M- operations are oriented more to the form of the text — for example, moving a word, sentence, or paragraph at a time.

When you customize emacs, you will probably start by binding different commands to different keys. The simplest macros are just scripts of keypresses. Later you learn to develop your own commands using the basic commands and the macro language. You can bind either kind of macro to a key combination.

# 7.3 Beyond Key Combinations

Emacs has more predefined commands than simple meta-key and Ctrl-key combinations. The first level of extension to the basic command keys is gained through C-x (think of eXtended command). For example, the sequence to exit emacs is C-x C-c. Most C-x combinations are associated with window, file, and buffer operations.

The second level of extension is through M-x. This key combination is the portal to *all* the emacs commands because it prompts you with a colon (:) at the bottom of the screen, to which you respond with *any* emacs command.

You don't have to remember the exact and complete names for the more than one-hundred commands. The emacs editor helps by completing unambiguous beginnings of commands. For example, you can enter the command help-with-tutorial by entering it altogether, or you can abbreviate it as he and press the space bar. Because help-with-tutorial is the only command that begins with the letters *he*, any ambiguity has been resolved and the command name is completed. This facility, called *completion*, is not limited to command names. If you start entering a command name (or one of the other values that emacs helps you complete) and you want to know what options are available, enter a hook (?) as the next character. A window opens with your options. After you enter your command, the window closes and you return to your normal editing screen.

Another helpful facility in emacs, called *apropos*, helps you find the correct command for the job. The apropos command is usually bound to the key sequence C-h a. Apropos is an index of the help files. Suppose, for example, that you want to know about all the operations related to files. Use the key word *file* with apropos. Assuming that apropos has a key binding of C-h a, enter C-h a file. The screen shows a window briefly describing all the commands related to files.

# 7.4 Starting emacs

To begin editing a file with the emacs editor, the command is as follows:

emacs *file-list*

(You exit emacs with C-x C-c. It is good to know this before you get stuck in it and can't figure a way out.)

## Screen Regions

If you are editing only one file, you see three screen regions, as shown in Figure 7-1.

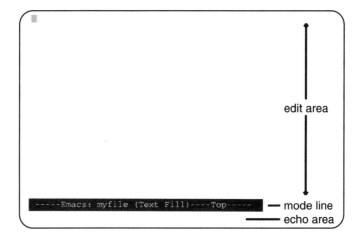

edit area

------Emacs: myfile (Text Fill)----Top----- — mode line
—— echo area

The large region at the top is the editing area. This is the area in which your text appears. (There is no text in figure 7-1.)

At the bottom of the screen is the *echo area*, from which emacs prompts you for commands, file names and other directions. The echo area is also where emacs displays any single-line messages.

The line between the edit area and the echo area is called the *mode line*. This line is usually displayed in reverse video. When your screen is divided into multiple windows, there is a mode line at the bottom of every window. The emacs editor displays the name of the buffer (more on buffers later) and its status on the mode line. Among the status indicators are your relative position in the file (a percentage) and whether the file has been modified (asterisk—*) or not (dashes). Another status item, the editing *mode*, appears here.

## Edit Modes

Different kinds of files require different kinds of editing facilities. For example, if you edit a C language program, you might want the editor to automatically indent whenever you open a curly brace and return to the previous indent level when the braces close. Text editing should probably wrap to the next line whenever you reach the right margin. But rather than using a different editor for each of these styles of editing, you can use `emacs` to edit a particular kind of file in the appropriate *mode*. In fact, `emacs` looks at the suffix in the file name to determine what kind of file it is. If, for example, it sees a `.c` at the end of the file name, it assumes that the file is a C language program and automatically goes into the mode for C language programming.

If the editor cannot determine what kind of file you are editing, it goes into *fundamental mode*, a simple editing mode. There are both *major* and *minor* editing modes; fundamental mode is major. The major modes are exclusive: `emacs` can be in only one major mode at a time. Other major modes include Lisp, C, Text, Nroff, TEX, and Outline.

Along with the exclusive major modes, `emacs` has three common minor modes. These modes are not exclusive, meaning that they can run alongside any major mode or any other minor mode. Common minor modes include *Auto-fill*, *Overwrite*, and *Abbrev*. The most common mode for text is Auto-fill, which makes the editor wrap automatically to the next line. Toggle Auto-fill mode ON and OFF with the following command:

```
M-x auto-fill-mode<CR>
```

Because `emacs` can complete commands, you need enter only `M-x au<space>f<space>`.

MicroEMACS has the sequence `C-x m wrap-<CR>` to achieve the same effect. This is a fine example of how various companies that have implemented `emacs` have completely different ways of doing things. Making generalizations about a program that appears in so many diverse forms can be difficult.

The default line length after which `emacs` wraps is 80 characters. You will probably want to change this to 65 characters. There are two ways to change this position. One is to enter the value 65 as a parameter to the `set-fill-column` command, in this case `M-65 C-x f`. `M-65` is the value; `C-x f` is the key binding for `set-fill-column`. The other method is to move the cursor to the horizontal position at which you want to wrap and issue the set-fill-column (`C-x f`) command without any parameters.

### Entering and Editing Text

To enter text, just start typing. There is no command/text-entry switch. You are always in text-entry mode.

Any C- or M- combination is interpreted as a command. You can, however, enter and edit text that includes these characters. To do so, preface the control character with C-q (quoted-insert).

If emacs has been properly installed on your computer, you can use the arrow keys for moving the cursor. Otherwise, you must use the "standard" cursor motion keys: C-f (forward one character); C-b (back one character); C-p (previous line); and C-n (next line). (See fig. 7-2.)

**Fig. 7-2:**
The basic cursor-motion keys for emacs.

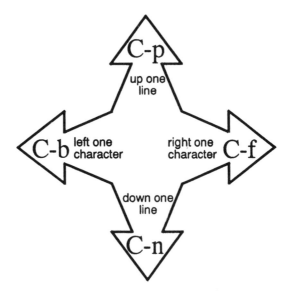

Unless your Control key is located conveniently, you will have to adjust your style of typing. Of course, people nowadays are used to moving around the screen with a mouse. The emacs editor works with mouse movements under the control of the X Window System.

A few other cursor motions that speed your movement through a file are M-f (forward one word), M-b (back one word), C-a (beginning of line), C-e (end of line), C-v (forward one screen), and C-z (back one screen).

## Multiplying the Commands

Like the vi editor, emacs commands can include a multiplier. But because you are always in text mode, you must enter the meta-key to indicate that you want a multiplier. In other words, M-*any number-any operation* multiplies whatever you wish, including entering the next literal character. For example, to move forward one hundred words, the command sequence is M-100 followed by M-f, the command to move forward by a word. To add a string of 20 equal signs, the command sequence is M-20 followed by the equal-sign (=).

You can give any command a multiplier of 4 by prefixing the command with C-u. In fact, you can prefix C-u with C-u for additional powers of 4 (16, 64, 256, 1024, etc.) In other words, each time you enter C-u in succession, you increase by a power of four the number of times the following command will be executed.

## Changing and Deleting

Unless you are an exceptional thinker and typist, you will probably have to change and delete text. The simplest method for making corrections is to backspace over the error and enter the correction. In contrast to vi, you do not have to go in and out of text-entry mode. With emacs you just move the cursor to the mistake, backspace, and re-enter.

An alternative is to edit in *overwrite mode*. The overwrite mode is a minor mode and therefore not exclusive. You must enter overwrite mode by name unless you have bound it to a key combination, for example, C-x ov-<space>. Because it is the only command that starts with the letters OV, you can use command completion rather than spell out the whole command. To return to text-insert mode (overwrite mode off), reenter the command C-x ov-<space>. It works like a toggle.

Sometimes you will want to delete to the end of a line, or delete several lines of text. The generic name for deleting text is *kill* and the command is kill-line. The key binding is C-k. To kill an entire line of text and delete the remaining space, you must enter the command twice: C-k C-k. The first instance kills to the end of the line; the second removes the new-line character at the end. You do not wipe out the characters to the left of the cursor, even after issuing the command twice. To remove the line completely, you must place the cursor at the beginning of the line. Figure 7-3 illustrates the process as follows:

1. Place the cursor at the beginning of the area to be deleted (panel a)

2. Enter C-k to delete to the end of the line (panel b)

3. Enter C-k again to delete the new-line character (panel c)

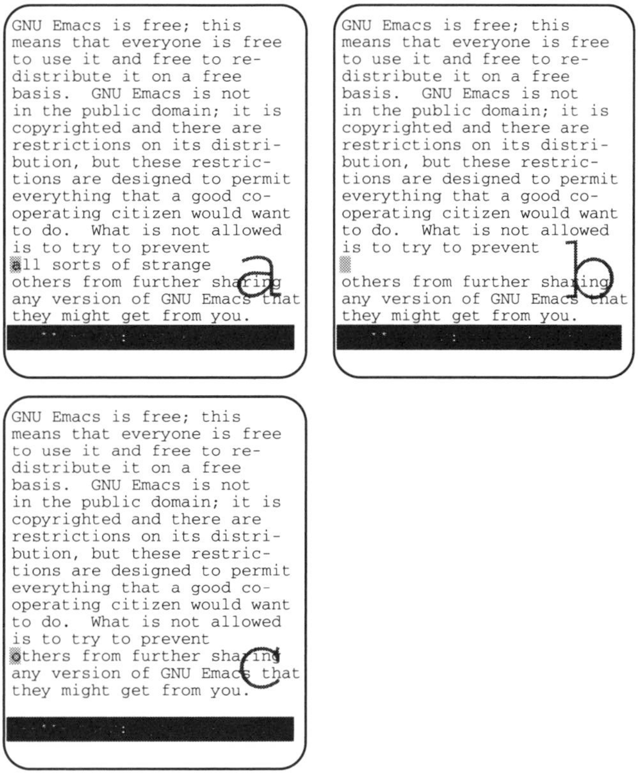

**Fig. 7-3:**
Killing a line
with C-k.

GNU Emacs is free; this
means that everyone is free
to use it and free to re-
distribute it on a free
basis.  GNU Emacs is not
in the public domain; it is
copyrighted and there are
restrictions on its distribution, but these restrictions are designed to permit
everything that a good co-
operating citizen would want
to do.  What is not allowed
is to try to prevent
all sorts of strange
others from further sharing
any version of GNU Emacs that
they might get from you.

*a*

GNU Emacs is free; this
means that everyone is free
to use it and free to re-
distribute it on a free
basis.  GNU Emacs is not
in the public domain; it is
copyrighted and there are
restrictions on its distribution, but these restrictions are designed to permit
everything that a good co-
operating citizen would want
to do.  What is not allowed
is to try to prevent
others from further sharing
any version of GNU Emacs that
they might get from you.

*b*

GNU Emacs is free; this
means that everyone is free
to use it and free to re-
distribute it on a free
basis.  GNU Emacs is not
in the public domain; it is
copyrighted and there are
restrictions on its distribution, but these restrictions are designed to permit
everything that a good co-
operating citizen would want
to do.  What is not allowed
is to try to prevent
others from further sharing
any version of GNU Emacs that
they might get from you.

*c*

The kill-line command is a common target of the M-*number* command prefix
for accomplishing multiples. To kill the next ten lines, place the cursor at the
beginning of the first line to be removed and enter M-10 C-k.

There are other kill commands: kill word (kill-word or M-d), kill to end of
sentence (kill-sentence or M-k), and kill region.

## Point, Mark, and Region

The current cursor location in a buffer is called *point*. The emacs editor keeps
track of point, not by its line number (as in vi), but by its character position in the
buffer. The character base of emacs is the second-most elemental difference
between it and the vi family of editors. (The most elemental difference is that
emacs is a single-state editor whereas vi is a dual-state editor.)

As with vi, emacs has many commands for moving around within a buffer, or in
other words, moving point. (See Table 7-1.)

**Table 7-1.   Commands for moving point.**

| Command | New point location |
|---------|--------------------|
| C-a | The beginning of the line |
| C-e | The end of the line |
| C-f | Forward one character |
| C-b | Backward one character |
| M-f | Forward one word |
| M-b | Backward one word |
| C-n | Down to next line |
| C-p | Up to previous line |
| C-v | Next windowful |
| M-v | Previous windowful |
| C-l | Scroll to center of window |
| M-< | Beginning of buffer |
| M-> | End of buffer |

You can also tell emacs to keep track of a second position in the buffer, the *mark*. The default position of the mark is the beginning of the file. To move the mark to the current point position, enter C-space or C-@. Later you can return to the new mark by entering the command C-x C-x (exchange point and mark). As the name of the command implies, you can then return to your former cursor position by re-issuing the C-x C-x key combination.

The mark and the point together define a *region*. Many emacs commands act on a region. For example, you can kill a region with C-w. You can copy the region into a *kill buffer* with M-w (see the section on "Files and Buffers" later in this chapter), or you can write the region to a file with C-x w. If your lines become wildly uneven in length, you can reformat them with the fill-region command.

## Searching

The searching functions of emacs are so good that, even if you don't want to use it as your editor, you might want to use it for scanning and searching text.

The basic and most common search method is the *incremental search*, invoked with C-s. When you are in incremental search mode, the point moves to the next occurrence of the characters you have entered. In contrast to the vi search routine, emacs does not require that you guess what is necessary to specify the search and then completely enter the regular expression. With incremental searching, the search begins as you enter a character. Figure 7-4 shows a sample incremental search that works as follows:

1. Point is at the beginning of the text; C-s begins the search (panel a).

2. Pressing the letter *e* makes point move to the first occurrence (panel b).

3. Entering very after the e takes the cursor to the first occurrence of every (panel c).

4. Entering C-s again takes point to the next occurrence of every (panel d).

**Fig. 7-4:**
An incremental search.

As another example of incremental search, assume that you start the search by entering the letter *a*. Point moves forward to the first *a* (below its current position). Then, if you add the letter *l*, point moves to the first *al* combination. An additional *t* moves point to an *alt*. If you enter characters for which there is no match, the search routine returns a message to that effect. You can either backspace, removing the specific letter and returning the match for the shorter string, or press the Delete key to abort the search.

To find the next occurrence of your target, enter C-s again. To search in reverse, use C-r. Even after you have found your target and manipulated the text, you can recall the last search by issuing the command twice: C-s C-s or C-r C-r (a single search command starts a new search). Also, if you fail to find an occurrence of the target in the direction you are searching, you can continue searching back around to your starting point by adding a C-s or C-r when you receive the Not Found message.

By default, the search string is literal. In other words, there are no magic characters other than the C- and M- keys. The hook (?), dot (.), and asterisk (*) have no special meaning. You can search for literal control characters by prefacing the control character with a C-q (quoted-insert).

You can use regular expressions if you wish. The command isearch-forward-regexp (incremental search forward with regular expressions) is usually bound to the sequence C-M-s. (The C- and M- keys are used together. If your meta-key is Alt, press both Alt and Ctrl at the same time. On the other hand, if your meta-key is Esc, press that first and then follow it with the C- combination.) The incremental regular expression search is similar to the simple incremental search, except that the former uses *magic characters*. (See Chapter 5 for information about regular expressions.)

## Search and Replace

The obvious extension to searching is replacing text. This is an operation for which vi is sadly missing depth. The emacs editor, on the other hand, is well equipped in this area. There are the global and unconditional search-and-replace commands: replace_string and replace-regexp. (These usually do not have key-bindings.) The more common search-and-replace commands are query-replace (bound to M-%) and its regular expression counterpart, query-replace-regexp (no key binding).

All the search-and-replace commands use roughly the same format. After invoking the command, you see a prompt for the search string. After you enter the search string terminated by Enter, you see a prompt for the replacement string, also terminated by Enter. The global and unconditional forms of these commands continue from the current point to the end of the file, making the replacements without any interactive support from you. The "query" forms stop after every occurrence of the target to request your approval of the replacement. At this point you can press the spacebar to approve the replacement, or the Delete key (this might be the backspace on some systems) to reject the replacement and continue on to the next occurrence of the target. Enter Esc to abort the search-and-replace command, dot (.) to replace at this point and exit, bang (!) to replace unconditionally throughout the rest of the buffer; or carat (^) to go back to the previous replacement.

Sometimes you'll want to replace the same word with more than one substitution, depending on the context of the target. To accomplish this, start a query replace operation with the most likely substitution. When you arrive at an occurrence that needs editing rather than a simple substitution, enter C-r. At this level of emacs, this key combination takes on a special meaning: *enter recursive editing level* (see the next section). There are other options also. For help on the replace options when in the midst of a search-and-replace, enter C-l to get a quick help line.

### Recursive Editing Levels

When in some emacs operations such as search-and-replace, you can create a *recursive editing level*, to do other emacs operations without exiting the first one. The first command is pushed into a sleeping state, and you can use emacs. When you exit the recursive level with C-M-c, the earlier command resumes where it left off. When you enter a recursive editing level, the state field of the mode line (at the bottom of the buffer window) is enclosed in an additional set of square brackets. You can even enter a recursive editing level from a recursive editing level. To exit all recursive editing levels *and* the original command from which you entered this state, enter C-] (abort-recursive-edit).

Recursive editing levels are not available as a regular emacs command. They are available only through other emacs commands.

## 7.5   Help!

The emacs operations we have covered so far can be a little overwhelming. Few people can recall all this information without some help. Earlier in this chapter, we discussed the emacs command apropos and name completion. As mentioned, however, there is more specific and detailed help. Two quickies are C-h k (describe-key) and C-h f (describe-function). The former gives a description of which command or function is bound to the M- or C- sequence that follows. The latter explains which key is associated with the command or function you specify.

When you find yourself totally lost in emacs and don't know how to accomplish a task, start with apropos. Then, use the command name to get detailed information with describe-function. After using emacs for just a few hours, you will rely more on the internal documentation than on a printed manual or this chapter.

## 7.6  Files and Buffers

You can edit the material in emacs buffers. (The vi editor does not allow this procedure.) In fact, in emacs, you are always in a buffer when you are editing. If you invoke emacs with more than one file, the editor allocates a buffer for each file.

The first buffer operation you need to learn is saving a buffer to a file. The command is C-X C-S. (The normal exit sequence is C-X C-S C-X C-C, save and exit.) Periodically, the emacs editor automatically saves a copy of the current buffer. When it does this, it does not overwrite your original file. The purpose behind auto-save is to prevent the loss of your work. The auto-save feature is activated by the number of characters you enter. The default is 300. You can turn this feature off or modify it.

You can view or edit other files while you are in emacs. The term *visiting* describes the action of copying the contents of a file into an emacs buffer. When you invoke emacs with a file name, you are *visiting* that file. To visit another file from within emacs, the command is C-x C-f. The emacs editor creates a new buffer and copies the file into it.

When trying to find a file, you can enter just the first few letters of the file name and press the spacebar; emacs attempts to complete the file name for you. If the characters you entered appear in more than one file name, emacs gives you a list of files to select from. You can see the possibilities by using a hook (?) instead of a space.

You will probably have some files (and buffers) that should not be altered. For example, you might have a finished report that you want to look over but not edit. To ensure that you can't change the file from emacs, issue the command C-x C-q. This is a toggle, but it works only if you have write permission on the file (see the discussion of chmod in Chapter 4).

### Using the Directory Tree: dired

The emacs editor has a special extension that allows you to move through the UNIX directories, pick files to edit, save (if you are editing a file), and even delete from the directory. To invoke the extension, enter the command dired (bound to the key sequence C-x d). What you see in the dired buffer looks very much like the output from the UNIX command ls -l. The main difference is that this file list is interactive. You move up and down in the file list with the same keys as in any other buffer. (You can also use the n and p keys without the Control key).

Recall that the name of the parent directory is dot-dot (..). Also recall that directories show up with d as the first character in the permission list. Therefore, to go up or down in the directory tree, move the cursor to the chosen directory, and press e; you enter that directory. If you press e when the cursor is on a regular file, you enter that file; in other words, you open an edit buffer for that file.

If while in dired you see a file you want to delete, press d. The dired utility will *mark* that file for deletion. The file is not deleted until you enter an x. You can mark as many files for deletion as you wish. If you change your mind on any file, you can remove the delete flag with u (undelete).

## Switching Buffers

The question now is, How do you get back to the edit buffer from the dired buffer? More generally, how do you switch between the different buffers? The answer is, just think *b* for buffers as you enter C-x b (change-buffer). When you invoke the change-buffer command, note that a buffer name appears along with the prompt. This is the name of the previous buffer you were editing; it is the default buffer. To switch back to the previous buffer, press Enter.

Name completion is available when you enter the buffer name; enter a hook (?) if you want to see a list of all existing buffers. To look at a list of only those buffers associated with files, enter C-x C-b, list-buffers.

When you look at the list of buffers, note that there are more buffers than open files. There are *kill buffers* for any text that you have deleted. There might be help buffers, because when you use any help facility, a help buffer is created to hold the screen. Some of these buffers are read-only (such as the help buffers), but most can be edited.

Create your own temporary buffer by giving the C-x b (switch-to-buffer) a name that does not already exist. Then use this buffer for whatever you want, such as making notes to yourself, combining pieces of files, or copying text from other buffers. This buffer becomes an additional workspace. To save the contents of the buffer to a file, use the same write command as for a buffer that is associated with a file, C-x C-s. The emacs editor prompts you for a file name, and the buffer becomes a file.

## The Buffer Menu

You can investigate and manipulate the buffers with buffer-menu. This facility is similar to dired, the file/directory editor. The buffer-menu commands are as follows: d or k to tag the buffer for deletion, s to tag the buffer for saving, u to untag the buffer, and x to perform any actions specified by the tags you placed.

On some emacs implementations, the buffer-menu is automatically invoked if you try to exit without saving all your modified buffers. Normally you invoke the buffer-menu with M-x buffer-menu, but you might bind it to a simpler key combination if you find that you use it often.

## The Kill Buffers

When you delete text, whether by killing words, lines, or regions, the text is moved into a *kill buffer*. To insert the contents of the last-used kill buffer, move the cursor to the position where you want the text and issue the command C-y (yank). The contents of the kill buffer are inserted just before the cursor position (point).

You can also copy text into the kill buffer without deleting it from the buffer. The command copy-region-as-kill is more easily invoked with M-w. This is roughly equivalent to killing the region and then yanking it back to its original position. The effect of both methods is to retain a copy of the region in the kill buffer.

There is actually more than one kill buffer. Repeated kills at the same position in the buffer are accumulated in the same kill buffer and can be yanked as a single block; however, if you move to a new position, a new kill buffer is used to accumulate the text. You are not just overwriting the earlier text in the buffer, you actually have a new buffer, well, an *almost*-new kill buffer. The truth is, there are only six kill buffers. After you use the sixth one, the oldest one is re-used next. This process is called the *kill buffer ring* (sounds like a dangerous criminal organization, doesn't it?). The whole point of multiple kill buffers and the way they are organized is to have the facility to do complex block-editing operations.

To yank back a kill buffer other than the most recent one, rotate through the ring of kill buffers by entering M-y after you have used C-y (yank). The order of the kill buffer ring does not change; it is always from the most recent to the oldest.

There is one set of kill buffers for any editing session. Therefore, they may be used for moving text around from edit buffer to edit buffer, or file to file. When you work on more than one buffer simultaneously, put all the buffers on the screen at the same time, so that you can jump back and forth both visually and with the cursor. Use the window commands of the emacs editor to open the windows you need.

# 7.7 Windows

The easiest and most useful feature of `emacs` is its capability of splitting the editing screen into multiple windows. Instead of marking a position in the file, moving to another area of the file to make some changes or review what was there, and returning to the original position (as you would with `vi`), you can open a new window on the same buffer (and file) and use that for your diversion. One window holds your former place; the second holds your new place. With windows, you can be in *two places at the same time*. Or you can be in two files at the same time. In fact, you can have more than two windows and do more than just a few things at a time. With facilities like these, you too can master multitasking.

Most window commands belong to the extended command set (`C-x`) and include a digit. For example, you can create another window with `C-x 2` (see fig. 7-5). Note that the windows can show different parts of the same file (panel c of figure 7-5) or different files (panel d of figure 7-5).

**Fig. 7-5:**
*Splitting a window with* `C-x 2`.

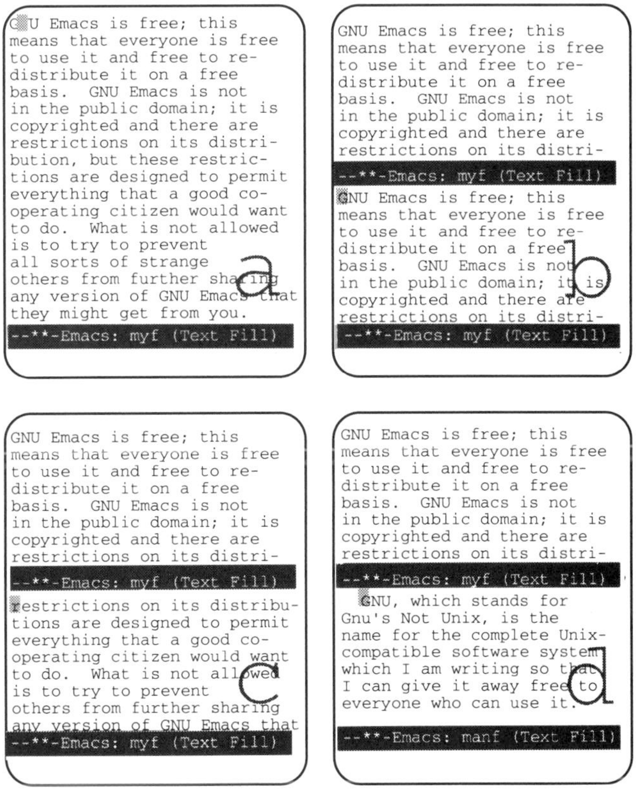

Both windows default to displaying the same buffer; if you are showing the same area of text in each window, your text changes will appear in both windows. You can scroll and operate the windows separately. Therefore, you can edit and view two completely different parts of the same file simultaneously. You can also bring up another buffer (C-x b) or visit another file (C-x C-f). To toggle between the windows, enter the commands C-x o (lowercase letter o) and C-x p (previous window). Table 7-2 summarizes the window commands in emacs.

**Table 7-2.** The emacs **window commands.**

| Command | Purpose |
| --- | --- |
| C-x 2 | Split vertically |
| C-x 5 | Split horizontally |
| C-x o | Select other window |
| C-M-v | Scroll next window |
| C-x 0 | Kill current window |
| C-x 1 | Kill all but current window |
| C-x ^ | Grow current window vertically |
| C-x } | Grow current window horizontally |

Each additional C-x 2 operation subdivides the current window. You can delete the current window with C-x 0 and delete all other windows with C-x 1. As you can see from table 7-2, there are also commands for resizing the windows and creating side-by-side windows. All these windows work well both on character-based terminals and on workstations. Users of the X Window System version of emacs (xemacs) can use the mouse for many window and point operations.

# 7.8 Working With the Shell

The emacs editor has many shell operations as part of its normal set functions. You can get the date, sort text, and read and write mail. emacs also provides several levels of interaction with the shell. For example, to run a shell command and display the output in a temporary buffer, enter M-! -*command* (shell-command). You can pipe a region through a shell command with M-| -*command*.

You can run a subshell within an emacs buffer, capturing all the input and output. (This is useful for writing books about UNIX, because you can capture examples as you write.) You create a *shell buffer* with the obvious command, shell. (As with other unbound commands, invoke it with M-x shell.)

Besides the fact that you are still inside emacs and have not fully escaped to a shell, there are a few other differences between a shell buffer and a real shell. For one, as far as the operating system is concerned, there is no terminal attached to the shell process (your screen will tell you otherwise). So, you cannot run ps or any commands that have to know the characteristics of a terminal, for example, vi. The other characteristics are a result of the way emacs interacts with the shell.

When you use the shell buffer, you are actually in an emacs buffer. The only time you are actually connected to a shell is when you are at the end of the buffer and enter a new line. What you enter on the new line is directed out to the standard input of a shell. The standard output and error are redirected to your emacs buffer. (For a better understanding of standard input, output, and error, see Chapter 8, "Processes.")

When you have to send more than just characters to the shell (for example, to interrupt a process), use the emacs command C-c C-c (interrupt-shell-subjob). The mnemonic here might seem obscure to a new UNIX user, but it is clear to old-timers: to the shell, Ctrl-C means *interrupt*. The other emacs shell commands follow the same pattern: C-c C-z for stopping, C-c C-d for end-of-file. There are other special emacs shell-command controls, but these are the basic ones.

The most complete shell from emacs is a complete escape to the shell, C-z (suspend-emacs). Depending on which version of UNIX you are running, re-enter emacs with exit (Bourne shell and System VR3) or %emacs (C shell on Berkeley and System VR4).

# 7.9 *Personalizing* emacs

As with any well-designed, interactive UNIX program, there are many ways to customize emacs to your tastes. But emacs comes close to being the granddaddy of them all, because it is an *extensible* program. In other words, you can extend the program with the internal and underlying language of the program. In the case of GNU emacs, this language is a version of the threaded programming language LISP. The Lugaru editor, *Epsilon*, uses a language nearly identical to the C programming language.

You do not have to program in order to customize emacs, or even to extend it a little here and there. By capturing keystrokes into a macro buffer, naming that key macro, and binding that named key macro to a shortened key sequence, you have extended the editor with your own commands. Before we go into the details of that process, let's look at how to modify emacs by changing what commands are bound to which keys.

## Key Bindings

All the emacs editing actions have underlying commands with names. The ever-popular C-f (to move the cursor to the right) is actually the "forward-char" function; C-b is "backward-char," C-e is "end-of-line," and so on. What makes all these commands available with the C- and M- combinations is *key binding*. Most of these relationships are defined within the emacs program, but all of them can be changed. There is a system-wide definition file that your system administrator created when he or she installed emacs. But you can have your own definitions that emacs will use instead of the system-wide definition file. Any key bindings you do not define revert to those that are part of the program.

To bind a key to a function just for an editing session, invoke it with M-x global-bind-key <CR> <the keypress> <CR> <the function>. The only differences between defining the macro interactively and as a LISP macro are that you do not use the parentheses of the LISP macro language, and you enter the actual keypress to which you want to bind. If you want the key binding to be active on only one of your buffers, the command is local-set-key.

You can define your default key bindings in a file named .emacsrc. A typical .emacsrc file contains text like this:

```
(global-set-key "\M-a" apropos) (global-set-key "\C-xz"
shell)
```

The editor runs the .emacsrc file whenever you start a new emacs session. You can have several of these. The emacs editor looks first in the directory from which you start your session, your *present working directory*. If it doesn't find an .emacsrc file there, it looks in your *home directory*. If you have none there, the editor reverts to the system-wide emacs startup file.

## Keyboard Macros

A keyboard macro is just a recording of keystrokes that you can replay any time you want. To tell emacs to record your keystrokes, begin with a C-x ( (open parenthesis — the command is start-kbd-macro). To tell it to stop recording, end with a C-x ) (close parenthesis — this command is end-kbd-macro). Everything between is copied to macro memory. Then, when you want to replay the keypress, issue the command C-x e (call-last-kbd-macro).

As with any other `emacs` command, you can invoke the macro any number of times by prefacing it with M-*number*, in which *number* is the number of iterations you want.

An example of a keyboard macro is the following sequence; it surrounds the current word with the expressions !MONO and !ENDMONO:

```
C-x(M-bMONOM-fENDMONOC-x)
```

M-b moves point back to the beginning of the word, where you enter MONO. Follow this with M-f to move forward to the end of the word, where you enter ENDMONO. To define it as a macro, the entire operation is enclosed in C-x ( and C-x ). The trick here is to capture only those keystrokes that can be re-used just about any place you might want to invoke the macro.

Now you can move to the middle of any word to be enclosed in the typesetting directives MONO and ENDMONO, press C-x e, and the keystrokes are replayed.

When you define another keyboard macro, you overwrite the earlier one unless you give the keyboard macro a name:

```
M-x name-last-kbd-macro macro-name
```

For the preceding example, the name might be:

```
M-x name-last-kbd-macro make-mono
```

After you have given the keyboard macro a name, you can bind the macro to a key, generate other keyboard macros, and even save the macro so that you can use it during other editing sessions.

If you don't save the keyboard macro, it disappears when you exit `emacs`. To save it, you must first create a file for macros. The file can be your .emacsrc file or any macro file (see the section on LISP macros that follows). Once you have switched to the buffer for macros, execute as follows:

```
M-x insert-kbd-macro macro-name
```

The `emacs` editor generates the LISP code from your keypresses. Don't forget to save this buffer before you exit.

### Macro Files and `emacs` **LISP**

To say that `emacs` has an underlying structure of commands is not quite precise. The underlying structure of `emacs` is a LISP interpreter. Most of the commands are actually LISP statements. (The LISP engine and some of the extremely repetitive operations are written in the C language.) The LISP engine is what allows you to extend the emacs editor.

The LISP programming language is used primarily for research in Artificial Intelligence, the field of computer science focusing on the attempt to give computers common sense (something they totally lack). But on the way to this apparently impossible goal, many good products have been developed; emacs is one of them.

It is not necessary to go into a detailed explanation of LISP here, but you should know that LISP is an excellent language for handling lists and for modeling other computer (and human) languages. If you look at the text that you edit as a list of characters and words, you can see how well suited LISP is to the job. If the engine of the editor is inherently good at modeling language, it is also good at dealing with complex operations of the language.

Two characteristics of LISP are immediately obvious when you look at a program or emacs macro: there are a lot of parentheses, and this isn't algebra.

```
(defun protect-innocence-hook ()
  (if (and (equal (file-name-nondirectory buffer-file-name) "sex.6")
           (not (y-or-n-p "Are you over 18? ")))
      (progn
       (clear-visited-file-modtime)
       (setq buffer-file-name (concat
                (file-name-directory buffer-file-name) "celibacy.1"))
       (let (buffer-read-only) ; otherwise (erase-buffer) might bomb.
         (erase-buffer)
         (insert-file-contents buffer-file-name t))
       (rename-buffer (file-name-nondirectory buffer-file-name)))))

(or (memq 'protect-innocence-hook find-file-hooks)
    (setq find-file-hooks (cons 'protect-innocence-hook find-file-hooks)))
```

The .emacsrc file is automatically loaded when the program initializes. To execute other LISP files, use M-x load-file. Your LISP extensions to emacs can be enhanced for faster loading and less memory by precompilation: M-x byte-compile-file. If your source files use the suffix .el, the compiled files have the suffix .elc.

As you develop your LISP extensions to emacs, you will want to work with the LISP interactively. The emacs editor has emacs-lisp-mode and a debugger. The most general commands for evaluating LISP expressions in a buffer are eval-region and eval-current-buffer.

You don't have to be a programmer to use emacs, but you will become one if you extend it. In a sense, you end up doing programming to extend any editing program. In truth, emacs and LISP are the easiest and most versatile combination for creating your perfect editor.

## 7.10 Summary

Even though the emacs editor is not part of the standard UNIX distribution, it is found on many systems. It is a single-state text editor; you are always in text-entry mode. Commands are invoked through control-key combinations.

The emacs editor maintains positions in terms of characters (rather than lines, as the vi editor does), although some commands are specific to words and lines. A region is defined as the text between a *mark* and the *point*, the current location of the cursor. Mark and point are maintained as character positions. Block operations (such as cut, move, and copy) are performed with a region.

The emacs editor has incremental searching. In this kind of search, the point (cursor position) immediately moves to the first occurrence of the characters entered in the search string. You can also search with regular expressions as you do in vi.

The emacs editor has multiple, named buffers you enter and edit separately from your main buffer. You can use buffers to edit separate files at the same time. You can have more than one window in the edit screen at one time; the separate windows can be on the same or different buffers.

The emacs editor is self-documented. It is also extensible; you can customize it and extend it using a macro language — usually a form of LISP, but sometimes the C programming language or another language specific to the implementation of emacs.

## Review Questions

1. What is the major operating state of the emacs editor?

2. How many files can you edit simultaneously?

3. What is required to issue a command while editing with emacs?

4. What is key-binding, and what does it represent in the structure of emacs commands?

5. What is the standard key combination used to save the current buffer and exit emacs?

6. How do you invoke a command by name?

7. What is *name completion*?

8. What does the apropos command do?

9. What does auto-fill-mode do?

10. How do you multiply a command or give it a value?

11. How do you delete to the end of a line, and what happens to the text you delete?

12. How do you retrieve text from the kill buffers?

13. How do you define a region?

14. What is an incremental search, and how do you start one?

# Exercises

Use the emacs editor to enter the following text in a file named "part2:"

```
Martha leaned back and put her ear against the rough bark of
the ancient maple. She could hear centuries of the tree's
history, great storms, winters with ten feet of snow, count-
less generations of birds and squirrels. Was it the sap
running in the tree or her own blood flowing in her veins?

Borgonne became numb as he was drawn inside by the cold
light of an alien energy field. He was conscious, but lacked
sensation. His only awareness was of the brumb-buba-rumba
sound.

His mental plea for help became faint and finally faded
away.
```

Go to the beginning of the text and do an incremental search for the word *fade*. Watch where the cursor moves as you enter each character.

Using mark and point, define a region around the last two paragraphs.

Cut the region and move it to the beginning of the example.

Split the screen into two windows. Delete the sentence, *He was conscious, but lacked sensation*, and watch the other window.

Save the file and exit.

## Further Reading

*Emacs, the Extensible, Customizable Self-Documenting Display Editor*, AI memo 519a, Publications Department, Artificial Intelligence Lab, 545 Tech Square, Cambridge, MA 02139, USA.

*A Cookbook for an Emacs*, Craig Finseth, Publications Department, Laboratory for Computer Science, 545 Tech Square, Cambridge, MA 02139, USA.

# 8

# Processes: Concepts and Connections

## Contents

## Objectives

In this chapter you will learn

1. The importance of multitasking

2. How to connect tasks

3. How to use background tasks

A *process* is a running program, whether the shell, a utility, or an application. The input of a process can be from your keyboard, a file, or another program. Similarly, the output can go to the screen, a file, or another program.

UNIX utility programs are designed to work in combination with each other. Because UNIX is a multitasking operating system, it is particularly efficient when running programs that are connected. In this chapter, we explore the multitasking environment, the advantages of tying utilities together, and having multiple processes running at the same time.

# 8.1   Process Input and Output

The connection between a program and its source of information or control is the *standard input*. If you invoke a program in the simplest way, your keyboard is assumed to be the standard input. By default, the output and errors from a utility usually go to your terminal. These two streams of output are called the *standard output* and *standard error*, respectively (see fig. 8-1).

**Fig. 8-1:**
Standard input, standard output, and standard error.

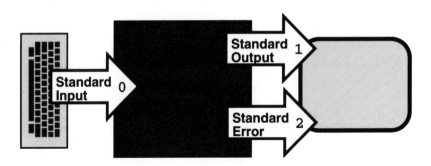

Programs that take a file name as a command-line parameter might actually be changing their standard input from the keyboard over to the file. The file, rather than the keyboard, becomes the input for the program. For example, if you have a file my list that you wish to see as a sorted list, enter the following:

```
sort mylist
```

The sort command assumes that you want to sort the content of the file mylist. If, however, you invoke sort without any command-line arguments, the program expects the input from the default standard input, the keyboard. You could enter words (one per line) as input. When you finish entering all the words, enter the end-of-file character, Ctrl-D, at the beginning of a line, and sort does its work.

As an example, use the sort command to sort the following four names: Tony, Barbara, Harry, Dick. Instead of first entering the names into a file, enter them directly from the terminal:

```
$ sort
Tony
Barbara
Harry
Dick
<CTRL-D>
Barbara
Dick
Harry
Tony
$
```

Because no file name is specified to the sort command, the input is taken from the standard input, the terminal. After the fourth name is entered, you use Ctrl-D to signal the end of the data. At that point, the sort command sorts the four names and displays the results on the standard output device, your terminal screen. (The sort utility is discussed in greater detail in Chapter 9, "A Collection of Utilities.")

## Output Redirection

Under the UNIX system, the output from a command normally intended for standard output, the terminal, can be easily diverted to a file instead. This capability is known as *output redirection*.

When the notation > *filename* is appended to *any* command that normally writes its output to standard output, the output of that command is written into the specified file rather than to your terminal (see fig. 8-2).

The following command line causes the who command to be executed and its output written to the file users.

```
$ who > users
```

**Fig. 8-2:**
*Redirecting
standard
output to a
file.*

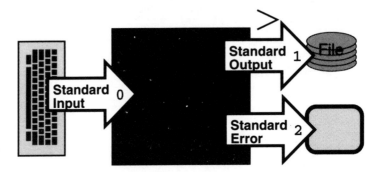

Note that no output appears at the terminal. No output appears because it has been *redirected* from the default standard output device (the terminal) into the specified file. You can now examine the contents of the users file with the cat command to see whether the redirection did in fact work:

```
$ cat users
oko             tty01   Sep 12 07:30
ai              tty15   Sep 12 13:32
ruth            tty21   Sep 12 10:10
pat             tty24   Sep 12 13:07
felix           tty25   Sep 12 13:03
$
```

As another example of output redirection, store the current date and time inside a file called now as follows:

```
$ date > now
$ cat now
Tue Jan 12 14:20:26 EDT 1990
$
```

The echo command also writes to standard output, which means that it, too, can be redirected as follows:

```
$ echo line 1 > x
$ cat x
line 1
$
```

If a command redirects its output to a file that already contains some data, that data is lost. Consider the following example:

```
$ echo line 1 > x
$ cat x
line 1
$ echo line 2 > x
$ cat x
line 2
$
```

The contents of x (the line line 1) are lost when the second echo command is executed.

Now consider the following example:

```
$ echo line 1 > x
$ cat x
line 1
$ echo line 2 >> x
$ cat x
line 1
line 2
$
```

The second echo command uses a different type of output redirection, indicated by the characters >>. This character pair causes the standard output from the command to be *appended* to the specified file. Therefore, the previous contents of the file are not lost, and the new output is added onto the end.

## More on the cat Command

You might recall that one of the files in Chapter 4 was created by the command cat > names. Now you can understand precisely how that command worked. Like most other commands, the cat command takes its input from standard input and writes its output to standard output by default. This means that if no file name is supplied to the cat command, this command expects its input to come from the terminal. The following example illustrates this idea:

```
$ cat
line one
line one
line two
line two
```

```
etc.
etc.
<CTRL-D>
$
```

Because no filename argument was specified, `cat` read its input from the terminal. As each line was read, it was written to standard output. The net effect was to echo each line entered. Ctrl-D signaled the end of the input to `cat`. Redirection of the output with a command such as

```
cat > junk
```

would have caused the three lines entered to be redirected to the file `junk`.

By using the redirection append characters >>, you can use `cat` to append the contents of one file to the end of another, as follows:

```
$ cat file1
This is in file1.
$ cat file2
This is in file2.
$ cat file1 >> file2      —Append file1 to file2
$ cat file2
This is in file2.
This is in file1.
$
```

Recall that specifying more than one file name to `cat` results in the display of the first file followed immediately by the second file, and so on:

```
$ cat file1
This is in file1.
$ cat file2
This is in file2.
$ cat file1 file2
This is in file1.
This is in file2.
$ cat file 1 file2 > file3    —Redirect it instead
$ cat file3
This is in file1.
This is in file2.
$
```

Now you can see where the `cat` command gets its name: when used with more than one file its effect is to *concatenate* the files.

One thing you should note: a command such as

```
cat file2 file1 > file1
```

does *not* work correctly, and you lose the original contents of `file1`. To do this sort of thing, use a temporary file for the output and then `mv` the file where you want it. For example, to concatenate `file1` to the end of `file2` and have the result go to `file1`, use the following sequence:

```
$ cat file2 file1 > temp
$ mv temp file1
$
```

You can see how output redirection enables the `cat` command to be used for purposes other than displaying files.


## Input Redirection

Just as the output of a command can be redirected to a file, so can the input of a command be redirected from a file. Whereas the greater-than character ($>$) is used for output redirection, the less-than ($<$) character is used for input redirection of a command (see fig. 8-3).

**Fig. 8-3:**
Redirecting standard input to come from a file.

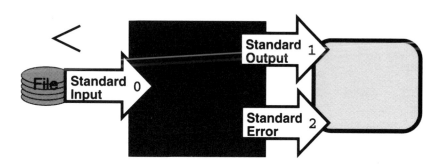

Of course, only commands that normally take their input from standard input can have their input redirected from a file in this manner.

To redirect the input of a command, enter the < character followed by the name of the file from which the input is to be read. For example, to count the number of lines in the file `names`, you could execute the command `wc -l names` as follows:

```
$ wc -l names
       5 names
$
```

Or you can count the number of lines in the file by redirecting the input of the `wc` command from the terminal to the file `names`:

```
$ wc -l < names
       5
$
```

Note that there is a difference in the output produced by the two forms of the `wc` command. In the first case, the name of the file `names` is listed with the line count; in the second case, it is not. This points out the subtle distinction between the two commands. In the first case, `wc` knows it is reading its input from the file `names`. In the second case, it knows only that it is reading its input from standard input. The shell redirects the input from the terminal to the file `names`. Therefore, `wc` doesn't know whether its input is coming from the terminal or from a file!

Some commands do not take file names in their parameter list. To use these on a file, you *must* redirect the standard input. For example, the command for doing character translations, `tr`, takes only two strings in its parameter list. The first string is the list of characters to be remapped, and the second is the character to which they are to be mapped. Therefore, to map all lowercase characters to uppercase, use the command `tr '[a-z]' '[A-Z]'`. Apply this to the file `names` as follows:

```
$ tr '[a-z]' '[A-Z]' < names
SUSAN
JEFF
HENRY
ALLAN
KEN
$
```

## Input and Output Redirection

As you might expect, you can simultaneously redirect the input and the output of a command — provided of course the command reads its input from standard input *and* writes its output to standard output.

```
$ cat names
Susan
Jeff
Henry
Allan
Ken
$ tr '[a-z]' '[A-Z]' < names > uppercase
$ cat uppercase
SUSAN
JEFF
HENRY
ALLAN
KEN
$
```

In this example, the sort command's input is redirected from the file names and its output is redirected to the file uppercase.

## Redirecting the Standard Error

If you have attempted any of the redirection commands we have looked at, you might have noticed that some of the output did not end up in the files but went to the screen instead. This is the text that is directed to *standard error*.

```
$ cat names xxx > allout
cat: can not open xxx
$ cat allout
Barbara
Dick
Harry
Tony
$
```

The problem is how to capture that error message along with the output. (This problem becomes more relevant when you work with background processes and shell scripts.) The Bourne and Korn shells differ from the C shell in the syntax.

The Bourne and Korn shells specify the use of digits representing the internal file descriptor numbers for the standard input, standard output, and standard error:

0, 1, and 2, respectively. The standard error is represented by the digit 2. Therefore, to redirect the standard error to the file errors, the following syntax is used: 2> errors (see fig. 8-4).

**Fig. 8-4:**
*Redirecting standard error to standard output and that to a file.*

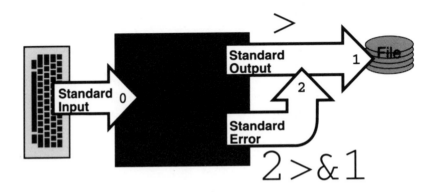

The following is an example:

```
$ cat names xxx 2>errors
Susan
Jeff
Henry
Allan
Ken
$ cat errors
cat: cannot open xxx
$
```

Now, how do you capture both the standard error and the standard output in one file? The technique is not so obvious; first you must redirect standard output to a file, then redirect standard error to standard output. But standard output is not a file. What are you to do? The key is in using the ampersand (&) before the file number. Recall that standard output is file descriptor number 1. Our example becomes:

```
$ cat names xxx > output 2>&1
$ cat output
Susan
Jeff
Henry
Allan
```

```
Ken
cat: cannot open xxx
$
```

The last line, the error statement, is actually part of the `output` file. There are a few points to remember when you use redirection of this sort. The first is that there cannot be any spaces between the file descriptor number (0, 1, 2) and the redirection symbol. Otherwise the file descriptor number is interpreted as a file name. The second point is that you *must* redirect the standard output before you redirect the standard error to it.

The syntax for redirection in the Korn shell is exactly the same as with the Bourne shell. The C shell is different only when it comes to dealing with the redirection of standard error. The redirection of standard error along with standard output is done in a single expression >&. The file descriptor number is not used at all. The syntax and order become much simpler. The previous example demonstrated with the C shell appears as follows:

```
1% cat names xxx >& output
2% cat output
Susan
Jeff
Henry
Allan
Ken
cat: cannot open xxx
3%
```

Even with the C shell, keep the ampersand right next to the redirect character; otherwise, it might be confused with a second use, that of putting the process in the background (explained later in this chapter). There is no way to redirect only the standard error when using the C shell.

# 8.2  Pipes

Recall that the file `users`, created previously, contains a list of all the users currently logged onto the system. Because you know that there will be one line in the file for each user logged onto the system, you can easily determine the *number* of users logged in by counting the number of lines in the `users` file:

```
$ who > users
$ wc -l < users
5
$
```

This output indicates that there are five users logged in. There is another, easier approach to determining the number of logged-in users without using a file. The UNIX system allows you to effectively connect two commands. This connection is known as a *pipe*; it enables you to take the output from one command and feed it directly into the input of another command (see fig. 8-5).

**Fig. 8-5:**
How a pipe
works.

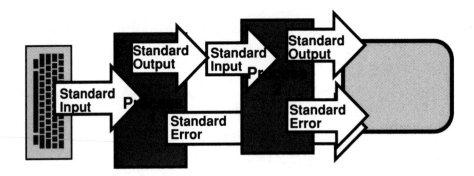

A pipe is effected by the character | , which is placed between the two commands. To make a pipe between the who and wc -1 commands, enter who | wc -1:

```
$ who | wc -1
          5
$
```

When a pipe is set up between two commands, the standard output from the first command is connected directly to the standard input of the second command. You know that the who command writes its list of logged-in users to standard output. Furthermore, you know that if no filename argument is specified to the wc command, it takes its input from standard input. Therefore, the list of logged-in users that is output from the who command automatically becomes the input to the wc command. Note that you never see the output of the who command at the terminal, because it is *piped* directly into the wc command.

A pipe can be made between *any* two programs under the UNIX system, provided the first program writes its output to standard output, and the second program reads its input from standard input.

As another example of a pipe, suppose that you wanted to count the number of files contained in your directory. The `ls` command displays one line of output per file; therefore, you can use the same type of approach as in the previous example:

```
$ ls | wc -l
       10
$
```

The output indicates that the current directory contains 10 files. (Although Berkeley implementations of `ls` display multiple columns as the default, they are affected by redirection of the standard output. If the output is redirected, the Berkeley `ls` will output the file names in a single column; otherwise, it will be in multiple columns. The `ls | wc -l` command will still give you the expected result, the number of files.)

As another example, you can use `who` and `sort` in the following pipeline to get a sorted list of logged-in users:

```
$ who | sort
adn          tty27   Feb 22 08:56
ai           tty05   Feb 22 09:43
clf          tty11   Feb 22 08:59
ben          tty04   Feb 22 09:00
dianne       tty14   Feb 22 08:45
dji          tty20   Feb 22 09:44
fes          tty22   Feb 22 09:31
jcm          tty06   Feb 22 08:19
rcc          tty37   Feb 22 08:27
ruth         tty17   Feb 22 09:44
felix        tty15   Feb 22 08:45
ws           tty13   Feb 22 08:25
$
```

To save the sorted list of users in a file called `users`, use output redirection on the `sort` command: `who | sort > users`.

Pipes are the most important glue in UNIX. Having many single-purpose utilities is valuable because you can tie these utilities together. If you explore a really complex UNIX utility such as `calendar`, a program that notifies you of pending commitments, you find that it is actually just a few lines of utilities tied together with pipes.

## Pipes and Standard Error

For the same reasons that you might want to combine the standard error with the standard output for redirected output, you might want to combine the two to send them to a pipe. Things would be very confusing, however, if the standard error were redirected after the pipe character (|). Therefore, the Bourne and Korn syntax is predictable:

*command* 2>&1 | *command*

and the C syntax is as follows:

*command* |& *command*

A common use of redirection through pipes is with the screen pager commands pg and more. For example, you can use the following command to view the statistics in the /usr/bin directory along with any error messages that might be generated:

```
$ ls -l 2>&1 | pg      – Bourne shell version
```

or

```
% ls -l |& pg      – C shell version
```

Clearly, the C shell syntax for redirection is the simpler of the two. But you should make clear notes to yourself as to how to do these operations for the Bourne and Korn shells. When you learn to write shell scripts, you will find that the Bourne and Korn shells are applicable on more systems.

## Copying the Output to a File: *tee*

We have stressed the fact that output from a command that gets piped into another command is not seen at the terminal. Sometimes you might want to save the output produced in the middle of a pipe. The format of this command is simple enough:

```
tee file
```

The tee command copies the data coming in on standard input to standard output and saves a copy in the specified *file*. Figure 8-6 gives you a better understanding of how this command works and where it gets its name.

As you can see in the following example, you can insert the tee command right after the who in the pipeline to save the user names in a file. This pipeline works

**Figure 8-6:**
The tee splits
out a copy to
a file.

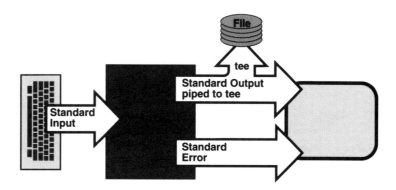

the same way as the simple pipe, except that in this case the tee command saves
the output of the who command in the file users:

```
$ who | tee users | wc -l
        4
$ cat users
ampsphw tty08    Feb 27 09:03
ampsoko tty11    Feb 27 14:39
ampssgk tty15    Feb 27 08:40
ampsclf tty18    Feb 27 10:26
$
```

Some interesting uses of tee involve interactive programs. One example involves
UNIX's somewhat primitive interactive communications program, cu. (See
Chapter 11, "Advanced Utilities," for more on this program.) The cu program can
conduct an interactive session on a remote machine. The one thing it lacks is an
internal way to capture the session to a file. You can, however, redirect it, because
everything you enter is echoed off the remote machine and then combined with
the responses and output from the remote machine through the standard output of
cu. If you use only the greater-than symbol (>) to redirect to a file, you do not see
the output on your local screen. Everything ends up in the file, but you operate
blindly. The tee solves the problem. Assume, for example, that the machine you
want to call is named bytepb. The command to issue is as follows:

```
cu bytepb | tee log
```

Because the pipe doesn't have a command (other than tee) on the right, the data
ends up on the standard output; however, a copy is made in the file log.

An even more interesting application involves capturing keystrokes but *not* the output from an interactive program; in other words, capturing the standard input. You might want to test or automate an interactive program. By replaying the keystrokes later, you can recreate the entire session. Using the ex editor program as an example, the command to capture the standard input is as follows:

```
tee keystrokes | ex testfile
```

Note that due to the way vi handles the standard input, using a tee on the input does not work as well as with ex. Some commercial UNIX programs do work surprisingly well with keypress-log testing.

The standard input is copied to the file keystrokes and simultaneously piped to the standard input of ex. The entire procedure might look like the following:

```
on $ tee keystrokes | ex testfile
"testfile" [New file]
a                                              — Going into append mode
This is text that is being entered into
the file testfile. The next line will
be deleted after it has been entered.
Delete this line.
$                                              — Look at last line
Delete this line.
d                                              — Delete the line
be deleted after it has been entered.
1,$p                                           — Display first through last
This is text that is being entered into
the file testfile. The next line will
be deleted after it has been entered.
w                                              — Write (save) the file
"testfile" [New file] 3 lines, 117 characters
q                                              — Quit the editor
$ cat keystrokes                               — Look at the keystrokes file

a
This is text that is being entered into
the file testfile. The next line will
be deleted after it has been entered.
Delete this line.
$
d
1,$p
w
q
$ cat testfile                                 — Look at the text created
```

```
This is text that is being entered into
the file testfile. The next line will
be deleted after it has been entered.
$ mv testfile o.testfile          — Move the file aside so we can test
$ ex testfile < keystrokes        — Run the editor using keystrokes file
$
```

## Stringing Commands Together

You can string several commands together, without writing a shell script. To issue
a single line with several commands (without piping the output of one into the
other), separate the commands by a semicolon ( ; ), as follows:

```
$ mv file3 filex; mv file2 file3; mv file1 file2; mv filex file1
$
```

There is no real connection between the commands in the list. Whether or not the
previous command succeeds, the next command is attempted.

You can allow a command connection to be controlled by the success or failure
of one or more commands. The special symbols are &&!EM and ||. (Don't
confuse these symbols with the single pipe (|) used for piping the output of one
command to the input of another, described previously, and the single ampersand
(&) used to send a command to the background, described later in this chapter.)

```
on $ echo "one" && echo "two"
one
two
$ echo "one" || echo "two"
one
$ ls -l all && echo "previous command succeeded"
-rw-r--r--   1 ben        group         110 Jan 28 16:55 all
previous command succeeded
$ ls -l xxx || echo "previous command failed"
"xxx" not found
previous command failed
$
```

As you can see from the examples, you can issue commands so that a second
command executes only if the first command succeeds. You do this by joining the
commands with &&. By joining the two commands with ||, you can ensure that
if the first command fails, a second command "cleans up."

Note that not all commands return a correct *exit status*. Some, even when successful, actually return random values which are usually interpreted as a *failure*.

As you can see, these *plumbing parts* — pipes and tees — really enhance the UNIX utilities. When we explore the subject of shell scripts in Chapter 12, "Basic Shell Scripts," you will see some more process plumbing.

# 8.3  Processes — Parents and Children

You might wonder how UNIX creates all those processes that make it multitasking and multiuser. Without going into the details of the system boot (startup) sequence, we can say that UNIX knows how to *spawn*. (And you thought that a genderless operating system was sterile!) One process can create several other processes. You have probably already guessed which is the parent process and which are the children. These terms, *spawn*, *parent*, and *child*, are actually the standard expressions for describing the relationship of processes in UNIX. Don't personify these ideas too much, however, or you will be horrified to learn that you must sometimes *kill* a process.

## Escape to a Shell

Many interactive programs, `vi` and `emacs` included, allow you to escape to the UNIX shell. If you escape to the shell and invoke `ps` to see what processes are running, you see that you have more than just `ps` and a shell, as in the following example:

```
$ ps
   PID TTY   TIME COMMAND
   552  1a  0:01 sh
   612  1a  0:00 vi
   613  1a  0:00 sh
   614  1a  0:00 ps
$
```

When you escape to a shell, you create a child process. The `ps` (process status) command is valuable for seeing what is running on your system. The process family relationship is revealed when you use `ps` with the `-l` (long) option:

```
$ ps -l
  F S   UID   PID  PPID  C PRI NI  ADDR  SZ   WCHAN TTY  TIME CMD
  1 S   201   552     1  0  30 20   217  28   11734  1a  0:01 sh
  1 S   201   612   552  0  30 20 196136      117dc  1a  0:00 vi
  1 S   201   613   612  0  30 20   396  28   1192c   1a  0:00 sh
  1 R   201   614   613  4  52 20   2cc  24            1a  0:00 ps
```

This infomation is far more than we need. We are interested in the following columns: S (state), PID (process ID), PPID (parent-process ID), and CMD (command).

The other columns are: F (flag), UID (user ID), C (CPU), PRI (priority), NI (nice), ADDR (memory address), SZ (process size), WCHAN (wait channel), TTY (communications port), and TIME (CPU time). We won't go into these processes here.

The status flags are S for sleeping processes and R for running processes. The fact that there is only one running process, the ps command, in the example does not mean that there cannot be others. Actually, this process list is limited to those that are at your terminal; other users might be running many other processes.

Look at the process ID (PID) for the ps command. It is 614. Its parent process ID (PPID) is 613. That is the process ID for one of the sh (shell) commands. Whenever you start a command by entering the command at the shell prompt, that command is created as a *child* of the shell.

Continuing back through the process list, matching parent process IDs with process IDs, you see that the second shell is the child of the vi command, and vi is the child of the first sh.

You return to the parent process (in this example, the vi editor) by using the exit command.

To escape to a new shell from your current shell, start a shell like any other command. For example, to start a Bourne shell, use sh; a Korn shell, ksh; and a C shell, csh. The original shell is asleep while you work in the new shell. The two most common reasons to do this are to maintain your place in the file system and your history while you go out and do some other task, and to temporarily change the kind of shell you are using. The C shell and the Korn shell have commands to keep track of the directories you visit, a sort of directory history like the command history. The Bourne shell, however, has no such facility. In any case, running errands is easier if you create a child shell. When you finish, exit the temporary shell and you are right back where you started.

On many UNIX systems both the C and Bourne shells are available. Experienced users often use the Berkeley shell for their regular activities and switch to the

Bourne shell for interative programming and some of the complex commands discussed in Chapter 12, "Basic Shell Scripts." The C shell can do iterative operations, but the Bourne shell syntax for iterations is easier to remember if it is the first one you learned. With the Korn shell available on increasing numbers of systems, users just use the Korn shell. The Korn shell is standard in System V Release 4. It provides the advanced features of the C shell with the simple syntax of the Bourne shell.

## Replacing the Current Process: *exec*

Rather than make a temporary child process and build up your process tree, you can actually switch to a new process, completely *replacing* the old process with the new one. To do so, preface the new command with the shell internal command exec. The current shell is replaced by the new process. If you are operating from the lowest level shell, the one you receive when you first log in, then when the process terminates, you are logged off of the system.

When you exec a command or shell, no new process is created, as the following example shows:

```
$ ps
   PID TTY   TIME COMMAND
   868  1a   0:01 sh
   922  1a   0:00 ps
$ exec csh
% ps
   PID TTY   TIME COMMAND
   868  1a   0:01 csh
   924  1a   0:00 ps
% exit

login:
```

Note that the process ID (PID) for the csh is the same as that for the earlier sh. You will discover some uses for execing when you start writing shell scripts. For now, you will find it useful for changing shells without carrying around the baggage of parent shell processes, and for invoking commands that automatically log you out when they terminate. As with so many other operations in UNIX, however, there are better ways of dealing with processes that don't need interaction: *background* processes.

# 8.4 Processes — Foreground and Background

We have been talking about how UNIX is multitasking, but so far we haven't done anything to take advantage of this feature, or even demonstrate it. The techniques we have used so far put one process to sleep while another process runs. True multitasking involves more than one process actively running simultaneously. To prove that this actually happens, use the ps command with the -el option (BSD systems use the -g option), as in the following example:

```
$ ps -el
  F S   UID    PID   PPID  C PRI NI  ADDR SZ   WCHAN  TTY   TIME CMD
  3 S     0      0      0  0   0 20    64  0   1aefa   ?   0:00 swapper
  1 S     0      1      0  0  30 20    9b 16   10ffc   ?   0:02 init
  1 S     0    746      1  0  28 20   17b 24   1a1a4  01   0:00 getty
  1 S     0    747      1  0  28 20   1f5 24   1a204  02   0:00 getty
  1 S     0     28      1  0  26 24   1fd 16    5fa4   ?   0:00 logger
  1 S     0     27      1  0  40 20   1f1 12 6000000   ?   0:04 update
  1 S     0     56      1  0  28 20   1c5 24   1a264  03   0:00 getty
  1 S     0     30      1  0  26 20   1d0 24    ed22   ?   0:00 cron
  1 S     0    916      1  0  28 20   18a 24   1c6d8   ?   0:00 getty
  1 S     0     57      1  0  28 20   20c 24   1a2c4  04   0:00 getty
  1 S     0    770      1  0  28 20   199 24   1a564  11   0:00 getty
  1 S     0     59      1  0  28 20   211 24   1a5c4  12   0:00 getty
  1 S   201    925      1  0  30 20   217 36   11734  1a   0:01 sh
  1 R   201   -936    925 19  59 20 26d204           1a   0:02 epsilon
  1 S    14    440      1  0  30 20   380 24   11884   ?   0:00 lpsched
  1 R   201   -938    936  0  26 20   27f  8           1a   0:00 epsilon.
  1 S    14    908    440  0  30 20   28a 24   119d4   ?   0:00 lpsched
  1 S    14    118      1  0  26 20   349 24    c5c2   ?   0:00 lpsched
  1 S    14    909    908  0  29 20   37c 20   1f024   ?   0:00 sh
  1 S   201    939    936  0  40 20   33d  8 6000000  1a   0:00 epsilon.
  1 S   201    940    936  0  30 20   1d4 32   11c74   ?   0:00 sh
  1 R   201   -942    940  3  51 20   31e 24           ?   0:00 ps
$
```

Note that the three processes 936, 938, and 942 are all in the R (running) state.

This feature is particularly useful when you use commands that are slow to execute, such as text formatters and typesetters, large sorts, and file filters. You can create your own active background process by following any command with the ampersand (&), as in the following example:

```
$ ps
   PID TTY   TIME COMMAND
   946  1a   0:00 sh
   947  1a   0:00 ps
$ nroff -mm 8-all | lp
 948
 949
$ ps
   PID TTY   TIME COMMAND
   946  1a   0:00 sh
   948  1a   0:00 lp
   949  1a   0:02 nroff
   951  1a   0:00 ps
$
```

Normally you enter a command and wait for the results to be displayed at the terminal. Typically the wait is short — maybe a second or two. However, you might have commands that take many seconds or even minutes to execute. In such cases you must wait for the command to finish executing before you can proceed, *unless you execute the command in the background* (or have another window in which to work).

If you enter a command followed by the ampersand (&), that command no longer ties up your terminal, and you can proceed with other work. The standard output from the command is still directed to your terminal; in most cases, however, the standard input is dissociated from your terminal. If the command tries to read any input from standard input, it will be as if Ctrl-D (end-of-file) were entered.

```
$ sort data > out &            — Send the sort to the background
1258                           — Process ID
$ date                         — Your terminal is immediately available
Thu Apr 26 17:45:09 EST 1988
$
```

When a command is sent to the background, the UNIX system automatically displays the process ID for that command. In the previous example, 1258 was the process ID assigned by the system. This number uniquely identifies the command you sent to the background, and can be used to obtain status information about the command. Use the ps command to obtain this information.

As noted previously, the process of freeing your terminal for other work by sending a command to the background for execution is most often used for commands that require a significant amount of time to execute. Do not abuse this feature if you have more than one user logged in to your system. Having many commands executing in the background is discourteous to other users, because you use a disproportionate amount of the computer's resources.

## C-Style Process Control

Until UNIX System V Release 4, the only systems that offered real process control were those running BSD UNIX or that had incorporated the BSD process structure into their implementation of the operating system. It is not enough to have the C shell running. The underlying kernel must also have the appropriate facilities. If your UNIX system has these facilities, you can move processes back and forth between the foreground and the background, put them to sleep, and awaken them.

The simplest operation, that of creating a running process and placing it in the background, is the same for all the shells: use the ampersand (&) at the end of the command line. But with the C shell and Korn shell you can also put the current process to sleep by hypnotizing it with Ctrl-Z. After a Stopped message, you are given a new shell prompt — not a new shell, just a new prompt. You have not escaped to a new shell, but have escaped to your original shell. You have not terminated the process, just put it to sleep. If you try to log out without first terminating the sleeping process, you are warned: There are stopped jobs. Exit jobs properly, or at least kill them before you exit. (See the "Removing Unwanted Processes" section near the end of this chapter.)

Bring jobs back into the foreground with fg. Without an argument, this command awakens the sleeping command. fg even brings running background processes into the foreground, which you might not want to do. To be sure of which jobs (processes) are in which states, use the jobs command.

```
% jobs
[1]     +    Stopped    vi chapter8
[2]     -    Stopped    mail phw
[3]          Running    emacs example
%
```

The notation at the beginning of each line brings us back to the subject of using fg with parameters. The complete syntax is as follows:

    fg *jobid*

in which *jobid* can take several different forms such as the following:

    %*job-number*
    %*name-prefix*
    %+
    %-

The percent (%) is not the shell prompt; it is part of the syntax for *jobid*. The *job-number* comes from the list output from jobs. The *name-prefix* is conceptually similar to the C-shell bang (!) command; in this case you need enter only enough of the job's name to identify it. Using the previous jobs example, the following is enough to revive the sleeping vi:

```
% fg %v
```

The %+ is always the job most recently put in the background or to sleep. This is the default if you don't specify a job. The %- is the second-most recent job. Therefore, the three equivalent versions of the command to revive the mail session are:

```
% fg %m
% fg %2
% fg %-
```

There is one more process-control command: bg. This command is almost identical to the fg command, but when it awakens the sleeping command it moves it to the background rather than the foreground.

In summation, there are three possible job states: running in the foreground, running in the background, and sleeping (stopped). The fourth possible state, dead, isn't considered a state because jobs leave behind no number when they meet their end.

There is one other state, which results from errors in killing associated processes. This is the *zombie*, or *dead but lingering*, state. Fortunately, such occurrences are rare.

## Process Control with *shl*

As an alternative to the process control of the csh and sh shells under BSD systems, many systems based on UNIX System V Release 2 and 3 have a special shell manager, shl. This is not a shell of its own, but rather a shell-level manager. You create multiple concurrent shells with it. Its limitation is that only seven shells can run at one time.

To enter the shell layer manager, enter the command shl. There are no parameters, just the command. There are two levels of shl: the manager level, with the prompt >>>; and the shells, with a prompt that uses the layer's name or number. (If your SHELL environment variable is set to csh, you get your standard C shell prompt.)

When you first enter the shell layer manager, you have no shells running. You must create a shell by using the `shl` command: `create` *shell-name*. The *shell-name* is optional. The default name is the shell number.

When you are in a shell and wish to return to the manager or switch to another shell, use Ctrl-Z. From the manager level, you can resume any shell with `resume` *shell-name*, or toggle between the last two active shells with `toggle`. To terminate all the shell layers and return to the normal shell, the command is `quit`.

All shell layer manager commands can be abbreviated to as little as the single character with which they begin. The *shell-name* can be abbreviated to the first letter that makes the name unique.

A session using `shl` might look like this:

```
$ shl
>>> create comm
comm mail phw < chapter8
comm ^Z
>>> create calc
calc bc
scale=2
12456 / 2
6228.00
^Z
>>> toggle
comm who
$ who
felix          stx001       Apr 22 18:11
ben            ttyla        Apr 22 20:21
root           tty11        Apr 22 18:12
comm ^Z
>>> toggle
^D
calc exit
>>> resume comm
comm mail ben
   .
   .
   .
comm exit
>>> quit
$
```

You can terminate any shell layer and all its child processes with the manager level command, `delete` *shell-name*.

When you are in one shell layer, the *input* of the other shell layers is blocked but the *output* of the other layers is not. This means that any output from other shell layers still appears on your terminal. Although you might want this information, it can produce visual chaos. Therefore, `shl` has two additional commands (from the manager level): `block` *shell-name* and `unblock` *shell-name*.

Although `shl` might seem primitive when compared to the process control of C systems and System V Release 4, it is useful when the others are not available. The underlying structure has been more valuable than `shl` itself because it is the mechanism that allows many *virtual terminals* to operate. Virtual terminals are implemented on Santa Cruz Operations UNIX and Xenix as well as Interactive Systems UNIX, BSD UNIX, AIX, and many other UNIX licensees. They provide the console with the equivalent of many different terminals, all of which operate using the same screen and keyboard. You switch between the virtual terminals with a special key combination such as Alt-F (SCO's implementation). Each window in an X Window System screen is also a virtual terminal.

Because the `shl` doesn't have any facilities for maintaining the information for independent screen images for the different shell layers, it is not as popular as job control that is built into the shell.

## Removing Unwanted Processes: *kill*

When a program completes, the process dies. It no longer appears in the list of processes when you use the `ps` command. Some processes don't know when to die unless you tell them. For example, the shell continues to run until you enter the command `exit` or Ctrl-D.

You can kill a process in other ways as well, most directly with the `kill` command. Be careful what you shoot down, however, because when you kill a process, all its children die. Usually this is necessary when you have a runaway process or a program over which you have lost control.

There are some safeguards built in to the `kill` command. For one, you can kill only your own processes. (The system administrator, however, can kill any process. In fact, if you have a serious problem, you can contact the system administrator and ask that your whole session be killed, right back to the `login` prompt.)

By their nature, some programs are more resistant to `kill` commands than others. But with any process, you must know the process ID in order to kill. Then you can try the command with the following syntax:

`kill` *process-ID*

The usual way to do this includes first finding the process-ID with ps, issuing the kill command, and checking again with ps to see if you were successful. If you were not, it is time to send some strong signals. In fact, the term *signals* is appropriate because that is the nomenclature for one of the mechanisms that the UNIX kernel uses to communicate with processes. The syntax for sending a signal with a kill command is as follows:

kill  *– signal  process-ID*

Of the more than a dozen signals available, you need to know only a few. The gentlest is signal 15. This is the same as kill with no signal specified. It allows a program to die with warning so that it can settle any unfinished business before it terminates.

The kill  -2 command is equivalent to pressing the interrupt key (usually the Delete key) from within the process.

The command to kill without hesitation and overcome all defenses is kill  -9. You can even log yourself out this way. Just kill your most senior shell.

Occasionally you will find a process lingering on after its parent is deceased. The process doesn't seem to have any connection to the real world. This is a *zombie* process. This kind of process requires help from the system administrator. If your UNIX system software is old or poorly implemented, it might be necessary to bring the entire system down to kill off zombies. Hope that you never have one lurking about.

As a final note, the Korn shell and C shell support kill  [ *-signal- number* ] *jobid* and [ *-signal-name* ] *jobid*. An example is kill  -HANGUP %2.

# 8.5  Summary

UNIX processes have three ports with which they can be connected to devices, files, and other processes: the standard input, the standard output, and the standard error. Unless otherwise directed, the standard input comes from your keyboard and the standard output and error go to your screen.

Sending or receiving input and output with something other than the default device or with a file is called "redirecting." Connecting two processes is called "creating a pipe."

Processes can be temporarily halted and restarted. They can also be placed "in the background," where they continue to work without user interaction. On systems such as System V Release 4 and Berkeley, there are utilities for managing your processes, including reviving sleeping processes and moving background processes back into the foreground (interactive) state. All systems allow you to kill (prematurely terminate) processes.

## Review Questions

1. What is a process?

2. Why is UNIX called a multitasking operating system?

3. How do UNIX utilities take advantage of multitasking?

4. What are the three input and output *ports* of a UNIX utility?

5. What does it mean to redirect standard input, standard output, and standard error?

6. What is a pipe and how is it designated in UNIX?

7. What does the tee command do?

8. How do you specify (without using if) that one process is to run only if another process completes without errors?

9. How do you specify that one process is run only if another fails?

10. When you escape to a shell from a program like vi, how do you return to the parent process?

11. What is the command that displays the status of your processes?

12. How do you invoke a process so that it runs in the background?

13. What do you have to do to kill a process?

## Exercises

List the files in the directory /usr/bin to a file named ls.out in one of your directories (use the ls command).

List the files in the directory /bin, appending them to the ls.out file you used in the previous exercise.

List the files in the directory /usr/bin through either the pg or the more utility.

Sort the ls.out file as a background process using the command: sort ls.out &. Note that the output went to the terminal even though the process was in the background. Even though a process is in the background, the standard output still goes to the terminal unless you redirect it.

Do a ps and make a note of the PID (process ID) of the ps command. Try to kill this process. What happened? Now kill the sh (or csh or ksh). What happened this time?

# Further Reading

*An Introduction to Berkeley UNIX*, Paul Wang, Wadsworth Publishing Company, Belmont, CA, 1988. A useful textbook for programmers and students of operating systems. It covers both theory and practice.

*Kornshell Command and Programming Language*, Korn and Bolsky, Prentice Hall, Englewood Cliffs, NJ, 1988.

# A Collection of Utilities

## Contents

## Objectives

In this chapter you will

1. Become familiar with the most common UNIX utility programs

2. Learn how to manage information files

3. Be able to schedule jobs for periodic processing

We keep saying that UNIX is filled with wonderful utility programs, and so far we have looked at `sed`, `grep`, and a few others. This chapter discusses a broad collection of UNIX utilities, some of which are simple (such as `lp`, the print spooler) and some sophisticated (such as `diff`). Chapter 11 deals with even more complex utilities, such as `awk`. You might use some of these utilities every day; others you might never use.

This chapter does not cover all the UNIX utilities with an in-depth discussion of all their possibilities; it is just an introduction. The *Further Reading* list at the end of the chapter directs you to more texts with additional details. Appendix A attempts a complete listing of the utilities with a brief description of each.

## 9.1  Printing

Consider what might happen if several users on a UNIX system were to send different files directly to the printer at the same time. The printer, having no way of knowing that more than one file was sent to it, would probably mix them all up. Because of this problem, and because printers are much slower in producing their output, multiuser systems rely on *print spooling*.

The print spooler is the subsystem that manages printing tasks. As a user, all you need to know is the `lp` (line printer) command.

```
lp <file-list>
```

The files in the list are *spooled* to the printer. In other words, the print spooler queues up the requests and processes them one by one.

Receiving a shell prompt after the `lp` request does not necessarily mean that the job has been completed. To determine the status of your print job, use the `lpstat` command, as in the following example:

```
$ lp file[1-4]
request id is hpjet-1105 (4 files)
$ lpstat
hpjet-1105              ben              2259    Jan 28 11:08 on hpjet
$
```

Note that there is only one request pending, even though you asked to print four files. The spooler will not mix up your four files. It prints a header page at the beginning of each request. The header page identifies the user who requested the printer, along with the job number, the date, and the time. This page helps separate the jobs, and tells the person managing the printer who should receive the printed output. (Header printing can be disabled.)

Your system can have more than one printer attached. If you use lj2 with no destination specified, your printing job is directed to the default printer. To determine what other printers are attached to your computer, issue the lpstat command with the -s (system info) option:

```
$ lpstat -s
scheduler is running
system default destination: hpjet
device for hpjet: /dev/lp1
device for lj2: /dev/lp0
$
```

This system has two printers, lp and hpjet (the default). To direct your printing job to a printer other than the default printer, use the -d option and the destination. For example, to direct the output to the lj2 printer:

```
$ lp -dlj2 file1
request id is lj2-1106 (1 file)
$
```

If you change your mind after requesting a print job, cancel it with the cancel command. You can do so even while the job is printing. To cancel the job in the previous example you would enter:

```
$ cancel lj2-1106
request "lj2-1106" cancelled
$
```

Use the lpstat command if you forget your print-job number.

## 9.2  Simple Text Formatting

The lp command prints the file with no formatting or pagination (breaking text into separate pages). UNIX sites generally include several formatting programs, the output of which is sent to lp. The simplest of these is pr and the most elaborate is troff, used for complete typesetting.

## Pagination: *pr*

Simple pagination with headers is accomplished with the pr command. For example:

```
$ pr digits

Jan 28 14:43 1990   digits Page 1

1012
1013
1014
1015
1016
1017
1018
1019
1020
1021
1022
1023
1024
1025

$
```

You might discover that pr output scrolls off your terminal screen. Scrolling off occurs because the command defaults to the page length for printed output, 66 lines. You can change to the page length of your screen and include a screen pause option:

```
$ pr -123 -P
```

The l option (the letter *l*, not the number *one*) represents the number of lines. The P option is for pausing between pages.

pr is commonly used in making multiple-column output from single-column input. Enter the number of columns you wish, preceding that number with a hyphen, as in the following example:

```
$ pr -3 digits

Jan 28 14:43 1990   digits Page 1

1012                1017                1022
1013                1018                1023
```

```
     1014              1019              1024
     1015              1020              1025
     1016              1021

     $
```

## Date and Time

If you want the date and time, the command is date. If you use the date command to generate text for an editing program or within an automated report, you might want to control the format with command-line options.

```
$ date
Sun Jan 28 15:46:33 EST 1990
$ date +"%T %D"
15:47:28 01/28/90
$ date +"%r"
03:50:19 PM
date +"%h %d, 19%y"
Jan 28, 1990
$
```

Note that the format option is invoked with a plus sign rather than a hyphen. Because the date format option takes only one argument, the format must be encapsulated in quotes. Table 9-1 lists the format specifiers.

**Table 9-1.    The Format Specifiers for the Date Command.**

| Specifier | Format |
|-----------|--------|
| a | Abbreviated name of day of week |
| d | Day of the month |
| h | Abbreviated name of the month |
| j | Number of the day in the year (001-366) |
| m | Number of the month |
| n | Newline character |
| r | Time in 12-hour clock notation |
| t | Tab character |

*Table 9-1 continues*

**Table 9-1.   The Format Specifiers for the** Date **Command.** *(continued)*

| | |
|---|---|
| w | Number of day in the week (Sunday = 0) |
| y | Last two digits of the year |
| D | Date in mm/dd/yy format |
| H | Hour in 24-hour clock time |
| M | Minute |
| S | Second |
| T | Time in hh:mm:ss format |

UNIX also includes a calender-generating program, cal. On most systems, cal with no command-line arguments gives you the calendar for the previous, current, and following months. The optional arguments specify the month and year.

```
$ cal
Sun Jan 28 15:59:11 1990
         Dec                      Jan                      Feb
 S  M Tu  W Th  F  S      S  M Tu  W Th  F  S      S  M Tu  W Th  F  S
                1  2         1  2  3  4  5  6                     1  2  3
 3  4  5  6  7  8  9      7  8  9 10 11 12 13      4  5  6  7  8  9 10
10 11 12 13 14 15 16     14 15 16 17 18 19 20     11 12 13 14 15 16 17
17 18 19 20 21 22 23     21 22 23 24 25 26 27     18 19 20 21 22 23 24
24 25 26 27 28 29 30     28 29 30 31              25 26 27 28
31

$ cal 7 1945
    July 1945
 S  M Tu  W Th  F  S
 1  2  3  4  5  6  7
 8  9 10 11 12 13 14
15 16 17 18 19 20 21
22 23 24 25 26 27 28
29 30 31

$ cal 1990               —For the entire year of 1990
```

```
                                1990

            Jan                        Feb                        Mar
   S  M Tu  W Th  F  S         S  M Tu  W Th  F  S         S  M Tu  W Th  F  S
      1  2  3  4  5  6                     1  2  3                     1  2  3
   7  8  9 10 11 12 13         4  5  6  7  8  9 10         4  5  6  7  8  9 10
  14 15 16 17 18 19 20        11 12 13 14 15 16 17        11 12 13 14 15 16 17
  21 22 23 24 25 26 27        18 19 20 21 22 23 24        18 19 20 21 22 23 24
  28 29 30 31                 25 26 27 28                 25 26 27 28 29 30 31

            Apr                        May                        Jun
   S  M Tu  W Th  F  S         S  M Tu  W Th  F  S         S  M Tu  W Th  F  S
   1  2  3  4  5  6  7            1  2  3  4  5                           1  2
   8  9 10 11 12 13 14         6  7  8  9 10 11 12         3  4  5  6  7  8  9
  15 16 17 18 19 20 21        13 14 15 16 17 18 19        10 11 12 13 14 15 16
  22 23 24 25 26 27 28        20 21 22 23 24 25 26        17 18 19 20 21 22 23
  29 30                       27 28 29 30 31              24 25 26 27 28 29 30

            Jul                        Aug                        Sep
   S  M Tu  W Th  F  S         S  M Tu  W Th  F  S         S  M Tu  W Th  F  S
   1  2  3  4  5  6  7            1  2  3  4                              1
   8  9 10 11 12 13 14         5  6  7  8  9 10 11         2  3  4  5  6  7  8
  15 16 17 18 19 20 21        12 13 14 15 16 17 18         9 10 11 12 13 14 15
  22 23 24 25 26 27 28        19 20 21 22 23 24 25        16 17 18 19 20 21 22
  29 30 31                    26 27 28 29 30 31           23 24 25 26 27 28 29
                                                          30

            Oct                        Nov                        Dec
   S  M Tu  W Th  F  S         S  M Tu  W Th  F  S         S  M Tu  W Th  F  S
      1  2  3  4  5  6                     1  2  3                           1
   7  8  9 10 11 12 13         4  5  6  7  8  9 10         2  3  4  5  6  7  8
  14 15 16 17 18 19 20        11 12 13 14 15 16 17         9 10 11 12 13 14 15
  21 22 23 24 25 26 27        18 19 20 21 22 23 24        16 17 18 19 20 21 22
  28 29 30 31                 25 26 27 28 29 30           23 24 25 26 27 28 29
                                                          30 31

  $
```

# 9.3  Changing Text Without Editors

Because so much of the information we manipulate with computers is text, it is important to have good utilities to automate text handling. A stream editor such as sed is good for operating on words and lines, substituting and deleting them by rules specified with regular expressions. Some tasks involve cutting files into pieces either by line or by column. Other tasks involve merging separate files together, finding the differences in files, and other operations that use more than one file as input. These kinds of operations are usually done with UNIX utilities rather than editing programs.

## Translate Characters: *tr*

The tr filter, the simplest of the text tools, maps one character to another. You will find that tr is useful as a primitive in shell scripts filtering raw text from other systems.

The tr utility does not take file names in its argument list; it has three options and two arguments, the mapping lists. If you want to use a file for the source, you must redirect it to standard input. Each character in the first list is mapped to the character in the corresponding position in the second list.

```
$ cat source
MARY HAD A LITTLE LAMB.
ITS FLEECE WAS WHITE AS SNOW.
$ tr '[A-Z]' '[a-z]' < source > output
$ cat output
mary had a little lamb.
its fleece was white as snow.
$
```

In this example, standard input was redirected to come from the file source, and the standard output was redirected to output. Note that the strings used as parameters behave like regular expressions: [A-Z] expands to all the capital letters, and [a-z] expands to all the lowercase letters.

The tr utility is often used for deleting unwanted characters. When files have been moved to UNIX from MS-DOS systems, they contain unwanted carriage-return characters at the ends of the lines. (UNIX terminates lines with the line-feed character, whereas MS-DOS uses both the carriage return and the line feed. Even though the MS-DOS files appear to be fine when you cat or page them, they will cause you some grief. If you want to see a before-and-after example, just look at the original and translated versions of the file with vi or emacs.) To create this filter with tr, it is necessary to use an escape-to-octal notation to specify the carriage return (see the *Backslash* section in Chapter 5, "Regular Expressions"). The carriage return is ASCII octal 15; therefore, the filter is

```
$ tr -d '\015' <dos-file >unix-file
$
```

## Selecting Fields from a Line: cut

Suppose that you are interested in only certain character positions or columns from the output of a command or a file. For example, you want only the login ID and full name of each name in the system's password file, /etc/passwd, as in the following example:

```
$ cat /etc/passwd
root:E5jyLFPWxTKww:0:0:Super user:/:/bin/sh
sysadm:zPHjc7byON2rY:0:0:System Administration:/usr/sysadm:/bin/sh
network:NOLOGIN:12:12:Mail and Network administration:/usr/spool/micnet:
ben:jUZksaETDA/vc:201:50:Ben Smith:/usr/ben:/bin/csh
jrs:zwYea2DSxD1To:203:50:Johannes Smith:/usr/jrs:/bin/csh
infopro:QjzfhE2icgEyY:4:4:Infopro uucp :/usr/spool/uucppublic:/usr/lib/
uucp/uucico
linda:fUwdpPDDRjXsI:207:50:Linda Reneau:/usr/linda:/bin/csh
news:rrAWiOrmKkhio:209:52:News administration:/usr/lib/news:/bin/csh
david:wXqn3U6vZIrtQ:214:50:David Fiedler:/usr/david:/bin/csh
felix:pe09xljbSlMcE:215:50:Felix the cat:/usr/felix:/bin/sh
$
```

The fields you want are the first and fifth. The field *delimiter* (the character that separates fields) is the colon (:). The cut command gives you what you want:

```
$ cut -d':' -f1,5 /etc/passwd
root:Super user
sysadm:System Administration
network:Mail and Network administration
ben:Ben Smith
jrs:Johannes Smith
infopro:Infopro uucp
linda:Linda Reneau
news:News administration
david:David Fiedler
felix:Felix the cat
$
```

The basic formats of the cut command are as follows:

cut  -d*delimiter* −f*list files*
cut  −c*list files*

The delimiter (-d) option defaults to white space (spaces and tabs) if it is not included. The field list (-f option) is a list of numbers separated by commas and/ or connected by dashes. For example, to specify fields five, nine through eleven, and thirteen, enter 5,9-11,13.

Use the `-c` option to specify that you want to cut out specific character positions from *each* line of the specified *files*. *list* specifies which character positions to cut. For example, the command `cut -c1-3 /etc/passwd` cuts the first three characters of each line from the file `/etc/passwd`:

```
$ cut -c3 /etc/passwd
roo
sys
net
ben
jrs
inf
lin
new
dav
fel
$
```

Note that the Tab is only one character even though it spaces words out by more than one space.

To specify that a cut is to be made from a specified character position to the end of the line, leave out the ending number:

```
$ cut -c50- /etc/passwd

sr/sysadm:/bin/sh
tion:/usr/spool/micnet:
csh
/bin/csh
l/uucppublic:/usr/lib/uucp/uucico
a:/bin/csh
r/lib/news:/bin/csh
id:/bin/csh
ix:/bin/sh
$
```

As you might expect, `cut` takes its input from *standard input* and writes its output to *standard output* by default. This means, of course, that it can be used in a pipeline.

## Putting It Back Together with *paste*

A sister command to cut is paste. This command combines data from different files into one file. The only criterion used to match the two files together is the line number. In other words, line one of file A is pasted to line one of file B; line two is pasted to line two, and so forth. You can paste together as many as you wish.

```
$ cat digits
1012
1013
1014
1015
1016
1017
$ cat numbers
 one thousand twelve.
 one thousand thirteen.
 one thousand fourteen.
 one thousand fifteen.
 one thousand sixteen.
 one thousand seventeen.
$ paste digits numbers
1012     one thousand twelve.
1013     one thousand thirteen.
1014     one thousand fourteen.
1015     one thousand fifteen.
1016     one thousand sixteen.
1017     one thousand seventeen.
$
```

If one file runs out of lines before the other does, the paste operation continues without the shorter one. It continues until it reaches the end of the longest file.

By default, the files are pasted together with a tab separating each file. You can specify different delimiters. If you specify, for example, paste -d'|' digits numbers, the files are pasted together with a vertical bar (|) between each element. You can specify no delimiter or more than one; each delimiter separates the corresponding file records.

```
$ paste -d'[]' digits numbers digits
1012[ one thousand twelve.]1012
1013[ one thousand thirteen.]1013
1014[ one thousand fourteen.]1014
1015[ one thousand fifteen.]1015
1016[ one thousand sixteen.]1016
1017[ one thousand seventeen.]1017
$
```

## 9.4  Sorting

Although we used the `sort` command in some examples in previous chapters, we have not explored all its capabilities. The UNIX `sort` utility is a great deal more than a simple tool for giving order to lines of text. It is a sophisticated, self-optimizing, database tool.

As with many other UNIX utilities, you can include a source file name in the command arguments, as follows:

    sort *file*

The file name is optional. If you don't include it, the `sort` utility assumes that the data is coming from the standard input; in other words, it assumes that you are using pipes or redirection or are entering data.

As you can see from Table 9-2, there are many optional arguments to the `sort` utility.

**Table 9-2.    Optional Arguments to `sort`.**

| Argument | Function |
|----------|----------|
| -b | Ignore leading white space (tabs and spaces) |
| -c | Check for the input file before proceeding |
| -d | Sort in dictionary (rather than ASCII) order |
| -f | Fold case (ignore difference between upper- and lowercase) |
| -i | Ignore non-printing characters |
| -m | Merge sorted files |
| -M | Use first three characters as a sort field of abbreviated names of months |
| -n | Treat sort field as numbers rather than ASCII characters |
| -o *file* | Put output in *file* |
| -r | Sort field in reverse |
| -t*c* | Use *c* as field separator (default is Tab character) |
| -u | Output only unique lines |
| -y *memsize* | Use only *memsize* Kbytes of memory for the sort |

*Table 9-2 continues*

**Table 9-2   Optional Arguments to** `sort`. *(continued)*

| | |
|---|---|
| `-z` *length* | Limit record size to *length* bytes |
| +*pos1*-*pos2* | Sort field is specified by position *pos1* and (optionally) *pos2*. (See text for variations on this.) |

The `sort` utility always looks at each line as a separate sort item, a record. You can, however, tell it to use any part of the line as the key on which to sort. Therefore, for example, if you have the following file to sort:

```
bolts steel stainless 20
screws brass natural 15
nails steel common 100
tacks copper natural 85
rivets iron black 35
```

but you want to sort on the second word, the material, you would use `sort` as follows:

```
$ sort +1 list
screws brass natural 15
tacks copper natural 85
rivets iron black 35
nails steel common 100
bolts steel stainless 20
$
```

Why an argument of +1? To begin with, the first word is designated as field zero (the field delimiter is white space, by default). The +1 argument specifies that the sort key should begin at field one. Note that the sort key continues to the end of the record: *steel common* is placed before *steel stainless*.

You can also tell `sort` where to stop the sort key:

```
$ sort +1 -2 list
screws brass natural 15
tacks copper natural 85
rivets iron black 35
bolts steel stainless 20
nails steel common 100
$
```

The `-2` specifies that the sort key should stop before field 2.

Note what happens when you sort on field three, the numbers:

```
sort +3 list
nails steel common 100
screws brass natural 15
bolts steel stainless 20
rivets iron black 35
tacks copper natural 85
$
```

The list has been rearranged, but not exactly as you might expect. The problem is that the field is numeric and we have performed an alphabetic sort. You must specify a numeric sort for a numeric field:

```
sort +3 -n list
screws brass natural 15
bolts steel stainless 20
rivets iron black 35
tacks copper natural 85
nails steel common 100
$
```

You can specify more than one field as the key. For example, you can sort on the material (field 1) and the count (field 3, a numeric sort), all in one command:

```
sort +1 -2 +3 -n list
screws brass natural 15
tacks copper natural 85
rivets iron black 35
bolts steel stainless 20
nails steel common 100
$
```

The first, or primary, key starts at field one and continues up to the beginning of field two. It is a standard alphabetic sort. The secondary key starts with field three and continues to the end of the record. It is a numeric field. You might want to sort numeric fields in descending rather than ascending order. The -r argument reverses the order of the key field to which it is applied.

```
$ sort +1 -2 +3 -n -r list
screws brass natural 15
tacks copper natural 85
rivets iron black 35
nails steel common 100
bolts steel stainless 20
$
```

In this example, only the last two records have been rearranged because they are the only ones with a common material, field one.


## Flat Database Files

Although there are many excellent relational database programs for UNIX, many of your small data management problems can be solved with simple flat files — text files with fields delimited by a special character, and records delimited by a newline. UNIX system administration uses many of these kinds of files. The most obvious example is the /etc/passwd file that lists all the accounts on your system.

The most likely use of a flat file outside the system administration is a mailing list.

Using white space as the delimiter between fields is not very practical for this kind of data because some of the fields consist of more than one word. The database routines would be incapable of distinguishing between the spaces that separate words within a field and the field delimiter. Therefore, specify a delimiter such as the vertical bar (|). A record might look like this:

```
Migneault|Thomas P.|35A Highland St. |East Rochester|UT|97867|
    (801) 335-1484
```

The fields are as follows: (0) last name, (1) first name and optional initial, (2) street address, (3) city, (4) state, (5) zip code, and, (8) phone number. Now it is easy to sort the file on the zip code, field number five:

```
$ sort -t'|' +5 -6 +0 -2 mlist
Theriault|Kenneth|13 Gorham Street |Lawrence|MA|01841|
Basinow|Richard|P.O. Box 821 |Sanford|AZ|04073|
Hickman|David|64 4th Avenue |Goffstown|UT|97045|(801) 497-2413
Cilluffo|Paul|6 Hunter Lane |Hudson|UT|97051|
Bunce|Rosco|73 Tampa Street |Nashua|UT|97060|(801) 882-3980
Skinner|John|22 Elm Street |Nashua|UT|97060|
Soucy|Donald|P.O. Box 6677 |Nashua|UT|97060|(801) 888-5645
    .
    .

    .
Riordan Jr.|John L.|77 Pond Road |Derry|UT|97978|(801) 432-4414
Nichols|Robert|70 1/2 Tidy Road |Eliot|AZ|97997|(602) 748-1250
$
```

In this case, we sorted on the zip code, the last name, and the first name.

## Special Sorting Operations

There are two special capabilities of the UNIX `sort` program that should not be overlooked, especially for flat file operations, *merge sorts* and *unique sorts*.

The `sort` command with the `-u` (unique) options produces output where there are no duplicate records. If you are combining several different lists, this feature is invaluable. (If you wish to know how many duplications exist, use the separate `unique` command on a sorted file before you remove the duplicates with `sort -u`.)

Because they often have hundreds of thousands of records, large commercial mailing lists require more than UNIX utilities provide. The UNIX utilities, however, are still useful for sizable lists. The problem with even the best sorting routines is that they operate considerably more slowly on large lists. The UNIX `sort` command automatically splits a large file into small temporary sorted parts and then merges the parts for the final.

The UNIX `split` command takes a very large file and breaks it into pieces; the default is 1,000 lines each. You can specify how many lines maximum you want in each resulting file with the `-n` *lines* option:

```
split -n 10000 very_large_file piece
```

If `very_large_file` is 100,000 lines, you end up with ten files, `pieceaa`, `pieceab`, and so forth through `pieceaj`. The argument after the file name is the *root* (or prefix) of the file names of the pieces. If you don't specify a root, the default is the letter *x*. In other words, the default output names are `xaa`, `xab`, etc.

The `cat` command is the opposite of the `split` command. Whereas `split` breaks large files into pieces, `cat` concatenates pieces into one large file. Because the shell expands the asterisk (*) into an alphabetical list, you can reverse the split of `very_large_file` with the following:

```
$ cat piece* > very_large_file
```

The following exercise demonstrates the entire process of splitting, sorting, and merging. (The `pr` command is applied just to help you view the example files.)

```
$ pr -3 -t lnames
Balamotis         Freihette          Skinner
Colby             Basinow            Riordan Jr.
Bunce             Hickman            Theriault
Soucy             Paul               Aldrich
Daudelin          Sable              Cotterly
Allen             Caulfield          Booth
Anderson          Udall              Lantiegne
```

```
Hevey            Cilluffo          Tsoukalas
Nichols          Migneault         Kenyon
Robida
$ split -10 lnames
$ ls
lnames
xaa
xab
xac
$ sort xaa > p1          — Sort the first part
$ sort xab > p2          — Sort the second part
$ sort xac > p3          — Sort the third part
$ sort -m p1 p2 > t1     — Merge the first two parts
$ sort -m t1 p3 > t2     — Merge in the next part
$ pr -3 -t t2
Aldrich          Cotterly          Paul
Allen            Daudelin          Riordan        Jr.
Anderson         Freihette         Robida
Balamotis        Hevey             Sable
Basinow          Hickman           Skinner
Booth            Kenyon            Soucy
Bunce            Lantiegne         Theriault
Caulfield        Migneault         Tsoukalas
Cilluffo         Nichols                     Udall
Colby
$
```

You can merge all the steps into a single command. In the previous example, the command would be as follows:

```
sort -m p1 p2 p3 > result
```

Don't forget that the merge routine requires presorted source files, and the merge must be done with the same key fields as used for the sorts.

## A Database Classic: join

The join command extends the flat-file database concept of UNIX utilities a little toward relational database concepts. If you organize two database files so that they have a common key field, one of the files can be used as an extension of the other, providing detailed information organized around that key.

The classic example is a file of invoices and a file of customer information. The object is to get the customer information from the customer file and combine it with the invoices.

The key would be a unique customer key or account number. The customer file would have a single unique record for each customer key. The invoice file could have many entries with the same key. Both files must first be sorted on the key. The join command is not an option to the sort utility, but a separate command. Nevertheless, it is dependent on sort. A simplified demonstration follows:

```
$ cat invoice
5/8/90|SMITH901|32|reams|Xero-9 20lb White xerographic paper|IVN92313
5/8/90|JONES742|1|each|Adjustable typist chair, MONGO 486, blue|IVN92314
5/7/90|JONES742|12|pkgs|Avery T-5461 removable labels, light blue|IVN92315
5/7/90|SMITH901|3|pkgs|EPSON Thermal paper, HOORP-1|IVN92316
$ cat customer
GUERN113|Guernsey|Laura S.|Toledo Office|Manager
JONES742|Jones|Adam P.|Toledo Office|Front desk
SMITH901|Smith|Benjamin S.|Building #4|Room 241A
$ sort -t'|' invoice > t2
$ cat t2
JONES742|12|pkgs|Avery T-5461 removable labels, light blue|5/7/90
JONES742|1|each|Adjustable typist chair, MONGO 486, blue|5/8/90
SMITH901|32|reams|Xero-9 20lb White xerographic paper|5/8/90
SMITH901|3|pkgs|EPSON Thermal paper, HOORP-1|5/7/90
$ join -t'|' t2 customer
JONES742|12|pkgs|Avery T-5461 removable labels, light blue
     |5/7/90|Jones|Adam P.|Toledo Office|Front desk
JONES742|1|each|Adjustable typist chair, MONGO 486, blue
     |5/8/90|Jones|Adam P.|Toledo Office|Front desk
SMITH901|32|reams|Xero-9 20lb White xerographic paper
     |5/8/90|Smith|Benjamin S.|Building #4|Room 241A
SMITH901|3|pkgs|EPSON Thermal paper, HOORP-1
     |5/7/90|Smith|Benjamin S.|Building #4|Room 241A
$
```

The output lines have been wrapped in order to print them on the page. Without wrapping, there would be four continuous long lines.

Note that the entry for GUERN113 was not used in the output. This is because there was no corresponding entry in the invoice file.

We specified the field separator as the vertical bar; otherwise, join would have assumed white space (the default). We did not, however, specify which field to use as the key, because the default is the first field. In reality, the first field is seldom the key; join has options to specify which field of which file is the key. The format for specifying the key field is as follows:

```
-jn     m
```

in which *n* is the file number (1 or 2) and *m* is the field number (starting at 1 — inconsistent with `sort` field numbering).

You probably do not want all the fields of both files all the time. The default for `join` is to print all the fields; you can specify fields with the `-o` *field-list* specification. The format of each entry in *field-list* is *file-number.field-number*.

To illustrate these additional arguments to `join`, we rearrange the order of fields in the invoice file and then print only some essential fields, as follows:

```
$ sort -t'|' +1 -2 invoice > t2
$ cat t2
5/7/90|JONES742|12|pkgs|Avery T-5461 removable labels, light blue|IVN92315
5/8/90|JONES742|1|each|Adjustable typist chair, MONGO 486, blue|IVN92314
5/7/90|SMITH901|3|pkgs|EPSON Thermal paper, HOORP-1|IVN92316
5/8/90|SMITH901|32|reams|Xero-9 20lb White xerographic paper|IVN92313
$ join -j1 2 -j2 1 -o 2.3 2.2 1.1 1.3 1.4 1.5 -t'|' t2 customer
Adam P.|Jones|5/7/90|12|pkgs|Avery T-5461 removable labels, light blue
Adam P.|Jones|5/8/90|1|each|Adjustable typist chair, MONGO 486, blue
Benjamin S.|Smith|5/7/90|3|pkgs|EPSON Thermal paper, HOORP-1
Benjamin S.|Smith|5/8/90|32|reams|Xero-9 20lb White xerographic paper
$
```

Note that the order in which the fields are specified in the argument list is the order in which they print.

As you can see, combining the `sort` utility with a few others gives you the makings of a useful mailing-list manager.

# 9.5  Comparing Files: *diff*

If you have files with some common lines and some unique lines and you want to know the differences between the two, use the `diff` utilities: `diff`, `sdiff`, and `diff3`.

The syntax of `diff` requires the names of two files:

`diff` *oldfile newfile*

Keeping track of which file you consider the old file and which the new file is important; otherwise the `diff` report is confusing. The old file comes first in the argument list.

The default output is a list of line-number ranges and the lines that show a difference. None of the `diff` utilities indicates which word or character is different, only that the line is different. Assume that the following is the original file:

```
$ cat file.old
This is a sample of some of the things that you might
want to look at using the diff utilities. I used to
think that many of these utilities were of little use
to me, but over the years, I have found each of them
invaluable.

Here are a few lines to be deleted. I don't expect
that they will be missed very much.

But this line we will keep so that you can see some
of the different notation.

I shouldn't go on for too much longer. But I love to
chat.

And I'll end with this line.
$
```

And this is the edited version:

```
$ cat file.new
This is an example of some of the things that you might
want to look at using the diff utilities. I used to
think that many of these utilities were of little use
to me, but over the years, I have found each of them
invaluable.

But this line we will keep so that you can see some
of the different notation.

I shouldn't go on for too much longer. Just a few
more lines.

And I'll end with this line.

Well, in the edited version, I thought that I should
add a few extra lines. Now I will end.
$
```

We will use these two files for several examples. First, look at the default output format for diff, as follows:

```
$ diff file.old file.new
1c1
< This is a sample of some of the things that you might
---
> This is an example of some of the things that you
might
7,9d6
< Here are a few lines to be deleted. I don't expect
< that they will be missed very much.
<
13,14c10,11
< I shouldn't go on for too much longer. But I love to
< chat.
---
> I shouldn't go on for too much longer. Just a few
> more lines.
16a14,16
>
> Well, in the edited version, I thought that I should
> add a few extra lines. Now I will end.
$
```

The report consists of a list of actions and subject lines with right and left angle brackets (< and >) in the left column. The action-line format is as follows:

*range-in-old-file action range-in-new-file*

For example, the first action line is 1c1 and can be read as "line one in the old file is changed as shown in line one of the new file." The left-pointing angle bracket on the line following the action implies that the material is to be deleted. The next line has a right-pointing angle bracket, implying, "insert this material."

The next action line indicates that lines seven through nine have been deleted: 7,9d6. Because they no longer exist, the edited file is still at line six. The statement, 13,14c10,11, shows that two more lines have changed. Because we deleted two lines above, lines 13 and 14 are actually lines 10 and 11 in the edited file. Finally, you can see that lines 14 through 16 in the new version of the file have been added.

A practical use of diff is to send changes of large files to colleagues. If you generate the change report using the -e option, the result is an editing script rather than the former report. The script can then be applied to the original file to generate the new file. Though this method is not very efficient for the file in our example, it can be a great savings in data storage and transfer. There is one wrinkle in the system: you must add two commands at the end of the edit script, one to write the edited file, w, and one to quit the editor properly, q. You probably should add the lines using an editor, which you can do as shown in the following example, which redirects echo to append to the end of the diff/ed script:

```
$ diff -e file.old file.new > file.changes
$ echo "w\nq" >> file.changes
$ cat file.changes
16a

Well, in the edited version, I thought that I should
add a few extra lines. Now I will end.
13,14c
I shouldn't go on for too much longer. Just a few
more lines.
7,9d
1c
This is an example of some of the things that you might
w
q
$ ed file.old < file.changes
495
$ diff file.old file.new
$
```

You might want to save the ed result under a different file name. In that case, follow the w command with the new name.

There is a commonly found public program, patch, for taking the raw diff output and applying it to a file. In fact, patch is the heart of many software maintenance systems.

## Side-by-Side: sdiff

The sdiff command allows you to perform a side-by-side comparison of two files. This utility generates lines comprising lines from both sources. The default output is 130 characters wide. If you do not have a wide screen or printer for the output, use the width option, -w width, as follows:

```
$ sdiff -w 65 file.old file.new
This is a sample of some of th    |    This is an example of some
want to look at using the diff         want to look at using the
think that many of these utili         think that many of these u
to me, but over the years, I h         to me, but over the years,
invaluable.                            invaluable.

Here are a few lines to be del    <
that they will be missed very     <
                                  <
But this line we will keep so          But this line we will keep
of the different  notation.            of the different  notation

I shouldn't go on for too much    |    I shouldn't go on for too
chat.                             |    more lines.

And I'll end with this line.           And I'll end with this lin
                                  >
                                  >    Well, in the edited versi
                                  >    add a few extra lines. Now
$
```

The pipe character | flags lines with internal changes.

When comparing large files, use the -s option with sdiff; it suppresses the printing of identical lines, considerably reducing the amount of output.

## Comparing Three Files: diff3

Trying to see the differences among three files is not easy when you can see only two at a time. But diff3 shows you the differences among all three. The syntax (without options) is as follows:

diff3 *file1 file2 file3*

This utility can be useful when, for example, two people are editing a file, because you can see the results of their changes. In the following example we look at three little files side-by-side (using paste) before running the diff3 utility on them:

```
$ paste a b c
1 - cats        1 - cats         1 - cats
2 - dogs        2 - dogs         2 - dogs
3 - fish        3 - turnips      3 - turnips
4 - snakes      4 - snakes       4 - snakes
```

```
5 - mice          5 - seashells    5 - roses
6 - birds         6 - birds        6 - birds
7 - rabbits       7 - rabbits      7 - thunder
$ diff3 a b c
====1
1:3c
  3 - fish
2:3c
3:3c
  3 - turnips
====
1:5c
  5 - mice
2:5c
  5 - seashells
3:5c
  5 - roses
====3
1:7c
2:7c
  7 - rabbits
3:7c
  7 - thunder
$
```

There are three possible conditions. The first is that all three files are alike. The diff3 utility does not output anything for this condition. Lines 1, 2, 4, and 6 satisfy this condition.

The second possible condition is that one file is different and the other two alike. At the beginning of a region with this condition, diff3 specifies which file is different by breaking the output with the following notation: ====n, in which n is the number of the different file. The references to lines 3 and 7 show this notation. (Some implementations of diff3 use the same notation when only one file is different as when all three differ.)

The third possibility is that all three files differ from each other. At the beginning of the region in which all three files differ, diff3 inserts the ==== notation without a number. The reference to line 5 shows this notation.

The output between the region markers specifies the differences between the file(s). For example, the following section:

```
=====1
1:3c
  3 - fish
2:3c
3:3c
  3 - turnips
```

tells you that on line 3, file 1 has 3 - fish whereas files 2 and 3 have 3 - turnips.

Supposedly, the diff3 utility can also create scripts for the ed editor. The rules by which it generates these scripts are difficult to follow. I do not recommend that you use diff3 for that purpose. It is much simpler to keep track of what is happening by analyzing the output of diff3 and interactively applying diff based on which precedence you want to give the edits when they don't agree.

## Precise to the Character: cmp

A final utility in the diff category, the cmp program, identifies the first difference between two files. The files need not be lines of text; they can be binary data files. This utility is by far the simplest and quickest way to determine whether two files are different. The syntax is as follows:

cmp *file1 file2*

The cmp utility has two possible options: -l for listing differing bytes at positions, and -s, the silent version. The former is not very practical unless you are a programmer, because the output uses the octal (base 8) numbering system. The latter option does not return anything to the terminal, but it is useful in shell scripts because it returns an exit code. The following output shows a simple invocation of cmp and two optional ones:

```
$ cmp 9-2 9-2a
9-2 9-2a differ: char 9859, line 291
$ cmp -l 9-2 9-2a
  9859   40 145
  9860  156 144
  9861  157  40
$ cmp -s 9-2 9-2a
$
```

# 9.6  Advanced File Management

If you use your UNIX machine only on rare occasions, you might find that you have created only a few files. If you use the machine just to run a single application program which has its own file management, you don't have to be concerned about managing your files. Typically, however, a system is used for many different purposes: document writing, e-mail, scheduling, report generation, electronic news, and conferencing. You can easily end up with hundreds of different files.

Unless you're comfortable with chaos (in which case you will probably have all your files in your home directory), organize your files in your own directory tree. For example, if you have files relating to short-term jobs, you might have a subdirectory jobs under which you have other subdirectories specifying months (jun90, jul90, aug90, .., dec90). Under those you might have directories of files for each of the jobs.

The problem now becomes, how do you find files?

## Locating Files: *find*

This command has so many options and uses you will probably want to define it in an alias for your most common application: finding files in the directories below your present working directory. For this use the syntax is as follows:

```
find . -name file-name -print
```

The command-line arguments are as follows:

- Start the search at dot (.), the present working directory
- Search for the name of the file
- The name for which to search
- Print the path to the file (or files) when it is found

The first argument is always the directory from which to start the search. Therefore, to search the entire file tree, you could use the notation for the file tree root, slash (/), as in the following:

```
find / -print
```

To search your area of the file tree, use the environment variable $HOME (for more on environment variables see Chapter 10, "Networks") as follows:

```
find $HOME -print
```

Unlike most UNIX commands, which use single letters for their options, the find command uses full words for options (see Table 9-3).

**Table 9-3.** **Common options to** find.

| Option | Searches |
|---|---|
| -name *name* | Only files with *name*. You might use regular expressions, but you must enclose the *name* in quotes if you do. |
| -perm *octalnum* | Only files with permissions matching the octal permission code of *octalnum*. |
| -type *c* | Only files of type *c*, where *c* is:<br><br>b block special file<br><br>c character special file<br><br>d directory<br><br>p FIFO pipe<br><br>f plain file |
| -links *n* | Only files with *n* number of links |
| -user *userID* | Only files belonging to *userID* |
| -group *groupname* | Only files with *groupname* permissions |
| -size *n* | Only files of size *n* blocks |
| -size *nc* | Only files of size n characters |
| -atime *n* | Only files *accessed* in exactly *n* days. The *n* can be prefixed by + for "greater than" or – for "less than." |
| -mtime *n* | Only files *modified* in exactly *n* days. You can prefix as with -atime. |
| -ctime *n* | Only the files *created* in exactly *n* days. You can prefix as with -atime. |
| -newer *filename* | Only files modified more recently than *file* |
| -exec *cmd*{ }\e; | Execute *cmd* on each file matched. Find replaces the brackets ({ }) with the complete path of the matched file. |

*Table 9-3 continues*

**Table 9-3.   Common options to** `find`. *(continued)*

| | |
|---|---|
| `-ok`    *cmd*`{ }\e;` | Same as `-exec`, except that you will be prompted for confirmation before each action. |
| `-print` | Output each file matched. |
| `-cpio` *dev* | Write the files matched on the device *dev*. The `cpio` utility is used for file transfers and backup. |
| `-depth` | Descend each directory before acting on the parent directory. |

This subset of the `find` options makes it obvious that `find` is designed to work as the front end to other commands. In other words, the output of `find` is often piped (or otherwise directed) to the input of other commands. In Chapter 10 you will learn how to use it to remove old files.

## Comparing Directories: *dircmp*

To check two directories to see whether the files are identical, use the `dircmp` command. (The `dircmp` command is not on some BSD systems. It is often implemented as a shell script, and as such is a fine example of what you can do with shell scripts. See Chapter 10 for a discussion of shell scripts.)

The `dircmp` utility produces a two-part report on the directories. The first part is a list of files unique to either directory. The second report is a list of files that are the same. The following example shows the use of `dircmp`:

```
$ dircmp dir1 dir2

May 13 16:33 1990   dir1 only and dir2 only Page 1


May 13 16:33 1990   Comparison of dir1 dir2 Page 1

directory      .
same          ./customer
same          ./digits
same          ./fnames
same          ./invoice
same          ./invoice2
same          ./key'
```

```
same        ./passwd
same        ./streets
$
```

Use the -d option to direct dircmp to run diff on files that exist in both directories but are different.

## How Much Disk Space: df and du

Many commands give information about file systems. Two of the most useful are df and du.

The df command prints the number of free i-nodes and blocks on the mounted file system. An *i-node* is an entry in the UNIX system's table of files. The system configuration (done by your system administrator) determines the total number of i-nodes. The *blocks* on a system are units of disk space. In the file system reports, a block is 512 bytes. On BSD systems, a block is 1024 (1K) bytes.

```
$ df
/usr    (/dev/dsk/0s1  ):       138126 blocks      11675 i-nodes
/tmp    (/dev/dsk/0s3  ):        19184 blocks       2437 i-nodes
/       (/dev/dsk/0s0  ):         3066 blocks        670 i-nodes
$ df -t
/usr    (/dev/dsk/0s1  ):       138126 blocks      11675 i-nodes
                 total:  209792 blocks     25216 i-nodes
/tmp    (/dev/dsk/0s3  ):        19184 blocks       2437 i-nodes
                 total:   20000 blocks      2496 i-nodes
/       (/dev/dsk/0s0  ):         3066 blocks        670 i-nodes
                 total:    4000 blocks      2864 i-nodes
$
```

df with the -t option prints the total number of i-nodes and blocks as well. This command is most often used to see whether a file system is getting filled.

du prints a list of each directory in a file system and the number of blocks used by the files in that directory and its subdirectories. The du command is not file-system specific; it can be used on any directory structure. It is useful in determining *how* the space on a file system is being used:

```
$ du /usr
1762    /usr/bin/graf
5622    /usr/bin
453     /usr/lib/acct
2325    /usr/lib/spell
797     /usr/lib/uucp
```

```
16583    /usr/lib
695      /usr/mail
32       /usr/spool/lp
1        /usr/spool/uucppublic/oko
6        /usr/spool/uucppublic/weather
1        /usr/spool/uucppublic/tgd
10       /usr/spool/uucppublic
316      /usr/spool/uucp
455      /usr/spool
50794    /usr
$
```

Note that numbers are cumulative; in other words, each directory size includes the size of all its files *and subdirectories*.

If you receive reports that you are using more disk space than you should, check your directories to determine where that space is being used. Although both du and df are primarily for system administration, you can use them to help manage your own space. Unless all users on a UNIX system keep their spaces tidy, the system will grow so large as to degrade the performance of the machine.

# 9.7  Securing Your Information — *crypt*

You might be tempted to try to secure a file by encoding it through a simple character-substitution scheme and the tr utility. You could decrypt it using the reverse substitutions. The weaknesses of such a scheme are that substitution codes are easy to break, and that you probably want to have the aliases or shell script for encoding and decoding somewhere on your system. Anyone who had enough permissions to read the encrypted file could also find and use your substitution list.

The UNIX crypt utility is much more sophisticated; it uses a rotor algorithm and keyword for encryption. It is based loosely on Germany's Enigma encryption machine used during World War II. (To export the crypt utility outside the United States, you have to get permission from the U.S. State Department. There is, however, an equivalent public-domain version in Europe.)

Like the tr utility, crypt takes input only from standard input and sends its output to standard output. The syntax is as follows:

crypt *key* < *source* > *destination*

To decrypt the file, use the same key, but take the source from the encrypted file. If you use the wrong key, you end up with garbage.

Don't even think about using `cat` to display the result, and don't forget to redirect the output to a file or pipe. The result of `crypt` is 8-bit binary data — nasty stuff to try to display or print raw.

```
$ file mymessage
mymessage:       English text
$ crypt monkey! < mymessage > secret
$ file secret
secret: data
$ ls -l mymessage secret
-rw-r-r-   1 ben         group       139 Feb  5 19:33 mymessage
-rw-r-r-   1 ben         group       139 Feb  5 19:35 secret
$ crypt monkey! < secret > final
$ file final
final:  English text
$ cat final
This is a message for the Emperor. No one is to see it but
him. The message follows:

The Klingons are a bunch of wimps.

That is the message.
$
```

If you don't give `crypt` a key as an argument, it prompts you for one:

```
$ crypt < mymessage > secret
Enter key:                           — Not printed
$
```

This usage of `crypt` is better than entering the key on the command line, for two reasons. First, when the key is entered on the command line, it is printed on your terminal for everyone to see. If you let the computer prompt you for the key, `crypt` prevents the key from being printed on your screen. Second, if you enter the key on the command line, other users can look at it, by using the `ps -f` command. (Remember that `ps -f` prints the status of a process along with the command name *and any arguments*). `crypt` wipes out this information once it starts up, but there is a short period when it is available.

Normally, after you encrypt a file you should remove the original copy of the file, leaving yourself with only the encrypted version. This way the information in the file can be accessed only by someone who knows the key. Note that after removing the original, you must not forget the key! If you do, the information in the file is lost.

To make `crypt` security better and make life easier for users, most editors on the UNIX system have `crypt` built-in. The `-x` option to `ed` and `vi` tells them you are editing an encrypted file. The editor automatically reencrypts the file (using the same key) when it is written.

Without the `-x` option, you would have to decrypt the file before running the editor and reencrypt it after quitting. The disadvantage of this procedure is that the decrypted version of the file is left sitting around while it is being edited. With the `-x` option, there is no decrypted version of the file: the editor works directly on the encrypted file. To increase the security of your encrypted files further, use the `-x` option to the editor when you create the file. There will never be a copy of the file in the file system in its unencrypted form.

What was said in Chapter 2 regarding good and bad passwords for logins applies here to keys. Simple keys allow a decrypter to try various possibilities until the correct one is found. Nontrivial keys make trial-and-error decryption almost impossible. Of course, you have to use something you can remember, or you will not be able to decrypt your own files!

# 9.8   Numbers and Calculations: bc

The UNIX system has two programs that enable you to effectively convert your computer into a handy desktop calculator. One program is called `bc` and the other is `dc`. The latter program operates using so-called "Reverse Polish Notation" (familiar to Hewlett-Packard calculator users) but does not include any floating-point operations.

The `bc` calculation program can be used as an interactive program in a pipe or with a script. You build your own functions and extensions to it to automate some of your repetitive tasks. Unfortunately for those who are not familiar with C-language programming, the syntax of `bc` extensions is very much like that of C.

To start up the desk calculator program to run interactively, enter `bc`. As is typical for UNIX utilities, `bc` does not display any command prompt to let you know it has started — it just waits for you to enter your calculations. To terminate the program, enter Ctrl-D (the end-of-file character).

Once you've started `bc`, it's easy to use:

```
2 + 5
7
```

bc automatically displays the result of each operation; there is no need to hit an equals key.

The bc program recognizes the asterisk (*) as the multiplication sign, the slash (/) as the division sign, and the carat (^) as the exponent operator. Multiplication and division operations are done before addition and subtraction operations, if they appear in the same expression. You can always use parentheses if you want to change that:

```
753.25 * 2
1506.50
2^5
32
1 + 2 * 10
21
(1 + 2)*10
30
1 / 2
0
```

Notice what happens when you divide 1 by 2. Normally, bc automatically selects the number of decimal places for displaying results. However, for division operations, it won't display any decimal places unless you tell it to. To set the number of decimal places, set scale to the desired number. The upper limit is 99 decimal places.

```
scale=3
1 / 2
0.500
scale=40
5 / 17
.2941176470588235294117647058823529411764
```

To save the result of an operation, you can temporarily store it in any one of 26 *memories*, identified by the letters a - z. The value stored in a can be *recalled* by entering a. You can use its value in subsequent expressions.

```
a=1749.23 * 12
a
20990.76
a * 30
629722.80
```

bc provides many other features, including a math library for calculating logs, sines, cosines, etc. It even has some built-in programming capabilities.

## 9.9 Batch Processing

In Chapter 8, "Processes: Concepts and Connections," we discussed UNIX as a multiuser operating system in contrast to batch-processing systems. Being a multiuser system, however, does not exclude UNIX from doing batch processing as well. You are already familiar with background processing. Batch processing is simply *scheduled* background processing.

UNIX has a command for single-shot batches and a facility for repetitive batch processing. The appropriately named one-shot `at` command has an intelligent parameter syntax to specify the time for command execution. The commands you wish to batch are *not* included on the command line. You enter only the time for execution. Then, on following lines, enter the commands that you want executed. Terminate the list by starting a new line with the end-of-file character (Ctrl-D).

The execution time can be set as either a specific time or as an offset from `now`, the current time. If no date is specified, `today` is assumed. A few examples illustrate:

```
at now + 5 minutes
at now + 2 hours 30 minutes
at 10:30A
at 6:00P
at 4:45P Sunday
at 10:30A March 12
```

Typical uses include scheduling messages to other users (see `mail` in Chapter 10) and postponing computer-intensive tasks to a time when they won't burden the system. The `at` command redirects any standard output to your mailbox.

When you create an `at` job, a script file is created; it includes your present working directory and environment at the time you issue `at`. At the end of the file are the commands you specified. Another file tells the system when and where this script and any other scripts are to be executed. The operating system checks the list every minute to see whether it has any work to do. When the time arrives for the script to be executed, the operating system runs the script just as if you were there entering the individual commands. When completed, the script is deleted.

For regularly repeated tasks, use the facilities of the system scheduler, the `cron` daemon. (A *daemon* is a process that runs continuously in the background. Mail handlers and print spoolers are examples of daemons.) Like `at`, every minute `cron` reads any task tables that have been created using the `crontab` utility. Each line in a `crontab` entry consists of five fields for different units of time (minute, hour, day, month, and day-of-week), followed by the full path name of the task to be performed. Putting an asterisk (*) in a field signifies that the task is to be performed for all increments of that unit of time. For example, the following entry:

```
01 11 * * * /usr/bin/date
```

sends the output of the date command to your mailbox at one minute past eleven (24-hour clock) on every day of every month, any day of the week. You can use cron for any number of periodic tasks such as reminding you of periodic meetings, cleaning up your file area by compressing old files, and generating periodic reports. The UNIX system administrator uses cron to perform many routine administrative tasks such as notifying users when their passwords haven't been changed recently, polling other machines for mail and news, and backing up file systems.

# 9.10  Summary

The UNIX print spooler, lp (System V) or lpr (BSD), manages the sharing of a the printer among multiple users. Once you have sent a file to the print spooler, you can continue with your work while the spooler and printer do their work.

To substitute one set of characters for another (often uppercase for lowercase or vice-versa), use the tr utility.

The cut and paste commands break and build files by columns or fields. The UNIX sort can be used for complex, database-type sorting as well as simple word sorting. The join utility combines two sorted files based on matches between fields of the two files.

The diff, sdiff, and diff3 utilities are used to compare text files. The cmp utility can be used to see if two non-text files differ.

Although there are many options to the find command, and many are obscure, it is useful for locating files based on name, ownership, date last modified, or many other attributes of the files.

Other file-management utilities include: dircmp (for comparing directories), df (to see the amount of free disk space), and du (to determine how much of the disk is being used by a branch of the directory tree).

The crypt command makes information undecipherable. It is particularly useful in protecting electronic mail from prying eyes. The bc and cd programs are for numerical calculations.

UNIX provides two mechanisms for batch processing: at for one-time scheduling and crontab for periodic operations.

# Review Questions

1. How do you send a file to the print spooler?

2. What is the purpose of the print spooler?

3. What are two common uses of the `pr` command?

4. What command outputs a formatted string with the current date and time?

5. What does the `tr` command do?

6. How do you selectively output fields from a flat ASCII data file?

7. How do you combine multiple lists into a single data file where each of the source files represents a separate field?

8. What are the strengths of the UNIX `sort` command?

9. What does `join` do?

10. What is the difference between `diff` and `sdiff`?

11. Which UNIX command searches through the directory tree looking for the file names (and other information) specified in its arguments?

# Exercises

Using the print spooler, the `ls` command, and the `pr` command, generate a three-column printed report of all of the files in the `/usr/bin` directory of your machine.

Using `tr` and `cut`, and `pg` or `more`, display a list of all of the user ID on your system *in uppercase*.

Use `cut`, `sort`, and `paste` to create a sorted list of the users on your system. The final report should have the user's real name followed by the user ID, separated by a vertical bar ( | ).

Create three tables (flat data files) that represent contract information. File one should be a time sheet and have project numbers, charge codes (key for rates), times, and dates. The second table should have actual rates and the key for rates. The third should have a brief explanation (10 words or less) of the project and the project number. Now use `sort` and `join` to produce a single report showing the times, rates, and project description. (This takes more than one pass.)

Create three copies of a file with 20 (or fewer) character lines. Slightly edit two of the copies and analyze them with the `diff` commands.

Use `ls -i` in your home directory to see the i-node number of one of your files. Now use `find` starting at the root (/) to find the full path to that i-node.

Use `bc` to find 1024 to the 1024th power. (This might seem like a ridiculous problem, but it demonstrates the phenomenal power of an arbitrary precision calculator.)

Use `at` to `echo` the message "Howdy, partner!" in five minutes. After five minutes, check your e-mail. (See Chapter 11, "Advanced Utilities," for details on `mail`).

## Further Reading

*UNIX — The Complete Reference*, Stephen Coffin, Osborne/McGraw Hill, Berkeley, CA, 1988.

*UNIX Utilities, A Programmer's Reference*, R.S. Tare, McGraw-Hill, Hightstown, NJ, 1987.

*The UNIX Programming Environment*, Brian Kernighan and Rob Pike, Prentice-Hall, Englewood Cliffs, NJ, 1984.

# 10

# Networks, File Transfers, and Communications

## Contents

## Objectives

In this chapter you will learn

1. How UNIX computers and workstations communicate with one another

2. How to use UNIX computers on LANs (Local Area Networks)

3. How to use UNIX with a modem

4. About UNIX e-mail and network news

A *network* hooks two or more systems together to exchange information. In the UNIX environment, there are two common species of networks: *real-time* and *batch*. The obvious difference between the two is the time involved in communications between systems. Real-time networks are most commonly confined to a single computing site or campus, using *ethernet* or *token ring* communications. Real-time networks have data-transmission rates of roughly a million characters a second. Local area networks (LANs) are a form of real-time network. Dozens of machines share the network at the same time. Real-time networks can span the globe using expensive phone lines and satellite communications.

Batch networks are formed from individual systems connecting one-on-one over communication links, usually involving modems and a voice-quality phone line. The network is created by each machine logging into the other, often one at a time. The programs that are involved in this sort of network are called UUCP (for UNIX to UNIX Communication Program). The transmission speeds are slower. Therefore, the operations done on batch networks are a subset of those on real-time networks. We cover batch networks and their UUCP operations later in this chapter. Batch networks are more often used for spanning long distances, because they can use modems and standard phone lines.

## 10.1  Real-Time Networks

The most common real-time networks are LANs (local area networks), which can run over ethernet or token ring network hardware. The network might be as simple as two desktop machines beside each other on a table, or as complex as hundreds of workstations tied to different mainframes, each running different operating systems that are in turn tied into a large network server handling  millions of characters per second over specially designed communication links. Quite often, large networks are hybrids composed of several different types of smaller network. See figure 10-1 for a diagram in which computers and workstations continuously communicate with each other to share resources.

Commands to access a network can be as simple as ordinary UNIX commands (with the underlying UNIX system modified to use the network hardware) or as complex as a whole new set of commands for file transfer, remote command execution, interdepartmental mail, etc. The simple use of networks is the result of a complex amount of system administration and network administration that makes the file systems of remote machines appear as part of the file system on each local machine. As a user, you don't even have to know that you are part of a

**Fig. 10-1:**
A simple real-
time network.

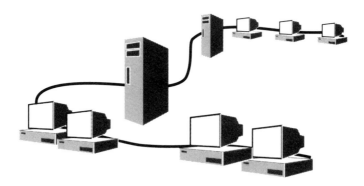

network. But you will find that your system resources far exceed what would otherwise be available from your local machine.

It is valuable to know what machines are part of your network. You will need this information for the machine-specific commands discussed later. The information is in the file /etc/hosts.

```
$ cat /etc/hosts
# Local network host addresses
#
#ident "@(#)hosts  1.1 - 88/05/17"
#
127.1 local localhost          —The default local address
192.1.1.1  bytenix opus
192.1.1.4  elwimpo
192.1.1.5  bytepb
192.1.1.6  iris
$
```

Machines listed in this file might not actually be connected or running. This is the list of possibilities.

The field with the numbers is called the *Internet address*. The names that follow it are names by which users know the machine and application programs. Each machine must have at least one unique Internet address. The machine names should also be unique for each machine.

Although you usually don't have to know the Internet addresses, the concept is simple. The first number is the network number. Each subsequent set of digits references a subnet. The last number in the series is the site number for the network or subnetwork. A machine might be on more than one network, in which case it would have more than one Internet address entry. Such a machine is a gateway between networks, passing data from one network to the other.

## Remote File Systems — NFS and RFS

The most common UNIX network facility you will use is the remote file system. You access files that exist on remote machines in exactly the same way you access files on your local machine. The remote file system is attached to your file tree in the same way as any local file system. (See fig. 10-2.)

**Figure 10-2:**
*A remote file system mounted on a local file system.*

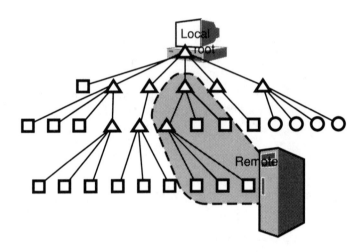

In fact, your Home directory might actually be on a remote machine, a *file server* (described later in this chapter). As with any multiple-file system, you cannot link (ln) files across two separate file systems, but you can read, write, copy, and move files. The only limitation on remote file-system operations is that you cannot rename directories using mv. Accessing files on remote machines might be slightly slower than on your local machine because the data has to travel over the network.

The remote file system might be attached to (mounted on) your local machine's directory tree using the AT&T RFS or the Sun Microsystems NFS. The major differences are apparent to only the system administrator. (NFS is designed for heterogeneous networks, whereas RFS is designed for homogeneous networks.) You might find that an RFS file system is faster than an NFS file system.

## Remote Commands for Remote Machines

The `rlogin` command allows you to log into a remote system over the network. The `telnet` command is another popular program used to log in to remote systems on local area networks. The `rlogin` command always requires you to log in. The two commands are very similar. On some networks the system administrator can allow you to log onto other machines (through the network) without re-entering a login name or password, as long as your name appears in the remote system's `/etc/passwd` file. If you do not have an account on the remote system, or if the systems are not set up to allow equivalency of login names between systems, you are required to give the login name and password. When the session on the remote system is over, log off in your usual way.

```
$ hostname
bytenix                         — The name of the current machine
$ rlogin elwimpo                — Log into elwimpo
login: felix                    — elwimpo doesn't know felix
Password:
-- elwimpo welcomes you --
-- system scheduled to be down Sunday 1AM-3AM

0 messages in your mailbox
$ pwd
/usr/felix
$ hostname
elwimpo
$ exit                          — Leave elwimpo
Closed connection.
$ rlogin ronin                  — Log into ronin
login: felix                    — ronin knows felix
Smith Design — One Reynolds Drive, Peterborough, NH 03458 —

$ pwd                           — ronin knows felix
/usr/people/felix
$ ls
bin
memos
sources
$ ~.                            — Another way to exit network connections
Closed connection.
$
```

You can use `rlogin` and `telnet` to reach from one machine to another, and from that to still another. If the connections in the network are set up for regular use, you should be able to log directly into the destination machine.

## Remote Shell — *rsh*

To execute commands on a remote machine without logging into that machine, use the `rsh` command. (On some versions of UNIX, `rsh` is used by a program that is a restricted shell rather than a remote shell. The `rsh` you want will probably be in a directory that has the name `/usr/ucb` or `/usr/berkeley`. It might also be linked to the command `remsh`, remote shell. You might want to change your directory-search path, as explained in Chapter 12, so that the remote shell `rsh` is found in your path before the restricted shell.)

The syntax for executing commands on a remote machine without logging in is as follows:

```
rsh host command
```

For example, to find out who is using the `ronin` machine, you would execute the following:

```
$ rsh ronin who
ben     tty2a     Feb 16 07:30
root    tty02     Feb 15 07:46
ben     tty04     Feb 15 07:49
ben     tty01     Feb 15 07:43
$
```

The `rsh` command allows you to combine computing resources of several machines into one operation. For example, to take the list of files on the `elwimpo` machine, sort them on `bytenix`, and print them using the local print spooler, enter the following:

```
$ rsh elwimpo 'find / -type f -print' | rsh bytenix sort | lp
$
```

Notice that the command parameter of the `rsh` directed to `elwimpo` is enclosed in quotations. This is necessary whenever the command being sent out to the remote machine has its own parameters or there are any wildcards to be expanded by the shell on the remote machine.

## Copying files — *rcp*

Use `rcp` to copy remote files. It works similarly to the `cp` command, except that a path name can begin with *system*. The following example shows how to specify that the file or directory is on the remote system *system*:

```
$ rcp elwimpo:/usr/felix/file1 file1$
$ rcp file2 elwimpo:/usr/felix/file2$
$
```

This sequence copies file1 from the directory /usr/felix on the system elwimpo to file1 in the current directory. Similarly, the second copies file2 from the current directory to /usr/felix on the system elwimpo.

rsh and rcp work only if your user id exists on the remote system and the remote system allows equivalency of login names.

# 10.2  Operating System Independent Transfer: ftp

There is more than one way to transfer files. If all the easy ways of moving files seem to be unavailable when you are probing around your network, you can fall back on the ARPANET standard File Transfer Protocol and its user interface program, ftp. The ftp utility is an interactive program, unlike the other file-moving methods, which require only command-line arguments.

The basic routine for moving files with ftp is as follows:

1. Open the connection to the remote machine with open *machinename*.

2. Locate the directory on the remote machine into which or from which you want to transfer files. The commands are cd, pwd, and dir. The first two are like their counterparts in standard UNIX; the latter is like ls -l.

3. Move the files with get (copy from the remote machine) and put (copy to the remote machine). The get and put commands move only one file at a time, but they have multiple-file counterparts, mget and mput.

A typical ftp session appears as follows:

```
$ ftp iris
Connected to iris.
220 iris FTP server (SGI 3.2 version 4.160 Aug 19 1989 04:53) ready.
Name (iris:ben): ben
331 Password required for ben.
Password:
230 User ben logged in.
ftp> pwd                        — Display current remote directory
257 "/usr/people/ben" is current directory.
ftp> cd logo                    — Change remote directory to logo
250 CWD command successful.
```

```
ftp> dir                              — List files in remote directory
200 PORT command successful.
150 Opening data connection for /bin/ls (ascii mode) (0 bytes).
total 6228
-rw-r--r-- 1 user      334 Mar 20 15:03 Makefile
-rw-r--r-- 1 user     1435 Mar 19 10:37 byte1.c
-rw-r--r-- 1 user      801 Mar 9 12:41 circle.c
-rw-r--r-- 1 user    13339 Mar 30 15:44 draw4.c
226 Transfer complete.
348 bytes received in 0 seconds (.33 Kbytes/s)
ftp> mget *.c                         — Get multiple files
mget ./byte1.c? y                     — Confirm that you want this file
200 PORT command successful.
150 Opening data connection for ./byte1.c (ascii mode) (1435 bytes).
226 Transfer complete.
local: ./byte1.c remote: ./byte1.c
1534 bytes received in 1 seconds (1.5 Kbytes/s)
 mget ./circle.c? y                   — Confirm that you want this file
200 PORT command successful.
150 Opening data connection for ./circle.c (ascii mode) (801 bytes).
226 Transfer complete.
local: ./circle.c remote: ./circle.c
843 bytes received in 0 seconds (0.82 Kbytes/s)
mget ./draw4.c? y                     — Confirm that you want this file
200 PORT command successful.
150 Opening data connection for ./draw4.c (ascii mode) (13339 bytes).
226 Transfer complete.
local: ./draw4.c remote: ./draw4.c
14177 bytes received in 1 seconds (14 Kbytes/s)
ftp> put test.c                       — Put local file on remote system
200 PORT command successful.
150 Opening data connection for test.c (ascii mode).
226 Transfer complete.
local: test.c remote: test.c
654 bytes sent in 0 seconds (0.64 Kbytes/s)
ftp> bye                              — Log off remote connection and exit ftp
221 Goodbye.
$
```

To reduce the number of messages, issue the ftp toggle command verbose.

To see the entire ftp command set, use the ftp command help:

```
ftp> help
Commands can be abbreviated. Commands are:
```

```
!           cr          ls          prompt      runique
$           delete      macdef      proxy       send
account     debug       mdelete     sendport    status
append      dir         mdir        put         struct
ascii       disconnect  mget        pwd         sunique
bell        form        mkdir       quit        tenex
binary      get         mls         quote       trace
bye         glob        mode        recv        type
case        hash        mput        remotehelp  user
cd          help        nmap        rename      verbose
cdup        image       ntrans      reset       ?
close       lcd         open        rmdir
ftp>
```

The help command also gives you a short explanation for each command:

```
ftp> help proxy
proxy       issue command on alternate connection
ftp> help bell
bell     beep when command completed
ftp>quit
$
```

As you can see, the quit command closes the connection with the remote machine and exits ftp. There is some redundancy in ftp commands. For example, the exit command does just about the same thing as quit.

The ftp command binary specifies that the transfers include non-ASCII bytes. You should use binary transfers for transfers from UNIX to MS-DOS and MS-DOS to UNIX.

# 10.3  Server Services

Modern application programs are designed to take advantage of real-time networks. These programs divide applications' tasks into two elements: *client* tasks and *server* tasks. The server tasks serve the requests of the client tasks. Both the server and client tasks can exist on the same machine as separate processes that carry on a relationship through the operating system's resources for interprocess communications. The relationship, however, does not have to be private; several clients can be served by the same server. Nor does the relationship have to be intimate; the server can be on one machine and the clients on others.

A typical application that profits from the client and server model is a database management system. The server is the real manager of the data. It prevents more than one client from writing to a data record at one time. More germane to this chapter is the `rlogin` utility, which starts up a client process on the local machine and a server process on the remote machine.

Machines designed for special work such as database operations, intensive computing, or managing large file systems are also called servers: database servers, compute servers, file servers. You might keep all this straight by thinking of the graphic workstation as the graphics window server because it is specially designed for this sort of work. However, you might also find it confusing that the concept of clients and servers is applied to many applications programs that use similar multi- process designs. For example, a database program that has several concurrent users usually consists of a database manager, the server, and the users' separate requests, the client processes. At times, there are advantages to having different server programs running on separate computers on the network, spreading the workload around. Often, however, both the client and server process exist on the same machine.

The popular X Window System uses the client/server model for its operations. In a sense, however, the relationship of client and server is reversed, because the host runs the client applications and the local workstation (or X terminal) runs the server program. In the case of X Window System applications, the services provided are the facilities of the screen and detection of activity at the keyboard and mouse. The client applications use the server. For example, assume that a session involves many X programs running simultaneously (and not necessarily locally), all of which are sharing the resources of the same physical screen, keyboard, and mouse. You would typically have a window manager such as the Motif window manager (`mwm`), an `xterm` or two, and maybe even `xclock`, all running at the same time.

Most real-time network resources are intentionally transparent — nay, invisible. If you want to know more about them, talk to your network manager.

## 10.4  Batch Networking — UUCP

The UUCP commands create what is known as the *dial-up UNIX network*. This kind of network is rather limited in scope, and it is used mainly for exchanging mail and news messages between member systems. What it lacks in utility, however, it makes up for in the complexity of connections. The dial-up UNIX network currently consists of tens of thousands of UNIX systems throughout the world. It connects millions of users. The topology of the network is unbelievably complex, spanning every continent in the world.

If your UNIX system has dial-out capability — the capability to make calls as well as receive them — your system can call other systems and exchange data using UUCP. Communications between machines take place only as needed, usually through modems and over phone lines. Modems convert the digital data of a computer to and from an audio signal that can be carried on phone lines. (See fig. 10-3.)

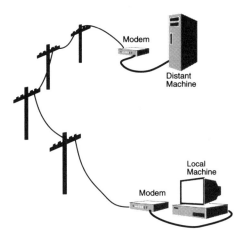

**Fig. 10-3:**
A batch mode network.

In UNIX lingo, UUCP refers to the collection of programs for intersite communications. UUCP is the acronym for UNIX-to-UNIX-CoPy. The UNIX command uucp is the basic utility for copying files from one UNIX system to another. The entire collection includes uucico, uux, uuxqt, uustat, uuclean, uuto, and uupick. The actual work is done by the UUCP daemons: uucico, uuxqt, and uusched. (Daemons are programs that run *invisibly* in the background.) Figure 10-4 diagrams how some of this works. All you execute is the uucp command; the system does the rest.

## Basic Utilities

It is easy to copy files from one system to another. You do not have to enter a communications program, establish communications with another computer, and

**Fig. 10-4:**
*Copying files
from remote
systems with
UUCP.*

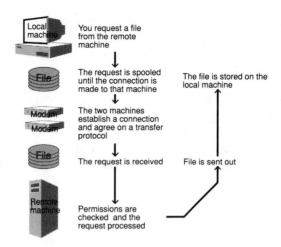

then transfer files using *upload* or *send file* as you would on an MS-DOS machine. On a UNIX machine, you do only the following:

    uucp *sourcefiles destination*

The only real difference between using this utility and copying files from one subdirectory to another within the same system is that the *sourcefile* or the *destination* can contain a site name or *address*. For example, to copy the source for the Notesfile system (the file name is Notes.tar.Z) from the UUNET machine in Virginia to the Notes subdirectory on your machine, issue the following:

```
$ uucp uunet!/usr/spool/ftp/news/Notes.tar.Z /usr/spool/
uucppublic/Notes
```

The directory /usr/spool/uucppublic is the traditional directory for file exchanges. (As the name implies, it is a public directory to which everyone has read, write, and execute permissions. In other words, everyone has permission to put files there and delete them, depending on file permissions. A common abbreviation for this directory in UUCP, Korn shell, and C shell is ~nuucp; another is ~uucp.)

The only complexity in the previous command is the directory path to the file. The ! (*bang* in computer vernacular) is appended to site names to distinguish them from subdirectory names.

To abbreviate the directory paths, use the tilde (~) to represent the "home" directory of a login. The home directory for UUCP is the public file exchange area, in this case `/usr/spool/ftp`, but more often `/usr/spool/uucppublic`. The use of the tilde abbreviation resolves site-specific differences. The simplified command with abbreviated path names becomes:

```
$ uucp uunet!uucp/news/Notes.tar.Z ~/Notes
$
```

As soon as you have issued the `uucp` command, you can continue with other work at your terminal or workstation window. UUCP works in the background without interrupting you or slowing you down.

The UUCP commands do the actual call-ups and file transfers between systems, maintain usage statistics, and ensure security.

When you send files via `uucp`, they will be readable and writable by *everyone* on the receiving system. If you are sending files that should *not* be accessible to everyone, pack and encrypt them using `pack` or `compress` and `crypt`. Not only does this prevent others from reading your files, it also reduces the size of the files and the amount of time required to transmit them. Even if you do not want to encrypt your files, consider packing them to reduce transmission overhead (particularly if you are sending files over a long-distance telephone connection).

After you run the `uucp` command to send a file to another system, you might have to wait several minutes for the file transfer to take place. When you get a $ after running `uucp`, you are being informed that the file transfer has been *queued*, or placed in line to be sent. (There might be other file transfers waiting to be performed before yours.) To determine whether the file has been sent, the command `uustat` can be used. Without arguments, `uustat` will tell you the job number of any pending UUCP requests; for example, copying local files to the remote system `bytepb`:

```
$ uucp log bytepb!~nuucp          — ~nuucp is an abbreviation
                                    for /usr/spool/uucppublic
$ uucp parts bytepb!~nuucp
$ uustat
bytepbN750a   05/28-14:33 S bytepb felix 11478 /usr/ben/sbs/ch10/log
bytepbN750b   05/28-14:33 S bytepb felix 13275 /usr/ben/sbs/ch10/parts
$
```

To cancel jobs, use `uustat` again, but this time with the arguments `-k` *job-num*. For example:

```
$ uustat -k bytepbN750b
Job: bytepbN750b successfully killed
$
```

Once the jobs have been processed, uustat returns nothing. However, if you wish to confirm that the transmission took place, use the uulog command. For example, the status of all uucp transfers for the system remote1 can be determined by using the uulog command with remote1 as an argument:

```
$ uulog remote1                          —Or uulog -s remote1
uucp remote1 (12/7-19:19:30,3524,0) SUCCEEDED (call to remote1 )
uucp remote1 (12/7-19:19:32,3524,0) OK (startup)
uucp remote1 (12/7-19:19:33,3524,0) REMOTE REQUESTED
(remote1!/usr/users/pw/sources/xfer.c —> local!/test/ (felix))
uucp remote1 (12/7-19:19:49,3524,1) REMOTE REQUESTED
(remote1!/usr/users/pw/sources/xfer.c —> local!/test/ (felix))
uucp remote1 (12/7-19:20:02,3524,2) OK (conversation complete tty0 39)
uucp remote1 (12/8-10:27:08,214,0) FAILED (LOGIN FAILED)
uucp remote1 (12/8-10:27:08,214,0) CONN FAILED (LOGIN FAILED)
uucp remote1 (12/8-10:27:42,223,0) SUCCEEDED (call to remote1 )
uucp remote1 (12/8-10:27:45,223,0) OK (startup)
uucp remote1 (12/8-10:27:46,223,0) REMOTE REQUESTED
(remote1!/usr/journal/v2n1/color.inset —> local!/journal/ (felix))
uucp remote1 (12/8-10:28:12,223,1) OK (conversation complete tty0 37)
uucp remote1 (12/8-11:13:39,247,0) SUCCEEDED (call to remote1 )
uucp remote1 (12/8-11:13:41,247,0) OK (startup)
uucp remote1 (12/8-11:13:42,247,0) REMOTE REQUESTED
(remote1!/usr/journal/v2n1/tips.figs/figs.ps —> local!~/journal/ (felix))
uucp remote1 (12/8-11:13:53,247,1) OK (conversation complete tty0 22)
uucp remote1 (12/8-18:40:16,976,0) SUCCEEDED (call to remote1 )
uucp remote1 (12/8-18:40:19,976,0) OK (startup)
felix remote1 remote1N3a5e (12/8-18:40:20,976,0) REQUEST
(local!/tmp/names —> remote1!~/john (felix))
uucp remote1 (12/8-18:40:57,976,1) OK (conversation complete tty0 49)
$
```

On some older versions of UUCP the uustat might require you to specify the system name as an option. The option is -s *system-name*.

The last four lines of output from uulog show the transfer of the file /tmp/names from the local system to remote1. The SUCCEEDED line says that the call (dialing) from the local system to remote1 succeeded. The OK (startup) line says that uucp successfully managed to log into and start communications with remote1. The REQUEST line says that the system has requested permission to start copying /tmp/names to ~/john. The OK (conversation complete... line signifies that the send was successful and that uucp is finished.

A REMOTE REQUESTED line signifies that the remote system is sending a file to the local one, whereas a REQUEST line signifies that the local system is sending a file to the remote one. A FAILED line means that the transfer somehow failed.

Usually this happens because uucp was unable to log into the remote system; that is, the system was down or all its telephone lines were busy.

Left to its own devices, uulog will print the entire log for the specified system. For a busy system, this can amount to hundreds or thousands of lines. To get just the most recent log entries from uulog, use the *-num* option. The option will be passed to tail along with the output of uulog:

```
$ uulog -5 remote1uucp remote1 (12/8-11:13:53,247,1) OK
(conversation complete tty0 22)
uucp remote1 (12/8-18:40:16,976,0) SUCCEEDED (call to
remote1 )
uucp remote1 (12/8-18:40:19,976,0) OK (startup)
felix remote1 remote1N3a5e (12/8-18:40:20,976,0) REQUEST
(local!/tmp/names -> remote1!~/john (felix))
uucp remote1 (12/8-18:40:57,976,1) OK (conversation
complete tty0 49)
$
```

## Interactive Dialup: *cu*

The cu command allows you to call another UNIX system, log in, and use it *while you are still logged into your original system.* It resembles the real-time network command rlogin. It works by using your UNIX system's dial-out ability and connecting your terminal to the outgoing modem; all you have to do is tell it what system or telephone number to call, as follows:

```
$ cu 386585
Connected
login:
```

or

```
$ cu remote1
Connected
login:
```

At this point, you can log in and use the system you called. Note that you have not logged off the system you were on before entering cu:

```
$ cu remote1                        —Call up remote system
Connected
login: felix                        —Log in as felix
Password
```

```
      Printer "qlaser" is now available. See "news."
      Maint. shutdown 3AM-5AM Sundays.

      $ who am i                          —Are we really felix?
      felix tty08 Dec 3 13:2
      $ pwd                               —Enter a few commands
      /usr/feli
      $ l
      file
      name
      uucpfile
      $ <Ctrl-D>                          —Log off
      login:
```

After doing some work on the other system, you decide to log off and continue working on your original system. Logging off is not enough, however, because the terminal is still hooked up to the outgoing modem, which is still dialed into the other system. You have to tell the cu command to disconnect you from the other system. This is done by entering ~. *at the beginning of a line*, followed by the Enter key. The session illustrated previously ends with the following:

```
      $ <Ctrl-D>
      login: ~[local].                    —Disconnect
      Disconnected
      $
```

[local] is printed by cu to indicate that the command you are entering will affect you on the local system. Note that you should always log off the remote system before disconnecting. Some systems will not log you off automatically when you disconnect, so that the next user who comes along on that line can be given access to your login.

cu is useful if you regularly use more than one UNIX system, because it lets you use another system without logging off the system you're already on. cu is also useful when you want to transfer small text files between your UNIX system and another. It has some built-in commands that use the communications link established when you call another system to transfer the files. The commands are ~%take and ~%put, which take files from and put files onto the other system, respectively. To take a file (that is, copy it) from the other system, you call it up, log in, and then enter:

   ~%take *source dest*

in which *source* is the name of the file on the other system and *dest* is the name you want for the file on your regular system. The *dest* file name is optional; cu will use the source file name if the *dest* file name isn't given. For example, assume that you want to copy the file file1 from another system:

```
$ cu remote1
Connected
login: felix
Password:
Printer "qlaser" is now available. See "news."
Maint. shutdown 3AM-5AM Sundays.

$ ~[local]%take file1                    —Copy file1 from another system
stty -echo;mesg n;echo '~>':file1;cat file1;echo '~>'; mesg y;stty echo\ ~>\:file1
123+
128 lines/2088 characters
$ Ctrl-D
login: ~[local].Disconnected
$ ls
file1                                    —It has been copied
test
$
```

The three lines following the ~%take are the control lines that go to the other UNIX system to transfer file1. As cu transmits the file, it prints a number when it starts to send each block of 1,024 bytes; therefore, the numbers in the line 123+ are printed one at a time as the transfer proceeds. The last line is printed when the transfer is complete; it tells you the number of lines and characters transferred.

Similarly, if you want to copy the file test to another system, use the ~%put command:

```
login: felix
Password:
Printer "qlaser" is now available. See "news."
Maint. shutdown 3AM-5AM Sundays.

$ ~[local]%put test     —Copy test to remote system
stty -echo; cat - > test; stty echo
1+
5 lines/30 characters
$
```

This file-transfer method is really useful only for small files, because the terminal is locked during the transfer; a 50,000-byte file transferred at the rate of 120 characters per second (1200 baud) takes about seven minutes to send. Also, there is no checking performed for errors in transmission, so there is a greater probability that large files might be garbled. The uucp copy utility described earlier has error checking and recovery built in, and is therefore more reliable for transferring large files. Also, cu sends and receives text files only. uucp can handle both text and binary files.

## NetNews

NetNews is not a news service like United Press International; it is more the actual activity of the developers and users of high technology than people reporting the news. The messages are not journalism, but the source of journalism. This is active conferencing, such as what happens on PC-oriented conferencing systems such as BIX (BYTE Information eXchange) and Compuserve.

There are four commonly used programs for reading and responding to the news: readnews, vnews, rn, and Notes. If you are new to reading news, use readnews; it is the simplest. If, however, you need the power of macros and the flexibility to customize the system, rn is for you. All four programs allow you to respond to messages, reply to the author directly with e-mail, and file and save messages. They also use lists in your home directory to keep track of what subjects you are interested in reading and which messages you have already read (so that you do not waste time rereading old messages).

The messages are organized as separate articles within *newsgroups*. Newsgroups are organized in a hierarchical structure with only a few newsgroups at the top of the structure. Each major newsgroup has several subnewsgroups. Each of these can, in turn, have its own subnewsgroups, and so on, sometimes to four levels of organization. For example, the messages relating to bug fixes for BSD 4 UNIX are found in comp.bugs.4bsd.ucb-fixes. The periods divide the subgroups. This organization not only facilitates finding special newsgroups, but also provides the file structure for the actual messages.

In many ways, sending news is like sending mail. Rather than sending the message to an individual, however, you send the message to a news group. Reading the news, however, can be a big task, not because it is any more complicated than reading and replying to mail, but because of the sheer volume of news on the system. You select which articles you want to read from the list of article headers. Discussions within a newsgroup are tied together by the subject in the article headers. You can follow an entire conversation within a news group before going on to read another conversation within that same group. Or you can mark a subject for rejection.

For instance, if you are interested in the subject of Atari ST computers, you would join the news group comp.sys.atari.st. If there were a conversation about MIDI programs and devices for which you had no interest, you could make the news-reading program kill all new articles with the key words *MIDI* and *music*. Similarly, you might be interested in data acquisition/analysis, and you could automatically save all articles with these key words.

All news messages are copied onto the local machine. You and all other local users peruse them on your local machine without each person dialing up to a remote machine. This is another example of how resources are shared on UNIX systems. One call serves all.

NetNews messages have a header describing the e-mail address of the originator of the message, which news groups the message belongs to, the subject of the message, the date the message was posted, and a unique message id.

### Information Overload

The computers and communications lines can handle the heavy load of electronic mail and news, but can we? Are we doomed to information overload? Many of us already suffer from severe information indigestion. Using these "free" UNIX communications and news utilities is very appealing, but they can be like swimming in a dangerous undertow.

Because the UUCP programs open our machines to oceans of new information, it is best to start with just a little at a time. The most useful facility is the ability to send electronic mail through the Usenet. You will also want to share documents with other UNIX sites.

If you decide to become involved in NetNews, start with subscribing to just one specific news subgroup. Learn to use the news-reading program of your choice. Don't let your excitement over the Usenet resources make your appetite for information exceed your capacity to digest it.

On the other hand, NetNews is as pure an example of *social networking* as you will find. It is great fun to meet and talk to others about your interests without having to join a club or society. If you are doing research or looking for help with a problem, NetNews can give you answers in hours to questions that might otherwise take months or years to solve.

## 10.5 Electronic Mail and Conversations

One of the phrases you hear most often when someone talks about office automation is *electronic mail*, commonly known as *e-mail*. Electronic mail allows you to send messages, memos, or any type of document to other users electronically — that is, without using paper. The other person can be on your local machine or on another machine that connects either by a real-time network or by a UUCP connection. The mail system does all the work of delivering the mail in the same way that the Postal Service directs a letter or the phone company routes a phone call.

To carry on an interactive conversation with another user who is currently logged in to your system or another machine in your real-time network, use the `write` and `talk` programs.

With electronic mail, the mail is automatically kept by the system until the user issues the necessary command to read his or her mail. Some people send electronic messages using the following approach: If the user is logged in, they use the `write` or `talk` command to talk to the user directly. If the user is not logged in, they use the `mail` command to send the message. The disadvantage of the first method is that you might interrupt what someone is doing. `mail` is the more polite method.

## Using mail

Under the UNIX system, either the `mail` or `mailx` command can be used to send and read electronic mail. (A well-written, popular, and freely distributed e-mail program is `elm`. If your system has this mail program, you will find it much easier to use than either of the other standard mail programs, although you should learn them anyway.)

The `mailx` command has more powerful features than the mail command. It allows you to review your messages and file them quickly in different *folders*. However, because the `mail` command is much simpler, we describe that one in this text. The fundamental principles we show here using `mail` also apply to `mailx`.

The format of the command to send mail to a user is simple:

```
$ mail user
```

in which *user* is the user ID of the person you want to send the mail to. Once this command line has been entered, the `mail` program waits for you to enter the message you want to send. Enter as many lines as you like. When you finish, enter Ctrl-D to tell the `mail` program the message is completed. `mail` then takes your message and "mails" it to the specified user.

Periodically, the shell automatically checks to see whether you have received any new mail. If you have, the following message is displayed at your terminal:

```
you have mail
```

This check is also performed when you log in.

Reading mail is even easier than sending it — simply enter the command `mail` with *no* arguments. This causes the `mail` program to display any mail sent to you. As each item of mail is displayed at your terminal, the `mail` program displays a ? and waits for you to give a *filing disposition* for that piece of mail. Normally, after you enter your disposition, the next piece of mail is displayed. After reading your last piece of mail, the `mail` program returns you to the shell command level.

The most common mail dispositions are summarized in table 10-1.

**Table 10-1.  Commonly used `mail` dispositions.**

| Key | Meaning |
|-----|---------|
| `Enter` | No disposition on this piece of mail; it will still be there the next time `mail` is read. Display next piece of mail. |
| `d` | Delete this piece of mail. Display next piece of mail. |
| s*file* | Save this piece of mail in *file*. Display next piece of mail. |
| `*` | Print a list of disposition commands. |
| `q` | Quit reading mail; any unread pieces will be there next time mail is read. |
| `x` | Exit reading mail; any pieces of mail that might be deleted will be restored. |

Note that on some systems the disposition ? is used rather than * to obtain a list of commands. (Some systems accept both!)

Take a look at an example of `mail`. We assume here that the user `felix` wants to send some mail to `ruth`. We assume also that `ruth` is not logged in at the time that Felix sends the mail.

```
$ mail ruth
```

After Felix enters the command `mail ruth`, he enters his message to Ruth. The `mail` command takes every line he enters before the Ctrl-D as the message to be mailed.

```
$ mail ruth
ruth,
I wanted to remind you that
we have a meeting scheduled for
Monday (3/27) at 1pm.
felix                                        — Felix types in his message
<CTRL-d>
$
```

Entering Ctrl-D causes Felix's message to be mailed to Ruth. It also returns his command prompt, to indicate that the `mail` command has finished execution.

Now assume that Ruth arrives at work and logs in as follows:

```
login: ruth
Password:
you have mail

Good morning.
There are 4 users logged in.
$
```

Upon logging in, Ruth is automatically told that she has mail. To read her mail, all Ruth has to do is enter the command `mail`:

```
Good morning.
There are 4 users logged in.
$ mail
From felix Fri Mar 24 13:27 EST 1989
ruth,
I wanted to remind you that
we have a meeting scheduled for
Monday (3/27) at 1pm.
felix

?
```

Ruth reads her mail; the `mail` program waits for her to enter a disposition:

```
There are 4 users logged in.
? d                                          — Delete the message
$
```

She decides not to save it, so she enters d (for delete).

The mail program inserts a *postmark* at the front of each piece of mail, telling where the mail came from and the time and date it was sent.

Had Ruth had more mail, the next piece would have been displayed after she entered her d disposition. Because she had no more mail, she received her command prompt instead.

There are some additional points worth noting about the mail command. First, you can enter mail at your terminal at any time to see whether you have mail. If you have none, the message No mail. is displayed, as follows:

```
$ mail
No mail.
$
```

To send the same piece of mail to more than one user, list each user on the command line, as in the following:

```
$ mail tony fred leela alice ben
```

Because mail reads the message to be sent from standard input, you can redirect its input from a file. Therefore, to send the contents of the file reminder to ruth, use the following:

```
$ mail ruth < reminder
$
```

If you must send a long message to someone, this technique comes in handy. First, enter your message in a file using a text editor such as emacs or vi, make any necessary changes, and then mail the contents of the file. That way you can even keep a copy of the message for yourself.

On many systems, the emacs editor has its own interface to the mail system. If you are an emacs user, read the emacs help on mail.

## Other Mail Commands

To refresh your memory of the entire set of mail commands, enter the hook (?) command. You will see the following output:

```
? ?
#              display message number #
-              print previous
+              next (no delete)
```

```
! cmd           execute cmd
a               position at and read newly arrived mail
dq              delete current message and exit
d [#]           delete message # (default current message)
h a             display all headers
h d             display headers of letters scheduled for
                deletion
h [#]           display headers around # (default current
                message)
m user          mail (and delete) current message to user
n               next (no delete)
p               print
q               quit
r [args]        reply to (and delete) current letter via
                mail [args]
s [file]        save (and delete) current message (default
                mbox)
u [#]           undelete message # (default current mes
                sage)
w [file]        save (and delete) current message without
                header
x               exit without changing mail
y [file]        save (and delete) current message (default
                mbox)
```

As you can see, you escape to the shell with the bang (!) command. Another useful command is h, which displays the headers of the mail messages in your mailbox.

## Mail Addresses

When you send mail to a user on another system, you use mail (or mailx) just as if you were sending mail to someone on your local system. In other words, the user interface is the same, whether you send mail to someone on your local computer, to someone on your LAN, or to someone across the world. The only difference is how you address the mail.

There are two general formats for addressing mail to users on other machines. The first uses *bang paths*. For this you prefix the name of the recipient with his or her address. The address is a list of machines to route the mail through, each site name appended with a bang (!). For instance, if I want to send mail to George Bond on the bixpb computer, I issue the command mail bixpb!gbond (or uunet!bixpb!gbond, if my local computer connects to the bixpb through uunet).

The second address form is that of a *domain address*. A domain address consists of a user name, the "at" symbol (@), and the machine at which the user can be found. For example, George Bond would have the address gbond@bytepb.byte.COM. If you were on the same local area network as bytepb.byte.COM, you could shorten the address to gbond@bytepb.

With either addressing scheme, you compose the mail message in the usual way. George finds the mail message on his machine just as if someone local had sent him a mail message. He can reply without being concerned about the source of the message, because the mail header has the address of the original correspondent. His machine sends the response back in the same way your machine sent the original message. If there are intermediate machines, their names are included in the address string.

You can contact any individual with access to any machine that links to Usenet. There are direct links to ARPANET (Advanced Research Projects Agency Network), the Centre For Mathematic and Computer Science in Amsterdam, which acts as the common node between Usenet and the EUnet (the European UNIX network), New Zealand, Bangkok, Seoul, Toronto, and several-hundred other sites around the world. UNIX users often give their Usenet addresses whenever they give out their regular mail address and phone number. It is not uncommon to see these addresses on business cards and the "bios" of articles and technical papers.

Because of the complexity of Usenet, bang path addresses can get ridiculously long, as in the following example:

```
bixpb!uunet!lll-winken!lll-ncis!helios.ee.lbl.gov!\
pasteur!ucbvax!agate!bionet!csd4.milw.wisc.edu!uxc!\
uxc.cso.uiuc.edu!m.cs.uiuc.edu!aguest
```

This is actually one very long string. This address was probably generated by an inefficient mail-routing routine. The message would originate in New Hampshire, go to Virginia, work its way to California, go to Wisconsin, and eventually end up on the appropriate machine. The sites that have long names broken by dots (.) are local networks; each element is a node or domain in the local network.

As with most tedious and error-prone tasks that you might encounter on UNIX machines, there are quick and efficient ways to generate addresses. First, the UUCP system (UNIX mail system) has aliases for long addresses. That is, you can address mail with a nickname; a table supplies the full address path and real name. Second, there are mail-routing functions on "Backbone" site machines. On these machines and most of the "leaf" machines UUCP consults a map of all intermediate sites, and it can figure out a path for your message. All you supply is the path to a backbone site and the name of the destination machine. The monstrous address shown previously can be reduced to the following:

```
bixpb!uunet!m.cs.uicuc.edu!aguest
```

or with domain addressing as follows:

```
aguest@m.cs.uicuc.edu
```

If you have to communicate with this account more than once, you might want to create a nickname for it, an alias.

## Mail Aliases

Both the `mailx` program and the `elm` version of mail allow you to build aliases for users with whom you exchange electronic mail. Like the `alias` of the Korn and C shells, mail aliases are abbreviate the complex name and address strings you might need to direct your messages. You can also use the mail-alias function to use a single name to designate a group of people.

In the `mailx` program, you create an alias using the following syntax:

```
alias nickname recipient-list
```

The alias lasts only as long as your `mailx` session. To make the list permanent (or set other `mailx` parameters), enter the `alias` function in the mail initialization file in your home directory. The name of the file is `.mailrc` and might look like the following:

```
alias us tyager, ben, gbond, judell, rickg
alias david david@infopro.UUCP
alias pat ronin!pipeline!phw
```

The `elm` mail system's front end maintains its own alias database and has commands for searching, adding, and deleting entries in the table.

## Electronic Conversation with *write*

Sometimes you might want to send a message to a user who is logged in on another terminal of the same system as you are. That terminal might be located in another office on the floor, or even in another location, making it inconvenient for you to talk directly to that person. As an alternative to calling the person on the telephone, use the `write` command. `write` allows you to send a message to any other logged-in user. The message you send appears on that user's screen. The user has the option to send you a reply by initiating a `write` command from his or her own terminal. With this technique, two users can effectively have a "conversation" through their terminals.

The general format of the `write` command is as follows:

```
write user tty
```

in which *user* is the user id of the logged-in user and *tty* is an optional terminal ID. This latter information is needed when there is more than one logged-in user with the same user id — the *tty* number designates the terminal to which the message is to be sent. (To find out what terminal the user is logged in at, use the `who` command. To determine your own terminal ID, enter the `tty` command.)

As an example, the command:

```
write pat
```

tells the UNIX system that you wish to start a conversation with the user `Pat`. If Pat is not currently logged in, then the following occurs:

```
$ write pat
pat is not logged on.
$
```

If Pat is logged in, the `write` command prints the following on Pat's terminal (it will also "beep" Pat's terminal a few times to alert him in case he fell asleep):

```
Message from felix on depta (tty02) [ Fri Mar 24
14:20:35 ] ..
```

(Here we assume that the `write` command was initiated by Felix.) The actual format of this line might differ slightly on your system.

After initiating the write, the system waits for you to enter your message. This message can contain as many lines as you like. Each line you enter is displayed on Pat's terminal. When you finish entering your message, enter Ctrl-D as the first and only character on the line. This terminates `write` and displays the line <EOT> on Pat's terminal to tell him you are finished.

If Pat decides to answer your message, he can initiate his own `write` command from his terminal:

```
$ write felix
```

Any lines that Pat now types are automatically displayed on Felix's terminal. When Pat finishes his message, he too must enter Ctrl-D to terminate his `write`.

With write commands simultaneously active on both Pat's and Felix's terminals, you can see how these two users can carry on a conversation. As a matter of convention, most UNIX users end their message lines with the characters -o (as in "over") to tell the other user that their message line is finished and they are (possibly) awaiting a reply. The characters -oo are often used to signal the end of the conversation (as in "over and out").

The following sequence of screens depicts a typical conversation. Felix's screen shows:

```
$ date
Fri Mar 24 14:32:30 EST 1990
$ who                                — Felix checks to make sure that Pat is logged in
ben    tty06 Mar 24 08:53
pat    tty08 Mar 24 13:01
felix  tty02 Mar 24 13:19
$ write pat                          — Now he initiates a conversation with him
```

Pat's screen shows:

```
$ pwd
/usr/pat/tp
Message from felix on depta (tty02) ..
```

Felix types his message. Felix's screen shows:

```
Hello, Pat
I'm trying to find the file
fopen.c. Do you know what
directory it's in? -o
```

Back on Pat's terminal:

```
Hello, pat
I'm trying to find the file
fopen.c. Do you know what
directory it's in? -o
write felix                          — Pat uses write to respond.
Yes. You can find it in
/usr/src/lib/libc/port/stdio -o
```

Pat gets the question and sends his response. When both parties are finished with their conversation and have decided to hang up, they exit write with the end-of-file character, Ctrl-D.

## Inhibiting Messages with the mesg Command

Sometimes you might decide that you do not want to receive any messages. For example, you might be running a particular program and you don't want your screen to get messed up when someone writes to you. The perfect example is when using a screen editor such as vi. If someone tries to write to you while you are in the middle of editing a file, the incoming text overwrites information on your screen, turning your screen into a royal mess. Don't be alarmed, however, as the problem is only temporary; all you have to do to restore your screen to its previous state is enter the screen-refresh command, Ctrl-L.

To tell the UNIX system that you do not want to receive messages, use the mesg command. This command takes a single argument, n or y. The former specifies that you do not want to receive messages; the latter specifies that you do. Therefore, to inhibit incoming messages while you are editing a file, enter the command

```
$ mesg n
```

before you enter the editor. After your edits are complete, tell the system that you are willing to resume receiving messages, by entering the following command:

```
$ mesg y
```

If other users try to write to you while you have messages inhibited, the message Permission denied. will be printed at their terminal, as in the following example:

```
$ write felix
Permission denied.
$
```

To find out your current message-receiving status, enter mesg with no arguments.


## Real-Time Conversations: talk

The talk utility is another that came out of Berkeley. Like write, talk is a communication program which copies lines from your terminal to that of another user and vice-versa. But talk is more visual; the screen is divided into two separate regions. The top region is for your side of the conversation; the bottom region is for the other user's side.

You can use talk to converse with people on your local machine as well as with remote users. Begin with the following:

```
talk user@host
```

or

```
talk host:user
```

If the other user is on your local machine, you need not use the host name to specify the address. If the other user is logged on to more than one terminal, append the terminal name as follows:

```
talk user@host tty
```

in which *tty* is the name of the terminal connection to which you want to communicate.

To find out who is logged on and where (before you try to contact them), use the `finger` command. (There is a higher-level utility, `fingered`, which gives you a list of who is logged on to remote machines — just in case you want to talk, but don't know with whom.)

The syntax for `finger` is:

```
finger name
```

Once you have sent the invitation to talk, your screen is divided into two windows. The target user receives a message indicating that you wish to talk and a message telling how to respond. For example:

```
Message from TalkDaemon@iris...
talk: connection requested by felix@bytepb
talk: respond with: talk felix@bytepb
```

In this example, if the target user wishes to talk, she enters the following command:

```
$ talk felix@bytepb
```

and the conversation proceeds.

While you are in `talk`, if your screen becomes garbaged up for some reason, use Ctrl-L to refresh it. Either party can terminate the conversation with the interrupt character, usually Del or Ctrl-C.

Some programs disallow `talk` messages while they are running. This is done so that their output will not be intermingled with requests to `talk`. If you try to contact someone who is running one of these programs, you receive a message to that effect. As with `write`, permission to talk can be denied or granted by use of the `mesg` command (see previous discussion).

# 10.6 Summary

UNIX connectivity takes two forms: real-time networks and batch networks. Local area networks (LANs) are real-time networks.

The most common operations with real-time networks are: `rlogin` and `telenet` (for UNIX sessions on remote machines), `rsh` (for executing individual commands on remote machines), and an extension to UNIX called network file service (NFS) which makes parts of remote filesystems appear on the local machine. The `rcp` and `ftp` are utilities for copying files from one sytem to another. `ftp`, has been implemented across many operating systems and on many wide-area networks. It is actually an entire language.

The utilities used for batch networking are grouped under the heading UUCP. Most UUCP networks are connected using modems and voice-grade telephone lines. The element for remote login under UUCP is `cu`; for copying, it is `uucp`.

Two popular networking products are network news and electronic mail.

# Review Questions

1. What is the difference between a real-time network and a batch network?

2. What is the path and name of the file that contains the list of computers to which your computer can connect in a local area network?

3. What are the two most common commands used to log in to remote machines in UNIX LAN?

4. In real-time networks (LANs), how do you execute a program on a remote machine?

5. If the file system of a remote machine is not mounted on your local machine but the machines are connected by a real-time network, which two network commands are available for copying files to and from the remote machine?

6. What is the name given to the group of utilities used for batch networking?

7. Which UUCP program is used to copy files from one system to another?

8. Which UUCP utilities are used to determine the status and success of UUCP transfers?

9. What is the usable (though primitive) dialup communications program that is part of the UUCP set? The program lets you dialup and log in to remote machines. How do you terminate a session with this program?

10. What is NetNews?

11. Of the two methods of communication, electronic mail and interactive conversations, which creates the least interruption to other people's work?

12. What are the two ways to address electronic mail (e-mail) to users on remote machines?

# Exercises

Use `cat` to display `/etc/hosts`. Then, run a remote shell command on two of the machines. If there is no `/etc/hosts` file on your machine, you are probably not part of a real-time UNIX network.

If you are part of real-time network, try to copy a file to another machine's `/usr/tmp` directory. Copy the file back to your machine. Try doing this with `rcp` and then `ftp`.

Try to copy a small file to the `/usr/spool/uucppublic` directory on one of the remote machines. Use `uustat` and `uulog` to monitor the progress. Enter your mail system to send a mail message to yourself. After sending the message, logout. Log back in and see whether your system notifies you that you have mail. Read the message you left for yourself, and delete it from your mailbox.

# Further Reading

*UNIX System Networking*, P.H. Wood and S.G. Kochan (eds.), Howard W. Sams & Company, Indianapolis, IN, 1989.

*UNIX Communications*, B. Anderson, B. Costales, and H. Henderson, Howard W. Sams & Company, Indianapolis, IN, 1987.

*Using UUCP and Usenet*, Tim O'Reilly, O'Reilly & Associates, Newton, MA, 1986.

# 11

# Advanced Utilities

## Contents

## Objectives

In this chapter you will learn

1. How to format data with awk

2. How to control projects with make

3. How to format and typeset text

With the exception of the editors and the shell, all the UNIX utilities introduced so far have had single, narrow uses. The breadth of UNIX utilities comes from the variety of programs and how they can be combined. This chapter introduces some utilities with a broad spectrum of uses, and with corresponding complexity of syntax.

# 11.1   *Report Generation* — awk

When you first start working with awk, you might be tempted to confuse the utility with Donald Duck's exclamation, "AAK!" After you gain more experience with this useful and powerful report-formatting language, you will give it the respect it deserves.

Although it is possible to invoke both awk and its directives on the command line, this is done for only the simplest of tasks. Usually the tasks and formatting are described in a directives file. Therefore, the usual syntax for invoking awk is as follows:

awk -f *<directives file> <source data file>*

Each directive consists of a regular expression followed by the actions to take when the expression is met by a line in the source data. The actions are enclosed in curly braces ( { } ). If no regular expression is associated with an action list, awk assumes that the actions are to be applied to every line. A trivial example prints every line in its entirety, as follows:

```
{ print; }
```

By default, white space (tabs and space characters) separates the information of each line into pieces. In the language of databases, each line of the data file can be thought of as a record, and each group of characters (other than white space) becomes a data field. Each field can be treated separately within the awk script: the first is $1; the second, $2; and so on. (The entire line is referred to as $0.)

```
$ cat test.dat
NEW     Watson   A12345   10.45
OLD     Jones    A2343    135.02
OLD     Smith    B1414    89.34
NEW     Chess    A1324    12.35
$ cat test.awk
/NEW/   { print $2, $4; }
$ awk -f test.awk test.dat
Watson 10.45
Chess 12.35
$
```

For every line with the key word NEW, the second and fourth fields are printed. This is just a demonstration of the basics of awk.

If all awk did was separate lines into fields and selectively print them, you could just as well use a combination of grep and cut. The awk program allows you to create and use variables without regard to how they might be used. In addition, there are two predefined conditions for action: BEGIN, the condition before data is read; and END, the condition after the data has been read. Put it all together and you have the parts for a little accounting report, as follows:

```
$ cat test2.awk
BEGIN  { total = 0.00; }
/NEW/  { print $2, $4; total += $4; }
END    {print "TOTAL", total;}
$ awk -f test2.awk test.dat
Watson 10.45
Chess 12.35
TOTAL 22.8
```

Note that each action in a group is terminated by a semi-colon. The actions associated with a condition can get complex, running on many lines and having conditions with their own group of actions. The rule is, all groups of actions must be enclosed in curly braces.

The awk program has many functions for both arithmetic operations and string operations. For example, the action total += $4; is a way of saying, "Add the contents of the fourth field to the total variable." Earlier, in the BEGIN condition statement, zero was assigned to the total variable. Although awk does not require you to declare and initialize variables before you use them, doing so is a good practice. Table 11-1 lists the arithmetic functions and operators in awk.

**Table 11-1.   The arithmetic functions and operators of** awk.

| Operator | Arithmetic Function |
|----------|---------------------|
| + | Add |
| - | Subtract |
| / | Divide |
| * | Multiply |
| % | Modulo |
| ^ | Exponentiate |
| ++ | Increment by one |

*Table 11-1 continues*

**Table 11-1.    The arithmetic functions and operators of** awk. *(continued)*

| | |
|---|---|
| `--` | Decrement by one |
| `=` | Assign value on right to variable on left |
| `+=` | Add by value on the right and assign to variable on the left |
| `-=` | Subtract by value on the right and assign to variable on the left |
| `*=` | Multiply by value on the right and assign to variable on the left |
| `/=` | Divide by value on the right and assign to variable on the left |
| `%=` | Modulo by value on the right and assign to variable on the left |
| `^=` | Use value on right as exponent and assign to variable on the left |
| `\|\|` | Logical OR |
| `&&` | Logical AND |
| `!` | Logical NOT |
| `<` | Less than |
| `<=` | Less than or equal to |
| `==` | Equal to |
| `!=` | Not equal to |
| `>=` | Greater than or equal to |
| `>` | Greater than |
| `( )` | Grouping |
| `atan2(y,x)` | Arctangent of $y/x$ (from $-\pi$ to $+\pi$) |
| `cos(x)` | Cosine of $x$, with $x$ in radians |
| `exp(x)` | Exponentiation function of $x$, $e$ to the $x$ |
| `int(x)` | Integer part of $x$ |
| `log(x)` | Natural (base $e$) logarithm of $x$ |
| `rand()` | Random number $r$, where $r$ is between 0 and 1 |
| `sin(x)` | Sine of $x$, with $x$ in radians |
| `sqrt(x)` | Square root of $x$ |
| `srand(x)` | Seed random-number generator with $x$ |

The format of the output from the previous example leaves a little to be desired. Using print might be easy, but you do not have much control over the format. The alternative is the printf function (borrowed from the C programming language). The syntax is as follows:

```
printf ( "<format string>", <argument list>);
```

The *format string* is an explicit model of the format. The position for argument substitution is indicated by a percent sign followed by an optional number of character positions and a required data type abbreviation, such as f (digits of a floating point number), g (variable-length floating point), s (character string), d (decimal integer), and a few others that are seldom used. The previous example is improved by the following:

```
$ cat test.awk
BEGIN   { total = 0.00; }
/NEW/   { printf("%10s %10.2f0, $2, $4); total += $4 }
END     {printf("%10s %10.2f0, "  TOTAL", total);}
$ awk -f test.awk test.dat
    Watson      10.45
     Chess      12.35
     TOTAL      22.80
$
```

Note that the format description for the floating point values has two parts. The first describes how many character positions are reserved to the left of the decimal value (including the position for the decimal point). The second part describes how many positions are to the right of the decimal point. All formatted fields default to right justification. A negative number in the format indicates left justification (for example, %-10s).

## String Data

The string capabilities of awk are not limited to output formatting. Table 11-2 lists the many functions awk has for handling string data.

If your data contains text, you do not want the field separator to be defined as white space; if so, the text will be divided into separate fields. You can change the field separator to any character you wish by redefining the internal FS variable in your BEGIN statement; for example, FS='|'. Other useful internal variables include RS (the record separator, default is newline), FILENAME (the name of the current input file), NR (the current record number), and NF (the number of fields in the current record). There are others, too.

**Table 11-2.** Awk **string-handling functions and operators.**

| Operator | Function |
|---|---|
| ~ | Test whether string on right matches string on left |
| !~ | Test whether string on right does not match string on left |
| > | Test whether string on left is (alphabetically) greater than string on right |
| < | Test whether string on left is (alphabetically) less than string on right |
| <space> | Concatenate strings (space character is operator) |
| gsub(*s1,s2*) | Substitute string *s2* for *s1* globally in input line, $0 |
| gsub(*s2,s3,s1*) | Substitute string *s3* for *s2* globally in string *s1* (returns number of substitutions made) |
| index(*s1,s2*) | Return position value of first occurrence of string *s2* in *s1* |
| length(*s1*) | Return length of string *s1* |
| match(*s1,s2*) | Test to see whether substring *s2* is in string *s1* |
| split(*s1,as*) | Split string *s1* into an array of substrings; similar to the relationship of $1, $2, . . . to the full record $0 (returns number of fields made) |
| split(*s1,as,fs*) | Split in the same way as above, but use fs as the field separator (returns number of fields made) |
| sprintf(*fmt,exps*) | Return a string using the same formatting rules as printf() |
| sub(*s1,s2*) | Substitute string *s2* for first occurrence of *s1* in full record, $0 |
| sub(*s2,s3,s1*) | Substitute string *s3* for first occurrence of *s2* in string *s1* (returns number of substitutions made) |
| substr(*s1,bp*) | Return the substring of *s1*, from position *bp* to end of original string |
| substr(*s1,bp,len*) | Return the substring of *s1*, from position *bp* for a length of *len* |

## Building an Application

When you are learning a programming language, building an application is usually an interactive process with many small steps. (As you become more proficient, there will be fewer and larger loops.) Test new methods one at a time using a small subset of the data that you plan to use later.

The following application is developed in steps. The first attempt has some new concepts: looping within a record and changing the record separator as well as the field separator.

A common application for awk is mailing-list formatting. Mailing lists can come from many different sources. The awk language can handle almost anything as long as it is text. In the following example, the source is assumed to be formatted as one *field* per line. Records are delimited by blank lines.

```
John Jones
2139 E. Grasshopper Road
Norton, AK 99872

Dr. Josef Kruchikakin
San Pedro Clinic
451 West Ridge Blvd.
Pecos, AZ   23145 USA

Armando Chumford
West Didley Street
Norton, NH 03411

Brandon Products, Inc.
2241 Elm Street
South New Brunswick, ND 77563

Uriah Heep, Esq.
Green Glass Works
Bottle Wash Alley
New London, CT 01234
```

The task is to convert the raw data to a format appropriate to sorting; that is, one record per line. The following is a rough attempt to make this conversion:

```
BEGIN   { RS="" ; FS="\n"; }
        {                  # for all records
              for ( i=1; i <= NF; ++i )
              {
```

```
                    printf("%s|", $i);
              }
              printf("\n");
       }
```

Let's take this item by item. The BEGIN action changes the record separator (RS) from the newline to the null string (""), and changes the field separator to the newline (\n).

The for statement causes the statements within the curly braces ({ }) to repeat. The expression in parentheses after for controls the loop. In the example, the controlling expression says, "Repeat the statements for each field in the current record." There are three elements to the controlling expression. These elements are separated by semicolons.

The first element, i=1, is the initialization. This operation happens only once, when the for statement begins. In this case, the counter, i, is assigned the value of 1.

The second element of the controlling expression is the test that determines when the for loop should run. When this test fails, the loop ends and the script continues with the next statement after the loop. In this case, the for loop will continue as long as the counter, i, is less than or equal to NF, the predefined awk variable for the number of fields found in the current record.

The third element of the controlling expression is the controlling action performed for each iteration of the loop. In this case, the counter is incremented by one.

The loop-controlling expression can be literally translated as, "Repeat the statements, starting with i equals 1, while i is less than or equal to the number of fields in the current record, incrementing i each time the statements in the loop are executed."

For example, there is only one statement in the following loop:

```
       printf("%s|", $i);
```

As mentioned earlier, printf is an awk command for *formatted* printing. The expression inside the parentheses describes *how* and *what* to print. A comma separates the elements of this expression.

The first element, the *how*, is a string of characters enclosed in double quotations. It uses the construction %s to indicate that a string variable is to be printed. The vertical bar character (|) is taken literally. You could read this format to mean, "Print some string variable followed by a vertical bar."

The second element, the *what*, is the name of the variable to be used. There should always be the same number of variables listed after the *how* string as the number indicated within it. In the awk utility, if a numeric variable, such as i in our example, is prefixed by the dollar sign, the value returned is field of that numeric position. Therefore, when i equals 5, the $i means the fifth field. (If the printf statement had used i rather than $i, awk would have printed the number 5 rather than the fifth field.

After the for loop in our example, there is another printf statement. This one has no variables; it is used just to print a new line ("\n").

Applying this awk script produces the following:

```
$ awk -f mlist.awk mlist.dat
John Jones|2139 E. Grasshopper Road|Norton, AK 99872|
Dr. Josef Kruchicakin|San Pedro Clinic|451 West Ridge Blvd.|Pecos, AZ USA|
Armando Chumford|West Didley Street|Norton, NH 03411|
Brandon Products, Inc.|2241 Elm Street|South New Brunswick, ND 77563|
Uriah Heep, Esq.|Green Glass Works|Bottle Wash Alley|New London, CT 01234|
$
```

The first draft managed to merge the multiline entries into single-line records, but output is not ready for sorting. The problem is that we want to sort on the ZIP code and the last name. Both of these fields are embedded in other fields. It is not hard to come up with rules for plucking the ZIP code off the last field; just look to see whether the last word in the field contains numerals. If it does, move it to the right of the last delimiter. (The method might not be apparent, but the rules are.)

Common to both the ZIP code and last-name problems is the requirement that we subdivide a field into subfields; in this case, words. The awk language includes many functions for string operations. The most appropriate function for this operation is:

split(*string, array, field-separator*)

An array is a variable with depth. A one-dimensional array (the only kind that awk implements) is like a list, each element of which has an index: 1, 2, 3, etc., analogous to fields within records.

The script in listing 11-1 builds on the awk script we have been developing. It splits the first field — the name field — into its parts, making each part a separate element in the output. (The line numbers are not part of the script. They are included for reference in the text.)

```
1   BEGIN   { RS="" ; FS="\n"; }
2     {
3        for ( i=1; i <= NF; ++i)
4        {
5            if( i == 1) # the first field, the name
6            {
7                count = split($i,subfield," ");
8                # print the last subfield first as a
9                # separate field
10               printf("%s|",subfield[count]);
11               for( j= 1; j < count; ++j)
12               {
13                       printf("%s ",subfield[j]);
14               }
15               printf("|"); # field delimiter
16           }
17           else
18           {
19                   printf("%s|", $i);
20           }
21       }
22       printf("\n\");
23   }
```

Lines 1 through 4 and 21 through 23 are right out of the little version of mlist.awk. The material inside the loop has changed considerably, however. The first addition is the following statement in line 5:

```
if( i == 1)
```

This statement is a *conditional*, a test (enclosed in the parentheses) which determines whether the following block of instructions (enclosed in the curly braces) is to be run. The test is, "Is the variable i equal to 1?" If it is, the statements in lines 6 through 16 are executed by awk. Note the key word else, line 17, followed by another smaller (and familiar) block. In other words, if the field number (i) is equal to 1, perform lines 6 through 16; otherwise, perform lines 18 through 20. This is how awk knows that it has to do something special on the first field. All other fields are handled the same old way: printf("%s|", $i);.

Now look at the instructions applied to first field (when i == 1). Line 7 says, "Split the field $i (in this case, $1 ) into an array, subfield, using the space character as the delimiter for determining where to break up the string. Put the number of elements of subfield in the variable count." Because we are dealing with the parts of a name, we could say, "Break the whole name into parts, each part in a separate element of the array subfield."

Now that the name is broken into parts, we can rearrange it. First print the last part, subfield[count], followed by a vertical bar (line 10). Then print the rest of the name, from the first to the last (lines 11 through 14). Finally, print another vertical bar (line 15).

The result of this version of the script is as follows:

```
$ awk -f conv1.awk mlist.dat
Jones|John |2139 E. Grasshopper Road|Norton, AK 99872|
Kruchicakin|Dr. Josef |San Pedro Clinic|451 West Ridge Blvd.|Pecos, AZ USA|
Chumford|Armando |West Didley Street|Norton, NH 03411|
Inc.|Brandon Products, |2241 Elm Street|South New Brunswick, ND 77563|
Esq.|Uriah Heep, |Green Glass Works|Bottle Wash Alley|New London, CT 01234|
```

The ZIP code is still part of the city-and-state field. See whether you can ascertain the difference between the way we deal with the first field and the way we deal with the last field (marked with asterisks) in listing 11-2.

---

***Listing 11-2.*** Mlist.awk *with statements to split out the ZIP code.*

---

```
 1   BEGIN   { RS="" ; FS="\n"; }
 2           {
 3                   for ( i=1; i <= NF; ++i)
 4                   {
 5                           if( i == 1) # the first field, the name
 6                           {
 7                                   count = split($i,subfield," ");
 8                                   # print the last subfield first as a
 9                                   # separate field
10                                   printf("%s|",subfield[count]);
11                                   for( j= 1; j < count; ++j)
12                                   {
```

*Listing 11-2 continues*

*Listing 11-2.* *(continued)*

```
 13                                          printf("%s ",subfield[j]);
 14                                   }
 15                                   printf("|"); # field delimiter
 16                            }
*17                     else if ( i == NF )  # the last field
*18                     {        # use a similar technique
*19                            count = split($i,subfield," ");
*20                            for( j= 1; j < count; ++j)
*21                            {
*22                               printf("%s ",subfield[j]);
*23                            }
*24                            # print the last subfield as
*25                            # a separate field
*26                            printf("|%s",subfield[count]);
*27                     }
 28                     else
 29                     {
 30                            printf("%s|", $i);
 31                     }
 32              }
 33              printf("\n");
 34       }
```

The program is growing fast. The result is the following:

```
$ awk -f mlist.awk mlist.dat
Jones|John |2139 E. Grasshopper Road|Norton, AK |99872
Kruchicakin|Dr. Josef |San Pedro Clinic|451 West Ridge Blvd.|Pecos, AZ |USA
Chumford|Armando |West Didley Street|Norton, NH |03411
Inc.|Brandon Products, |2241 Elm Street|South New Brunswick, ND |77563
Esq.|Uriah Heep, |Green Glass Works|Bottle Wash Alley|New London, CT |01234
$
```

Let's refine it some more. As you can see from the last two records, getting the last name into a field at the beginning is not as easy as we thought. Two obvious conditions make it an important problem. The normal, anticipated situation puts the last name as the last word of the first field. But what if the name field sometimes contains the name of a company? And what about titles that might be at the end of the name field, for instance, *M.D.* and *Jr.*? Because they include the dot used with abbreviations, we can recognize a good percentage of these variations. For the rest, a little empirical evaluation will help.

Now let's take this script to a solution of all these cases, just to deal with the simplest ones. This process will demonstrate a few points and show how quickly a simple script grows in complexity as finer details are addressed. Our latest result is shown in listing 11-3.

---

**Listing 11-3.**   Mlist, *with even more refinement.*

---

```
BEGIN     { RS="" ; FS="0; }
          {
                  for ( i=1; i <= NF; ++i)
                  {
                          if( i == 1) # the first field
                          {
                                  count = split($i,subfield," ");
                                  # print the last subfield first as a
                                  # separate field
                                  if( subfield[count] !~ /[.]/) # no dot
                                  {
                                          printf("%s|",subfield[count]);
                                          for( j= 1; j < count; ++j)
                                          {
                                          printf("%s ",subfield[j]);
                                          }
                                          printf("|"); # field delimiter
                                  }
                                  else # leave as is
                                  {
                                          printf("%s|", $i);
                                  }
                          }
                          else if ( i == NF ) # the last field
                          {       # use a similar technique
                                  count = split($i,subfield," ");
                                  for( j= 1; j < count; ++j)
```

*Listing 11-3 continues*

**Listing 11-3.** *(continued)*

```
                                {
                                        printf("%s ",subfield[j]);
                                }
                        # print the last subfield as
                        # a separate field
                        # if there are any digits (ZIPCODE)
                        if(subfield[count] ~ /[0-9]/)
                        {
                                printf("|%s",subfield[count]);
                        }
                        else # some plain text -
                                who knows what
                        {
                                printf("%s ",subfield[j]);
                        }
                        }
                        else # just a regular field - leave
                                as is
                        {
                                printf("%s|", $i);
                        }
                }
        printf("0);
        }
```

The result is as follows:

```
$ awk -f mlist3.awk mlist.dat
Jones|John |2139 E. Grasshopper Road|Norton, AK |99872
Kruchicakin|Dr. Josef |San Pedro Clinic|451 West Ridge Blvd.|Pecos, AZ USA
Chumford|Armando |West Didley Street|Norton, NH |03411
Brandon Products, Inc.|2241 Elm Street|South New Brunswick, ND |77563
Uriah Heep, Esq.|Green Glass Works|Bottle Wash Alley|New London, CT |01234
$
```

Some final words about this application before we continue. It would seem that once we have properly created the fields, we are ready to send the output to sort -t'|' +3 +0 (sort on the 4th and 1st field using the pipe as the field delimiter). The ZIP code is the last field, whether there are four fields or eight. The sort utility does not do well on key fields that float about. (The keys must be in constant positions or field numbers.) We need to move the ZIP code to the first field, by putting each of the fields in an array (reserving the first array position for the ZIP code) rather than outputting each field as it is read in. Then, after all the fields have been input and the array is filled, we output the entire record at one time.

The other option is to pass the output of one awk run into another. The second invocation of awk rearranges the fields before passing the output of that on to the sort utility. (Who said this was going to be easy?) The awk utility is useful, flexible, even powerful; but even with all that, and the corresponding complexity, awk might not be enough to solve what appeared (at first glance) to be a simple problem.

# 11.2  Managing Complex Projects — make

UNIX is well-known for its rich environment for programmers; many of its utilities have migrated to other systems. Some of the tools originally designed for software development have also migrated to other uses. One of these is a facility for managing the control of complex projects in which some elements of the project are dependent on changes in other elements. These kinds of relationships are common outside the programming world as well; for example, managing a research project or the design and fabrication of a building. The texts on UNIX software development document how to use the make dependency-tracing facility for programming. Here we will demonstrate how to use the same make utility for more generic purposes.

The make utility automatically keeps track of files that have changed and takes action on dependent files when necessary. The make program uses a file, known as the *makefile*, to describe dependencies and actions as follows:

- The names of the files that make up a system
- Their interdependencies
- How to regenerate the system when there are changes

This file is conventionally named makefile or Makefile, although any file name will do. However, if you use a different name, you must supply the name as an argument whenever you execute the make command.

Once you have described the necessary information in the file, the make program can take over and do the rest. Entering the command make causes the program to examine your makefile and regenerate the system according to the *rules* you have laid out in the file.

This automated method of program generation saves you the bother of having to keep track of the files you change and rebuilding each level yourself. Furthermore, it is common for several source files to depend on another source file. If you change the source file, you would need to rebuild all the files that depend on it. By specifying this dependency in the makefile, make will take care of rebuilding the necessary files whenever that particular file is changed.

The following example will show how make works. Assume that you have a project called bison that is dependent on the following four files: funding, staffing, research, and computing. If any of the four files changes, bison needs to be regenerated by collecting the four into a new version.

```
bison: funding staffing research computing
    collect funding staffing research computing > bison
```

The goals are on the left side of the colon (:); the dependencies are on the right side of the colon. The action(s) necessary to reach the goal are on subsequent lines, each prefixed by a tab. In the above example, collect is a program that uses the four dependent files to generate bison.

Also assume the following relationships: funding is dependent on the budget, expenses, and deposits (all data files); schedule is dependent on personnel and calendar (also data files); staffing is dependent on funding and another data file, personnel; and so on. The tree of dependencies is depicted in figure 11-1.

Note that the tree in figure 11-1 is not a simple tree; several elements affect more than one other element.

Listing 11-4 is the makefile.

**Fig. 11-1:**
*The dependency graph of the "bison" project.*

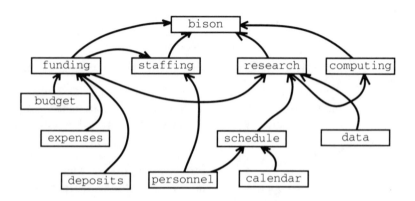

---

**Listing 11-4.** Makefile *for the bison project.*

---

```
# dependencies for the Bison Research Project
# Ben Smith — March 1, 1990

# "report," "balance" and "combine" are scripts for
# generating the appropriate files
#
# the source files are:
# calendar budget personnel deposits expenses data

bison: funding staffing research computing
        collect funding staffing research computing > bison

funding: budget expenses deposits
        balance budget expenses deposits > funding

schedule: personnel calendar
        report personnel calendar > schedule

staffing: funding personnel
        report funding personnel > staffing

research: funding schedule data
        report data > research

computing: research
        compute research > computing
```

---

Assume that the current directory contains the makefile and the source files previously mentioned. You can see what happens when you make the bison system by entering make bison:

```
$ make bison
        balance budget expenses deposits > funding
        report funding personnel > staffing
        report personnel calendar > schedule
        report data > research
        compute research > computing
        collect funding staffing research computing > bison
$
```

Entering the command `make bison` initiates execution of the `make` program. First, `make` looks for a file called either `Makefile` or `makefile` in your current directory. If either is found, it is taken as the file that tells what it is supposed to do. `make` scans `makefile`, looking for a line containing `bison` (the argument to `make`) followed by a colon. When it finds the following line, it looks to the right of the colon to see what files `bison` depends upon:

```
bison: funding staffing research computing
```

We specified that `bison` needs `funding`, `staffing`, `research`, and `computing`. Therefore, `make` starts with the first file in the list, `funding`, and scans `Makefile` to see whether a line containing `funding` to the left of a colon exists in the file. The following line:

```
funding: budget expenses deposits
```

tells `make` that `funding` depends on `budget`, `expenses`, and `deposits`. Again, each of these is the object of a search, but `makefile` has no instructions for these files. Now `make` searches to see whether these files exist (and they do). The last modification time, or time stamp, of each of these is compared to that of the dependent file, `funding`. If `funding` is older than any of these file or does not exist, the indented command lines below the dependency line are executed:

```
balance budget expenses deposits > funding
```

The `staffing` file, and then `schedule`, `research`, and `computing` are all created in the same fashion. Now, all the files on which `bison` are dependent are ready. Finally, it is all `collected` into `bison`:

```
collect funding staffing research computing > bison
```

For the initial run, all the files (except the basic data) had to be created. Now, however, everything is in order. Each dependent file is newer than the files on which it depends. The proof is as follows:

```
$ make bison
$
```

Nothing happened. This is as it should be. Now `touch` some of the files and run `make`. (The `touch` command updates the file's time stamp to the current time.)

```
$ touch funding
$ make bison
        report funding personnel > staffing
        report data > research
        compute research > computing
        collect funding staffing research computing >
```

```
bison
$ touch research
$ make
        compute research > computing
        collect funding staffing research computing >
bison
$ touch schedule
$ make
        report data > research
        compute research > computing
        collect funding staffing research computing > bison
$ rm bison
$ make
```

By comparing the messages from make with the makefile, you can confirm the logic of how it works.

You can ask make to make any goal that is defined, and it will make up to, but not beyond, that level of definition. For example, we could have ordered make computing, and the processing would not have included collecting the files into bison.

The most general definition is made nearest to the beginning of the file. The final definitions are for the subordinate goals on which others depend. It is common to have some independent operations included with the main one, just as a convenience. For example, you could define a goal, clean, that does not result in creating a file, but instead removes temporary ones. Just do not put it in the dependency list of any other goals. The clean goal is as follows:

```
clean:
      rm -f funding staffing schedule research computing bison
```

You can also collect lists of files into macros and define the operations using a special set of variable names and notations.

# 11.3  Text Formatting and Typesetting

Although text formatting and typesetting are single-function UNIX utilities, they are very complex and sophisticated subjects. Traditionally, UNIX text is formatted using nroff, a descendant of runoff, the original text-formatting program that inspired (sired?) many word processors and other text formatters. In typesetting, which requires font control and precise control of vertical and horizontal position, you use troff (typesetting roff) or its more modern child, `ditroff` (device independent `troff`). The general syntax of all these is the same. Lines that begin with a dot indicate controls for formatting and typesetting. We will restrict our discussion to this family of formatters, but they are not the only ones found on UNIX systems.

Another, quite different, text-formatting and typesetting system/language is TeX (TYPESET with a drop *e*, pronounced "tech"; the final character is the Greek letter "Chi"). Although the original intent of this system was to facilitate the typesetting of technical papers with complex mathematics, it has become popular on many different operating systems and in many environments outside academia.

Now much work is done with elaborate WYSIWYG (What You See Is What You Get) typesetting/desktop-publishing programs such as Frame and Interleaf. These programs use the high-resolution displays of workstations to show what your typeset output will look like, *as you enter and modify the text*. These expensive systems facilitate much of the production of the advertising literature that you see in magazines. Some magazines and newspapers are produced entirely on this kind of system, but neither `troff` nor desktop publishing systems can be easily pushed to generate the extremely high level of control required for this kind of publishing. Books and technical papers are another matter. Many, if not most, UNIX books are typeset using `troff`.

## The Traditional *nroff*

As we mentioned in the previous section, the `nroff` program controls the way a document looks when printed. This control is achieved by interspersing `nroff` "commands" throughout the actual text wherever such control is desired. There are about 90 different `nroff` commands enabling you to specify everything from the length of each line to the spacing to use between each line of the document. We will give you a brief introduction to `nroff` in this section by describing about a dozen basic commands. With this small set of commands you will be able to use `nroff` to format letters, memos, and even small documents.

## Setting Up the Page

The first thing to learn is how to tell `nroff` about the page you want the document printed on. Specifically, you should tell `nroff`:

- Where to set the left margin
- Where to set the right margin
- What the length of the page is

Set the left margin by using the page-offset command .po (*all* nroff commands start with a . that must be entered in the first column of the line). The .po command takes a parameter, the distance from the left edge of the paper you want as the margin. As a general rule, specify a unit of distance; for example, P for picas, i for inches, and c for centimeters.

Setting the right margin is a little different. Instead of specifying the distance from the right margin, you specify the total length of a line of text. You do this with the line length command .11. For example, assume that you are dealing with 8 1/2 by 11-inch paper. If you want both the left and right margins to be 1 inch wide, your line length should be set to 8 1/2 - 2, or 6 1/2 inches.

Now we come to the last command for specifying the physical layout of the page, .pl. This command specifies the length of the page. So, for 8 1/2-by-11-inch paper, you would write:

```
.po 1i          — 1-inch margin on the left
.11 6.5i        — 1-inch margin on the right
.pl 11i
```

## Filling and Adjusting Text

To make your document look better, try to make each line appear as uniform as possible. That is, try to align your right margin precisely. You can fill each line with as many full words as possible; you might hyphenate the last word to make the right margin even more uniform, and even add spaces between the words to ensure that the right margin is truly flush. The first action is known as *filling* the text; the second is *enabling hyphenation*; and the third is *adjusting* the text.

We will take a small sample of text to see the differences among these three actions. The sample is as follows:

```
$ cat sample
.11 50
.nf
Here is some sample text.
In the first case,
We'll show fill on,
in the second,
fill and hyphenation on,
and in the third fill,
```

```
hyphenation,
and adjust.
It is not necessary to have
hyphenation to get adjust
to work, just more pleasing.
$
```

The following output samples include a description of the formatting used. (The formatter does not print the descriptions, because the dot occurs in the first column.)

The output with fill on, but no hyphenation or adjust:

```
Here is some sample text. In the first case, we'll
show fill on, in the second, fill and hyphenation
on, and in the third fill, hyphenation, and
adjust. It is not necessary to have hyphenation
to get adjust to work, just more pleasing.
```

The output with fill and hyphenation, but no adjust:

```
Here is some sample text. In the first case, we'll
show fill on, in the second, fill and hyphenation
on, and in the third fill, hyphenation, and ad-
just. It is not necessary to have hyphenation to
get adjust to work, just more pleasing.
```

We ended up hyphenating only one word, but every little bit helps. Now, the output with the works — fill, hyphenation, and adjust:

```
Here is some sample text. In the first case, we'll
show  fill on, in the second, fill and hyphenation
on, and in the third fill,  hyphenation,  and  ad-
just.  It is not necessary to have hyphenation to
get adjust to work, just more pleasing.
```

Not bad at all! Note that a space has been added on the second line between the words *show* and *fill*. Three spaces were added to the third line, one to the fourth, and the last line was left as it was. After all, the last line is the end of the paragraph.

When you invoke the formatters, the default settings are the following: fill on, adjust on, and no hyphenation. Table 11-3 lists the filling, adjusting and hyphenation commands.

**Table 11-3.**  Nroff **filling, adjusting, and hyphenation commands.**

| Command | Function |
|---------|----------|
| .fi | Fill each line and wrap text into paragraphs |
| .nf | Don't fill lines, leave text in exact format of source file |
| .ad | Adjust text so that margins are in a line. This command can take the following arguments to describe how to fill: |
| |   l      Adjust left margin only |
| |   r      Adjust right margin only |
| |   b      Adjust both margins (default) |
| |   c      Center filled line between margins |
| .hy 0 | Automatic hyphenation off |
| .hy *n* | Automatic hyphenation on when *n* is any combination of these values: |
| 1 | Hyphenation on at all times |
| 2 | Do not hyphenate last line on a page |
| 4 | Do not hyphenate after the first two characters in a word |
| 8 | Do not hyphenate before the last two characters of a word |

## Skipping Lines

To skip a line in your text, insert a blank line at the appropriate point in your file. To skip more lines, just insert more blank lines in the file, or else use the nroff command, .sp, designed specifically for skipping lines. This command takes an optional parameter, the number of lines to skip. The following example shows how to skip four lines:

```
$ cat sample
.pl 1.5i
Skip 4 lines
.sp 4
```

```
here
$ nroff -Tlp sample
Skip 4 lines



here
$
```

## Centering Text

It is easy to center text within the line length. For a single line, place the .ce command before the line to be centered. You can center more than one consecutive line of text without including separate .ce commands before each line. Use a single .ce immediately before the group of lines to be centered. In that case, the .ce takes the following form:

.ce *n*

in which *n* is the number of lines to be centered, as in the following example:

```
$ cat sample
.ll 3.5i
.pl 1.5i
.ce 4                          —Center the next four lines
Ben Smith
Smith Design
17 Coyote Trail
Fairbanks, AK 99701
$ nroff -Tlp sample
                    Ben Smith
                  Smith Design
                 17 Coyote Trail
               Fairbanks, AK 99701



$
```

## Underlining Text

To underline text in nroff, use the .ul command. On the next line after this command, enter the word or words to be underlined, as in the following example:

```
$ cat text
.ll 3.5i
.pl 1.51
Underlining a
.ul
word
in the middle of a sentence is easy.
.ul
Underlining an entire sentence is just as easy.
$ nroff -Tlp text
Underlining a word in the middle of
a sentence is easy. Underlining an
entire sentence is just as easy.
$
```

Any text entered on the line following the .ul will be underlined by nroff. *Note:* beware that some printers might not directly support this capability. You might have to use a special filter program to get your text printed properly. See your system administrator if you run into problems with this command.

## Double-Spaced Output

To get double-spaced output, place the following command:

```
.ls 2
```

at the beginning of your text. You can actually supply any number you desire after the .ls. So, .ls 3 would give you triple-spaced output, whereas .ls 1 would produce single-spaced output (the default).

## Indenting Text

The .in command makes it easy to indent text. The number that immediately follows .in specifies the distance to indent from the left margin. The indentation remains in effect until another .in command is issued, as in the following example:

```
$ cat sample
.ll 3.5i
```

```
.pl 1.5i
Indentation is useful for setting off
certain portions of text.
.in .5i
Here we indent a half-inch from the
left margin.
.in 0i
And then we go back
$ nroff -Tlp sample
Indentation is useful for setting
off certain portions of text.
     Here we indent in a half-inch
     from the left margin.
And then we go back


$
```

## Going to a New Page

To start some text at the top of a new page, use `.bp`, which stands for *break page*.

## Give Me a Break

Normally, when `nroff` is operating in fill mode, it tries to fit as many words on a line as possible, by bringing in words from the subsequent lines. However, due to the effects of certain commands, there are times when `nroff` will not do this, even while operating in fill mode. In `nroff` terminology, these commands are said to cause a *break*. For example, the line-space command `.sp` causes a break. `nroff` will not use words that follow the `.sp` to fill the line before the break. Because this line will not be filled, it will not be adjusted either. The following example shows this effect:

```
$ cat sample
.ll 3.5i
.pl 1.5i
.fi
Here is some text to show the effect
of causing a break.
.sp
Notice that words from this line were
not used to fill in the previous line.
```

```
Also notice that the line before
the .sp was not filled or adjusted.
$ nroff -Tlp sample
$ nroff -Tlp fill1
Here  is  some  text  to  show  the
effect of causing a break.

Notice that words  from  this  line
were   not  used  to  fill  in  the
previous line. Also notice that the
line  before the .sp was not filled
or adjusted.


$
```

Breaks can also be caused in other ways. A blank line in your text causes a break, as does any line that *begins* with a blank space (but *not* a tab). .ce (center text) places a break after every line that is centered.

When you want to force a break, use the .br command. This command causes a break but has no other effect, as in the following example:

```
$ cat sample
.ll 3.5i
.pl 1.5i
.fi
This file is a demonstration of
the .br command, which is used
to create a break between filled
or adjusted lines.
This line is part
of the filled section.
This is as well.
.br
But this line is after the break.
.br
As is this.
$ nroff -Tlp sample
This file is  a  demonstration  of
the  .br  command, which is used to
create a break  between  filled  or
adjusted  lines. This line is part
of the filled section. This  is  as
well.
But this line is after the break.
As is this.
```

## Command Summary

To refresh your memory, table 11-4 summarizes the nroff commands described in this section. The third tells whether the command causes a break.

**Table 11-4.** Basic nroff Commands

| Command | Description | Breaks? |
|---------|-------------|---------|
| .ad | Adjust text (provided fill mode has not been turned off) | No |
| .sp 4 | Go to top of next page | Yes |
| .br | Cause a break in fill | Yes |
| .fi | Fill text (and adjust if .ad) | Yes |
| .ce $n$ | Center next $n$ lines of text (default 1 line) | Yes |
| .hy | Hyphenate text | No |
| .in $n$ | Indent $n$ from the left margin | Yes |
| .ll $n$ | Set line length | No |
| .ls $n$ | Set line spacing | No |
| .na | Do not adjust text (turn .ad off) | No |
| .nf | Do not fill (or adjust) text | Yes |
| .pl $n$ | Set page length | No |
| .po $n$ | Set left margin | No |
| .sp $n$ | Skip $n$ lines (default 1 line) | Yes |
| .ul $n$ | Underline next $n$ lines of text (default 1 line) | No |

## A Small Example

Now we are ready to look at a small, complete example. We will show how to format a letter using the nroff commands discussed in this section.

Assume that we have letterhead only 5 inches wide and 5 inches long. We will leave a 1/2-inch margin on both sides of the page.

The `nroff` input for the sample letter is as follows:

```
.po .5i                          — 1/2-inch left margin
.ll 4i                           — 1/2-inch right margin
.pl 5i                           — Length of page is 5 inches
.hy                              — Hyphenate words
.nf                              — Don't fill lines
.in 2.5i                         — Indent in 2.5 inches
July 1, 1990
.in 0i                           — Indent back
.sp 3                            — Skip three lines
Karl Flaccus
Howard M. Billete & Company
4302 W. 62nd Street
Indianapolis, IN 46268
.sp 2                            — Skip two more
Dear Karl:
.sp 2                            — And two more
.fi                              — Now fill and adjust
Here is my latest draft of the book
"Kittens at the Keyboard."  I hope you
appreciate the hard work that went into
getting this to you on time. I prefer
Scotch whiskey over warm milk, but will drink
either.
.sp
Please call me if you have any questions.
.sp 3                            — Skip 3 lines
Sincerely yours,
.sp 2                            — Skip 2 lines
Fritz Feline
.br
Author
```

We entered "no-fill" mode at the start so that the address lines were not filled by `nroff`. Later, when we were about to start the text of the letter, we turned fill mode back on. Because we never explicitly turned off adjust mode, all subsequent lines were filled *and* adjusted. (Remember, lines can be adjusted only if they are also filled. As long as adjust mode is not turned off with `.na`, lines will always be adjusted whenever fill mode is enabled.)

Running this text through `nroff` produces the following:

```
$ nroff -Tlp letter1
                        July 1, 1990




        Karl Flaccus
        Howard M. Billete & Company
        4302 W. 62nd Street
        Indianapolis, IN 46268


        Dear Karl:


        Here is my latest draft of the book
        "Kittens at the Keyboard."  I hope you
        appreciate the hard work that went into
        getting this to you on time. I prefer
        Scotch Whiskey over warm milk, but will drink
        either.

        Please call me if you have any ques-
        tions.



        Sincerely yours,


        Fritz Feline
        Author
```

## Formatting Larger Documents

The previous example shows how easy it is to format small documents with `nroff`. Actually, it is just as easy to format larger documents, except that when you deal with such documents you will need some features not provided by the commands we have discussed. The most obvious feature is page numbering; `nroff` does not number your pages for you. In fact, it does nothing special at all at the start of a new page. This can be annoying if you have to format multipage documents. Also, `nroff` does nothing special at the bottom of a page. It will just keep printing all the way to the bottom without leaving a margin.

To format multipage documents, insert the following lines at the start of the document:

```
.lt 6.5i                    -Change this to your line length
.de hd
.if \\n%>1 \{\
'sp .5i
.tl "-%-" \}
'sp |1i
.ns
..
.de fo
'bp
..
.wh 0 hd
.wh -1i fo
```

These nroff commands cause each page after the first to be numbered using the format -*n*-, in which *n* is the page number. This will appear centered on the page, 1/2 inch down from the top. These commands also cause 1 inch to be left at the bottom of each page.

## Add-On Packages

If you need still more text-processing features such as automatic footnote processing, the ability to define a block of text that cannot be split across two pages, automatically numbered lists, and so on, you will have to use the special nroff add-on package known as mm, which stands for Memorandum Macros. As the name implies, this add-on package was developed for the express purpose of formatting technical documents; in particular, memoranda. To find out how to use the MM formatting package, read *UNIX Text Processing*, listed in the "Further Reading" section at the end of this chapter.

The MM package is not the only commonly used macros package. Another one to try is MS. It is easier to use.

## Typesetting Text: *troff*

This entire book was preview typeset by a program that is nearly identical to nroff. Called troff, this program differs from nroff primarily in that it produces its output for higher-resolution devices such as laser printers and photo-typesetters. Because the commands for nroff and troff are highly compatible, nroff can be used to debug text before it is sent off to the laser printer or phototypesetter for printing.

Among the programs that work with troff are the following:

- tbl. Allows you to format tables for troff (and nroff).

- eqn. Allows you to describe complex equations using a simple language.

- grap. Allows you to include graphs in your documents. Graphs are described in a special language and then run through the grap program.

- pic. Allows you to include figures in your document. The figures are described in a special language and then run through the pic program.

- cip. Allows you to draw figures interactively on a Teletype 5620 terminal. The output from cip is actually a pic description of the figure.

- picasso. An advanced version of pic.

Initially, troff was designed with a specific phototypesetter in mind: the Wang Laboratories, Inc. C/A/T phototypesetter. Now, however, troff is device-independent; that is, it can be used to produce high-quality output on a variety of devices provided that they have the necessary hardware capabilities and support software. For example, with the proper software filters, troff output can be previewed on terminal screens and can be printed on laser printers such as Hewlett-Packard's LaserJet and Apple's LaserWriter.

### The Documenter's Workbench System

As of System V, the programs related to formatting text have been grouped into a package known as the Documenter's Workbench system. These programs include nroff, troff, device-independent troff, pic and sroff (a faster version of nroff). Also included is the MM memorandum macros package and picasso.

## 11.4 Summary

The awk utility/language is used to format reports from tables of information. It includes many mathematical functions and character-string search and format operations.

The make utility is used to manage projects with a complex array of interdependencies. A control file, the Makefile, describes the relationships and operations required to produce the intermediate and final goals.

The standard UNIX text formatting and typesetting programs are `nroff` and `troff`. They have nearly identical syntax, the commands of which are specified with lines that begin with a dot (`.`). Although you can create your own formatting macros, the MM (memorandum macros) and MS macros can fill most of your needs for pagination, paragraph formats, and list formatting. There are also other utilities such as `tbl` (for formatting tables) and `pic` (for generating diagrams).

# Review Questions

1. What is `awk` used for?

2. What are the two parts of all `awk` statements?

3. What string-pattern matching rules are used in `awk`?

4. What is the default field separator used by `awk`?

5. What two input conditions can be used to define actions to be taken at the start and finish of `awk` input?

6. In `awk`, how do you redefine the field separator to be a colon (`:`)?

7. What UNIX utility is used to take a file describing file dependencies and perform actions based on these relationships?

8. What is the default name for the file that describes dependencies?

9. What are the three parts of a dependency statement?

10. What are the names of two major UNIX programs used to format or typeset text?

11. The standard UNIX formatting and typesetting programs use commands in the text to control the format. What is the form of these commands?

12. What are the commands to turn text fill on and off?

13. What are the commands used to specify left margin (page offset) and line length?

14. How do you force a new page?

15. What is the MM package?

# Exercises

Build a small mailing list with last name, first name, one address line, city, state, and ZIP code. Separate each field with a vertical bar ( | ), and start each record on a new line. Have at least five entries in the list. Now use `awk` to create mailing labels that are always six lines long.

Enter the `bison makefile` in your system. Use `touch` and `make` to see all the different combinations of processes possible.

Copy half a page from this book in a raw format; in other words, do not pay attention to where the lines break within a paragraph. You can indicate where each paragraph begins by indenting a few spaces. Now use `nroff` and the line length and fill commands to see the different effects. Try at least four different line lengths with fill and adjust modes.

# Further Reading

*The AWK Programming Language*, Aho, Kernighan, and Weinberger, Addison-Wesley, Reading, MA, 1988.

*Managing Projects with Make*, Steve Talbott, O'Reilly & Associates, Inc., Newton, MA, 1987

*UNIX Text Processing*, Dale Dougherty and Tim O'Reilly, (Kochan and Wood, consulting editors), Hayden Books, Indianapolis, IN, 1987.

*Text Processing and Typesetting with UNIX*, David Barron and Mike Rees, Addison-Wesley, Reading, MA, 1987.

# 12

# Basic Shell Scripts and the Shell Environment

## Contents

## Objectives

In this chapter you will learn

1. The basics of how to write shell scripts for the Bourne shell

2. More about shell variables and environment variables

3. How to use variables and command-line arguments in shell scripts

4. How to control input and output of scripts

This chapter goes into more detail about the operation of the Bourne shell. It also introduces the unique shell programming language. In Chapter 3, "User Interfaces," you learned that the shells are the UNIX system's command interpreters. But shells can actually do much more than just start up other programs. They can manage your UNIX operations any way you want.

This chapter introduces the concepts of shell variables, environment variables, and the real power of the shell — shell scripts. Because the traditional shell is the Bourne shell, this chapter discusses these concepts using the Bourne shell's grammar and vocabulary. Chapter 13, "Advanced Shell Scripts," continues with more advanced shell script writing, still focusing on the Bourne shell. Then, Chapter 14, "Programming Other Shells," describes how the Korn shell and C shell differ from the Bourne shell and explains some tricks of shell scripts that take advantage of the special capabilities of each of the shells.

Shell scripts are nothing more than files that have shell commands in them. The shell takes its commands from the file rather than from your input at the command line. In this chapter, you are introduced to shell scripts that set up your environment when you first log in. Then you learn how to create your own commands with shell scripts, and how to make an interactive shell script.

# 12.1 Summary of the Bourne Shell

You must be well grounded in the grammar and vocabulary of the shell before you can use it effectively to construct compound command statements and shell scripts.

## Program Execution

Just about everything you enter at the terminal is interpreted by the shell. While waiting for you to enter a command, the shell displays your prompt, $. After you enter your command and press Enter, the shell analyzes the line you entered. This line is commonly called the *command line*.

Every command executed under the UNIX system has the same general format, as far as the shell is concerned:

*command arguments*

The shell treats the first word on the line as the name of a command to be executed. The rest of the line is interpreted as the command's arguments. Arguments are separated by spaces or tabs. So, for example, in the following command, grep is the command and Fox and phone_book the arguments:

```
grep Fox phone_book
```

As you saw in Chapter 5, "Regular Expressions," quotations can be used to group space-separated characters together into a single argument:

```
grep "Felix the Cat" phone_book
```

Here grep also has two arguments: Felix the Cat and phone_book.

The shell is responsible for ensuring that the arguments you enter are properly "handed over" to the program being executed. The shell then starts execution of the program. After the program has completed execution, control goes back to the shell, which displays the prompt and awaits your next command.

## File Name Substitution

If file name substitution is specified on the command line with the characters *, ?, or [...], the shell performs the substitution. Any substitution happens before the program is executed; the program itself is not involved.

## I/O Redirection

The shell also handles input and/or output redirection specified on the command line (by <, >, >>, or &). On input redirection, the shell opens the file for reading and "connects" it to the standard input of the program. Again, this connection happens before execution of the program begins, so the program does not even know (or care) that its input is redirected. The program merely reads its input from standard input; the shell takes care of the rest.

When output redirection is specified, the shell creates the file if necessary and "connects" it to the program's standard output. If the file already exists, its previous contents are lost unless the append characters >> are used for the redirection. As with input redirection, the program itself never has to worry about output redirection; it just writes its output to standard output, as usual.

### Pipeline Hookup

If the command line contains two programs connected by a pipe, as follows:

```
who | wc -l
```

the shell takes responsibility for connecting the standard output of the first program to the standard input of the second. It then starts execution of both programs. As with I/O redirection, neither program is aware that a pipe connects them: the first program simply writes its output to standard output, and the second program reads its input from standard input.

## 12.2  Shell Variables

As you learn to do more complex shell operations, you will find that you need a way to keep track of information that may change depending on the situation. *Shell variables* are the tool you need. The UNIX system and your application programs use a similar tool, *environment variables*, for the same purpose. Conceptually, both kinds of variables are the same.

A variable is an abstraction for data. It is a place to hold information or data. A simple analogy is a bucket and its contents. The bucket can contain water, paint, oil, or nothing at all. When you ask your assistant to "fetch the bucket," you are implying that you want the contents of the bucket, whatever that may be. Assigning a value to a variable is like filling the bucket. You are putting something in the variable.

Many programming languages have different variables for different information, such as integers, floating point numbers, strings of characters, and so on. The shell has only one kind of variable, the string of characters. You can still do numeric operations on a string of digits, but the operation must be capable of converting the string of digits to actual numeric (digital) values. Programs such as bc, the calculator, and test (see Chapter 9, "A Collection of Utilities") are examples of common utilities that can make this conversion.

### Variable Names

Like many computer applications and all programming languages, the shell allows the user to define *variables* and to assign values to them. A shell variable name begins with a letter (upper- or lowercase) or underscore character optionally followed by an sequence of letters, underscore characters, or numeric characters.

```
i5
length
Input_file
HOMEDIR
_cflag
```

The preceding examples are valid shell variable names, whereas the following examples are invalid names for the reasons stated:

| | |
|---|---|
| `5i` | — *Cannot begin with a numeric character* |
| `.length` | — *"." is not a valid character* |
| `file name` | — *Embedded spaces are not permitted* |

## Assigning Values to Variables

You can assign values to shell variables by writing the variable name followed by the assignment operator =, which is in turn followed by the value to be assigned to the variable:

```
length=80
```

This statement assigns 80 to the shell variable `length`. Note that embedded spaces are *not* allowed either before or after the equals sign. The following shell command assigns `ai.memo` to the shell variable `file_name`:

```
file_name=ai.memo
```

When you assign a string of characters to a shell variable, you should enclose the string within a pair of *double* quotations. In fact, if the string of characters contains embedded spaces, then the quotations are *mandatory*:

```
message="The system will be shut down at 18:00 for PM"
```

## Displaying the Value of a Shell Variable

Now that you know how to assign values to shell variables, you can see how to use these variables. The first thing to learn is how to access the value stored in a shell variable. The shell is unlike most other programming languages in how you reference the data stored in a variable. To access the value stored inside a shell variable, you must place a dollar sign immediately before the name of the variable, as in `$length` or `$file_name`.

To display the value assigned to a shell variable at the terminal, use the echo command. To assign 80 to the shell variable length and then display its value using the echo command, you could use the following sequence:

```
$ length=80
$ echo $length
80
$
```

The first command assigns the value 80 to the shell variable length. In the next line, the echo command displays the value of this variable. The following example uses the same technique:

```
$ message="System shutdown in 5 minutes."
$ echo $message
System shutdown in 5 minutes.
$
```

Wherever the shell encounters a dollar sign followed by a variable name, the shell substitutes the value of that variable at that precise point. This explains the output from the following sequence of commands:

```
$ length=80
$ echo The length is $length
The length is 80
$
```

Now see what happens when you try to display a shell variable that was never assigned a value:

```
$ echo $noval

$ echo :$noval:
::
$
```

The last echo demonstrates that an unassigned variable has no value. In shell programming terminology, this is known as the *null* value.

### Using Shell Variables

Shell variables are frequently used as command arguments, as in the following example:

```
$ file="ai.memo"
$ wc -l $file
        115 ai.memo
$
```

First, the string ai.memo is assigned to the shell variable file. Then the wc command is executed. The value of the shell variable file provides the file name argument to the command. Because you assigned the string ai.memo to this variable, the number of lines contained in the file ai.memo is counted and displayed at the terminal, exactly as if the following command were entered instead:

```
wc -l ai.memo
```

The option could be stored in a variable as well as the file name, as in the following example:

```
$ option="-l"
file="ai.memo"
$ wc $option $file
        115 ai.memo
$
```

As a final example along the same lines, consider the following, in which even the command itself is stored in a variable:

```
$ command="wc"
$ option="-l"
$ file="ai.memo"
$ $command $option $file
        115 ai.memo
$
```

You can assign the value of a shell variable to another shell variable as follows:

```
$ file="ai.memo"
$ save=$file
$ echo $save
ai.memo
$
```

A shell variable should almost always be preceded by a dollar sign, except when it appears on the left side of an equals sign, as in the following example:

```
$ file="ai.memo"
$ option="-l"
$ command="wc $option $file"
$ echo $command
wc -l ai.memo
$ $command
        115 ai.memo
$
```

Another common use for shell variables is assigning symbolic names to directory paths. For example, recalling the directory structure from previous chapters, suppose that you had to do a lot of work between two directories, such as the misc directory and the proposals directory. Your command sequence might include the following types of commands:

```
$ cd /usr/felix/documents/proposals
$ cp sys.A /usr/felix/misc/sys.A_save
$ ls /usr/felix/misc
        .
        .
        .
$ cd /usr/felix/misc
        .
        .
        .
```

Even when you use relative path names, the typing can get a little tedious when you perform operations between directories, such as moving or copying files or simply switching between them.

You can assign path names to shell variables and then use them in subsequent commands to help reduce typing, as in the following example:

```
$ p=/usr/felix/documents/proposals
$ m=/usr/felix/misc
$
```

The path name /usr/felix/documents/proposals is assigned to the shell variable p, and the path name /usr/felix/misc is assigned to the shell variable m. Now you can avoid some typing in future commands:

```
$ ls $p
new.hire
sys.A
$ cd $m
```

```
$ pwd
/usr/felix/misc
$
```

The next example shows how easily you can move or copy a file between the two
directories:

```
$ cp $p/sys.A $m
$ ls $m
sys.A
$
```

You usually should use more meaningful variable names than those shown,
particularly when you write command files. Meaningful variable names help
make your shell programs more understandable — both to you and others.


## Arithmetic Operations with Shell Variables

The Bourne shell provides no built-in mechanisms that enable you to perform
arithmetic operations on shell variables. If you think the absence of such
mechanisms is unusual for a programming language, you're right; but then, no
one ever claimed that the shell was your usual programming language!

Suppose that you had a shell variable called count and you set it equal to 0 with
the following statement:

```
count=0
```

If you attempt to add 1 to count, the result is as follows:

```
$ count=$count+1
$ echo $count
0+1
$
```

Once again, unlike most programming languages, the shell does not know how to
add 1 to a variable. All is not lost, however, because there is a command called
expr that shell programmers use to evaluate expressions in shell programs. Let's
experiment with this command:

```
$ expr 1 + 2
3
$ expr 5 "*" 10
50
```

```
$ expr 1+2
1+2
$ count=100
$ expr $count + 1
101
$
```

The `expr` command evaluates the expression given by its arguments and writes the result to standard output. In the first case, `expr` is given three arguments, 1, +, and 2. The `expr` then displays the result of the addition: 3.

In the second example, the * operator — used to multiply two integers — *must* be enclosed by quotations to prevent the shell from substituting the names of all of the files in the current directory on the command line. You could not place quotations around the entire expression, as in the following:

```
expr "5 * 10"
```

because `expr` would see this as only *one* argument rather than three.

The third example shows that `expr` does not interpret the following as you might expect:

```
1+2
```

This example relates to the same point made in the previous sentence: `expr` expects to see each term and operator as separate arguments. Arguments must be separated by white space.

The fact that `expr` writes its result to standard output is the key to performing arithmetic operations in the shell. By using the grave accent (`` ` ``) you can assign `expr`'s result to a shell variable because this is the mechanism you use to substitute the result (standard output) of a command as an element within another command:

```
$ result=`expr 1 + 2`
$ echo $result
3
$
```

(Note that the grave accent is *not* the apostrophe.)

The following example shows how you can use `expr` to add 1 to a shell variable:

```
$ count=100
$ count=`expr $count + 1`    —Add 1 to count
```

```
$ echo $count
101
$
```

Note that the Korn shell, ksh, does provide built-in integer arithmetic operations and also allows you to work with integers expressed in different bases.

# 12.3 Environment Variables

Environment variables are like shell variables except that they have special
significance to the programs you run. Application programs, editors, and some
utilities use the values in environment variables to set up how they behave. These
are the basic values that make a UNIX system unique to your needs.

You can see what your environment is by invoking the command env:

```
$ env
HOME=/usr/felix
PATH=/bin:/usr/bin:/usr/felix/bin:\
   /usr/local/bin:/usr/lbin:/usr/games:/usr/informix/bin:
TERM=ansi
HZ=50
TZ=EST5EDT
SHELL=/bin/csh
MAIL=/usr/spool/mail/felix
NAME=Felix the Cat
ORGANIZATION=<White Pine Club>
LOGNAME=felix
RNINIT=/usr/felix/.rninit
EPSPATH=./:/usr/felix/:/usr/lib/epsilon
MODEM=/dev/tty1A
E=/usr/felix/explore
EPSRUNS=Y
$
```

There are shell variables that are specific to the user. For example, there is a shell
variable HOME that contains the path to your HOME directory; another variable called
PATH describes to the UNIX system the directories to be searched whenever a
command is executed; and two shell variables called PS1 and PS2 describe your
first and second "level" command prompts. This section takes a little detour from
the subject of shell scripts to discuss the most common environment variables.

### There's No Place Like *HOME*

The shell variable HOME is automatically set to your HOME directory path when you log into the system. Try printing the value of this variable at your terminal and see what happens:

```
$ echo $HOME
/usr/felix
$
```

Several UNIX commands use the HOME variable to locate your HOME directory. For example, recall that entering the command cd with no argument places you in your HOME directory. The cd command determines where this directory is by examining your HOME variable. Study the following example:

```
$ pwd
/usr/felix/documents
$ cd                        — Change to HOME directory
$ pwd
/usr/felix
$ HOME=/usr/felix/misc      — Change the value of HOME
$ cd                        — Now see what happens
$ pwd
/usr/felix/misc
$
```

As you can see, changing the value of the shell variable HOME affects the execution of the cd command. Be careful: the operation of other commands might be affected as well.

### PS1 and PS2

By now you are accustomed to receiving a dollar sign prompt whenever the shell is waiting for you to enter a command. But what if you don't want your prompt to be a dollar sign? Well, you can easily change your prompt character at any time by changing the value of the shell variable PS1. First, see the current value of this variable:

```
$ echo "prompt is $PS1"
prompt is $
$
```

Now see what happens when you change it:

```
$ PS1=">"
>date
Mon Mar 20 16:16:05 EST 1989
>
```

(Recall from the discussion on quotations in Chapter 5, "Regular Expressions," that you must include > in quotations when assigning it to PS1; otherwise, the shell thinks you are trying to redirect output.) Note that as soon as you change the value of PS1, the value is changed to become your new prompt character for *all* subsequent commands. You can change the command prompt to any characters at all, as the next few examples illustrate:

```
>PS1="> "              — Add an extra blank space to the end
> date
Mon Mar 20 16:19:55 EST 1989
> PS1="=> "
=> PS1="Enter your command: "
Enter your command: date
Mon Mar 20 16:20:25 EST 1989
Enter your command:
```

The last prompt, Enter your command:, might seem a little extreme, but it does illustrate the point.

As you probably guessed, the prompt that is printed whenever the shell is expecting more input (normally >) can also be changed.

This prompt character is stored in the variable PS2:

```
Enter your command: echo $PS2
>
Enter your command:PS1="$ "          — Change this back
$ PS2="====> "                        — Now change this one
$ for n in 1 2 3
====> do
====> echo $n
====> done
1
2
3
$
```

(Chapter 13, "Advanced Shell Scripts," discusses the for command.)

Any value assigned to either PS1 or PS2 remains in effect throughout your login session. Next time you log in, the default returns to the values of $ and >. You will soon see how you can retain these changes across login sessions.

The shell commands we have used so far require only one line to be complete. The looping and switching commands introduced in Chapter 13, "Advanced Shell Scripts," require more than one line. If you are entering a very long command at the prompt, you can continue it on the next line by ending the incomplete command line with a backslash (\). The shell prompts you with the secondary prompt (normally >), and you can continue the command on the new line.

## Your PATH

Probably the most important shell variable is the one called PATH. This variable tells the shell exactly *where* to find *any* command you execute. Whenever you log in, your PATH variable is set to some default value, as in the following example:

```
$ echo $PATH
PATH=.:/bin:/usr/bin:/usr/felix/bin:\
/usr/local/bin:/usr/lbin:/usr/games:/usr/informix/bin
$
```

The PATH variable contains a list of *all* directories searched when you enter the name of a program to be executed. It also specifies the order in which the search is performed. The directories listed in the PATH variable are searched by the shell from left to right. A colon (:) separates one path from the next in the list. A colon at the end of the list means that the current directory is to be searched last.

The value of the PATH variable shown indicates that seven directories are to be searched whenever you enter the name of a program to be executed. First the present directory is searched, then the directory /bin, then /usr/bin, and so on. As soon as the shell finds the program in one of these directories, it executes it. If the shell fails to find the program, however, it prints the following message:

*command:* not found.

The nice thing about the PATH variable is that you can change its value to control the order of the search or to add new directories to be searched. You might have some of your personal utilities in your subdirectory /usr/felix/programs:

Without using the PATH mechanism, you must tell the shell explicitly where to find these programs. Assuming that you have a utility called nu (to count the number of users on the system) in the directory /usr/felix/programs, note what happens when you use the following command:

```
$ echo $PATH
PATH=:/bin:/usr/bin:/usr/felix/bin:/usr/local/bin:/usr/lbin:.
$
$ pwd
/usr/felix/documents/memos
$ nu                    — Execute the program  nu
nu: not found           — The shell couldn't find it
```

When you tried to execute nu, the shell used the PATH variable to determine where to search for the program. First it looked inside the /bin directory for nu. Because no executable file of that name was in that directory, the shell continued its search through the directory /usr/bin, then through the directory /usr/felix/bin, and so on through the list, looking in the local directory last. Because nu could not be found in these directories either, the shell printed its not found message at the terminal.

Now you can try it again, this time specifying a full path to the nu program as follows (a relative path could be used as well; see Chapter 4, "Files"):

```
$ /usr/felix/programs/nu
There are 9 users logged in.   — This time the shell found it
$
```

The shell went directly to the directory /usr/felix/programs to find nu, because specifying a path to a program always overrides the PATH variable.

Instead of having to tell the shell explicitly where to find nu each time you want to use it, however, you can add the programs directory to your PATH so that the shell automatically searches this directory. Assign the new search path to PATH by "tacking" your new directory onto the end of the existing PATH, as follows:

```
PATH=$PATH:/usr/felix/programs
```

Now you can execute a program contained in your programs directory from *anywhere*:

```
$ pwd
/usr/felix/documents/memos
$ echo $PATH
PATH=:/bin:/usr/bin:/usr/felix/bin:/usr/local/bin:\
    /usr/lbin:.:/usr/felix/documents/memos
$ nu
There are 9 users logged in.   — This time the shell found it
$
```

Note that PATH specifies only directories to be searched for programs and not for other files. Unless a relative or full path name is specified for a file, only the current working directory is searched for that file. But your shell scripts and many application programs can use environment variables to get paths to their special subdirectories. The following environment variables are examples of this use:

```
MAIL=/usr/spool/mail/felix
EPSPATH=./:/usr/felix/:/usr/lib/epsilon
CDPATH=$HOME
```

Before leaving this discussion, note that the shell uses the PATH variable to find standard UNIX commands as well. These are stored in the directories /bin and /usr/bin. If you did something naughty such as assign the null string to PATH, the system could not find *any* command.

## Exported Variables

Whenever you execute a shell program, the shell creates an entirely separate environment for that program to run in. This means the program gets its own distinct set of *shell* variables. The program cannot access or change any shell variables you assigned values to before executing the program. Also, when the program finishes execution, its environment goes away with it. Therefore, any variables set by that program do not exist after that program has completed execution.

```
$ cat > foo          — Quickly generate a shell script to display the value of x
echo :$x:
Ctrl-d               — End the file
$ chmod +x foo       — Make it executable
$ x=100              — Assign a value to x
$ echo $x
100
$ foo
::
$
```

The foo program could not access the value of x. Furthermore, had foo assigned a value to the variable x (which was already assigned the value 100), x would not change. Its value would still be 100 after execution of foo was completed.

There is a way to access the value of a shell variable from another program. A shell statement called export must be used. Its format is as follows:

```
export variable-list
```

In this format, *variable-list* is a blank-separated list of variables (*not* preceded by dollar signs). Any program subsequently executed can access the value of the exported variables — but the program still cannot permanently change the values. *Exporting is how we create global environment variables in the Bourne shell.*

Now go back to the `foo` program:

```
$ echo $x
100                          — It's still there
$ export x
$ foo
:100:                        — This time foo knows about x
$
```

## Your .profile

Assume that you have made several changes to your environment and you want to save them to be there the next time you log in. To be capable of saving the changes, the shell has the following convention: Every time you log in, the shell automatically looks in your HOME directory for a file called .profile. This is a shell script, which the next section discusses in more detail. If .profile is in the directory, the shell automatically executes the shell script. Because .profile is executed differently than other shell programs, any variables set or exported inside .profile remain in effect even after execution of .profile (that is, the program is executed as if it were entered at the terminal).

If your default shell is the Bourne shell or the Korn shell, you probably have a .profile right now without even knowing it! But assuming that you don't have one, let's set one up to do the following: include the programs directory in your PATH; change PS1 to "=>"; change your erase character from # to Backspace (Ctrl-H); print a salutation; and then tell us how many users are logged in. The process is as follows:

```
# Add "programs" to the search path and
# export it so other programs know about it

PATH=$PATH:/usr/felix/programs
export PATH

# Now change PS1
```

```
PS1="=>"

# Set erase character to Backspace

stty echoe erase Ctrl-h

# Print salutation

echo "Howdy! Great day for computing!"


# Tell how many people are logged in

nu
```

The shell can find the nu program because your PATH will be changed by the time you execute this program.

# 12.4  Shell Scripts

A shell script is nothing more than a text file with UNIX commands in it. The .profile, .login, .cshrc, and .logout files are examples of shell scripts. As you learned in Chapter 9, "A Collection of Utilities," some UNIX commands can get complex with all the arguments. Because shell commands also can get complex, it is usually easier to enter them in a file as text and then execute them with the following general form:

sh *scriptfile*

When you create a new file using an editor, the default permissions usually do not include *execute*, only *read* and *write*. To add execution permission to a file, you must use chmod. For example, to make the file dir executable, use the following:

```
$ chmod +x dir
$
```

So, for a simple example, you could have a file named dir:

```
$ cat dir
ls -l | cut -c30-
$ sh dir
sh dir
```

```
2039 May 21 13:58 part1
3998 May 21 14:00 part2
5226 May 21 14:08 part3
2696 May 21 15:32 part4
2523 May 21 15:35 part5
  47 May 21 13:50 title
  18 May 21 21:10 dir
 398 Feb 10 09:19 outline
$
```

You can simplify the act of invoking a shell script by changing the permissions on the script file to include execution. Then you need enter only the file name as a command. The caveat is that you must be running the same type of shell (Bourne, C, or Korn) as that for which the script is written. (Simple scripts might have the same syntax for all three shells.) Alternatively, you can specify in the script that the script is to be executed from a shell by entering the shell on the first line in the format of the following example:

```
$ cat dir
#!/bin/sh              — How to execute this file
ls -l | cut -c30-
$ chmod a+x dir        — Give the file execute permission
$ dir p*
```

```
2039 May 21 13:58 part1
3998 May 21 14:00 part2
5226 May 21 14:08 part3
2696 May 21 15:32 part4
2523 May 21 15:35 part5
  47 May 21 13:50 title      — Note that the argument was ignored
  18 May 21 21:10 dir
 398 Feb 10 09:19 outline
$
```

Not all UNIX systems and shells support the #! directive. For example, SCO Xenix and UNIX require that the first line be the shell "no operation" command, the colon (:), to force the Bourne shell interpretation.

You should put comments in your script files. Any text to the right of a hash mark (#) is treated as a comment, and the shell command interpreter does not try to execute it as a command. Of course, the exception is the #! directive on the first line.

Shell scripts are regular text files containing a list of shell commands. (They are also known as command files or shell programs.) There is nothing special about the commands in these files. They are the same commands that you enter interactively to the shell prompt.

Now that we have created a personalized directory listing command, we should give it a little more control and allow it to use command-line arguments.

# 12.5   Passing Arguments to Shell Programs

Arguments greatly increase the flexibility and usefulness of any program. Your shell programs can take arguments the same way other UNIX commands take them. When the program is executed, list the arguments on the command line in the usual way. To reference arguments from inside a shell program, use the following notation:

```
$i
```

In this notation, *i* is an integer from 1 through 9 that identifies the first through ninth arguments, respectively. For example, the first argument is referenced as $1, and the fifth as $5. (Actually, the first argument is the name of the script or program that is being invoked. It is referred to as $0. So, if you have a script named ap and you invoke it as ap cat dog, then $0 is ap, $1 is cat, and $2 is dog.)

```
$ cat args
echo ":$1: is the first argument"
echo ":$5: is the fifth argument"
$ args a bumblebee in her bonnet
:a: is the first argument
:bonnet: is the fifth argument
$
```

## Globally Referenced Variables

You can reference all the variables at once with the following notation:

```
$*
```

In the following example, p* is expanded to the names of all files that begin with p:

```
$ ls
args
part1
part2
part3
part4
part5
$ args p*
:part1: is the first argument
:part5: is the fifth argument
$
```

The first name in the list, part1, gets assigned to $1. Therefore, you could pass all of the arguments to the dir example by changing it as shown in this new version:

```
$ cat dir
ls -l $* | cut -c30-                    — Now we use arguments
$ dir p*
        2039 May 21 13:58 part1
        3998 May 21 14:00 part2
        5226 May 21 14:08 part3
        2696 May 21 15:32 part4
        2523 May 21 15:35 part5
$                                        — Note that all the arguments were honored
```

Now you can see a practical use of a shell program that takes an argument. Recall the phone directory file called phone_book (from Chapter 5, "Regular Expressions"):

```
$ cat phone_book
Farber, Ethan        555-4343
Iansito, Toby        555-1232
Levy, Steven         (907) 555-4432
Mead, John           555-5378
Sander, Rick         555-2109
Smith, Ben           555-2205
Snellen, Bart        555-9974
Weather info         555-1212
Wood, Pat            555-3193
Wood, Sam            555-3321
$
```

You saw how the grep command could be used to look up an entry in this file:

```
$ grep "Iansito, Toby" phone_book
Iansito, Toby  555-1232
$
```

Here is a simple shell program that takes a name as its argument and does a *lookup* of the name inside the phone_book:

```
# lookup a person's phone number    — A comment line
grep "$1" phone_book
```

The quotations around $1 are needed so that grep sees a name with embedded blank spaces as a single argument.

If these lines are in a file called lu (for lookup), and the mode on the file is "executable," you can use the script in the following way:

```
$ lu "Iansito, Toby"
Iansito, Toby  555-1232
$ lu "Master, Rich"
$
```

The last example shows what happens when a name is not found in the phone book: the command prompt returns.

Now that you have a shell program to look up phone numbers, you also like to have a program for adding a new entry to the phone book. The program should be straightforward enough. You can have it take two arguments: the name and the number to be added. These two arguments can be appended to the end of the phone_book file:

```
#
# add a name and number to the phone book
#

echo "$1\t\t$2" >> phone_book
echo "$1 has been added to the phone book."
```

The \t tells the echo command to insert a tab character at that point in the string. Now enter the shell program just shown into the file add, change its mode, and execute it:

```
$ add "Gualtieri, Dave" 555-5394
Gualtieri, Dave has been added to the phone book.
$ lu Gualtieri
Gualtieri, Dave      555-5394
$
```

The program seems to be working just fine. Take a closer look at the new phone book file:

```
$ cat phone book
Farber, Ethan        555-4343
Iansito, Toby        555-1232
Levy, Steven         (907) 555-4432
Mead, John           555-5378
Sander, Rick         555-2109
Smith, Ben           555-2205
Snellen, Bart        555-9974
Weather info         555-1212
Wood, Pat            555-3193
Wood, Sam            555-3321
Gualtieri, Dave      555-5394
$
```

Gualtieri was added to the end of the file, as we intended. However, note that the file is no longer in alphabetical order. This is not necessarily a problem, but you could modify your add program to sort the phone book after adding a new entry:

```
#
# add a name and number to the phone book
#

echo "$1\t\t$2" >> phone_book        # add name and number
sort phone_book -o phone_book        # sort the phone book
echo "$1 has been added to the phone book."
```

Because of the way output redirection works, the output of the sort cannot go directly to phone book; standard output cannot be directed to an input of the same command. The -o option on sort takes care of that problem.

Note what happens when you add another entry to the phone book:

```
$ add "Barker, Barry"    555-7776
Barker, Barry has been added to the phone book.
$ cat phone book
Barker, Barry            555-7776
Farber, Ethan            555-4343
Gualtieri, Dave          555-5394
Iansito, Toby            555-1232
Levy, Steven             (907) 555-4432
Mead, John               555-5378
Sander, Rick             555-2109
Smith, Ben               555-2205
Snellen, Bart            555-9974
Weather info             555-1212
Wood, Pat                555-3193
Wood, Sam                555-3321
$
```

### Predefined Script Variables

Besides the $* variable (for all the arguments), the shell has another variable, $#, that is automatically set when you execute a shell program. $# is set to the *number* of arguments passed to the program. For example:

```
cat num                          — An illustrative script
echo Number of arguments is $#.
$ num one                        — Now let's experiment
Number of arguments is 1.
$ num one two three
Number of arguments is 3.
$ num "one two three"
Number of arguments is 1.
$ num
Number of arguments is 0.
$
```

$# tells you the number of arguments that were passed to the program. This information is useful when you write a shell program that expects a precise number of arguments. You will soon see how to test the value of this variable to find out whether the correct number of arguments were supplied to the program.

## 12.6  Interactive Output and Input

You will often need the shell script to interact with you when it is running. The most commonly used command for generating output to the terminal is echo, and the most commonly used command for reading input from the terminal is read. These two commands give you what you need for interactive scripts. (Both the echo and read commands are internal to the shell, and therefore behave a little differently depending on which shell you are running.)

As demonstrated in the previous example of the script that added a name and number to a phone book, the echo command gives special meaning to certain characters that are preceded by a backslash \. These characters are quite useful because they give you more flexibility and control in your output displays.

### Moving to the Next Line: \n

If the echo command sees a backslash character followed immediately by the letter n, the cursor goes to the beginning of the next line. The following examples help make this point clear. A word of caution before you proceed: to remove the backslash character's special meaning to the shell, these special echo characters *must* be enclosed in quotations (either single or double).

```
$ echo "one\ntwo\nthree"
one
two
three
$ echo this is what happens\nif you forget the quotes
this is what happensnif you forget the quotes
$ echo 'skip a\n\nline'
skip a

line
$
```

In this example, the first \n causes the cursor to move to the beginning of the next line, and the second one causes it to go down another line. The net effect is to insert a blank line between skip a and line.

### Staying on the Same Line: \c

Normally, after echo displays its last argument, it goes to the beginning of the next line; that is, echo outputs a newline as its last action. This action is usually what you want. However, suppose that first you want to display one part of a message, and later in the program you want to display another part of the message *on the same line*. Or, as you will see later, suppose that you want to display a message and then enter some data right after that message on the same line.

If you tack the characters \c to the end of an echo command, echo does *not* automatically go to the beginning of the next line; instead, the command stays right where it is.

```
$ echo "stay on this line\c"
stay on this line$
```

The \c causes the echo command to suppress the newline. Therefore, the shell's prompt is printed right after the last character displayed by echo.

Enter the following commands into a file called testx:

```
echo "one\c"
echo "two\c"
echo "three"
```

Now change the mode on the file so that it can be executed; then run it.

```
chmod +x testx
$ testx
onetwothree
$
```

As a final example, enter the following lines into a file called test2:

```
for i in 0 1 2 3 4 5 6 7 8 9
do
        echo "$i\c"
done

echo
```

Then execute the file:

```
$ chmod +x test2
$ test2
0123456789
$
```

The string $i\c is enclosed in double quotations rather than apostrophes so that the shell substitutes the value of the shell variable i. (Of course, you could use $i"\c" or $i'\c' instead.)

The purpose of the last echo is to go to the next line. If the echo had not been included, then the shell's prompt, $, would appear right after the 9.

### *Moving to the Next Tab Stop:* \t

Try pressing the Tab key on your keyboard and see what happens. (If your keyboard does not have this key, press Ctrl-I instead.) If your terminal is like most others, then each time you press this key, the cursor moves across the screen. On most terminals, the cursor moves over eight character positions each time the Tab key is pressed. The first tab position is column 1, the second column 9, the third column 17, and so on. Tabs are useful for aligning data in columnar format. You can move to the next tab position on the line in an echo command by using the characters \t.

### *Reading Data from the Terminal*

Your shell program might require the user to enter some data from the terminal. The shell statement read exists for this purpose. Its general format is simple enough:

    read *variable-list*

Execution of this statement causes the shell to read in a line from the terminal and assign the values that are read to the shell variables specified in *variable-list*. If only one variable is listed, the entire line is assigned to that variable. Values entered are delimited by blank spaces or tabs.

```
$ read a b c
one   two   three
$ echo ":$a:$b:$c:"
:one:two:three:              — Blanks were removed
$ read line                  — Only one variable
this is a line of text
$ echo "$line"
this is a line of text       — Entire line was assigned
$ read a b
first and then the rest
$ echo ":$a:$b:"             — Rest of line assigned to last variable
:first:and then the rest
$
```

Now put the `read` statement to work in an actual program. The purpose of this program is to show how you can develop your own commands that prompt the user for information. You will create a program called `copy` to copy files. The program does not take arguments; rather, it prompts the user for the names of the source and destination files. After the user has entered this information, the `copy` program calls the `cp` command to copy the files.

```
#
# Program to copy files
#

echo "Source file: \c"
read source

echo "Destination file: \c"
read destination

cp $source $destination
```

The `\c` characters are placed in the two `echo`s so that the user can enter the data on the same line as the prompt message.

Now, to test it:

```
ls                              — Let's see what's around
names
names1
names2
$ copy
Source file: names
Destination file: test
$ ls
names
names1
names2
test                            — The new file is there
$ sdiff -s names test            and it's identical to the original
$
```

A subtle point worth noting about the `copy` program: Because you were careful *not* to enclose the shell variables `destination` and `source` inside quotations in the `cp` command, the shell performs file name substitution on these arguments if specified:

```
$ ls *2
names2
$ copy
Source file: *2
Destination file: test2
$ sdiff -s names2 test2
$
```

Some interesting modifications can be made to the copy program to make it more useful. For example, you can enable the user to enter the arguments on the command line if desired. The program can test for this condition and directly call the cp command with the arguments entered on the line (remember $* ?).

Another worthwhile change is to test whether the destination file already exists. If it does exist, the program could ask the user whether to proceed with the copy. If the user decides not to proceed, the program could simply ignore the copy request. Novice UNIX users would find this modification helpful to keep them from accidentally overwriting their files. (You can even make your own version of the mv command to do the same type of check.)

The main point to remember is that the UNIX system provides you with the power and flexibility to effectively customize UNIX commands. The fact that cp is a built-in UNIX command, whereas copy is a custom-written command, can remain unknown to other users.

# 12.7  Summary

Shell variables, environment variables, and command-line arguments to a shell script are all handled much the same way within shell scripts.

Your .profile file (in your HOME directory) is a shell script that is automatically run when you log in (provided that the Bourne shell is your default shell).

Simple shell scripts are no more than a text file containing a list of commands as they might be typed to the shell command-line interpreter.

To make shell scripts interactive, use the echo and read commands for output and input, respectively.

# Review Questions

1. What is a shell script?

2. Which part of the UNIX system is responsible for ensuring that the arguments you enter at the command line are properly "handed over" to the program being executed?

3. What happens to the characters *, ?, and [...] when they are included (not enclosed in quotations or escaped) on the command line?

4. What part of the system is responsible for handling input/ouput file redirection? (Kernel? Shell? Application program?)

5. What is used to hold information or data for the shell or a computer program?

6. What is a user's *environment*?

7. How do you output newlines with echo? How do you output newlines with tabs?

8. What command is used to read from the terminal?

# Exercises

Write a Bourne shell script that takes two words from the command line and displays them in reverse order.

Write a Bourne shell script that displays the number of *different* users currently on the system. You need to use pipes and sort -u among other things.

Write a Bourne shell script that displays a sorted list of all of your environment variables.

Write a shell script that asks for a file name and then searches for all occurrences of the name, printing the location of each of the occurrences.

# Further Reading

*UNIX Shell Programming, Revised Edition,* Stephen G. Kochan and Patrick H. Wood, Hayden Book Company, 1990.

# 13

---

# Advanced Shell Scripts

## Contents

## Objectives

In this chapter you will learn

1. How to use the Bourne shell's facilities for selectively processing commands and blocks of commands

2. How to use loops (iterations) in your shell scripts

3. Some ways to control the flow of a shell script

The purpose of shell scripts is to automate your work and make your life easier, not more complex. Shell scripts give the repetitive work to the computer, leaving the interesting and serious work for you. But shell scripts are programs. Although this book is for UNIX *users*, not programmers, you have written some programs if you have come this far, and it is time to add some sophistication to your programs (scripts).

The scripts in Chapter 12 consisted of a list of instructions for the shell. When the shell executed the script, it started at the top of the list and executed each command until it reached the end of the list. In this chapter you learn how to make your scripts selectively and repetitively execute commands; this is called *flow control*. Again, we focus on the Bourne shell. The other shells are discussed in Chapter 14.

# 13.1  Compound and Complex

In Chapter 8, "Processes: Concepts and Connections," you were introduced to conditional program execution using the && and the || notations. Far more flexible and widely applicable shell command constructs exist, however. The first of these is the `if ... then ... fi` construct. Other conditional and looping constructs alter the otherwise linear processing of script statements; they are referred to as *flow-control* statements.

These command constructs can be used on the command line. Because you cannot edit the Bourne shell command line (other than to delete or re-enter), however, you use most of these constructs inside shell scripts — files of shell commands. Even so, for these first examples we assume that you are a perfect typist and know exactly what you are doing. In other words, the examples show what happens if you enter the flow-control constructs at the shell prompt.

### The *if Statement*

Computers can produce results quickly, but they are not intelligent. The "smarts" of a computer come from the skill of the person giving the instructions. The computer's capability for making decisions is usually built into the lowest levels of its hardware. It can make the wrong decision, however, just as fast as it makes a correct one. It doesn't know (or care) which way the decision falls. Of course, you *do* care. Therefore you must give the computer explicit instructions as to how to make decisions.

The if statement implements the decision process in the shell language. In its basic form, the if statement allows you to make the script take an alternate path: "If some condition exists, then follow these instructions." With the Bourne shell, the general format of the if statement is:

```
if condition
then
        command
        command
        . . .
fi
```

The *condition* is a command that executes with an error status. Think of it this way: if the value of *condition* is valid, or True (error status of zero), then the commands enclosed between then and fi (the body) are executed; if the condition is False, they are skipped. (See figure 13-1 for a diagram of the basic if statement. When the if condition is true, block B is executed; otherwise the script flows directly from block A to block C.)

**Fig. 13-1:**
The basic if statement.

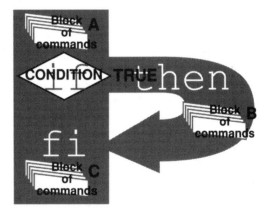

Any command can be used as a condition. If the command exits with a zero exit (error) status, it is equivalent to true; a non-zero status is equivalent to false. You can also use the key words true or false to force a condition. When the command used as a condition returns an error, it is interpreted as false.

## Determining a Condition with test

The *condition* might be a test to determine the value of a shell variable or the existence or permissions of a file. These tests are enclosed in brackets. A space separates the brackets from the test, and the space is absolutely necessary because the left bracket is actually the `test` command, which is external to the shell. The space separates `test` from its arguments. The general format is as follows:

[ *test-expression* ]

or

*test test-expression*

The following sequence displays the message `Hello, felix` if the value of the variable `user` is equal to `felix` (assume here that it is):

```
$ echo $user
felix
$ if [ $user = felix ]
> then
>        echo Hello, felix
> fi
Hello, felix
$
```

The *condition*, [ `$user = felix` ], tests whether the shell variable `user` is equal to the character string `felix`. If it is, the `echo` command is executed; otherwise it is ignored. The process starts at the top of the diagram and flows along either the left or right branch, depending on the condition returned by the `test` ([).

There are other *relational operators* you can use besides the equality operator =. The more commonly used operators are summarized in Table 13-1.

**Table 13.1.   The operators of the test command.**

| Operator | Meaning |
| --- | --- |
| -r *string* | Is *string* the name of a readable file? |
| -w *string* | Is *string* the name of a writable file? |
| -x *string* | Is *string* the name of an executable file? |
| -f *string* | Is *string* the name of a regular file? |
| -d *string* | Is *string* the name of a directory? |
| -s *string* | Is *string* the name of a file that is not empty? |

**Table 13.1.  The operators of the test command.** *(continued)*

| | |
|---|---|
| -z *string* | Is *string* a null string (length zero)? |
| -n *string* | Is *string* not a null string? |
| *string* = *string* | Are *strings* identical? |
| *string* != *string* | Are *strings* different? |
| *string* | Is *string* not a null string? |
| *value* -eq *value* | Are *values* equal? |
| *value* -ne *value* | Are *values* not equal? |
| *value* -gt *value* | Is *value* on left greater? |
| *value* -ge *value* | Is *value* on left greater or equal? |
| *value* -lt *value* | Is *value* on left less? |
| *value* -le *value* | Is *value* on left less or equal? |
| ! | Not |
| -a | And |
| -o | Or |
| ( ) | Parenthesis for grouping subexpressions |

Many of the file attribute tests are not covered in this book, but are covered in *UNIX Shell Programming* and *UNIX System Administration.*

An expression can be joined with either the *and* operator, -a, or the *or* operator, -o. The following expression:

```
[ $i -gt 5 -a $i -le 100 ]
```

is true only if the value of the shell variable i is greater than 5 and less than or equal to 100. The following expression:

```
[ $env = UNIX -o $group = GP ]
```

is true if the shell variable env equals UNIX *or* the variable group equals GP.

You should enclose shell variables (on either side of a relational operator) within double quotations. Otherwise, the shell issues an error message if the variable is null or contains blanks:

```
$ user=""                              – Intentionally set user null
$ if [ $user != felix ]
> then
>              echo I was expecting felix
> fi
test: argument expected
$
```

When the condition of an if statement is false, the flow of the script *continues on immediately after the terminating* fi, unless you have included an else.

### The *else* Clause

The Bourne shell provides an else clause to the if. You can use else to execute statements when the if condition proves false. When you use the else construct, you create an either/or situation. The diagram of the if ... then... else ... fi construct, shown in figure 13-2, shows that when the if condition is true, block B is executed; when false, block C is executed. Both continue with block D.

**Fig. 13-2:**
*The* if *statement with the* else *alternate.*

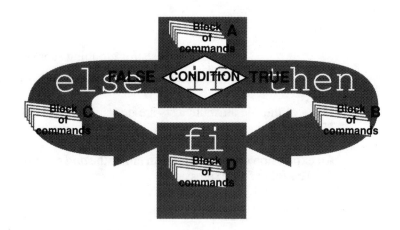

The general format of the if-else is as follows:

```
if condition
then
   command
   command
   ...
else
```

```
        command
        command
          . . .
   fi
```

If the result of *condition* is true, the commands enclosed between the `then` and `else` are executed; otherwise, the statements between the `else` and `fi` are executed. In either case, only one set of commands is executed, never both.

The script in listing 13-1 is an example of the use of the `else` and `$#` variables (see Chapter 12). It is a modification of the lookup program `lu` (also from Chapter 12) that includes a test to ensure that exactly one argument is supplied on the command line.

---

**Listing 13-1.**   Lu *version 2.*

---

```
# lookup a person's phone number in the phone book

if [ $# -ne 1 ]
then
     echo "\nUsage: lu name\n"
else
     grep "$1" phone_book
fi
```

---

If the number of arguments does not equal 1, the `echo` command displays the proper command usage; otherwise, the `grep` is invoked to search phone book for the specified name.

```
$ lu

Usage: lu name

$ lu Iansito, Toby

Usage: lu name

$ lu "Iansito, Toby"
Iansito, Toby    937-1232
$ lu "Master"
$
```

This version of lu reminds you that the program displays nothing if a name is not found in the phone book. You might want to change the program to make it display a message when it cannot find someone's name.

You know that grep produces no output when it finds no lines that match the given pattern. Using this fact and the grave accent (`), you can assign the output of the grep to a shell variable and then test the variable to see whether it is null (that is, has zero length). If it is null, you know that grep could not find the name in the file. In that case, you can display an appropriate message at the terminal. If it is not null, the variable contains the result of grep, so you can simply display it at the terminal.

Listing 13-2 is the once-again modified version of lu.

---

**Listing 13-2.**   Lu *with some error handling.*

---

```
# lookup a person's phone number in the phone book

if [ $# -ne 1 ]
then
        echo "\nUsage: lu name\n"
else
        output=`grep "$1" phone_book`

        if [ -z "$output" ]
        then
                echo "I couldn't find $1 in the phone book"
        else
                echo "$output"
        fi
fi
```

---

As you can see in listing 13-2, including ifs inside other ifs is perfectly valid. In fact, the nesting can go as deep as you like. Just remember that for each if you must include a corresponding fi.

```
$ lu Sander
Sander, Rick     343-2109
$ lu Archer
```

```
I couldn't find Archer in the phone book
$ lu Wood
Wood, Pat                           421-3193
Wood, Sam                           778-3321
$
```

The output from the last example explains why you include $output inside double quotations in the echo command of the program. If you do not do this, the shell removes the newline characters from output before giving the argument to echo, which results in, for example, two Wood entries on the same line.


### Multiple Choice with *elif*

Some scripts have to determine one condition from many possibilities. The construct might look something like this:

```
if condition
then
    command
else
    if condition
    then
        command
    else
        if condition
        then
            command
        else
            command
        fi
    fi
fi
```

This construct can be simplified with elif, a combined else and if:

```
if condition
then
    command
elif condition
then
    command
elif condition
then
    command
```

```
else
        command
fi
```

Suppose, for example, that you want to create a shell program displaying the salutation "Good morning" when it is after midnight; "Good afternoon" from noon to 6 p.m.; and "Good evening" from 6 p.m. to midnight. The structure should look something like the following:

```
if          it's after midnight and before noon
then
            display Good morning.

        elif  it's after noon and before 6 PM
        then
                display Good afternoon.
        else
                display Good evening.
        fi
fi
```

To translate the previous example into a shell program, you must first figure out how to make the tests on the time of day. You know that the date command gives you the time (plus some other information);

```
$ date
Sun Mar 19 13:43:00 EST 1989
$
```

All you really need to know is the hour of the day. You can use the cut command to get the hour of the day out of date because the hour always appears in columns 12-13 of date's default output:

```
$ date | cut -c12-13
13
$
```

You could also just use the date format option to limit the output to the hour. There is usually more than one way to solve a problem.

Listing 13-3 is a script (named salute) that uses the date to print the salutation.

**Listing 13-3.**   *The* salute *script.*

```
#
# shell program to execute date and then display
# Good morning, Good afternoon, or Good evening, as
# appropriate
#

hour=`date | cut -c12-13`

if [ $hour -ge 0 -a $hour -lt 12 ]
then
        echo "Good morning."
elif [ $hour -ge 12 -a $hour -lt 18 ]
then
        echo "Good afternoon."
else
        echo "Good evening."
fi
```

Let's see whether salute works for the present time:

```
$ date
Sun Mar 18 13:59:11 EST 1990        — We know it's afternoon
$ salute
Good afternoon.                     — Seems okay
$
```

## Multiple Choice with case

The shell case statement is useful when you want to compare a value against a whole series of values. This comparison can be done with an if-elif statement chain, but the case statement is more concise and is also easier to write and read. The general format of this statement is as follows:

```
case value
in
        pattern1 )  command
                        command
                        ...
                        command;;
        pattern2 )  command
```

```
                              command
                                ...
                              command;;
            ...
      patternx )   command
                              command
                                ...
                              command;;
    esac
```

Operation of a `case` statement proceeds as follows: *value* is successively compared against *pattern1, pattern2,* and so on through *patternx.* When a match is found, the commands listed after the matching patterns are executed until a double semicolon ( ; ; ) is reached. At that point, the `case` statement is terminated. If *value* does not match any of the specified patterns, no action is taken and the entire `case` is effectively "skipped." If the pattern * (the catch-all) is included as the *last* pattern in the `case`, the commands that follow are executed when none of the preceding patterns match.

As a simple example of a `case` statement, the program in listing 13-4 displays the English equivalent of a number from 0 through 9. This number is given as an argument to the command. If a value other than 0 through 9 is specified, the program displays the message `Invalid argument`.

---

**Listing 13-4.**   `Digit`, *a script for English equivalents of digits.*

---

```
    #
    # Display the English equivalent of a digit
    #

    case "$1"
    in
        0 )              echo zero;;
        1 )              echo one;;
        2 )              echo two;;
        3 )              echo three;;
        4 )              echo four;;
        5 )              echo five;;
        6 )              echo six;;
        7 )              echo seven;;
        8 )              echo eight;;
        9 )              echo nine;;
        * )              echo Invalid argument;;
    esac
```

---

Running the `digit` script looks like the following:

```
$ digit 5
five
$ digit x
Invalid argument
$ digit 8
eight
$
```

The `case` statement is frequently used by shell programmers to write programs that take options. Again, looping statements are valuable for this kind of processing.


# 13.2    Iterative Statements — Loops

*Honor all ancestors. Strike while the iron is hot. Stir until well mixed.* Instructions like these imply processing a list, or repetition while or *until a condition is met.* All programming languages provide mechanisms enabling you to repeatedly execute a set of statements. The Bourne shell is no exception; it has three such iterative constructs: the `for`, the `while`, and the `until`.


# 13.3    Looping with *while* **and** *until*

The `while` statement allows you to repeatedly execute a set of commands *while* a specified condition is true. Figure 13-3 illustrates the flow, showing that as long as the condition is true, block B is executed; a `break` in block B causes the loop to terminate and start block C.

The format of the `while` loop is as follows:

```
while condition
do
        command
        command
        . . .
done
```

The *condition* section is the same as for the `if` statement. It is tested first when the `while` loop starts. If it is true, the commands enclosed between the do and done are executed. Each time the commands are about to be executed, *condition* is again tested. The commands enclosed between the do and done continue to be executed until *condition* proves false, at which time the while loop terminates. It is therefore necessary that some inevitable operation will make *condition* fail. (The commands between do and done are indented only to make the structure of the loop easier to read. This is called the *body* of the loop.)

**Fig. 13-3.**
*The* while
*loop.*

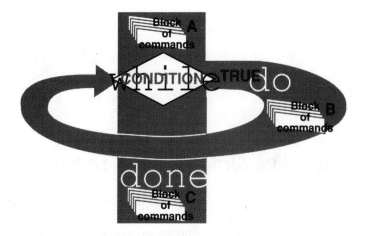

Programmers commonly create infinite loops which terminate with a signal or an exit. This procedure is explained later in this chapter.

The following example shows one use of the while loop and also the method outlined for performing arithmetic (expr) with shell variables.

```
$ count=1
$ while [ "$count" -le 10 ]
> do
>       echo $count
>       count=`expr $count + 1`
> done
1
2
3
4
5
6
7
8
9
10
$
```

The Bourne shell also provides a statement called `until` that is similar in operation to the `while`. The syntax is as follows:

```
until  condition
do
        command
        command
        . . .
done
```

`until` differs from `while` in that it loops until *condition* proves true. In other words, `until` loops as long as the condition is false — the opposite of a `while` loop.

# 13.4   Looping with `for`

Almost every procedural programming language has a `for` statement, used for counting and controlling loops. The shell is more oriented to handling lists than handling numeric values; therefore, its use of `for` is more along those lines. The general format of the `for` statement in the shell is as follows:

```
for  variable  in  list
do
        command
        command
        command
        . . .
done
```

*Variable* is any shell variable you choose. It is listed *without* a leading dollar sign. The number of items specified in *list* determines the number of times the *commands* enclosed between the do and done will be executed. Each time the loop is executed, the next value in *list* is assigned to *variable*.

As an example of `for`, consider the following:

```
for index in 1 2 3 4 5
do
        echo $index
done
```

In this example, *list* consists of the five values 1, 2, 3, 4, and 5. Therefore, the loop is executed a total of five times. Each time through the loop, the next value in *list* is assigned to the shell variable `index`.

See what happens if you enter this `for` loop at the terminal:

```
$ for index in 1 2 3 4 5
> do
>         echo $index
> done
1
2
3
4
5
$
```

Execution of the `for` begins with `index` being assigned the first value in the list: 1. The body of the loop — the `echo` command — then executes. This step causes the number 1 — the value of `index` — to be displayed at the terminal.

After the `echo` command has been executed, the next value in the list, 2, is assigned to `index`. The `echo` command executes again, displaying the value of `index`, and execution of the loop continues. The last time through the loop, the value 5 is assigned to `index`, the `echo` command displays its value at the terminal, and the loop terminates.

A common use of the `for` loop is to apply commands to a group of files. Assume that you have files `names`, `names1`, and `names2` in your current directory. You could do the following to operate on each file individually:

```
$ ls name*
names
names1
names2
$ for file in names names1 names2
> do
>         echo $file
> done
names
names1
names2
$
```

The next example shows how file name substitution can be used in the list specification:

```
$ for file in name*
> do
>        echo $file
> done
names
names1
names2
$
```

As explained in the section on file-name expansion in Chapter 5, "Regular Expressions," even though there appears to be only one item in the list, the shell sees the * in name* and expands it into names, names1, and names2. This is verified by the output of the echo commands.

In the following example, the contents of the files names, names1, and names2 are sorted separately:

```
$ for file in name*
> do
>        sort $file
> done
Bill
Pat
Ruth
Tony
Bill
John
Pat
Ruth
Tom
Tony
John
Pat
Ruth
Tom
Tony
$
```

Well, we got some results, but they are not very readable! The following is an improvement:

```
$ for file in name*
> do
>           echo "===================================="
```

```
>           echo "          Sorted contents of $file"
>           echo "===================================="
>           sort $file
>           echo
> done
====================================
          Sorted contents of names
====================================
Bill
Pat
Ruth
Tony


====================================
          Sorted contents of names1
====================================
Bill
John
Pat
Ruth
Tom
Tony


====================================
          Sorted contents of names2
====================================
John
Pat
Ruth
Tom
Tony

$
```

The purpose of the echo after the sort is to insert a blank line in the result.

In a shell script that uses for, it is not unusual to see $* used as the list specification; for instance, to sequence through each of the arguments. The shell program in listing 13-5 takes any number of file arguments. Each argument is the name of a file to be sorted, preceded by an appropriate heading.

**Listing 13-5.**   Sortf — *A shell program to sort files.*

```
#! /bin/sh
for file in $*
do
        echo "======================================="
        echo "          Sorted contents of $file"
        echo "======================================="
        sort $file
        echo
done
```

The following shows the possible outcome of executing the sortf script:

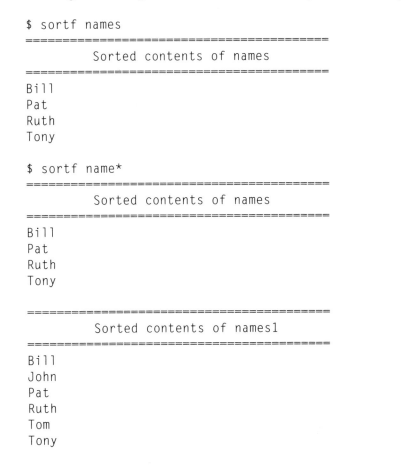

```
$ sortf names
=======================================
          Sorted contents of names
=======================================
Bill
Pat
Ruth
Tony

$ sortf name*
=======================================
          Sorted contents of names
=======================================
Bill
Pat
Ruth
Tony


=======================================
          Sorted contents of names1
=======================================
Bill
John
Pat
Ruth
Tom
Tony
```

*Listing 13-5 continues*

*Listing 13-5.* ` Sortf ` — *A shell program to sort files. (continued)*

```
=============================================
          Sorted contents of names2
=============================================
John
Pat
Ruth
Tom
Tony

$ sortf
$
```

The last example shows what happens when no arguments are supplied. In that case, the value of `$*` is *null*, so the `for` statement inside `sortf` has an "empty" list. The shell ignores the entire `for` statement if the list is empty, and there is no output.

As indicated earlier in this chapter, the `case` statement is often combined with the `for` statement. The example in listing 13-6 combines the `for` loop with the `case` statement to handle the options `-l`, `-c`, and `-w`, plus a list of file-name arguments. The `for` surrounding the `case` enables you to supply any number of options and arguments, in any order.

*Listing 13-6.* ` Coop ` — *A script that handles options.*

```
#! /bin/sh
loption=""
coption=""
woption=""
filelist=""

for arg in $*
do
        case $arg
        in
                -l)             loption=1;;
                -w)             woption=1;;
                -c)             coption=1;;
```

**Listing 13-6.** Coop — *A script that handles options. (continued)*

```
                                        # otherwise it must be part
                                          of the file list
                                        # so build a copy of the
                                          file list in a variable
                    *)                  filelist="$filelist $arg";;
                esac
        done
```

This script assumes that any file argument entered on the command line that is not
-l, -w, or -c is a file name. At the end of execution of these statements, the shell
variable loption is set to 1 if -l is used. The variable woption is set to 1 if -w
is used, and the variable coption is set to 1 if -c is used. The shell variable
filelist contains a list of files entered on the command line.

```
coop -w -c file1
coop -w f* -c -l
coop -l
coop file1 file2 name*
```

The patterns specified inside a case statement are matched by the shell the same
way file names are. This means, for example, that the pattern na* would match
any value that begins with na; the pattern ?x would match any two-character value
that ends in x; and the pattern [a-z] would match any lowercase letter.

An *OR*ing of patterns is effected by separating patterns with a vertical bar |.
Therefore, for example, the following pattern matches the value red *or* blue *or*
yellow:

```
red | blue | yellow)
```

As a final example, the following pattern matches any values that begin with the
characters fig *or* tbl:

```
fig* | tbl*)
```

By combining acceptable responses in this way, you can handle sets of conditions
with a single body of statements.

# 13.5 Functions

You can define a *function* within a shell script, in the same way as you create a shell script to perform a special task. A function is a block of instructions with a name. If your shell script has the same commands repeated at several places in the script, it might be simpler to write those lines once, give them a function name, and use that name wherever the commands occur in your script.

Functions are not limited scripts. You can also define functions on the command line and use them in subsequent commands, much like the C shell and Korn shell alias. A function used in this way is faster than the equivalent shell script because it remains in your shell's memory rather than having to be invoked from a file (with the usual additional overhead of another shell to run it). Unfortunately, functions cannot be exported; you cannot define functions in a shell script and make them available outside that script or shell.

The syntax for defining a function is:

*function-name* ( ) { *command*; ... ; *command*; }

Assume, for example, that you have a standard way of prompting the user for confirmation of different operations, as follows:

```
echo "Confirm some-string ([n] or y)? \c"
read response
```

You could define a function to prompt the user, embedding an appropriate string in the request for confirmation.

Functions can take arguments in a fashion similar to the way scripts do, but the $n use of positional parameters within a function refers only to the arguments passed to the function, *not to the arguments passed from the shell to the script*. (The use of functions was not fully implemented until System V Release 3. Although it might exist in earlier versions of the Bourne shell, some of its behavior might be unpredictable.)

The confirm ( ) function might look like the following:

```
confirm () {
        echo "Confirm $1 ([N] or y)? \c"
        read response junk
        case "$response"
                in
                [Yy]*) return 0 ;;
                [Nn]*) return 1 ;;
```

```
                          *) return 1 ;;
        esac
        }
```

Note the use of return rather than exit. If you use exit in the function, you exit not only from the function but from the entire script. The return command allows you to pass a result back to the command calling the function. Therefore, for example, you could use this function in a script used to delete files, as in listing 13-7.

---

**Listing 13-7.** *A demonstration of functions.*

---

```
#! /bin/sh
# the function
confirm () {
        echo "Confirm $1 ([N] or y)? \c"
        read response junk
        case "$response"
                in
                [Yy]*) return 0 ;;
                [Nn]*) return 1 ;;
                   *) return 1 ;;
        esac
}
# the main part of the script. It uses the confirm function.
for f in $*
do
        if confirm "deleting $f"
        then
                echo "Deleting $f"
        else
        echo "Not touching $f"
        fi
        shift
done
```

---

The rm command actually has the confirmation facility built in. It is the -i option.

Functions are useful in large scripts, but they are especially useful in the Korn shell, as you will see in Chapter 14.

# 13.6 Traps and Tricks

It might seem as if you have already read all you will ever want or need to read about Bourne shell scripting facilities. With the material in Chapter 12 and the preceding part of this chapter, you can perform input, output, and flow control. For most of your daily work, the material up to this point is sufficient. The discussion of shell scripts would not be complete, however, without a look at some traps and tricks.

## Long Command-Line Lists and *shift*

In Chapter 12, you learned that you can reference the arguments given to a shell script with $1, $2, $3, etc. It was not pointed out, however, that you can go up to only $9. (This limitation does not pertain to the number of items in a for list.) Although 10 might seem a reasonable limit to the number of arguments that you would ever want to enter on a command line, don't forget that wild cards such as asterisk (*) are expanded *before* a program or script receives them.

The solution to this trap comes with the shift command. (The shift command causes no action outside shell scripts.) Every time a shift is made, the parameter list is shifted down one position number. The previous parameter $1 is tossed, and the previous $2 becomes the new $1. The previous $3 becomes the new $2, etc. The previously inaccessible tenth parameter becomes the new $9.

The shift command is particularly valuable when you are developing scripts handling both options and file lists. By shifting off each option as you process it, you eventually end up with only the file list. The example in listing 13-8 takes the idea of option handling (seen in the previous option-handling script) one step farther; it handles options and file lists in different ways.

---

**Listing 13-8.** *Handling an arbitrary number of options using* shift.

---

```
loption=""
coption=""
woption=""
for arg in $*
do
        case $arg
        in
                -l)             loption=1;;
                -w)             woption=1;;
                -c)             coption=1;;
```

```
                          *)              break;;
          esac
          shift
  done
  filelist=$*              #the filelist is everything that is
                          left over
```

Listing 13-9 is a slightly different version you use to plug in your own code.

**Listing 13-9.** Shifter — *handling options and file lists.*

```
#! /bin/sh
source=""
dest=""
format_file=""

# first take care of all options
while [ -n "$1" ] # a parameter exists
do
        case $1
        in
                        # two shifts to get past the associate value
             -s)        source=$2
                        echo "SOURCE $source"
                        shift; shift;;
             -d)        dest=$2
                        echo "DESTINATION $dest"
                        shift; shift;;
             -f)        format_file=$2
                        echo "FORMAT FILE $format_file"
                        shift; shift;;
             -*)        echo "SHIFTER: bad option $1"; exit 1;;
              *)        break;; # not an option: leave loop
        esac
done
```

*Listing 13-9 continues*

***Listing 13-9***   Shifter — *handling options and file lists. (continued)*

```
# now take care of the file list without rebuilding it
for f in $*
do
            #     put your process here
            echo "PROCESSING: $f"
done
```

Running this script looks like the following:

```
$ shifter -f myformat -s mysource *
FORMAT FILE myformat
SOURCE mysource
PROCESSING: file_1
PROCESSING: file_2
PROCESSING: file_3
PROCESSING: file_4
    ...
PROCESSING: file_32
$
```

Note that this type of option handling does not require you to rebuild the file list in a variable. A trick used in these scripts is a loop that can be terminated from within — in this case, by either an exit or a break.

## Getting Out of Trouble: *break* **and** *exit*

You can make good use of break or exit if you are in trouble, or if you just want to stop processing at the level your script has taken you.

The break command terminates whichever loop it is part of. That is, if you have loops within loops, break stops the loop that is directly part of the body. In the example in listing 13-9, the loops were not nested; the break merely allowed the program to flow on to the rest of the script. The example in listing 13-10 uses nested loops to build combinations of variables in the outer and inner loops.

**Listing 13-10.** Looper — *breaking out of nested loops.*

```
#! /bin/sh
limit="4"

# the outer loop
first="1"
while true
do
        # the inner loop
        second="1"
        while true
        do
                echo "OUTER: $first   INNER: $second"
                second=`expr $second + 1`
                if [ $second -gt $limit ]
                        then break
                fi
        done
        first=`expr $first + 1`
        if [ $first -gt $limit ]
                then break
        fi
done
```

There is a far more elegant way to produce the same loops as looper: replace the while true with while [ $first -le $limit ] (or $second, as the case may be). With these substitutions, the if statements are no longer needed. But looper is used here to illustrate break. Elegance is set aside.

A run of looper appears as the following:

```
$ looper
OUTER: 1   INNER: 1
OUTER: 1   INNER: 2
OUTER: 1   INNER: 3
OUTER: 1   INNER: 4
OUTER: 2   INNER: 1
OUTER: 2   INNER: 2
OUTER: 2   INNER: 3
OUTER: 2   INNER: 4
OUTER: 3   INNER: 1
```

```
OUTER: 3   INNER: 2
OUTER: 3   INNER: 3
OUTER: 3   INNER: 4
OUTER: 4   INNER: 1
OUTER: 4   INNER: 2
OUTER: 4   INNER: 3
OUTER: 4   INNER: 4
$
```

The exit command is not as delicate as break. exit not only interrupts loops (if there are any), but also interrupts *the script*! Without a parameter (by itself), your script terminates with the status of the last expected command (within the script). If there was no error, this last command is zero. To force your script to terminate with no error (0) or a specific error, enter a number with the exit command (as shown in listing 13-7). UNIX uses many error numbers for flagging different problems. The most common for your use is either the value 1, a general failure, or the value 2, a file permissions/access failure.

### And There is More

When programming with the Bourne shell, you can define functions within shell scripts; limit changes to environment variables; trap signals from the operating system and other programs; and await completion of other processes. There are even shell options for debugging shell scripts. We do not go to that depth in this book. If, however, you are interested in getting even deeper into shell scripts, read the books listed in *Further Reading* at the end of this chapter.

Chapter 14 extends the ideas of Chapters 12 and 13 with the Korn and C shells. Although this is not the last chapter of the book, it is the climax. You have reached the top step in *UNIX Step-by-Step*. Now it is time for you to explore this plateau! If you look off in the distance, you can see some higher peaks. You will find *UNIX System Administration*, by Fiedler and Hunter, an enjoyable guide to one of those mountain ranges. Many others are listed in Appendix A.

## 13.7  Summary

With the Bourne shell, the if and case constructions provide you with a method of writing shell scripts that do different things in different situations or during different states. The if construction is a basic element of *flow control*, the facility to have different parts of a program operate depending on *conditions*. A condition is a true or false (no-error or error) result of a command. The most common command used for setting a condition is test, which is used to evaulate numeric and string comparisons as well as the existence and state of files. The if construction can be combined with else to create either/or decisions and operations. The if construction can be combined with elif statements for nested sets of operations.

Commands (or blocks of commands) can be repeatedly run by using the while construction or the until construction. Another looping construction is the for loop, which uses a list of items for processing as its control.

Long lists of command-line arguments require use of the shift command because only 10 arguments can be handled by a shell script at one time. Further flow control is offered by the break and exit commands, which interrupt looping and the entire script, respectively.

# Review Questions

1. What is meant by flow control?
2. The if statement includes a condition and a body. What is required of the condition for the body to be executed?
3. What different things does the test command test for?
4. How does the Bourne shell use the square brackets in a condition?
5. What is the Bourne shell case used for?
6. What is meant by *looping* in a script or program?
7. What three commands in the Bourne shell produce looping?
8. What controls the number of loops of a for statement?
9. How do you exit a loop?

# Exercises

Write a Bourne shell script that uses the if statement to tell whether a file can be executed but not written to by you.

Write a Bourne shell script that uses the until loop to print the message "Waiting..." repeatedly until the minute changes in the date command.

Write a Bourne shell script using `for` to echo each command line parameter with its parameter number on a separate line, as in the following:

```
Parameter 0: command
Parameter 1: parameter
Parameter 2: parameter
etc.
```

Using the `for` loop and the `case` statement, create a script that counts the number of files (given as parameters) and lists the permissions for the owner, group, and others (read, write, and execute).

# Further Reading

*UNIX Shell Programming — 2nd Edition*, Stephen G. Kochan and Patrick H. Wood, Hayden Book Company, 1989.

*Tricks of the UNIX Masters*, Russell G. Sage, Howard W. Sams & Company, Indianapolis, IN, 1989.

# 14

![chapter number 14]

# Programming the Other Shells

## Contents

## Objectives

In this chapter you will learn

1. How to apply the concepts of Chapters 12 and 13 to the C shell and the Korn shell

2. Some of the programming strengths and weaknesses of the C shell and Korn shell

If you have the Korn shell or the C shell on your system, you might find it advantageous to write your scripts in these shells rather than in the syntax of the Bourne shell. Both the Korn and C shells have internal math operations that are faster and more convenient than calling the `expr` utility. The shell variables can be more than just strings of characters. These shells have other useful features (such as aliases). Keep in mind, however, that Korn shell scripts can be from two to ten times faster than C shell scripts.

# 14.1 Korn Shell Scripts

The Korn shell's capability to handle almost all the commands of Bourne shell scripts without any change is one of its greatest features. There are differences in syntax, but only on aspects of shell programming that are not covered in this book; for example, the use of $(*variable*) for shell-variable substitution.

One difference between the Bourne and Korn shells relates to exporting variables. The Korn shell does not require you to make an assignment and then export the variable. You can do it all in one statement:

```
$ export NAME="Felix the Cat"
$ env | grep NAME
NAME=Felix the Cat
$
```

If you are programming the Korn shell specifically, you might want to take advantage of its features.

## Built-in Integer Arithmetic: let

Because the Korn shell does not rely on `expr` to do integer math, creating counted loops is simpler and faster.

The built-in command is `let` (similar in concept to its namesake in BASIC). The syntax for assigning the result of an operation to a variable is as follows:

let *variable=expression*

in which *expression* can be any arithmetic expression using the following:

| | |
|---|---|
| + | Add |
| - | Subtract or (unary) minus |
| / | Divide |

| | |
|---|---|
| * | Multiply |
| % | Modulo (remainder) |
| = | Assignment |
| < | Less than |
| > | Greater than |
| == | Equal to |
| != | Not equal to |
| <= | Less than or equal to |
| >= | Greater than or equal to |
| ( ) | Parenthesis for grouping |

Variables used in a `let` statement do *not* have a leading $ even though they are on the right-hand side of the assignment (=). Nor do you need to separate the variables and operators with white space (spaces and tabs). As you can see in the following example, more than one operation can be included in a single `let` statement:

```
let a=a+1 b=a*10 c=a+b
```

If you include white space in your expressions, enclose the expression in quotes so that the `let` command does not interpret the elements as separate expressions. For example:

```
let "a = a + 1"  "b = a * 10"  "c = a + b"
```

The internal arithmetic operations can be used in place of `test` to provide the conditions for flow-control statements such as `if` and `while`. When you use the operations for this purpose, enclose the condition within double parentheses as follows:

```
(( expression ))
```

You do not have to quote expressions within the double parentheses. Listing 14-1 is a rewrite of listing 13-9 from Chapter 13, this time with all the elegance of the Korn shell applied.

---

**Listing 14-1.**  `Looper2` — *nested loops with arithmetic.*

---

```
#! /bin/ksh
let limit=4

# the outer loop
let first=0
while (( (first=first+1) <= limit ))
```

*Listing 14-1 continues*

*Listing 14-1.* Looper2 — *nested loops with arithmetic. (continued)*

```
do
    # the inner loop
        let second=1
        while (( (second=second+1) <= limit ))

        do
                echo "OUTER: $first  INNER: $second"
        done
done
```

Note that the conditional expressions within the double parentheses include assignments.

The output of this concise shell script is identical to that of 13-9, as follows:

```
$ looper
OUTER: 1  INNER: 1
OUTER: 1  INNER: 2
OUTER: 1  INNER: 3
OUTER: 1  INNER: 4
OUTER: 2  INNER: 1
OUTER: 2  INNER: 2
OUTER: 2  INNER: 3
OUTER: 2  INNER: 4
OUTER: 3  INNER: 1
OUTER: 3  INNER: 2
OUTER: 3  INNER: 3
OUTER: 3  INNER: 4
OUTER: 4  INNER: 1
OUTER: 4  INNER: 2
OUTER: 4  INNER: 3
OUTER: 4  INNER: 4
$
```

To speed up the math functions, tell the shell that certain variables are numeric values before you use those variables. For example, listing 14-1 could start with the following:

```
integer limit first second
```

The `integer` command is a predefined alias to the `typeset -i` Korn shell command. Declaring a variable is only one of many control options that the Korn shell provides.

## Arrays

An array is a variable that holds more than one value at a time. Think of the command-line parameter list as an array of parameters. Each value in an array is called an *element*. The command-line parameter $0 can be thought of as the first element in that array. It is the name of the script file that is running. The first parameter after the command name is $1; the next is $2, etc.

The arrays you define in the Korn shell are referenced slightly differently; the *index* (the element number) is enclosed in square brackets after the variable name. For example, name[5], would be element number six of the array name. The first element in that array would be name[0].

Why wouldn't you just create different variables with different names? Arrays offer several conveniences in programming: for one, they group associated data. Also, you can access each of the elements of an array by incrementing the index rather than having to use a list of names. For example, assume that you have an array of names, name[0] through name[22]. You can display the list using a loop, as follows:

```
integer idx
idx=0
while [ -n "$name[idx]" ]
do
        echo "NAME: $name[idx]"
        let idx=idx+1
done
```

In this example, you don't even have to predetermine how many elements you are using. (Note that the Korn shell does not allow more than 512 elements to an array.)

Arrays become particularly valuable when you are trying to coordinate information in two separate lists. Although the Korn shell provides for only one-dimensional arrays (two-dimensional arrays are lists of lists), you can coordinate two separate lists by having two separate arrays that use the same index variable.

## String Functions

There are a few UNIX utilities for deriving the substring of a larger string of characters (for example, basename), but the Bourne shell has no general-purpose, internal string-altering functions. The Korn shell complements its arithmetic functions with its capability to cut and chop strings into substrings that are based on either the desired length or the contents of the original string.

Many of the string functions are provided by the ubiquitous typeset command. typeset is used not only to create integer variables and force variable formats (as we show here), but also to determine variables for the environment (exported variables), define function names and how they are used, and a miscellany of other Korn-shell operations.

The syntax for typeset is as follows:

typeset -*options* *variable-list*

Table 14-1 lists the string-related *options*.

**Table 14-1. String-related options to typeset.**

| Option | Usage |
| --- | --- |
| u | Uppercase |
| l | Lowercase |
| L*n* | Left-justified, *n* specifies length. |
| R*n* | Right-justified, *n* specifies length. |

As you can see, you can assign a value to the variable when you define its attributes. The following examples illustrate the use of typeset with string variables:

```
$ typeset -u ab="Monster Mash"
$ echo $ab
MONSTER MASH
$ typeset -l ab
$ echo $ab
monster mash
$ typeset -L15 ab
$ echo "<$ab>"
<Monster Mash   >
$ typeset -L7 ab
$ echo "<$ab>"
<Monster>
$ typeset -R15 ab
$ echo "<$ab>"
<   Monster Mash>
```

```
$ typeset -R4 ab
$ echo "<$ab>"
<Mash>
$ typeset -uL15 ab
$ echo "<$ab>
<MONSTER MASH   >
$ typeset -R1 ab
$ echo $ab
M
$
```

You can strip characters from either end of a string by using the file-name wildcard, as described in Chapter 5, "Regular Expressions." Some of these characters include the familiar *, ?, [ ], and the OR subexpression designated by (*pattern\pattern*). The substring syntax takes four forms:

| | |
|---|---|
| ${*string#pattern*} | Remove smallest matching left pattern |
| ${*string##pattern*} | Remove largest matching left pattern |
| ${*string%#pattern*} | Remove smallest matching right pattern |
| ${*string%%pattern*} | Remove largest matching right pattern |

Another such function for strings is the kind of function that returns the length of a string:

${#*string*}

Examples of each of these functions follow:

```
$ string="Goat cheese is good"
$ echo ${string%s*}
Goat cheese i
$ echo ${string% *}
Goat cheese is
$ echo ${string%% *}                  — For the first word
Goat
$ echo ${string#* }
cheese is good
$ echo ${string##* }                   — For the last word
good
$ echo ${#string}
19
$
```

Combine all these features with what you know from the Bourne shell, and you will find that the Korn-shell environment is ideal for even the most complex tasks. Unfortunately, the Korn shell is not available on many systems. It is available on all HPUX (Hewlett Packard) systems and on all machines running UNIX System V Release 4.

### Aliases

As mentioned in Chapter 3, "User Interfaces," the Korn shell allows aliases. An alias creates a nickname for a command, a filename, a file path, or any shell text. The command can be complex and include parameters the same way a shell script does. For example:

```
$ alias dprint='pr -d $* | lp'
$ dprint myfile
request id is hpjet-264 (standard input)
$
```

The most common use of aliases is to customize your working environment by giving complex commands personalized shortcut names. Include these alias definitions in your .profile file, the file that is automatically executed when you first log in.

### Functions

The function definition is exactly the same as that used by the Bourne shell (see the latter part of Chapter 13), but the Korn shell has an advantage in that functions can be exported. Most Korn-shell users prefer to use the typeset -x *function-name* form rather than the export *function-name*. When you export a function, it is available to all subshells just as when you export an environment variable.

## 14.2 C Shell Scripts

If your UNIX system does not have the Korn shell, it probably has the C shell. (It is almost as widely available as the Bourne shell.) Most of the facilities of the Korn shell are available with the C shell. The shortcoming of the C shell is that nearly everything about C-shell scripts is different from Bourne-shell scripts.

## Variables

Whenever you give a value to a C shell variable, you must use the set command. (There is actually a set command in the Bourne shell as well, but it serves a very different function.)

To give a value to an environment variable (exported variables in the Bourne shell), you must use the command setenv, as in the following:

```
% set string="Are we in Kansas?"
% echo $string
Are we in Kansas?
% setenv BOSCO "Too much chocolate milk will make you dizzy."
%
```

Note that setenv does not use the equals sign for assigning values, whereas the set command does.

If your default shell is the C shell, there are three scripts in your home directory that take the place of the .profile script of the Bourne and Korn shells: .cshrc, .login, and .logout. The .cshrc script is executed when you start the C shell. The .login script is executed when you login. The .logout script is executed when you logout.

Here are some samples:

```
# The .cshrc file for Felix the Cat
# Commands here are executed each time csh starts up.

set history=20                            # save last 20 commands
# the aliases are abbreviations for common but complex commands
alias print 'jetpr :* | lp -dlp'          # print command alias
alias print2 'jetpr -2 -oland -sletter :* | lp -dlp' # format and print
alias h 'history'                         # look at history of commands
alias m 'messages'                        # check my mail
alias e 'epsilon :*'                      # nickname from my emacs editor
alias lc 'ls -FC :*'                      # an old and familiar Xenix command
# my environment variables
setenv NAME "Felix the Cat"
setenv ORGANIZATION '<White Pine Club>'
setenv LOGNAME felix
setenv RNINIT /usr/felix/.rninit
setenv EPSPATH "./:$HOME/:/usr/lib/epsilon"
setenv MODEM '/dev/tty1A'
setenv E /usr/felix/explore
```

```
# The .login script for Felix the Cat
# Commands here are executed for a login shell only.
set ignoreeof                      # don't let control-d logout
set path = (/bin /usr/bin $home/bin /usr/local/bin /usr/lbin   /usr/games
/usr/
informix/bin  $home/programs .)# execution search path
calendar                                # check my calendar whenever I login
messages                                # check my mail whenever I login
```

```
# .logout for felix the cat
clear                                   # clear the screen
# print some stats on session
echo "    Session started at `who am i | cut -c25-`"
echo "      Session ended at `date '+%h %d %H:%M'`"
```

Note the format difference for path in the .login file; the list is enclosed in parentheses, and the items are separated by spaces.

Another difference to note between the C shell and the others: when you add a directory to your PATH of executable files, the files do not become available immediately. The list of available executable files (outside your present working directory) is maintained only as a list in memory. You must issue the command rehash to have new executables added.

The Bourne shell also maintains a list in memory; however, if it cannot find the command in the memory-resident list, it automatically searches the directories in PATH.

This list is built when you start a C shell or when you execute the rehash command. So, for example, to add the programs in /usr/bin/X1 to your C-shell path, enter the following:

```
% set path=($path /usr/bin/X11)
% rehash
%
```

In the C shell, the path variable is linked to the PATH environment variable.

The C shell does not have integer data types or arrays, but it does have *lists*. A list is a multivalued variable similar to an array. The syntax for assigning values to a list and using them is demonstrated in the following example:

```
% set mylist = ( fox grain hen farmer boat river )
% echo $mylist[3]
hen
```

Your PATH in the C shell is a good example of a list.

You can create aliases to add and subtract elements from the list. These functions are not predefined in the C shell.

## Arithmetic

Like the Korn shell, the C shell has built-in integer arithmetic functions. The major difference is in the command name for arithmetic; the C shell uses the single character @ (the "at" symbol). As shown in table 14-2, there are a few more arithmetic operations as well.

**Table 14-2.    Arithmetic operations internal to the C shell.**

| Operator | Operation |
|----------|-----------|
| + | Add |
| - | Subtract or (unary) minus |
| / | Divide |
| * | Multiply |
| % | Modulo (remainder) |
| ++ | Increment by 1 (C shell only) |
| -- | Decrement by 1 (C shell only) |
| >> | Shift right |
| << | Shift left |
| = | Assignment |
| < | Less than |
| > | Greater than |
| == | Equal to |
| != | Not equal to |
| <= | Less than or equal to |

**Table 14-2** *continues*

| | |
|---|---|
| >= | Greater than or equal to |
| & | Binary AND |
| \| | Binary OR |
| ^ | Binary exclusive OR |
| ~ | Binary inversion |
| && | Logical AND |
| \|\| | Logical OR |
| ( ) | Parenthesis for grouping |

---

The following example shows the use of the @ to indicate that arithmetic operations follow:

```
% set sum = 495
% set count = 32
% set fudge_factor = 5
% @ avg = ( $sum / $count ) + $fudge_factor
% echo $avg
20
%
```

Don't forget that this is *integer* arithmetic!

## Flow Control with *if*

For the C shell, the simple if takes the following formats:

For one command:

```
if ( expression ) command
```

For a block of commands:

```
if ( expression ) then
        command
      command
      . . .
   command
endif
```

You can also include an else block as follows:

```
if ( expression ) then
        command
    command
    . . .
    command
else
        command
    command
    . . .
    command
endif
```

And, like the Bourne and Korn shells, you can nest ifs and elses.

The *condition* seems simple enough, but it can get messy because it must be a numeric value or expression. Non-zero evaluates as *true*; zero evaluates as *false*. Table 14-2 gives you the numeric-comparison (Boolean) operators, which you can easily use along with any arithmetic expression. The C shell also has built-in string-comparison operators:

( *string1* =~ *string2* )    *True* if two strings are *identical*

( *string1* !~ *string2* )    *True* if two strings are *different*

The problem starts when you try to get a numeric value that appropriately represents the performance or failure of a command or utility. The exit status of a command that succeeds is zero, whereas the exit status of one that fails is non-zero. Hence you have a conflict between what is required for a condition and the exit status of a command. The solution is the curly braces ({ }) numeric operator (not shown in table 14-2). The syntax is as follows:

{ *command* }

The curly braces return 1 if *command* succeeds (that is, if it exits with a status of zero). Otherwise, the curly braces return 0.

```
% @ return_val = { echo "Say cheese." }
Say cheese.
% echo $return_val
1
% @ return_val = { cat xxx }
cat: cannot open xxx
% echo $return_val
0
%
```

Now all that remains is to put the command inside a pair of parentheses so that it will be recognized as a condition.

```
% if ( { date } ) echo "It works"
Sun Jul  1 09:42:44 EDT 1990
It works
%
```

You can always use the `test` command to find file status. `test` is not internal to this shell, as it is to the Korn shell. Also, you must enclose it with curly braces.

```
% if ( { test -r myfile } ) echo "File is readable."
File is readable.
%
```

Be careful if you are using pipes or indirection; the curly braces don't know about indirection, as shown in the following example:

```
% cat ison
#! /bin/csh
if ( { who | grep "^$1" >/dev/null } ) then
        echo "$1 is on the system"
else
        echo "$1 isn't logged on"
endif
% ison ben
ben             tty02           Jun 30 13:25
ben             tty01           Jun 30 13:11
ben             tty03           Jul  1 09:18
ben             tty1a           Jul  1 07:48
root            tty11           Jun 30 13:12
ben isn't logged on
```

OOPS! Not only was the output of `who` not piped to `grep` to end up in standard output, the whole thing obviously failed. The problem occurred because the curly braces did not know what to evaluate. You must group the entire command, `who | grep "^$1" >/dev/null`, so that it appears to be a single entity to the curly braces. Another set of parentheses (inside the curly braces) does the job:

```
% cat ison
#! /bin/csh
if ( { ( who | grep "^$1" >/dev/null ) } ) then
        echo "$1 is on the system"
else
    echo "$1 isn't logged on"
endif
```

```
% ison ben
ben is on the system
```

The solution is not exactly intuitive, but the steps are necessary.

Listing 14-2 shows the `salute` script (from listing 13-2) done with C shell.

---

***Listing 14-2.*** Salute — *C shell version.*

---

```
#! /bin/csh
# shell program to execute date and then display
# Good morning, Good afternoon, or Good evening, as
# appropriate

set hour=`date +%H`            # much simpler than the version using cut
if ( ( $hour > 0 ) && ( $hour < 12 )) then
        echo "Good morning."
else if ( ( $hour >= 12 ) && ( $hour < 18 ) ) then
        echo "Good afternoon."
        else
                echo "Good evening."
        endif
endif
```

---

## Multiple Choice with C Shell *case*

The C shell also has a `case` command, but, typically, its use differs from that in the Bourne and Korn shells. The syntax is as follows:

```
switch ( string )
case pattern1:
        command
        command
        . . .
        breaksw
case pattern2:
        command
        command
        . . .
        breaksw
```

```
default:
        command
        command
        ...
        breaksw
endsw
```

Listing 14-3 is the C-shell equivalent of the digit script in listing 13-3.

---

*Listing 14-3.*  Digit — *a script for English equivalents of digits.*

---

```
#! /bin/csh
#
# Display the English equivalent of a digit
#
#! /bin/csh
switch ( $1 )
case 0:
        echo "zero"
        breaksw
case 1:
        echo "one"
        breaksw
case 2:
        echo "two"
        breaksw
case 3:
        echo "three"
        breaksw
case 4:
        echo "four"
        breaksw
case 5:
        echo "five"
        breaksw
case 6:
        echo "six"
        breaksw
case 7:
        echo "seven"
        breaksw
```

```
case 8:
        echo "eight"
        breaksw
case 9:
        echo "nine"
        breaksw
default:
        echo "Invalid argument"
endsw
```

Make sure that the command block does not start on the same line as the `case`.

## Looping with *while*

The C-shell version of the `while` loop looks like the following:

```
while ( condition )
        command
        command
        . . .
        command
end
```

## Looping with *foreach*

The C-shell counterpart to the `for` loop is `foreach`. Here the syntax is a little simpler than the Bourne shell's `for`:

```
foreach variable-name ( list )
        command
        command
        . . .
        command
end
```

Listing 14-4 is the C-shell equivalent of the `sortf` script in listing 13-4.

---

***Listing 14-4.*** Sortf — *C shell program to sort files.*

---

```
#! /bin/csh
foreach file ( $* )
        echo "========================================="
        echo "           Sorted contents of $file         "
        echo"========================================="
        sort $file
end
```

---

## Looping with *repeat*

The repeat loop is not found in either the Korn shell or Bourne shell. It is equivalent to a while loop with internal counters that break out of the loop. The repeat command iterates a command a specific number of times. The syntax is as follows:

repeat *count  command*

Repeat cannot act on a block of commands. It is sweet, but very simple. Our final example in this book shows the use of repeat:

```
% repeat 10 echo "The final example."
The final example.
The final example.
The final example.
The final example.
The final example.
The final example.
The final example.
The final example.
The final example.
The final example.
%
```

# 14.3 Summary

Although the C shell offers many features that are more advanced than those of the Bourne shell, it is more difficult to use in creating shell scripts. The syntax is significantly different for operating on shell variables and using flow-control commands and arithmetic.

The Korn shell offers all the interactive features the C shell does, and also maintains a high amount of compatibility with the Bourne shell for shell scripts. Also, the Korn shell runs scripts faster than the Bourne shell and the C shell, because of its construction and because it internally processes arithmetic operations and tests.

# Review Questions

1. Which shell is more like the Bourne shell, the Korn or the C shell?

2. Why would shell operations that use numeric values be faster with the Korn shell than with the Bourne shell?

3. What are arrays used for?

4. Which Korn shell command is responsible for setting most of the variable formats and types?

5. What is the command for internal arithmetic in the Korn shell?

6. What keyword is necessary whenever you assign a string to a C shell variable?

7. To use the internal arithmetic operations of the C shell, what single key character do you use?

8. What keyword ends the block of a C shell `if` statement?

9. What kind of expression must be used for the condition in all C-shell `if` and `while` statements? What value indicates a true condition?

10. In the C shell, how do you convert the result status of a command operation into a proper value for a condition?

11. Which keyword ends a C-shell `while` loop?

# Further Reading

*UNIX Shell Programming — 2nd Edition*, Stephen G. Kochan and Patrick H. Wood., Hayden Book Company, 1989.

*The Korn Shell — Command and Programming Language*, Morris I. Bolsky and David G. Korn, Prentice Hall, Englewood Cliffs, NJ, 1989.

*An Introduction to Berkeley UNIX*, Paul Wang, Wadsworth Publishing Company, Belmont, CA, 1988.

*C Shell Field User's Guide*, Anderson and Anderson, Prentice Hall, Englewood Cliffs, NH, 1986.

# Appendix A

## For More Information

There are many sources of information on the UNIX system, including manuals, books, periodicals, and technical papers.

## Books

There is one reference that you cannot do without. This is the UNIX documentation for your particular version. It gives detailed descriptions of the syntax and various options for each of the commands. A complete set of UNIX documentation is available from Prentice Hall/UNIX Press, the publishing arm of the UNIX Software Operation:

Prentice Hall/UNIX Press
Englewood Cliffs, NJ 07632

The complete System V, Release 4 set is 17 volumes:

- *System Administrator's Reference Manual*
- *Network User's and Administrator's Guide*
- *System Administrator's Guide*
- *Programmer's Guide: Networking Interfaces*
- *Programmer's Reference Manual*
- *Programmer's Guide: Systems Services and Application Packaging Tools*
- *Programmer's Guide: POSIX Conformance*
- *Programmer's Guide: Streams*
- *Device Drivers Interface/Driver-Kernel Interface (DDI/DKI) Reference Manual*

- *Programmer's Guide: Character User Interface (FMLI and ETI)*
- *Product Overview and Master Index*
- *Migration Guide*
- *ANSI C Transition Guide*
- *BSD/XENIX Compatibility Guide*
- *User's Guide*
- *User's Reference Manual*

As a regular user, you will need the last two: *User's Guide* and *User's Reference Manual*.


## Howard W. Sams & Company

The Hayden Press/H.W. Sams books on UNIX (of which this is one) are the best sources of information when you are exploring the facilities of UNIX. The address of the publisher is:

Howard W. Sams & Company
11711 N. College Ave.
Carmel, IN 46032

Books edited or written by Stephen G. Kochan and Patrick H. Wood:
*UNIX Shell Programming*, revised edition, 1990.
    A complete introduction to UNIX shell programming; it
    contains many practical programs that provide reinforcement
    for each new application.

*UNIX System Security*, 1985.
    A practical guide to system security, with methods for
    making sure your UNIX system is as secure as you want it to be.

*UNIX System Networking*, 1989.
    An in-depth look at the most popular UNIX networks. Each
    chapter is written by an expert on the subject.

*Exploring the UNIX System — 2nd Edition*, 1989.
    A tutorial that parallels this text. Many examples are
    similar.

*Programming in C*, 1988.
> A tutorial introduction to the C language; it contains many examples and teaches C in an organized fashion.

*Topics in C Programming*, 1988.
> The sequel to *Programming in C*; describes in detail some of the most difficult concepts in C as well as the UNIX system interface, curses, `make`, and debugging.

Other UNIX books from Howard W. Sams & Company:

*Tricks of the UNIX Masters*, Russell G. Sage, 1987.
> Many useful shell script utilities.

*UNIX Communications*, B. Anderson, B. Costales, H. Henderson, 1987.
> Step-by-step instructions on using UNIX facilities for electronic mail, USENET, UUCP, and more.

*UNIX Text Processing*, D. Dougherty and T. O'Reilly, 1987.
> An in-depth reference covering all aspects of text processing in the UNIX environment.

*UNIX System Administration*, D. Fiedler and B.H. Hunter, 1988.
> A practical guide to system administration.

## Other Notable Books on UNIX

*The UNIX System*, S.R. Bourne (Bell Laboratories), Addison-Wesley Publishing, Reading, MA, 1983.
> Although this book was written when there were but 3,000 UNIX systems in the world, and the current version from AT&T was not nearly as robust as it is now, this text remains a valuable resource, if for no other reason than that it was written by the developer of the Bourne shell (see Chapter 3). It is written for a technical audience.

*UNIX System: Readings and Applications Vol. I*, AT&T Bell Laboratories, Prentice Hall, Englewood Cliffs, NJ, 1987.
> Covers fundamentals such as real-time processing and microprocessor systems.

*UNIX System: Readings and Applications Vol. II*, AT&T Bell
Laboratories, Prentice Hall, Englewood Cliffs, NJ, 1987.
Covers graphics, security, networking, and portability.

*Life With UNIX*, Don Libes and Sandy Ressler, Prentice Hall,
Englewood Cliffs, NJ, 1989.
An enjoyable compilation of UNIX history, culture, and
esoteric information.

*The Design of the UNIX Operating System*, Maurice J. Bach,
Prentice Hall, Englewood Cliffs, NJ, 1986.
A technical textbook on the internal design and system
services of both System V and BSD UNIX.

*AT&T Open Look — Graphical User Interface, User's Guide*,
AT&T/Prentice Hall, Murray Hill, NJ, 1989.

*The Kornshell — Command and Programming Language*, Morris I. Bolsky
and David G. Korn, AT&T/Prentice Hall, Murray Hill, NJ, 1989.

*Vi — the UNIX Screen Editor*, August Hansen, Brady (Prentice
Hall) New York, 1986.
A thorough and easy-to-read reference text on `vi`,
exclusively.

*Guide to Vi Visual Editing on the UNIX System*, D. Sonnenschein,
Prentice Hall, Englewood Cliffs, NJ, 1987.

*Text Processing and Typesetting with UNIX*, David Barron and Mike
Rees, Addison-Wesley, Reading, MA, 1987.

*UNIX — The Complete Reference*, Stephen Coffin, Osborne/McGraw
Hill, Berkeley, CA, 1988.

*UNIX Utilities, A Programmer's Reference*, R.S. Tare, McGraw
Hill, Hightstown, NJ, 1987.

*An Introduction to Berkeley UNIX*, Paul Wang, Wadsworth Publishing
Company, Belmont, CA, 1988.

*The AWK Programming Language,* A.V. Aho, B.W. Kernighan, P.J.
Weinberger, Addison-Wesley, Reading, MA, 1988.
A complete description of the `awk` language.

*The UNIX C Shell Field Guide*, G. Anderson and P. Anderson,
Prentice Hall, Englewood Cliffs, NJ, 1986.
An in-depth reference to the C shell.

*Preparing Documents with UNIX*, C.C. Brown, J.L. Falk, and R.D.
Sperline, Prentice-Hall, Englewood Cliffs, NJ, 1986.
`nroff` and `troff` and the standard macros.

## Books from the Nutshell Series of Handbooks

*Managing Projects with Make*, Talbott, O'Reilly & Associates, Inc.,
Cambridge, MA 02140, 1987.

*Using Uucp and Usenet*, Grace Todino, O'Reilly & Associates, Inc.,
Cambridge, MA 02140, 1986.

*Managing Uucp and Usenet*, Grace Todino, O'Reilly & Associates,
Inc., Cambridge, MA 02140, 1986.

*Learning the Vi Editor*, Lamb, O'Reilly & Associates, Inc.,
Cambridge, MA 02140, 1987.

# Periodical Publications

*BYTE*, 1 Phoenix Mill Lane, Peterborough, NH 03458
A monthly magazine devoted to all aspects of computing (for
the experienced user). Although it is not devoted to UNIX,
it includes a monthly column on UNIX, occasional feature
articles about UNIX subjects, and unbiased reviews of
hardware and software.

*UNIX Review*, 500 Howard Street, San Francisco, CA 94105.
A monthly magazine devoted to UNIX; somewhat technical
in nature.

*UNIX World*, 444 Castro Street, Mountain View, CA 94101.
Another monthly magazine devoted to UNIX; less
technical than *UNIX Review*; lots of tutorial articles
and market information.

*UNIX Today!*, 600 Community Drive, Manhasset, NY 11030.
   A biweekly tabloid on UNIX; mostly news items and press
   releases.

*;login*, The USENIX Association, P.O. Box 2299, Berkeley, CA
   94710.
   A bimonthly newsletter for USENIX members. You must
   join to receive it.

*CommUNIXations*, /usr/group, 4655 Old Ironsides Drive, Suite
   200, Santa Clara, CA 95054.
   A bimonthly magazine for /usr/group members. You must
   join to receive it.

# Papers

Papers marked with an asterisk (*) are printed in the Berkeley 4.3 *UNIX User's
Supplementary Documents, UNIX Programmer's Supplementary Documents,* and
*UNIX System Manager's Manual,* available from the USENIX Association, P.O.
Box 2299, Berkeley, CA 94710.

*"The UNIX Time Sharing System," D.M. Ritchie and K.
   Thompson.
   The original paper written by Ritchie and Thompson
   describing the UNIX system.

"BC — An Arbitrary Precision Desk-Calculator Language," L.L.
   Cherry and R. Morris.

*"A Tutorial Introduction to the UNIX Text Editor," B.W. Kernighan.
   An introductory guide to ed.

*"Advanced Editing on UNIX," B.W. Kernighan.
   An advanced look at ed.

*"An Introduction to the UNIX Shell," S.R. Bourne.
   A complete, albeit terse, description of the UNIX
   shell.

*"SED — A Non-interactive Text Editor," L.E. McMahon.
   A complete description of the sed editor.

*"An introduction to the C shell," W. Joy.
An Introduction to the C shell and many of its commonly used commands.

*"An Introduction to Display Editing with VI," W. Joy.
An introductory guide to `vi`.

*"Ex Reference Manual," W. Joy.
A complete description of the `ex` text editor, which underlies `vi`.

*"A TROFF Tutorial," B.W. Kernighan.
A quick introduction to the `troff` typesetting program.

*"NROFF/TROFF User's Manual," J.F. Ossanna.
A complete description of the `nroff` and `troff` programs.

*"TBL — A Program to Format Tables," M.E. Lesk.
A description of the `tbl` preprocessor for `troff`.

*"A System for Typesetting Mathematics," B.W. Kernighan, L.L. Cherry.
A description of the `eqn` preprocessor for `troff`.

*"Make — A Program for Maintaining Computer Programs," S.I. Feldman.
An overview of `make`.

"A Loss of Innocence," P.H. Wood; "Tales of the Damned," K. Smith; "Assessing the Costs," V. Gligor and C.S. Chandersekaran; and "Interview with Roger Schell," T. Berson; *UNIX Review*, Vol. 6, No. 2 (February 1988), pp. 37-69.
Four articles on various aspects of UNIX security.

*"On The Security of UNIX," D.M. Ritchie.
An overview of UNIX security.

*"Password Security: A Case History," R.H. Morris and K. Thompson.
Many reasons for choosing good passwords.

"The UNIX System: UNIX Operating System Security," F.T. Grampp and R.H. Morris, *UNIX System: Readings and Applications Vol. II*, AT&T Bell Laboratories, Prentice Hall, Englewood Cliffs, NJ, 1987.
An overview of UNIX security.

"The UNIX System: File Security and the UNIX System Crypt Command," J.A. Reeds and P.J. Weinberger, *UNIX System: Readings and Applications Vol. II*, AT&T Bell Laboratories, Prentice Hall, Englewood Cliffs, NJ, 1987.
A description of how the `crypt` command was cracked.

"Further Cures for Business Ills, Part 2a," R. Farrow, *UNIX World*, Vol. III, No. 4 (April 1986), pp. 65-71.
An article on good security practices.

"Further Cures for Business Ills, Part 2b," R. Farrow, *UNIX World*, Vol. III, No. 5 (May 1986), pp. 65-70.
An article on some of the better-known security holes in UNIX.

"Making UNIX Secure," A. Filipski and J. Hanko, *Byte*, Vol. II, No. 4 (April 1986), pp. 113-128.
An article on making UNIX more secure.

*"A Dial-Up Network of UNIX Systems," D.A. Nowitz, M.E. Lesk.
An early description of the UUCP system.

*"Mail Reference Manual," K. Shoens.
A description of the Berkeley `mail` command, the model for AT&T's `mailx` command.

# *Appendix B*

## Overview of Commands

This appendix lists often-used UNIX commands. All commands are fully described in the *UNIX User's Reference Manual* and *UNIX System Administrator's Reference Manual*. Due to hardware constraints, not all the commands listed here will work on all the supported hardware configurations. (Portions of this overview were adapted from the document, *UNIX — Overview and Synopsis of Facilities*, by T. A. Dolatta, R. C. Haight, and A. G. Petruccelli.)

### *File and Directory Commands*

cat
Concatenates one or more files onto standard output. Mostly used for un-adorned printing, for inserting data into a pipe, and for buffering output that comes in pieces.

cp
Copies one file to another or many files to a directory. Works on any file regardless of its contents.

dd
Physical file format translator, for exchanging data with non-UNIX systems, especially OS/360, VS1, MVS, and so on.

mkdir
Makes one or more new directories.

rmdir
Removes one or more (empty) directories.

`cd`
Changes the working (that is, current) directory.

`find`
Searches the directory hierarchy for, and performs specified commands on, every file that meets given criteria specified as one or more of the following:

- A file name matching a given pattern
- The modified date in a given range
- The date of last use in given range
- Given permissions
- A given owner
- Given special file characteristics

Any directory can be the starting "node."

`cmp`
Compares two files, and reports disagreeing bytes.

`comm`
Identifies common lines in two sorted files. Output in up to three columns shows lines present in first file only, present in second file only, or present in both.

`cpio`
Copies a subtree of the file system (directories, links, and all) to another place in the file system. Can also copy a subtree onto a tape and later recreate it from tape. Often used with the `find` command.

`csplit`
Like `split`, `csplit` splits a large file into more manageable pieces, with the split occurring at a specified point.

`diff`
Reports line changes, additions, and deletions necessary to bring two files into agreement; can produce an editor script to convert one file into another.

`grep`
Prints all lines in one or more files that match a pattern of the kind used by `ed` (the editor). The kinds of patterns that `grep` can print are the following:

- All lines that fail to match
- Number of lines that match

`ln`

Links another name (alias) to an existing file.

`lp`

Sends file (or output) to the print spooler. This is the System V version of print spooling.

`lpr`

The Berkeley version of the print spooler (`lp`) command.

`more`

Prints files one screenful at a time. Available on BSD systems; System V, Release 3; and later releases of UNIX.

`mv`

Moves one or more files. Usually used for renaming files or directories.

`pg`

Prints files one screenful at a time. Note: this command is available in System V, Release 2 and later releases of UNIX.

`pr`

Prints files with title, date, and page number on every page with the following options:

- Multicolumn output
- Parallel column merge of several files

`rm`

Removes one or more files. If any names are linked to the file, only the name being removed goes away.

`sort`

Merges and/or sorts ASCII files line by line:

- In ascending or descending order
- Lexicographically or on numeric key
- On multiple keys located by delimiters or by position

Can fold upper-case characters together with lower-case into dictionary order.

`split`

Splits a large file into more manageable pieces.

sum

Computes the check sum of a file.

tar

Tape file archiver: tar saves and restores files and directory structures on magnetic tape.

tr

Does character translation according to an arbitrary code:

- Can "squeeze out" repetitions of selected characters

- Can delete selected characters

uniq

Deletes successive duplicate lines in a file:

- Prints lines that were originally unique, duplicated, or both

- Can give redundancy count for each line

Counts lines and "words" (strings separated by blanks or tab characters) in a file.


# Shell Commands

csh

The C shell (Berkeley) command language interpreter; it performs the same functions as sh (Bourne shell) except that the syntax is slightly different for many commands. It includes the following features that are not part of sh:

- Command history for replaying and using arguments from previous commands

- Alias of complex commands and paths to a single word without writing shell scripts

- Process control (on some systems)

echo

Prints its arguments on the standard output. Useful for diagnostics or prompts in shell procedures or for inserting data into a pipe.

expr

String computations for calculating command arguments:

- Integer arithmetic

- Pattern matching
- Like the `test` command, `expr` can be used for conditional side-effect

`ksh`

The Korn shell command language interpreter; it performs the same functions as `sh` (Bourne shell) with the same syntax. Although it has many of the features of `csh` (the C shell), it is much faster and more compatible with the standard Bourne shell. Its features include:

- Command history for replaying and using arguments from previous commands
- Alias of complex commands and paths to a single word without writing shell scripts
- Process control (on some systems)
- Arrays of variables
- Integer data type for faster arithmetic operations
- Full editing of the command line with either `emacs` or `vi` style of editing
- User-definable functions for scripts

`rsh`

Restricted shell; restricts a user to a subset of UNIX commands. The system administrator may construct different levels of restriction.

`sh`

The Bourne shell, the standard UNIX command language interpreter, understands a set of constructs that constitute a full programming language; it allows a user or a command procedure to do the following:

- Supply arguments to and run any executable program
- Redirect standard input, standard output, and standard error files
- Create a pipe, the simultaneous execution of separate processes with output of one process connected to the input of another
- Compose compound commands using the following:

      if...then...else
      case switches
      while loops
      for loops over lists
      break, continue, and exit parentheses for grouping.

- Initiate background processes
- Perform shell procedures (that is, command scripts with substitutable arguments)

- Construct argument lists from all file names matching specified patterns
- Take user-specified action on traps and interrupts
- Specify a search path for finding commands
- On login, automatically create a user-specifiable environment
- Optionally announce presence of mail as it arrives
- Provide variables and parameters with default settings

shl

Shell layer manager: shl enables a user to interact with more than one shell from a single terminal. Note: This command is available in System V, Release 2 and later releases of UNIX.

sleep

Suspends execution for a specified time.

test

Tests argument values in shell conditional constructs:

- String comparison
- File nature and accessibility
- Boolean combinations of the preceding

# Information

cal

Prints a calendar of any month or year.

date

Prints current date and time. Has considerable knowledge of calendrical and horologic peculiarities; can be used to set UNIX's idea of date and time. (As yet, cannot cope with Daylight Savings Time in the Southern Hemisphere.)

df

Reports amount of free space in file system.

du

Prints a summary of total space occupied by all files in a hierarchy.

file

Tries to determine what kind of information is in a file by consulting the file system index and by reading the file itself.

`help`
A brief explanation of commands.

`ls`
Lists the names of one, several, or all files in one or more directories:

- Alphabetic or chronological sorting, up or down
- Optional information: size, owner, group, date last modified, date last accessed, permissions

`man`
Prints UNIX manual entries at the terminal.

`pwd`
Prints name of your working (that is, current) directory.

`time`
Runs a command and reports timing information about it.

`tty`
Prints the "name" of your terminal (that is, the name of the port to which your terminal is connected).

`who`
Tells who is logged onto the system:

- Lists logged-in users, their ports, and time they logged in
- Can maintain an optional history of all logins and logouts
- Tells you who you are logged in as

# Editors

`ed`
Interactive line-oriented context editor. Random access to all lines of a file. It can do the following:

- Find lines by number or pattern (regular expressions). Patterns can include: specified characters, "don't care" characters, choices among characters, (specified numbers of) repetitions of these constructs, beginning of line, end of line
- Add, delete, change, copy, or move lines
- Permute contents of a line

- Replace one or more instances of a pattern within a line

- Combine or split lines

- Combine or split files

- Do any of the above operations on every line (in a given range) that matches a pattern

- Escape to the shell (UNIX command language) during editing

emacs

A popular screen editor that is found on many systems but is not part of the standard distribution of UNIX, either System V or BSD. Its features include:

- Is user modifiable and extensible using an underlying language, usually LISP

- Can have multiple buffers and screen windows open at the same time

- Is self-documented

sed

A stream (one-pass) editor with facilities similar to those of ed.

vi

Screen-oriented display editor for video terminals. When using vi, changes made to the file are reflected by what is displayed on the terminal screen. Note: this command is available in Berkeley UNIX and System V, Release 2 and later releases of UNIX.

# Text Formatting and Typesetting

nroff

Advanced formatter for terminals. Capable of many elaborate feats such as:

- Justification of either or both margins

- Automatic hyphenation

- Generalized page headers and footers, automatic page numbering, with even-odd page differentiation capability, etc.

- Hanging indents and one-line indents

- Absolute and relative parameter settings

- Optional legal-style numbering of output lines

- Nested or chained input files

- Complete page format control, keyed to dynamically planted "traps" at specified lines

- Several separately definable formatting environments (for example, one for regular text, one for footnotes, and one for "floating" tables and displays)

- Macros with substitutable arguments

- Conditional execution of macros

- Conditional insertion or deletion of text

- String variables that can be invoked in midline

- Computation and printing of numerical quantities

- String-width computations for unusually difficult layout problems

- Positions and distances expressible in inches, centimeters, ems, ens, line spaces, points, picas, machine units, and arithmetic combinations thereof

- Dynamic (relative or absolute) positioning

- Horizontal and vertical line drawing

- Multicolumn output on terminals capable of reverse line-feed or through the post processor `col`

### troff

This formatter generates output for a phototypesetter or other suitable graphics device. Its output is independent of the final printing device. Postprocessors are available to translate the `troff` output into a stream of device-specific codes that produce the correct representation. Devices presently supported by postprocessors are the Autologic APS-5 phototypesetter (`daps`), the Imagen Imprint-10 laser printer (`di10`), Imagen 8/300 (`di300`), Linotype 202 typesetter (`d202`), and the Tektronix 4014 graphics terminal (`tc`). The old version of `troff`, renamed `otroff`, produces output for the Wang CAT phototypesetter.

`troff` provides facilities that are upward-compatible with `nroff`, but with the following additions:

- Unlimited vocabulary of fonts (any ten simultaneously) in up to 100 different point sizes

- Character-width and string-width computations for unusually difficult layout problems

- Overstrikes and built-up brackets

- Dynamic (relative or absolute) point size selection, globally or at the character level

- Terminal output for rough sampling of the product

`pic`

A `troff` preprocessor for drawing pictures. Translates in-line pictures from a simple language into phototypesetter commands. The basic objects are box, line, arrow, circle, ellipse, arc, spline, and text.

`grap`

A `pic` preprocessor for drawing charts and graphs. Translates in-line graphs and data points from a simple language into pic drawing commands. Basic commands exist to add labels, tick marks, define alternate coordinates and transformations, and include data from files.

`eqn`

A mathematical preprocessor for `troff`. Translates in-line or displayed formulae from a very easy-to-type form into detailed typesetting instructions.

- Automatic calculation of point size changes for subscripts, superscripts, sub-subscripts, etc.

- Full vocabulary of Greek letters

- Vertical "piling" of formulae for matrices, conditional alternatives, etc.

- Integrals, sums, etc., with arbitrarily complex limits

- Diacriticals: dots, double dots, hats, bars, etc.

- Easily learned by nonprogrammers and mathematical typists

- Formulae can appear within tables to be formatted by `tbl`

`neqn`

A mathematical preprocessor for `nroff` with the same facilities as `eqn`, except for the limitations imposed by the graphic capabilities of the terminal being used. Prepares formulae for display on various Diablo-mechanism terminals, etc.

`MM`

A standardized manuscript layout macro package for use with `nroff` and `troff`. Provides a flexible, user-oriented interface to these two formatters. It is designed to be the following:

- Robust in face of user errors

- Adaptable to a wide range of output styles

- Extended by users familiar with the formatter

- Compatible with both `nroff` and `troff`. Some of its features are as follows:

  Page numbers and draft dates

Cover sheets and title pages

Automatically numbered or lettered headings

Automatically numbered or lettered lists

Automatically numbered figure and table captions

Automatically numbered and positioned footnotes

Single- or double-column text

Paragraphing, displays, and indentation

Automatic table of contents

`MV`
A `troff` macro package that makes it easy to typeset professional-looking projection foils and slides.

`tbl`
A preprocessor for `nroff` and `troff` that translates simple descriptions of table layouts and contents into detailed formatting instructions:

- Computes appropriate column widths
- Handles left- and right-justified columns, centered columns, and decimal-point aligned columns
- Places column titles; spans these titles as appropriate

`ptx`
Generates a permuted index, like the one in the *UNIX System User's Manual*.

`graph`
Given the coordinates of the points to be plotted, draws the corresponding graph; has many options for scaling, axes, grids, labeling, etc.

# Office Automation

`awk`
Pattern scanning and processing language. Searches input for patterns and performs actions on each line of input that satisfies the pattern:

- Patterns include regular expressions, arithmetic and lexicographic conditions, Boolean combinations, and ranges of these
- Data treated as string or numeric as appropriate
- Can break input into fields; fields are variables

- Variables and arrays (with nonnumeric subscripts)
- Full set of arithmetic operators and control flow
- Multiple output streams to files and pipes
- Output can be formatted as desired
- Multiline capabilities

bc

A C-like interactive interface to the desk calculator dc:

- All the capabilities of dc with a high-level syntax
- Arrays and recursive functions
- Immediate evaluation of expressions and evaluation of functions upon call
- Arbitrary-precision elementary functions: *exp, sin, cos, atan*

calendar

An automatic reminder service.

dc

Interactive programmable desk calculator. Has named storage locations, as well as conventional stack for holding integers and programs:

- Arbitrary-precision decimal arithmetic
- Appropriate treatment of decimal fractions
- Arbitrary input and output radices, in particular binary, octal, decimal, and hexadecimal
- Postfix ("Reverse Polish") operators: +, -, *, /, remainder, power, square root, load, store, duplicate, clear print, enter program text, execute

spell

Finds spelling errors by looking up all words from a document in a large spelling list. Knows about prefixes and suffixes and can cope with such rotten spellings as "roted."

# Security

chmod

Changes access permissions on a file(s). Executable by the owner of the file(s) or by the super-user.

`chgrp`
Changes group permission of a file(s).

`chown`
Changes owner of a file(s).

`login`
Signs on a new user:

- Adapts to characteristics of terminal
- Verifies password and establishes user's individual and group (project) identity
- Establishes working directory
- Publishes message of the day
- Announces presence of mail
- Lists unseen news items
- Executes an optional user-specified profile
- Starts command interpreter (shell) or other user-specified program

`newgrp`
Changes working group (project id). This provides access with protection for groups of related users.

`passwd`
Changes a password:

- User can change own password
- Passwords are kept encrypted for security

`su`
Allows a user to assume the permissions and privileges of another user or root (super-user) provided that the proper password is supplied.


# Communications and Networks

`ct`
Dials the phone number of a modem attached to a terminal and spawns a `login` process to that terminal.

cu

Dials a phone number and attempts to make an interactive connection with another machine.

elm

A popular, public-domain mail system front end. It is screen-oriented and offers many features not found in either `mail` or `mailx`.

ftp

An interactive utility with its own commands used for moving files to and from remote system on a heterogeneous network; solves many of the problems of moving files between completely different operating systems.

mail

The Berkeley version of `mail`.

mailx

Mails a message to one or more users. Also used to read and dispose of incoming mail. The presence of mail is announced by `login`. (System V version.)

mesg

Inhibits or permits receipt of messages from `write` and `wall`.

news

Prints current general information and announcement files.

NFS

Network File System. A software package for sharing files across a network. It allows users transparent access to remote files. Standard with most Berkeley and many System V, Release 3 UNIX systems. Networks may be heterogeneous.

RFS

Remote File Sharing. A software package for sharing files and resources across a network. It allows users transparent access to remote resources. Standard with System V, Release 3. Networks must be homogeneous.

rlogin

Login to remote machines on a real-time network.

send

Collects files together to be sent as a "job" to an IBM host.

telnet

Login to remote machines on a real-time network.

uucp
Sends files back and forth between UNIX machines.

wall
Broadcasts a message to all users who are logged in.

write
Establishes direct, interactive terminal-to-terminal communication with another user.

# Process Control

acctcom
Reports a chronological history of all processes that have terminated. Information includes:

- User and system times and sizes
- Start and end real times
- Owner and terminal line associated with process
- System exit status

at
Runs commands at specified times.

batch
Queues commands to be run when system load level permits.

cron
Runs commands on a regularly scheduled basis.

- Actions are arbitrary shell procedures or executable programs
- Times are conjunctions of month, day of month, day of week, hour, and minute. Ranges are specifiable for each

crontab
Command to allow user access to the cron. Note: this command is available in System V, Release 2 and later releases of UNIX.

kill
Terminates named process(es).

`nice`
Runs a command at low (or high) priority.

`nohup`
Runs a command immune to interruption from "hanging up" the terminal.

`ps`
Reports on active processes:

- Lists your own or everybody's processes
- Tells what commands are being executed at the moment
- Optional status information; state and scheduling information, priority, attached terminal, what the process is waiting for, its size, etc.

`tee`
Passes data between processes (like a "pipe") but also diverts copies into one or more files.

`wait`
Waits for termination of a specific process or of all processes that are running in the background.

# Terminal Control

`col`
Reformats files with reverse line-feeds so that they can be correctly printed on terminals that cannot reverse line-feed.

`stty`
Sets up options for control of a terminal:

- Erase and line kill characters
- Speed
- Parity
- Mapping of upper-case characters to lower case
- Carriage-return plus line-feed versus newline
- Interpretation of tab characters
- Delays for tab, newline, and carriage-return characters
- Raw versus edited input

tabs

Sets terminal's tab stops. Knows several "standard" formats.

# Programming

make

Controls creation of large projects. Uses a control file specifying source file dependencies to make new version; uses time last changed to deduce minimum amount of work necessary.

SCCS

SCCS (Source Code Control System) is a collection of UNIX commands (some interactive) for controlling changes to files of text. Some of the operations are

- Storing, updating, and retrieving any version of any source or text file
- Controlling updating privileges
- Identifying both source and object (or load) modules by version number
- Recording who made each change, when it was made, and why

# *Appendix C*

## Complete Command Summary

All the following commands are available on UNIX System V, Release 3. All commands marked with DWB are part of the DOCUMENTER'S WORKBENCH and are not distributed with System V, Releases 3 & 4 (although old versions of these commands are distributed with System V). DWB is usually available from UNIX vendors as an add-on package. Commands in the last section of this appendix (Berkeley UNIX Commands) are distributed by the University of California, Berkeley, and are available on many versions of System V.

| | |
|---|---|
| 300 | handle special functions of DASI 300 terminal (TC) |
| 300s | handle special functions of DASI 300s terminal (TC) |
| 4014 | paginator for the Tektronix 4014 terminal (TC) |
| 450 | handle special functions of the DASI 450 terminal (TC) |
| acctcom | search and print process accounting file(s) (I) |
| admin | create and administer SCCS files (SCCS) |
| ar | archive and library maintainer for portable archives (P) |
| as | assembler (P) |
| asa | interpret ASA carriage control characters (LP) |
| at | execute commands at a later time (PC) |

| | | | | |
|---|---|---|---|---|
| ATT | AT&T 5620 Support Programs | | M | Miscellaneous |
| COM | Communications | | OA | Office Automation |
| D | Directory Commands | | P | Programming |
| DWB | Documenter's Workbench | | PC | Process Control |
| E | Editing Commands | | SCCS | Source Code Control System |
| F | File Commands | | SEC | Security |
| FC | File Comparison | | SH | Shell Commands & Utilities |
| GR | Graphics | | TC | Terminal Control |
| I | Information | | TP | Text Processing |
| LP | Line Printer | | | |

| | |
|---|---|
| awk | pattern scanning and processing language (P) |
| banner | make posters (M) |
| basename | extract file name from path (SH) |
| batch | execute commands when system load is low (PC) |
| bc | arbitrary-precision arithmetic language (OA) (P) |
| bdiff | diff for big files (FC) |
| bfs | big file scanner (E) |
| cal | print calendar (OA) |
| calendar | reminder service (OA) |
| cancel | cancel request to an LP line printer (LP) |
| cat | concatenate and print files (F) |
| cb | C program beautifier (P) |
| cc | C compiler (P) |
| ccoff | convert a COFF file to local format (P) |
| cd | change working directory (D) |
| cdc | change the commentary of a delta (SCCS) |
| cflow | generate C flow graph (P) |
| checkmm | checks documents for proper use of MM macros (DWB) |
| chgrp | change group of a file or directory (D) (F) (SEC) |
| chmod | change mode of a file or directory (D) (F) (SEC) |
| chown | change owner of a file or a directory (D) (F) (SEC) |
| cip | interactive drawing program for 5620 (ATT) |
| clear | clear terminal screen (TC) |
| cmp | compare two files (FC) |
| col | filter reverse line-feeds (TC) (TP) |
| comb | combine deltas (SCCS) |
| comm | select or reject lines common to two sorted files (FC) |
| conv | convert archive and object files to different machine formats (P) |
| convert | convert archive files to common formats (P) |
| cp | copy files (F) |
| cpio | copy directory structures in and out (D) |
| cpp | the C language preprocessor (P) |
| cprs | compress object file (P) |
| crontab | user access to cron (PC) |

| | | | | |
|---|---|---|---|---|
| ATT | AT&T 5620 Support Programs | | M | Miscellaneous |
| COM | Communications | | OA | Office Automation |
| D | Directory Commands | | P | Programming |
| DWB | Documenter's Workbench | | PC | Process Control |
| E | Editing Commands | | SCCS | Source Code Control System |
| F | File Commands | | SEC | Security |
| FC | File Comparison | | SH | Shell Commands & Utilities |
| GR | Graphics | | TC | Terminal Control |
| I | Information | | TP | Text Processing |
| LP | Line Printer | | | |

| | |
|---|---|
| crypt | encrypt/decrypt files (SEC) |
| csh | C shell (SH) |
| csplit | context split (F) |
| ct | spawn getty to a remote terminal (COM) |
| ctrace | C program debugger (P) |
| cu | call another UNIX system (COM) |
| cut | cut out selected columns from each line of a file (F) (SH) |
| cxref | generate C program cross-reference (P) |
| daps | postprocessor for Autologic APS-5 phototypesetter (DWB) |
| date | print or set the date (OA) (I) |
| dc | desk calculator (OA) |
| dd | convert and copy a file between ASCII and EBCDIC (F) (FC) (SCCS) |
| delta | make a delta (change) of a file (SCCS) |
| deroff | remove nroff/troff, tbl, and eqn constructs (DWB) |
| di10 | postprocessor for Imagen Imprint-10 laser printer (DWB) |
| diff | print differences between files (FC) |
| diff3 | three file diff (FC) |
| diffmk | diff preprocessor for nroff/troff (DWB) |
| dircmp | compare directory contents (D) (FC) |
| dirname | extract directory name path (SH) |
| dis | disassembler (P) |
| disable | disable LP printers (LP) |
| ditroff | device-independent troff (TP) |
| du | summarize disk usage (D) (I) |
| dump | dump selected parts of an object file (P) |
| echo | print arguments (SH) |
| ed | text editor (E) |
| edit | Berkeley text editor for casual users (E) |
| egrep | search a file for a pattern (variant of grep) (F) (SH) |
| emacs | extensible screen editor (E) |
| enable | enable LP printers (LP) |
| env | set environment for command execution (SH) |

| | | | |
|---|---|---|---|
| ATT | AT&T 5620 Support Programs | M | Miscellaneous |
| COM | Communications | OA | Office Automation |
| D | Directory Commands | P | Programming |
| DWB | Documenter's Workbench | PC | Process Control |
| E | Editing Commands | SCCS | Source Code Control System |
| F | File Commands | SEC | Security |
| FC | File Comparison | SH | Shell Commands & Utilities |
| GR | Graphics | TC | Terminal Control |
| I | Information | TP | Text Processing |
| LP | Line Printer | | |

| | |
|---|---|
| eqn | format mathematical text for `troff` (DWB) |
| ex | Berkeley text editor (superset of `ed`) (E) |
| expr | evaluate arguments as an expression (SH) |
| f77 | FORTRAN 77 compiler (P) |
| factor | factor a number (M) |
| false | provide false value (SH) |
| fgrep | search a file for a pattern (variant of `grep`) (F) (SH) |
| file | determine file type (F) |
| find | walk a directory tree (D) (F) |
| fsplit | split `f77` files (P) (F) |
| ftp | network file transfer system (COM) |
| gdev | graphical device routines and filters (GR) |
| ged | graphical editor for TEKTRONIX 401X series terminals (GR) (TC) |
| gencc | create front-end to the `cc` command (P) |
| get | get a version of a file (SCCS) |
| getopt | parse command options (SH) |
| getopts | parse command options (SH) |
| glossary | give definitions of common UNIX terms and commands (I) |
| grap | `pic` preprocessor for drawing graphs (TP) |
| graph | draw a graph (GR) |
| graphics | access graphical and numerical commands (GR) |
| greek | terminal filter for `nroff` (TC) (TP) |
| grep | search a file for a pattern (F) (SH) |
| gutil | graphical utilities (GR) |
| head | print first lines of a file (opposite of `tail`) (SH) |
| help | ask for help (SCCS) |
| help | give information on common UNIX terms and commands (I) |
| hp | handle special `nroff` functions for Hewlett-Packard terminals (TC) (TP) |
| hpio | HP 2645A terminal tape file archiver (F) (TC) |
| hyphen | find hyphenated words (DWB) |
| id | print user and group id's and names (SEC) (I) |

| | | | | |
|---|---|---|---|---|
| ATT | AT&T 5620 Support Programs | | M | Miscellaneous |
| COM | Communications | | OA | Office Automation |
| D | Directory Commands | | P | Programming |
| DWB | Documenter's Workbench | | PC | Process Control |
| E | Editing Commands | | SCCS | Source Code Control System |
| F | File Commands | | SEC | Security |
| FC | File Comparison | | SH | Shell Commands & Utilities |
| GR | Graphics | | TC | Terminal Control |
| I | Information | | TP | Text Processing |
| LP | Line Printer | | | |

| | |
|---|---|
| ipcrm | remove a message queue, semaphore set, or shared memory id (M) |
| ipcs | report interprocess communication facilities status (M) |
| ismpx | return windowing terminal state (ATT) |
| join | relational database operator (F) (M) |
| jterm | reset layer of windowing terminal (ATT) |
| jwin | print size of layer (ATT) |
| kill | terminate a process (PC) |
| ksh | Korn shell (SH) |
| layers | start up 5620 windowing system (ATT) |
| lc | column form ls (D) |
| ld | link editor (P) |
| lex | generate programs for simple lexical tasks (P) |
| lf | horizontal ls (D) |
| line | read one line (SH) |
| lint | a C program checker (P) |
| list | produce C source listing from object file (P) |
| ln | link files (F) |
| locate | identify UNIX command using keywords (I) |
| login | sign on (M) |
| logname | print login name (SH) (I) |
| lorder | print ordering relation for an object library (P) |
| lp | send request to an LP line printer (LP) |
| lpr | send request to a Berkeley printer spooler (LP) |
| lpstat | print LP status information (LP) |
| ls | list contents of directories (D) (F) (I) |
| m4 | macro processor (P) |
| machid | provide truth value about your processor type (P) |
| macref | print cross-reference listing of macro files (DWB) |
| mail | send mail to users or read mail (OA) |
| mailx | Berkeley version of mail (OA) |
| make | maintain, update, and regenerate groups of programs (P) |
| makekey | generate encryption key (SEC) |

| | | | | |
|---|---|---|---|---|
| ATT | AT&T 5620 Support Programs | | M | Miscellaneous |
| COM | Communications | | OA | Office Automation |
| D | Directory Commands | | P | Programming |
| DWB | Documenter's Workbench | | PC | Process Control |
| E | Editing Commands | | SCCS | Source Code Control System |
| F | File Commands | | SEC | Security |
| FC | File Comparison | | SH | Shell Commands & Utilities |
| GR | Graphics | | TC | Terminal Control |
| I | Information | | TP | Text Processing |
| LP | Line Printer | | | |

| | |
|---|---|
| man | print entries in the *UNIX System User's Manual* (I) (TP) |
| mcs | manipulate comment section of an object file (P) |
| mesg | permit or deny `writes` to your terminal (OA) (I) |
| mkdir | make directory (D) |
| mkshlib | create a shared library (P) |
| mm | print/check documents formatted with the MM macros (DWB) |
| mmt | typeset documents (DWB) |
| more | print files one screen at a time (F) |
| mv | move files (F) |
| mvt | typeset view graphs and slides (DWB) |
| ndx | create a subject-page index for a document (TP) |
| neqn | format mathematical text for `nroff` (DWB) |
| newform | change the format of a text file (F) |
| newgrp | change to a new group (SEC) |
| news | print news items (I) |
| nice | run a command at low priority (PC) |
| nl | line numbering filter (F) (LP) |
| nm | print name list (P) |
| nohup | run a command immune to hangups and quits (PC) |
| nroff | text formatter (DWB) |
| od | dump file in octal, decimal, or hexadecimal (F) |
| omf | convert AT&T common object file format to Xenix object format module (P) |
| pack | compress files (F) |
| passwd | change password (SEC) |
| paste | merge same lines of several files or subsequent lines of one file (F) (SH) |
| pcat | print files compressed with `pack` (F) |
| pg | file scanning program for screen terminals (F) (TC) |
| pic | figure drawing preprocessor for `troff` (DWB) |
| pr | format files for line printer listings (F) (LP) |
| prof | display profile data for C programs (P) |
| prs | print an SCCS file (SCCS) |
| ps | report process status (PC) |
| ps | report process status (I) |

| | | | |
|---|---|---|---|
| ATT | AT&T 5620 Support Programs | M | Miscellaneous |
| COM | Communications | OA | Office Automation |
| D | Directory Commands | P | Programming |
| DWB | Documenter's Workbench | PC | Process Control |
| E | Editing Commands | SCCS | Source Code Control System |
| F | File Commands | SEC | Security |
| FC | File Comparison | SH | Shell Commands & Utilities |
| GR | Graphics | TC | Terminal Control |
| I | Information | TP | Text Processing |
| LP | Line Printer | | |

| | |
|---|---|
| ptx | permuted index generator for `nroff/troff` (TP) |
| pwd | working directory name (D) (I) |
| rcp | copy to a remote machine (COM) |
| red | restricted version of `ed` (E) (SEC) |
| regcmp | regular expression compile (P) |
| relogin | rename login entry to show current layer (ATT) |
| rlogin | login on remote machine (COM) |
| rm | remove files (D) (F) |
| rmail | restricted version of `mail` (OA) |
| rmdel | remove a delta (SCCS) |
| rmdir | remove directory (D) |
| rsh | restricted shell (SEC) (SH) |
| rsh | shell command for remote machine (COM) |
| sact | print current SCCS file editing activity (SCCS) |
| sag | system activity graph (I) |
| sar | system activity reporter (I) |
| sccsdiff | compare two versions of an SCCS file (SCCS) |
| sdb | symbolic debugger (P) |
| sdiff | side-by-side `diff` (FC) |
| sed | noninteractive stream editor (E) (SH) |
| see | list file showing nonprinting characters (F) |
| sh | shell, the standard command interpreter (SH) |
| shl | shell layer manager (SH) |
| size | print sizes of object files (P) |
| sleep | suspend execution for an interval (SH) |
| sort | sort and/or merge files (OA) (SH) |
| spell | find spelling errors (OA) |
| spline | interpolate smooth curve (GR) |
| split | split a file into pieces (F) |
| starter | give information on UNIX for beginning users (I) |
| stat | statistical commands useful with graphical commands (GR) |
| strip | strip symbol table and relocation bits from object module (P) |
| stty | set the options for a terminal port (TC) (I) |
| su | become super-user or another user (SEC) |
| subj | generate a list of subjects from a document (TP) |

| | | | | |
|---|---|---|---|---|
| ATT | AT&T 5620 Support Programs | | M | Miscellaneous |
| COM | Communications | | OA | Office Automation |
| D | Directory Commands | | P | Programming |
| DWB | Documenter's Workbench | | PC | Process Control |
| E | Editing Commands | | SCCS | Source Code Control System |
| F | File Commands | | SEC | Security |
| FC | File Comparison | | SH | Shell Commands & Utilities |
| GR | Graphics | | TC | Terminal Control |
| I | Information | | TP | Text Processing |
| LP | Line Printer | | | |

| | |
|---|---|
| sum | print checksum and block count of a file (F) |
| tabs | set tabs on a terminal (TC) |
| tail | print the last part of a file (F) (SH) |
| tar | tape archiver for directory structures (D) |
| telnet | login to a remote machine (COM) |
| tbl | format tables for nroff/troff (DWB) |
| tc | troff terminal filter for Tektronix 4014 terminal (DWB) (TC) |
| tee | send intermediate pipeline output to file (SH) |
| test | condition evaluation for shell programs (SH) |
| time | time execution of a command (I) |
| timex | better version of time (I) |
| toc | graphical table of contents routines (GR) |
| touch | update access and modification times of a file (F) |
| tplot | graphics filter for printing terminals (TC) (GR) |
| tput | shell program access to terminfo database (TC) |
| tr | translate characters (F) (SH) |
| troff | text formatting for phototypesetters (DWB) |
| true | provide truth value (SH) |
| tsort | topological sort for use with lorder in creating object libraries (P) |
| tty | get the terminal's name in /dev (TC) (I) |
| umask | set file-creation permissions mask (F) (SEC) |
| uname | print UNIX system name (I) |
| unget | ndo a previous get (SCCS) |
| uniq | report repeated lines in a file (F) (FC) |
| units | conversion program for weights and measures (M) (OA) |
| unpack | expand file compressed with pack (F) |
| usage | give usage information for UNIX commands (I) |
| uucp | UNIX-to-UNIX copy (COM) |
| uulog | print log of uucp actions (COM) (I) |
| uuname | print names of remote systems known to uucp (COM) (I) |
| uupick | get files from /usr/spool/uucpublic (COM) |
| uustat | uucp status inquiry and job control (COM) (I) |
| uuto | public UNIX-to-UNIX file copy (COM) |
| uux | UNIX-to-UNIX remote command execution (COM) |
| val | validate SCCS file (SCCS) |

| | | | | |
|---|---|---|---|---|
| ATT | AT&T 5620 Support Programs | | M | Miscellaneous |
| COM | Communications | | OA | Office Automation |
| D | Directory Commands | | P | Programming |
| DWB | Documenter's Workbench | | PC | Process Control |
| E | Editing Commands | | SCCS | Source Code Control System |
| F | File Commands | | SEC | Security |
| FC | File Comparison | | SH | Shell Commands & Utilities |
| GR | Graphics | | TC | Terminal Control |
| I | Information | | TP | Text Processing |
| LP | Line Printer | | | |

| | |
|---|---|
| vc | control version (SCCS) |
| vi | Berkeley screen editor (E) |
| wait | await completion of process (SH) |
| wc | character, word, and line count (SH) |
| what | identify SCCS files (SCCS) |
| who | print who is on the system (I) |
| write | write to another user (OA) |
| wtinit | download object file to 5620 terminal (ATT) |
| xargs | construct argument list(s) and execute command (SH) |
| xtd | extract and print window driver link structure (ATT) |
| xts | extract and print window driver statistics (ATT) |
| xtt | extract and print window packet traces (ATT) |
| yacc | yet another compiler-compiler (P) |

| | | | | |
|---|---|---|---|---|
| ATT | AT&T 5620 Support Programs | | M | Miscellaneous |
| COM | Communications | | OA | Office Automation |
| D | Directory Commands | | P | Programming |
| DWB | Documenter's Workbench | | PC | Process Control |
| E | Editing Commands | | SCCS | Source Code Control System |
| F | File Commands | | SEC | Security |
| FC | File Comparison | | SH | Shell Commands & Utilities |
| GR | Graphics | | TC | Terminal Control |
| I | Information | | TP | Text Processing |
| LP | Line Printer | | | |

| ATT | AT&T 5620 Support Programs | M | Miscellaneous |
| COM | Communications | OA | Office Automation |
| D | Directory Commands | P | Programming |
| DWB | Documenter's Workbench | PC | Process Control |
| E | Editing Commands | SCCS | Source Code Control System |
| F | File Commands | SEC | Security |
| FC | File Comparison | SH | Shell Commands & Utilities |
| GR | Graphics | TC | Terminal Control |
| I | Information | TP | Text Processing |
| LP | Line Printer | | |

# Answers to
# Review Questions

## Chapter 1

1. The fundamental purpose of an operating system is to provide a consistent interface between the hardware and the applications programs so that applications programs only need to address the hardware abstractly. The operating system is also expected to provide management of system resources.

2. UNIX is a multitasking, multiuser operating system. But beyond that, it offers many utilities. Enough, in fact, so that application programs might not be necessary for general use of the computer for handling text, calculation, and communications.

3. UNIX shells are command-line user interfaces to the operating system. They can differ in their syntax and internal facilities. The most common shells are the Bourne shell, the Berkeley shell, and the Korn shell.

4. The responsibilities of each user to other users on a multiuser system are to respect the privacy and needs of other users. If users do not behave responsibly, the system administrator might enforce stricter limitations on user accounts and freeze out some users from some of the resources.

5. UNIX was originally developed at AT&T Bell Labs by Brian Kernighan and Dennis Ritchie. Modern UNIX owes a great deal to the University of California, Berkeley and innumerable universities and computer companies who invested tremendous amounts of work in enhancing and refining the operating system.

6. UNIX was not always a commercial operating system. Bell Labs gave away early versions to universities. There is a strong contingent of users who are attempting to return UNIX to its original, freely available status.

7. UNIX owes much of its popularity to its hardware independence, and to its rich collection of utilities and the way they can be used together to solve complex problems.

8. Tradition is important to UNIX because written standards are relatively new to UNIX. Tradition is equivalent to *de facto* standards.

# Chapter 2

1. You have to log in to a UNIX system so that the system can distinguish you from other users. Each user has an area within the system with its own environment. Unless you identify yourself, the UNIX system does not know who you are. Logging in is the way you identify yourself to the UNIX system.

2. You log out to free resources for other users and to protect your files.

3. Accounts are password-protected to prevent unauthorized tampering with the UNIX system. If you don't have a password on your account, you are not only jeopardizing your files, but also weakening the security of the entire system.

4. End a session by entering exit as a command or entering Ctrl-D (End of file).

5. Change your password using the passwd command.

6. The man command allows you to view the on-line UNIX documentation.

7. The site advisor's job is to help users at a computing site. The system administrators set up accounts and maintain the system.

# Chapter 3

1. The shell is a command interpreter for the user's commands. Some of the commands result in activity by the shell alone; others are passed on to the UNIX kernel after they have been translated into operations that the kernel understands and can act on.

2. The Berkeley C shell defaults to a percent sign for its primary prompt.

3. Most UNIX command-line options are prefixed with the dash (minus sign, -).

4. Command history is the capability of a shell to record the command the user has executed. This list can be referred to for reissuing or editing new commands.

5. Command aliasing is the capability of a shell to give a name to a command or sequence of commands. The original file is not renamed, but the shell can use this "nickname" to execute the command.

6. The two most notable differences between the Bourne shell and the Korn shell are *history* and *aliasing*. The Bourne shell has neither; the Korn shell has both.

7. Operating system interfaces that use windows, menus, and icons rather than just a command line are called graphic user interfaces, or GUIs.

8. *Clicking on* means moving the pointer (usually an arrow) to an iconic object and pressing a mouse button.

9. *Dragging* means moving the pointer to an icon, pressing and holding a mouse button (usually the left), and moving the mouse to move the icon.

# Chapter 4

1. A tree structure with the root at the top.

2. A *directory* holds a collection of files.

3. The command for listing basic information about files within a directory is the `ls` command.

4. The command for copying files is the `cp` command; for creating links, `ln`; for moving (or renaming) files, `mv`; and for deleting unwanted files, `rm`.

5. The names are . (the current directory) and . . (its parent directory). These are read aloud as *dot* and *dot-dot*.

6. The `cat` command is one of the simplest commands for looking at small text files.

7. The two paging commands are `more` and `pg`. The command for printing a file on a printer is `lp`.

8. The *present working directory* is the current position in the file tree. The `pwd` command displays the path to that position. (Use it to get your bearings.)

9. Move about in the directory tree by using the `cd` command with a path to your destination directory. The path is absolute when you describe the relationship of the destination to the root directory; for example `/usr/felix/documents`. The path is relative when you specify the path in relation to the

present working directory; for example `../lists`. If you use a path that doesn't start with a slash (absolute path) or dot-dot, `cd` assumes the path is below the present working directory.

10. Create directories with the `mkdir` command.

11. The command to destroy a directory is `rmdir`; the directory must be empty before the command will succeed. You can eliminate a directory, all its files, subdirectories, and subsequent contents by using `rm -r`. This is DANGEROUS!

12. The three kinds of file permission are *read*, *write*, and *execute*.

13. The `chmod` is used for changing permissions; the `chown` is used to change ownership; and the `chgrp` is used for changing the group.

14. You must have *read* permission to see the names of files and programs in a directory. You must have *execute* permission to change directory (`cd`) into the directory or use it as part of a path down to another directory; that is, to use files in that directory. You must have *read* to add files to or remove files from the directory.

# Chapter 5

1. The asterisk character on the command line is a wildcard. In other words, it expands command-line arguments to include all files that match whatever conditions (characters) are issued with the asterisk. An asterisk surrounded by white-space characters expands to all the file names in the directory (with the exception of file names that start with the dot).

2. Almost all punctuation characters have a special meaning to one or more of the shells.

3. A shell variable provides temporary storage for pieces of information (usually small) to be used by the shell, the user, or a program.

4. The special meaning of non-ordinary shell characters can be escaped by prefixing them with the backslash, or enclosing the expression in apostrophes or double quotes. Some characters (for example, the dollar sign) still maintain their special properties within double quotes.

5. The shell treats each word on the command line as a separate argument unless the words are enclosed in quotations. All words bound by quotations are treated together as a single command-line argument.

6. The shell will act on anything enclosed in grave accents as a separate command line, the output of which is substituted in the command line with the grave accents.

7. A regular expression is an abstracted expression for a string that allows you to describe a set of strings through the use of regular characters combined with special characters.

8. The asterisk in a regular expression means any number, zero or more, of the previous character or subexpression.

9. The dot in a regular expression is the wildcard for any single character.

10. The carat (^) signifies the beginning of a line or string. The dollar sign signifies the end.

11. A set of characters for a single character position are enclosed in square brackets ([ ]).

12. The grep commands are used for doing global regular-expression searches on files.

# Chapter 6

1. Editors or word processors are used more than any other kind of application program.

2. A word processor reformats text as you write.

3. Editing programs usually produce the plainest text files. Word processors often embed special characters or commands in the text.

4. A line editor edits one line at a time, usually without using any of the capabilities of a terminal. It is well suited to printing terminals. A visual editor, on the other hand, does take advantage of a terminal's capabilities. The user can move the current position in a file by moving the cursor. A stream editor works from instructions on the shell's command line or from a file containing editing instructions. It is not an interactive editor.

5. The vi editor can be in either command mode or in text- entry mode. (The command mode comprises the vi and ex command modes. The text-entry mode comprises the *insert*, *append*, and *change* modes.)

6. You get into *insert* mode with the i command. You get into *append* mode with the a command. You return to command mode by pressing Escape.

7. The h key or the backspace moves the cursor to the previous character; l or the spacebar moves it to the next. The j key moves the cursor to the next line; k to the previous line.

8. The most common forms are cw for changing a word and uppercase C for changing to the end of the line. You may also change to a specified character with ct*x*, in which *x* is the character. You can also change a single character with r followed by the new character, and replace text with uppercase R.

9. The simplest delete command is x, used to delete a single character. Delete a word with dw; delete to the end of the line with uppercase D; and delete the entire line with dd.

10. If you prefix a command with a number, the command will be applied that many times.

11. Exit and save with either the single command ZZ or with the pair of (ex) commands :w and :q.

12. Search forward using a regular expression after the slash (/) command. Search backward by using the hook (?) in place of the slash. The next occurrence in the current search direction is found with lowercase n.

13. Ctrl-F takes you to the next screen; reverse the jump with Ctrl-B.

14. The jump to a line number is the uppercase G. Without a numeric argument, you jump to the end of the file. Any numeric argument takes you to that line number; therefore, an argument of 1 takes you to the beginning of the file.

15. The w moves you forward to the beginning of the next word; e to the end of the next word. The lowercase b takes you back to the beginning of the previous word.

16. You can undo (and then redo) the previous command with the u command.

17. When you delete text with any form of the delete commands, the text is automatically copied into the *delete buffer*. You can copy text into the buffer with the various forms of the yank (y or Y) command. You can then move to the new location and put the text in with p or P.

18. Mark a position with lowercase m followed by any letter. The letter becomes the name of the mark.

19. Marks can be used for simply jumping around in the file (grave accent and mark name), or for position marks for block operations.

20. Named buffers are semi-permanent areas for storing pieces of text. (They disappear only when you quit vi, but exist from file to file when you are editing more than one file.) You can delete, change, yank, and put with named buffers by prefixing the command with the double quote (") and the name of the buffer, a letter.

21. The vi editor is merely a visual shell around the ex editor. Many of the powerful editing commands of vi are actually ex commands. You can get all the power of these commands by dropping down to the ex editing level.

22. The colon (:) command from vi is used to preface any single ex command. If you want to work at the level of ex for more than a single command at a time, you can escape to ex with the uppercase Q from vi. To return to visual mode from ex, just enter vi as an ex command.

23. Ranges are defined by two references to line numbers separated by a comma ( , ). The line numbers can be specific numeric values, relative line numbers from any position (use a dot to specify the current line), or regular expression search strings delimited by slashes ( / ) or hooks ( ? ). You can also refer to marks by prefixing the mark name with a single quote ( ' ).

24. The command for reading in a file is r *filename*. The command for writing out to a file is w *filename*. If the filename is left off the write command, the write goes to the file currently being edited.

25. The sed editor is a *stream editor*. It is not interactive. It is used to filter text and automate repetitive editing tasks.

# Chapter 7

1. The emacs editor is always in the editing (text-entry) state. It is a single-state editor.

2. You can simultaneously edit as many files as you want.

3. All commands require either a Control-key or a meta-key combination to differentiate them from text you are entering. The meta-key might be an Escape-key combination or some other special key combination such as an Alt-key combination, depending on the keyboard you are using.

4. Under every command-key operation is a named command. *Key binding* is the relationship between a named command and the key combination that invokes it. The user can change the key bindings as desired.

5. The key combination used to save the current buffer and exit emacs is C-x C-s C-x C-c.

6. Invoke a command by name with M-x *command name*.

7. *Name completion* is the capability of emacs to complete the spelling of a command name, buffer name, or file name after you enter enough characters to differentiate that name from others of the same class. Invoke name completion with the spacebar or tab key. You can view your alternatives by entering the hook ( ? ).

8. The apropos command displays help based on key words.

9. The auto-fill-mode command turns automatic word-wrap on and off.

10. Multiply a command by prefixing it with the meta-key and a numeric value. This method is also used to give values to commands.

11. Delete to the end of a line with C-k. The text is copied into a kill buffer for possible use later.

12. Retrieve the last entry in the kill buffer with C-y. You can roll through the previous kill buffers with subsequent M-y commands.

13. Define a region by placing a mark (usually with M-space) and then moving the cursor (point). The region is the text between the mark and point.

14. An incremental search is fully interactive. In other words, as you enter characters in the search string, point moves to the next occurrence of the string. Start an incremental search with C-s.

# Chapter 8

1. A process is a program that is running.

2. UNIX is called a multitasking operating system because more than one task (process) runs simultaneously.

3. UNIX utilities take advantage of multitasking by being designed to be used together, in combination, with each utility's input and output being capable of connecting to another utility.

4. The three input and output ports are: standard input, standard output, and standard error.

5. To redirect standard input means to take the input for a program from a file rather than from the keyboard. To redirect standard output or standard error means to put the output or error messages in a file rather than on the terminal screen.

6. A pipe is the means by which the output of one process is directed into the input of another without using an intermediate file. A pipe is created by invoking both processes with a vertical bar character ( | ) between them. For example who | wc -l.

7. The tee command splits out a copy of the standard output to a file, but without otherwise affecting the normal flow.

8. When you join two program names with the double ampersand (&&), you indicate that the second command should execute only if the first completes without errors. The double ampersand acts like a logical AND.

9. Specify that one process is run only if another fails by joining the two commands with double vertical bars ( || ). This acts like a logical OR.

10. If you entered a child-process shell, use the exit command to kill the child and return to the parent. If, however, you have exited to the shell with Ctrl-Z, you must use fg to return the prior process to the foreground.

11. The command that displays the status of your processes is ps. On some systems, you might use the jobs command to see similar information. The

command `jobs -l` with the Korn shell gives the process ID also.

12. When you start a program by ending the command line with the single ampersand (&), the process runs in the background.

13. To kill a process, you must know the process ID. Get this information with the `ps` command. Use the `kill` command with the process ID.

# Chapter 9

1. Send a file to the print spooler with `lp` *filename*.

2. The print spooler is responsible for managing print jobs so that they don't conflict when being sent to the printer.

3. The `pr` command is used as `pr` *-n*, in which *n* is the number of columns you want. This command is also used to break files into pages with headers prior to sending to the print spooler.

4. The `date` command responds with the current date and time. You control the format with a format string.

5. The `tr` command does character substitution.

6. You selectively output fields from a flat ASCII data file using the `cut` command. If you don't specify a field separator, it assumes tabs or spaces are the field separators. Use the *-ffield-list* to specify which field you want.

7. `paste` combines lists from separate files into a single file.

8. The UNIX `sort` command can be used for multiple key sorting. The keys can be alphabetic and numeric. The command can also be used to merge previously sorted files.

9. The UNIX `join` command joins lines of two files that have common key fields. The files must have been sorted previously.

10. The `diff` command gives a report on the differences between two files, whereas `sdiff` compares them side by side.

11. The `find` command searches for whatever file information you specify.

# Chapter 10

1. A real-time network is connected for resource sharing and communications on immediate demand. Another name for a real-time network is a local area network (LAN). A batch network usually involves delays. Connections are made as needed. Most connections use serial communications through

modems and over telephone lines.

2. The name of the file that has the list of possible LAN connections is /etc/ hosts.

3. The two most common programs used to log in to remote machines in a LAN are rlogin and telnet.

4. The rsh command is used to execute commands on remote machines. The syntax is rsh *host command*.

5. The two commands for copying files are rcp (remote copy) and ftp.

6. The UUCP utilities are used for batch networking.

7. The UUCP program to copy files from one system to another (in batch networks) is uucp, the command from which the collection of utilities gets its name.

8. The utilities to determine status and success of UUCP transfers are uustat and uulog.

9. The primitive dialup communications program that is part of UUCP is cu. You terminate a session with cu by entering a tilde and a dot (~.).

10. NetNews is the UNIX conferencing network. You use the programs readnews, vnews, or rn to interact with this system. It works much like an electronic bulletin board, but is much bigger than any comparable system.

11. Electronic mail is less likely to interrupt other people's work. The interactive communications programs write and talk often display their messages in the middle of other users' displays.

12. The two ways to address e-mail are bang paths and domain addressing. Bang paths consist of a list of machines and a user name, each item separated by a bang, the exclamation point (!). The domain address consists of a user ID, the at-sign (@), and the domain name of the machine on which the user has an account.

# Chapter 11

1. The awk utility is a report generator. It is designed to take tables of information as input, search the information for patterns and fields, and produce a formatted output.

2. Each awk statement contains a condition and an action. The action is enclosed in curly braces ({ }). If the condition is null (blank), the action is applied to every line of input.

3. The awk utility uses regular expressions to define pattern matching.

4. The awk utility uses tabs and spaces as the default field separator.

5. The two special input conditions are BEGIN and END. These conditions can be used to define actions to be taken before any input is read and after all input is read.

6. In awk, you redefine the field separator by assigning the character(s) to the predefined variable FS. This is usually done in the BEGIN statement. Therefore, the statement would appear as follows: BEGIN { FS=':' ; }.

7. The UNIX make utility is used to initiate actions based on file dependencies.

8. The default name for the dependency file is Makefile or makefile.

9. The three parts of a dependency statement are as follows: target (or goal), dependency list, and action list.

10. The two programs for formatting and typesetting text are nroff (simple formatting) and troff (typesetting).

11. Almost all formatting and typesetting commands start with a dot (.) in the first column. The command usually consists of two characters, and the arguments (if any) are on the same line.

12. The command to turn text-fill on is .fi; to turn it off, .nf.

13. The command to set the left margin is .po *n*, in which *n* is the distance to set the margin. Similarly, the line length is set with .ll *n*.

14. Force a new page with .sp 4.

15. The MM package is a set of formatting and typesetting macros (higher-level commands) that help with standard page layout. MM stands for Memorandum Macros.

# Chapter 12

1. A shell script is a file consisting of commands for the shell to execute. For the shell script to be executed directly by the shell, it must have execute permissions.

2. The shell is responsible for ensuring that the arguments you enter are properly "handed over" to the program being executed.

3. If file name substitution is specified on the command line with the characters *, ?, or [ ... ], the shell performs the substitution. This happens *before* the program gets executed; the program itself never has to worry about it.

4. The shell handles input/output redirection even before execution of the associated application or utility begins.

5. A *variable* is used to hold information or data for a shell or a program.

6. A user's environment is defined by the shell variables that have been exported. These variables can be used by any application programs or utilities.

7. With `echo`, you output new lines by including a \n in your echo string. For tabs, use the \t.

8. The `read` command is used to read from the terminal. The command should be used with a variable, as in `read words`.

# Chapter 13

1. Statements that alter the otherwise-linear flow of processing of a script are referred to as *flow-control* statements.

2. The condition must be a command that executes and exits with a zero (no error) status for the body of the `if` to execute.

3. The `test` command tests strings to see whether they are identical; it tests numeric strings to determine inequality; and it tests files to determine their permission status.

4. The Bourne shell uses square brackets as one way to invoke the `test` command. The brackets must stand separate from other arguments in the line by at least one space character.

5. The Bourne shell `case` command is used to select a block of actions (commands) from many based on the comparison of a string against several alternative strings.

6. *Looping* means repeating a block of commands.

7. The three Bourne shell commands that produce looping are `for`, `while`, and `until`.

8. The `for` statement processes a list, item by item. When it has processed all the items in the list, it stops.

9. A loop exits when its controlling condition is no longer met or when a `break` is encountered.

# Chapter 14

1. The Korn shell is so much like the Bourne shell in its commands and syntax

that most Bourne-shell scripts will run unaltered as Korn-shell scripts.

2. The Korn shell is much faster with numeric operations because the integer arithmetic is built into the shell. In addition, the Korn shell has integer variables. The Bourne and C shells have only character-string variables.

3. Arrays are used to hold similar data together under one variable name. They facilitate iterative processing of groups of data.

4. The Korn shell command `typeset` is used to set many variable options, among which are the string length and justification, integer data types, and permissions on the use of the variables.

5. The `let` command is used in the Korn shell to indicate that an arithmetic expression follows.

6. All C-shell variable assignments begin with the keyword `set` or `setenv`.

7. The single key character used with C-shell arithmetic operations is the "at" sign (@).

8. C-shell `if` statements end with the key word `endif`.

9. The condition expression for the C shell must be an arithmetic expression. Any nonzero value indicates a true condition.

10. To convert the result status of a command into the proper value for a condition, enclose the command in curly braces.

11. C-shell `while` loops end with the keyword `end`.

# INDEX

:! command, ex editor, 128

## A

absolute file permission, 68
addresses, electronic mail, 256-258
Advanced Research Projects Agency Network (ARPANET), 257
    file transfer protocol, 239-241
aliases
    electronic mail, 258
    Korn Shell, 366
aliasing, Berkley C shell, 35
answers, review questions, 415-427
apostrophe (') quotation character, 82-84
applications, 2
apropos command, emacs help files, 142
arguments
    passing to shell programs, 318-322
    sort command, 206
arithmetic expressions, 360-361
    awk command, 267-278
arithmetic operations, C Shell, 369-370

arrays, Korn Shell, 363
artificial intelligence, LISP programming language, 160
ASCII character set, 82
assignments, keyboard, 21
asterisk (*)
    with files, 53
    with regular expression, 89
at command, 228-229
awk command, 266-279
    arithmetic functions, 267-268
    functions, 270
    operators, 270
    string data, 269-270

## B

b command, visual editor, 113-114
background process, 185-191
backslash (\) character, 86-87
Backspace key, 20
bang paths, 256
banner command, 84

# C